BEHIND the SCENES

BEHIND the SCENES

Contemporary Bollywood
Directors and their Cinema

EDITED BY

Aysha Iqbal Viswamohan
Vimal Mohan John

Los Angeles | London | New Delhi
Singapore | Washington DC | Melbourne

First published in 2017 by

SAGE Publications India Pvt Ltd
B1/I-1 Mohan Cooperative Industrial Area
Mathura Road, New Delhi 110 044, India
www.sagepub.in

SAGE Publications Inc
2455 Teller Road
Thousand Oaks, California 91320, USA

SAGE Publications Ltd
1 Oliver's Yard, 55 City Road
London EC1Y 1SP, United Kingdom

SAGE Publications Asia-Pacific Pte Ltd
3 Church Street
#10-04 Samsung Hub
Singapore 049483

Published by Vivek Mehra for SAGE Publications India Pvt Ltd, typeset in 10/13 pt Book Antiqua by Zaza Eunice, Hosur, Tamil Nadu, India and printed at Saurabh Printers Pvt Ltd, Greater Noida.

Library of Congress Cataloging-in-Publication Data Available

ISBN: 978-93-860-6239-0 (HB)

SAGE Team: Shambhu Sahu, Guneet Kaur, Apeksha Sharma and Ritu Chopra

When people ask me if I went to film school I tell them, no, I went to films.

—Quentin Tarantino

This book is dedicated to all those who go to films.

Thank you for choosing a SAGE product!
If you have any comment, observation or feedback,
I would like to personally hear from you.
Please write to me at **contactceo@sagepub.in**

Vivek Mehra, Managing Director and CEO, SAGE India.

Bulk Sales

SAGE India offers special discounts
for purchase of books in bulk.
We also make available special imprints
and excerpts from our books on demand.

For orders and enquiries, write to us at

Marketing Department
SAGE Publications India Pvt Ltd
B1/I-1, Mohan Cooperative Industrial Area
Mathura Road, Post Bag 7
New Delhi 110044, India

E-mail us at **marketing@sagepub.in**

Get to know more about SAGE

Be invited to SAGE events, get on our mailing list.
Write today to **marketing@sagepub.in**

This book is also available as an e-book.

Contents

Foreword

For a number of years, popular Hindi cinema was overlooked in studies of film and media, particularly in those accounts that were researched and written from the metropoles in the West and published via academic presses. Granted, there were articles that appeared sporadically and featured in scholarly journals arguing for the need to study and take seriously the popular commercial cinema of India in the hybrid Hindu–Urdu language format. It was not until the early to mid-1990s that 'Bollywood' as a term began to be used in common parlance as well as in academic discourse. In fact, for a number of years prior to this, popular Hindi cinema was often considered as kitsch, timepass or three-hour long weeping melodramas and, therefore, beyond the serious gaze of scholars and cinephiles as such. Thankfully, times have changed. There now exist over a dozen and more book-length studies of popular Hindi cinema and related popular cultures (as well as a smaller but rising number of studies on other cinemas from India), published by the leading academic presses around the world, and numerous refereed journal articles on the subject too. Hindi cinema has been studied and considered important not just for entertainment purposes and the relationships that it fosters with its millions of audiences around the world as a form of popular culture but it has also been explored along the lines of national identity, its representations pertaining to cultural identities such as gender and sexuality as well its increasing development in the era of contemporary globalization. The field of Indian cinema studies is growing and a healthy primary area within that might usefully be referred to as 'Contemporary Hindi Film Studies'.

The director is an important figure in the production of Bollywood films and alongside the star (who is often, though not exclusively, usually the male leading actor in the film) as well as the producer; these three are perhaps the most important protagonists in the making of contemporary Hindi films. Yet interestingly apart from biographies based on particular directors, serious scholarship on the roles, meanings and working practices of directors and other key personnel is much needed in the study of contemporary Hindi films. The collection of essays presented here and edited by Aysha Iqbal Viswamohan and Vimal Mohan John is a useful step in that direction in order to begin to situate and understand better the role and meanings of the work of Hindi film directors. Bringing together established and early career scholars from around the world, this book focuses on key names in the contemporary popular Hindi cinema industry providing textual readings of their work, placing their films in a wider social and cultural landscape of a globalizing India, as well as considering their legacies as film-makers. The attention given to women directors and issues related to the representation of gender in some of the chapters is also a welcomed addition and much needed in the scholarship in this area.

In terms of focus on directors in modern-day Hindi films, there exists a longstanding debate in cinema studies more broadly as to the role of a director in terms of his or her input as an auteur in the film-making process. In short, this debate has often to do with to what extent can an authorial imprint or signature be detected in a number of films as having been conceived, shaped and developed by the director. The debate also includes acknowledging the collaborative nature of film-making and poses further questions as to what extent, and in what ways, did the director work in tandem with other members of the cast and crew, on the film set and in post-production, in order to achieve the finished cinematic text? These questions are equally important for studies of Hindi film directors and their films, and this collection of essays helps us to start building a response to such queries.

From the men and women who make films and related products in the media and entertainment landscape that is contemporary

Hindi cinema to engaging with some of its varied and pleasurable filmic texts, *Behind the Scenes: Contemporary Bollywood Directors and Their Cinema* is a fruitful addition to the study of this exciting and complex cinematic form.

Rajinder Dudrah
Professor of Cultural Studies and Creative Industries
Birmingham City University, United Kingdom

Acknowledgements

Acknowledgements are due to Professor Bhaskar Ramamurthy, Director, Indian Institute of Technology, Madras, for his unstinting encouragement towards academic endeavours; Professor A. Ramesh, Chairman, Centre for Continuing Education, for the generous funding through the institute's Book Writing Scheme; and to the IIT Madras (IITM) administration, particularly Professor P. Sriram, Dean (Administration). Vimal and I also thank our respective departments and colleagues for their insightful observations during the making of this book.

Great thanks are due to Dr Rajinder Dudrah for graciously agreeing to write the Foreword for this book.

We owe it to all our contributors for their invigorating and wide range of essays.

We appreciate the library staff of Simon Fraser University, Vancouver (Canada); the British Council Library, Chennai; and English and Foreign Languages University, Hyderabad, for their support towards materials collection.

We thank the distinguished film-makers and members of the film fraternity who have been at IITM over the years and participated in our various film conferences and workshops. We do recognize the extent to which this book is enriched through the enlightening discussions we have had with our guests: Abhishek Chaubey, Anurag Kashyap, Atul Tiwari, R. Balki, Bejoy Nambiar, Dibakar Banerjee, Habib Faisal, Jaideep Sahni, (late) K. Balachander, Kamal Hasan, K.V. Anand, M. Nassar, Nagesh Kukunoor, P.C. Sreeram, Rana Daggubati, Ravi K. Chandran, (late) Rituparno Ghosh, Rakeysh Omprakash Mehra, Rohan Sippy, Shekhar Kapur, Sriram and Shridhar Raghavan, Santosh Sivan,

A. Sreekar Prasad, Shama Zaidi, Shimit Amin, Saurabh Shukla, Vikramaditya Motwane, Vishnuvardhan, Vetrimaaran, and many more.

We thank the SAGE team that facilitated this work through its inception till its conclusion, including Shambhu Sahu and others.

Thanks are due to my students for the course 'Film Theory and Practice', for bringing their dynamic perspectives on films and global media cultures.

Vimal and I are indebted to our respective families for their warmth and understanding. I would particularly like to give a very special thanks to my son Aneesh for his great good humour and unconditional affection.

Introduction

Aysha Iqbal Viswamohan

Behind the Scenes: Contemporary Bollywood Directors and Their Cinema is meant for those who think, read, teach and write about Indian cinema, particularly Bollywood,[1] as popular Hindi films are generally referred to. The impulse for this volume came from relating contemporary media and film studies with rapid developments in the sociocultural as well as the economic and technological landscape of India. The aim is to bring out a volume that offers an academic critique of those film-makers who have been active in the past two decades or so. Rather than providing a hagiographical account of these film-makers, the attempt is to acknowledge those who dared to march to a different beat, very often while working within the commercial framework, and within a certain temporal specificity.

The term 'contemporary' is defined, in the context of this work, as the period post economic liberalization in India. Though 1991 is earmarked as the year of liberalization, it was in the later part of the 1990s that Indian society, along with economic changes, witnessed major cultural and attitudinal shifts that found resonance in different aspects of life. Cinema is one cultural phenomenon, which, using its unique language and idiom, has come to embody these shifts in the most dynamic form.

Every decade of Hindi films has produced directors including early visionaries, such as Dadasaheb Phalke, Ardeshir Irani, K. Asif, Kamal Amrohi, Mehboob Khan and V. Shantaram. There were some known for their lyrical romanticism such as Guru Dutt and Raj Kapoor, while others were social commentators such as Bimal Roy and B.R. Chopra. There were the exponents of Indian noirs such as Raj Khosla and Vijay Anand; specialists of middle-of-the-road cinema, such as Basu Chatterjee, Basu Bhattacharya, Gulzar and Hrishikesh Mukherjee; creators of blockbusters, among whom are included prominent names such as Manmohan Desai, Ramesh Sippy and Prakash Mehra; experts of musical melodramas, such as Subhash Ghai and Rakesh Roshan; and there were also stark realists, such as Mrinal Sen, Shyam Benegal, Govind Nihalani, Saeed Akhtar Mirza, Ketan Mehta, Tapan Sinha, Aparna Sen and to some extent Mahesh Bhatt. It was this last category of film-makers whose works were feted and show-cased at international and national film festivals, won prestigious awards and got included in academic discourses.

However, during the last two decades the spotlight was turned on popular Hindi films. On one hand, the cinema of legendary mainstream film-makers is being enthusiastically revisited through retrospectives, revivals and remakes, and is considered worthy of academic attention. There is a proliferation of books, in English as well as regional languages, about the achievements of these leg-ends. At the same time, on the other hand, the current generation of Hindi film directors is fast attaining an international recall, and these directors have been regularly making their presence felt at international film festivals held at home and abroad. Film-makers such as Sudhir Mishra and Anurag Kashyap are no longer con-strained by the categories of 'art-house' cinema and regularly collaborate with big production houses, with the likes of Pritish Nandy Communications and Fox Star Studios. The proliferation of television channels has ensured that directors, and not just film stars, are given due coverage and are recognized (at least most of them) by their faces. Mainstream film magazines occasionally bring out 'Directors' Special' issues; select star directors are featured on the cover of magazines and directors are invited for interactive ses-sions, conferences and workshops and masterclasses at national and international universities and institutes of higher learning. Not content with just being behind the scenes, directors started becom-ing recognizable faces, and at times, even household names.

In recent times, Hindi film industry has rolled out an eclectic body of films, many of which have provided provocative and robust discussions among cinephiles. These films may be termed, for the sake of convenience, 'new age'; but, what is worth considering is the way film-makers of popular cinema have re-examined the formula and are balancing box office with more innovative films. This change is also perceptible in the works of Mumbai/ Bombay-based directors such as Farhan and Zoya Akhtar, Aditya Chopra and Sanjay Leela Bhansali who rub shoulders with 'Delhi' or 'small-town' migrant directors. The latter have consistently attempted to alter Bollywood cinematic grammar with films such as *Haasil* (Tigmanshu Dhulia, 2003), *Jab We Met* (Imtiaz Ali, 2007), *Oye Lucky! Lucky Oye!* (Dibakar Banerjee, 2008), *Gulaal* (Anurag Kashyap, 2009), *Ishqiya* (Abhishek Chaubey, 2010), *Band Baaja Baaraat* (Maneesh Sharma, 2010), *Ishaqzaade* (Habib Faisal, 2012), *Vicky Donor* (Shoojit Sircar, 2012) and many more. Apart from the employment of folk-based music, newer instruments/sounds and novel playback voices, we may consider these films for their representations of small towns (as well as cities other than Mumbai) and their lifestyles, diverse mindsets, spaces, dialect and the local colour. These films go easy on melodrama, glamour and gloss, and often challenge the popular notions about gender and community. This brand of cinema generally steers clear of the binaries and is more interested in mapping, through several quirky characters and the vicissitudes of human relations than understanding the conflict between 'good and evil'. Perhaps that explains why these films, though reasonably successful, are never record-breaking blockbusters. At the same time, formulaic films, such as *Om Shanti Om* (Farah Khan, 2007), *Dabangg* (Abhinav Kashyap, 2010), *Bajrangi Bhaijaan* (Kabir Khan, 2015), rework the traditional themes and tropes and still attempt to infuse them with new approaches. The 'new age' film-makers, most importantly, have given the audience a choice to decide what and who they want to watch. The changed audience and attitudes have compelled the stars to reassess the way in which they approach their work. Consequently, a star like Kareena Kapoor straddles a conventional *Bajrangi Bhaijaan* as well as *Ki & Ka* (R. Balki, 2016); Deepika

Padukone accommodates *Chennai Express* (Rohit Shetty, 2013) and *Piku* (Shoojit Sircar, 2015); and Shah Rukh Khan lends his star power to *Happy New Year* (Farah Khan, 2014) and *Fan* (Maneesh Sharma, 2016).

What remains most striking is the way Bollywood is finally re-examining the formula, while retaining its identity, thus bridging the gap between commercial and art-house cinema. Directors such as Imtiaz Ali and R. Balki can be seen as stellar examples (though there are several others as well) who have successfully achieved this balance. Ali consistently explores the motif of journey, physical as well as emotional, to underscore many conflicting human emotions. His most well-known films such as *Jab We Met* (2007), *Love Aaj Kal* (2009), *Rockstar* (2011), *Highway* (2014) and *Tamasha* (2015) are remarkable for their strong female protagonists. Ali invests his leads with the level of complexity and moral ambiguity that is often termed 'groundbreaking', which indeed is within the framework of commercial Hindi cinema. Likewise, a common theme that emerges in Balki's works is his preoccupation with the uncommon and unusual in human relationships. In *Cheeni Kum* (2007), he explores a romance between a 36-year-old woman and a 63-year-old man, with a feisty 80-plus matriarch thrown in. The film-maker also has a unique perspective on diseases and disabilities, where he eschews the traditional melodramatic sentiments.

So how and why does this period (1990s, 'post-liberalization'), which we use as a temporal marker, differs from the preliberalized cinema? There are several aspects to this trend. Much of the change happened as the new generation of urban cine-goers got exposed to international channels and films from various parts of the world. A sizeable section of film-makers started looking at the kind of cinema without the formulae commonly associated with the preceding decades, particularly the 1970s and the 1980s. The 'new age' cinema and its consumers (mostly in their 20s/30s) were ready for new stories in terms of form, style and themes. At the same time, 'stars' got younger, thus appealing to the demography between 15 and 35. Overseas markets too played a vital role in informing the style, content, music, production values and the overall texture of films. Global markets indeed offered film-makers the kind of freedom they had not experienced before, though its benefits belonged to the rather select group of stars and production houses. Due credit must also be given to directors such as Ram Gopal Varma and Nagesh Kukunoor as their early films are responsible for ushering in the winds of change. Kukunoor's *Hyderabad Blues* (1998) initiated the 'indie' movement in Hindi cinema. A deeply personal film (made on a shoestring budget), it traced the journey of an 'NRI' returning 'home' after a long stay in the United States. The film, though simplistic in its ideology, struck a chord with the audience.

At the heart of the contemporary Hindi film industry are the multiplexes, mostly housed in big shopping malls, the synapses and receptors of our post-liberalized times. It is 'multiplex films'[2] that have enabled the possibility of making a diverse range of works, as producer Elahe Hiptoola points out, 'It would have been difficult for *Hyderabad Blues* to fill a 1,000-seater every day, three shows a day, for eighteen weeks.... [I]t was meant for urban audiences, the multiplexes definitely came in there.' (Dwyer and Pinto 2011: 200) Without getting into arguments about single versus multiscreen theatres and urban/small-town dichotomy, it is certain that the appeal of contemporary 'niche' artists transcends the erstwhile established and accepted boundaries. As Rachel Dwyer points out, 'Just as India has been transformed during the last few decades, the Hindi film itself has changed in all areas — technology, marketing, viewing practices, audiences and consumption, as well as content, narrative, image and sound' (Dwyer 2014: 256).

By the first decade of the new millennium, films such as Dibakar Banerjee's *Khosla Ka Ghosla!* (2006), Anurag Basu's *Life in a Metro* (2007), R. Balki's *Cheeni Kum*, Shimit Amin's *Chak De! India* (2007) and Reema Kagti's *Honeymoon Travels Pvt. Ltd.* (2007) heralded the arrival of non-formulaic films on the commercial scene. Particularly worth noting was the blurring of distinctions between 'art' and 'commercial' cinema. Though cinema scholars consider commercial cinema derivational, the new brigade of Hindi film-makers is optimistic about appealing to a cultural demography and breaking away from geographical constraints.

These film-makers aspire to break into world cinema, rather than limit themselves to the NRI audience, and the ripple effects of these ambitions are visible (see Mishra 2006). Thus, if Karan Johar is known for melodramatic extravaganzas, he can also charter the unknown territory, as in *Bombay Talkies* (2013); likewise, Aditya Chopra, in his producer avatar, has been regularly giving us little gems, such as *Dum Laga Ke Haisha* (Sharat Katariya, 2015) — films that go against the kinds of film that the Yash Raj banner is known for. Another perceptible trend is women directors making a splash behind the camera. No longer restrained by the compulsion to make 'women's issues' pictures, these film-makers are confidently straddling the categories of 'art' and 'commerce', successfully telling local stories for an international audience.

While reviewing *Talaash* (Reema Kagti, 2012), Rachel Saltz (2012), *The New York Times* reviewer, observes, 'That's a lot of Cool Kids of New Bollywood talent, and it shows. "Talaash" isn't a radical departure (or a radical anything). It's very much a Hindi film, but updated and delivered with conviction and style.' The question whether the film-makers under discussion in the present volume can or even aspire to be considered as makers of world cinema still remains. In the last couple of years, films that have created ripples on the international forum, such as *Ship of Theseus* (Anand Gandhi, 2012), *The Lunchbox* (Ritesh Batra, 2013), *Masaan* (Neeraj Ghaywan, 2015), are conspicuously offbeat and belong to the art-house category. *Behind the Scenes: Contemporary Bollywood Directors and Their Cinema* focuses on those 'cool kids', whose works act as signposts of global Hindi cinema. The chapters grounded in interdisciplinary studies, vary in length and scope and lead towards well-articulated critiques of the works of select film-makers. Some key theories and concepts that provide the frameworks for the essays include mediated representations of class, gender, nation and spaces; stardom and entertainment; Hindi cinema and its global character; postcolonialism and South Asian studies; post-modernism and a new, vigorous interest in the noir; in addition to the elements of mise en scène, music and narratives. As expected, all contributors approach their essays through different perspectives, enabling us to see how divergent paths are taken, and are possible, in recent cinema.

To envisage an anthology that includes many directors of contemporary relevance is to embark on an ambitious venture, and we recognize the absence of certain prominent film-makers, a situation solely due to constraints of time and space, and not motivated by any sense of exclusion. Though some of the directors selected here are unapologetic about being 'mere' entertainers, several of them have adopted off-the-beaten-track approaches; in this regard, we have tried to represent both commercial and independent film-makers, who enjoy the varying degrees of position. While making no claims towards doing a canonical study, this edited volume attempts to locate the key to the magic kingdom of some of the movie-makers working today.

The editors, at this particular juncture, would like to draw the attention of the readers to the notion of 'auteur' that occurs at several places in this book. The term, though problematic, is a well-established one, and our contributors have channelled theoretical writings of the masters in the domain of auteurism. Though we recognize the limitations of the concept of cinematic authorship, we go by the conviction that contemporary Bollywood film-makers and their films are worth studying.

Structurally, this book is divided into three sections. In Part I, 'Cinema of Glamour and Celebration: The Post-liberalization Bollywood Auteur', the focus is on the directors of popular, glamorous and youth-oriented cinema whose transnational aesthetics have found them a place on the global scene.

We start with Ajay Gehlawat looking at the one of a kind Farah Khan in Chapter 1, '*Main Hoon* Farah: The Choreographer as Auteur'. The author follows Khan's fascinating trajectory from a groundbreaking choreographer to a sought after director, and posits that despite Khan's leanings towards populist entertainment, there is a presence of a distinct Brechtian element that makes her films much more than escapist fares. In Chapters 2 and 3, I focus on those two directors of our times whose films are known for authentic representation of youth culture in Bollywood. Though considered too Westernized for the early 1990s, there was a certain old-world charm in the films of Mansoor Khan. His films celebrated India in not so distant past and were nostalgic about times when India was at the cusp of liberalization. 'Nostalgia' and 'utopia' are at the core of Mansoor Khan's films, as is examined in 'Mansoor Khan: Narrative and Aesthetic Impulses of a Director in "Self" Exile'. 'Farhan Akhtar: Stardom of the Poster Boy of "New" Hindi Cinema' considers Farhan Akhtar as the 'It' boy of post-liberalization Hindi films. By employing the theories of stardom, this chapter provides an overview of the protean director's position as a star director.

Our next director's brand can be placed at the extreme end of the spectrum of cinematic aesthetics. It is well-documented how the extraordinary success of *Dilwale Dulhania Le Jayenge* (1995) had put the Yash Raj banner on the international map. In Chapter 4, 'Aditya Chopra's "Glamorous Realism"', Manjunath Pendakur maps the rise of Yash Raj Films as a global and cultural conglomerate. While doing so, he reflects on the emergence of Aditya Chopra as an auteur, whose particular brand of cinema combines superior understanding of Bollywood's 'masala' aesthetics with exceptional business acumen. The role of industry is discussed in Chapter 5 as well, with Sudhir Mahadevan's 'Authorship, Industry and the Intermedial Relay: The Films of Vidhu Vinod Chopra'. Mahadevan taps into Chopra's works, not just as a director but also as a collaborator on several projects. The writer tracks the director's involvement in commercial melodrama and the social from his early works till date. Mahadevan proposes that with influences such as the French New Wave, New Hollywood and also FTII generation, Chopra (along with his contemporaries) has produced interesting work that engages with cinematic modernism. Baradwaj Rangan in Chapter 6, 'Rajkumar Hirani: The Outsider', surveys the works of the director who has made satire popular, not to mention commercially viable. Arguably the most well-loved film directors of our times, Hirani has given us four consecutive blockbusters that have left a strong cultural impact on our collective consciousness. Through close readings of Hirani's films, Rangan identifies the major themes and motifs in the director's works that inform his films.

Chapter 7, Varsha Panjwani's 'Sanjay Leela Bhansali: In the Realm of Innovative Cinematic Experiences', puts the spotlight on recurrent themes in the director's works: disability and literary adaptation. His films may evoke strong responses but what is certain is that Bhansali has positioned himself as a director with strong visual aesthetics and has redefined the hues in Hindi cinema. Reading select films of Bhansali, Panjwani explains how through his unique style and cinematic grammar, Bhansali's films underpin certain provocative sociopolitical issues.

Part II titled 'Cinema of Commentaries and Interventions: History, Politics and Society in Bollywood' is concerned with understanding the issues related to globalization, neo-noir politics, social justice and nation building mainly through the perspectives of political and cultural theories. In Chapter 8, Jyotsna Kapur and Soumik Pal in their interestingly titled essay 'In the Morbid Interregnum: Vishal Bhardwaj's Realist Aesthetic and the Neoliberal Imaginary' trace the concept of auteurship in the age of neoliberalism. From his early association with Gulzar as the music director of *Maachis* (1996) till his recent *Haider* (2014), Bhardwaj has garnered equal doses of acclaim and controversies. Kapur and Pal, using a theoretical framework comprising the seminal works of Antonio Gramsci, Henri Lefebvre and Stephen Greenblatt, offer an intensive reading of Vishal Bhardwaj's cinema, with particular emphasis on *Maqbool* (2004).

Through her 'elements trilogy', Deepa Mehta has explored controversial social issues related to Indian society. Although not strictly 'Bollywood' (and, therefore, an exception in this volume), yet the Indo-Canadian director tells very Indian stories using popular stars and technicians from Hindi film world. Alka Kurian in Chapter 9, 'Post-colonial Transgression in Deepa Mehta's Feminist Quartet', examines the construction of the nation, subaltern and the marginal in the transnational director's films.

Whether it is urban or small town, discontent, despair and dread rule Anurag Kashyap's cinematic world. In Chapter 10, 'Sounding Dystopia: Anurag Kashyap's Films and Relocation of Popular Tropes', Madhuja Mukherjee reads Kashyap's films through the prism of 'neo-noir'. The essay that forms Chapter 10 of this anthology illustrates how the director creates a certain mood through his mise en scène, including shots, spaces, sounds and cinematography.

Luck by Chance (2009) introduced Zoya Akhtar as a film-maker whose films are conspicuous by their self-reflexivity and self-referentiality. In Chapter 11, 'Globalization, Reflexivity and Genre in Zoya Akhtar's Films', Nandana Bose provides an in-depth analysis of thematic and stylistic concerns in Akhtar's cinema. Bose posits that it is the collaborative nature of film-making, along with unusual promotional strategies, that underpins the director's works.

With *Is Raat Ki Subah Nahin* (1996), Mishra established himself as a director of urban claustrophobia and paranoia, whose films reflect the urgency of our times. Like Anurag Kashyap, Sudhir Mishra is also interested in creating moods on the silver screen. Pavithra Narayanan and Clare Wilkinson investigate Mishra's auteurial style in 'Urban Dreams: Sudhir Mishra's Representations of Social and Political Change', that is Chapter 12 of this volume. By examining Mishra's representative films, the authors infer that Mishra's films offer an intense humane perspective on contemporary India.

The role of films in nation building is as old as the history of cinema. In Chapter 13, Tutun Mukherjee analyses how films can link the past with the present through the mythical bond of the land and its people. Her essay, 'Ashutosh Gowariker: Narrativizing the "Nation"', seeks to determine how Gowariker's films can be seen in line with films such as *Mother India* (1957) and *Do Bigha Zamin* (1953), and fit in the category of nationalist narratives. The next director under scanner is someone whose films often betray a sense of sensationalism and melodrama, while they purport to offer correctives to various social ills that thrive beneath the glitter of our metros. From *Chandni Bar* (2001) onwards, his films stake a claim towards tackling socially relevant subjects and dealing with the seamier side of society, gender and sexuality. It is, therefore, not uncommon to refer to Madhur Bhandarkar's dark and often-disturbing films as 'realistic' cinema. Ulka Anjaria in Chapter 14, 'Madhur Bhandarkar and the New Bollywood Social' interrogates Bhandarkar's position as a film-maker through the lens of 'social' and 'realism'.

The key themes in Part III, 'Gendered Cinema: Bollywood's Women, Gender Politics and Representation', are gender, social justice and female agency.

With *Being Cyrus* (2005), Homi Adajania emerged as a new voice on the Hindi film scenario and provided an impetus to the independent cinema movement. Chapter 15, Sharanya's 'Finding Femininity: Homi Adajania and Representations of Urban Womanhood' tracks Adajania's output and highlights the director's thematic and stylistic preoccupations, including use of spaces, gender representation, dark humour and the politics of small communities. The writer reads Adajania's films primarily through the lens of mise en scène and locates him in a space that is slightly 'beyond Bollywood'.

With the release of *Ishqiya* (2010), Abhishek Chaubey arrived on the scene as a director capable of surprising his viewers with fresh characters and settings. Krupa Shandilya in Chapter 16, 'Gender Politics and Small-town India: The Cinema of Abhishek Chaubey', draws attention to the way Chaubey's cinema privileges gender construction and milieu of small town in present-day (north) India. The author argues that through his deployment of strong women characters as well as bold exploration of female sexuality, Chaubey represents a new genre that may be called 'desi feminist noir'.

Like Homi Adajania, Sriram Raghavan's films too feed on the darker edges of life and people. From *CID* (TV series, 1998) to *Badlapur* (2015), Raghavan has been preoccupied with neo-noir. Swetha Sridhar is interested in understanding the nodal points between film noir and globalization. In Chapter 17, 'Women in the Dark World: Sriram Raghavan and Hindi Film Noir', the author seeks to explore the facets of femininity and morality as embedded in Raghavan's noirish world.

A quick glance of Onir's output brings to attention the themes of family, fraternity and filiation. In Chapter 18, 'Our Brother Onir', Nandini Bhattacharya looks at the director's emergence as an independent 'indie' film-maker. Apart from understanding Onir's preoccupation with the constructs of hetero-patriarchy and heteronormativity, the writer also muses over the distinction between 'commercial' and 'non-commercial' film-making in today's Hindi film industry. In the final chapter, 'Location and Agency in Crafting Habib Faisal's Authorship', Monika Mehta illustrates the role of location and class in Faisal's films. Faisal's position as an auteur is also discussed in relation to his screenplays and dialogues.

Notes

1   'Bollywood' is an acceptable term for the popular variety of Mumbai cinema, and the term is a part of a universal lexicon despite fervid protests by several personalities from the Hindi film industry. For further details, see Dudrah (2006) and Rachel Dwyer and Jerry Pinto (2011).

2   In *The Multiplex in India: A Cultural Economy of Urban Leisure*, Adrian Athique (2010) comments on the new socio-economic order in India saying, '[T]he corporate populism expressed through the form of the multiplex represents a direct challenge to the classic anthropological understanding of India as culturally rich but economically backward.' He explains the multiplex phenomenon as something that 'demonstrates the necessity, and the utility, of an integrated approach to the symbolic and the material in researching social change' (p. 20).

References

Athique, Adrian. 2010. *The Multiplex in India: A Cultural Economy of Urban Leisure*. New York: Routledge.

Dudrah, R.K. 2006. *Bollywood: Sociology Goes to the Movies*. London: SAGE Publications.

Dwyer, R. 2014. *Picture Abhi Baaki Hai: Bollywood as a Guide to Modern India*. New Delhi/London: Hachette.

Dwyer, R. and J. Pinto (eds.). 2011. *Beyond the Boundaries of Bollywood: The Many Forms of Hindi Cinema*. New Delhi: Oxford University Press.

Mishra, S. 2006. 'Thirsting for Pyaasa.' *Outlook*. 4 December. Retrieved 11 October 2015, from http://www.outlookindia.com/article/thirsting-for-pyaasa/233289

Saltz, Rachel. 2012. 'The Dead Man Had an Oddly Familiar Name.' *The New York Times*. 29 November. Retrieved 11 October 2015, from http://www.nytimes.com/2012/11/30/movies/talaash-starring-aamir-khan.html

Part I

Cinema of Glamour and Celebration:
The Post-liberalization Bollywood Auteur

CHAPTER 1

Main Hoon Farah:
The Choreographer as Auteur

Ajay Gehlawat

There are not many, if any, directors like Farah Khan. A successful female film-maker in an industry overwhelmingly dominated by men, Khan is also one of the few choreographers who have migrated to the director's chair—as Tejaswini Ganti notes, '[She is t]he first (and only one of two) commercially successful female directors in the Hindi film industry' (Ganti 2013: 228).[1] This is no small feat in the segmented world of Hindi film production, in which directors have little oversight in the composition of the numerous song and dance sequences which populate and, by many accounts, quintessentially define the popular Hindi film form, more commonly known as Bollywood.[2] Khan began her career as a choreographer in the early 1990s, a period which also saw the liberalization of the Indian economy and its ensuing effects on the popular film industry. She quickly revolutionized the form of song and dance in Bollywood—as Baradwaj Rangan has observed, '[She] practically reinvented the way film songs are staged' (Rangan 2014: 380). Khan's experiences as a choreographer have crucially informed her approach as a film-maker, which commenced with *Main Hoon Na* (MHN), released in 2004.

Along with coming to define the style of contemporary Bollywood song and dance, she is, as one critic has noted, 'considered to be a master of the quintessential Bollywood repertoire' (Shresthova 2011: 158). Khan's choreography in over 90 films has influenced both her individual storytelling style (as a director) and, arguably, the work of other film-makers whose films' song and dance sequences she choreographed, both before and during her own career as a director. Similarly, Khan has continued working as a choreographer on her own films, including MHN, *Om Shanti Om* (2007, hereafter OSO), *Tees Maar Khan* (2010, hereafter TMK) and her most recent *Happy New Year* (2014, hereafter HNY). This dual function crucially informs Khan's auteurial style[3] and distinguishes her from her peers who, with few exceptions, leave song and dance sequences wholly in the hands of choreographers. More broadly, Khan takes a decidedly hands-on approach in the production of her films, involving herself not only with screenwriting and directorial decisions but also in what may seem like mundane activities such as costume and prop acquisition, location scouting, musical decisions and product placement. During the pre-production of her second film, OSO, for instance, Khan and her art director Sabu Cyril 'collected period furniture and props from the *chor bazaars* or flea markets and went to great lengths to research the "working model" of seventies Bombay cinema' (Sarkar 2013: 220). It is a testament to her proactive approach that three of her four films have been box office smashes (the one exception being TMK), in addition to the success of the numerous other films on which she has worked as choreographer (e.g., *Dilwale Dulhania Le Jayenge*, aka DDLJ [1995]; *Kabhi Khushi Kabhie Gham* [2001]; *Kal Ho Naa Ho* [2003]; etc.). Along with working in the Hindi film industry, Khan has also served as choreographer on a range of other films and productions, including Mira Nair's *Monsoon Wedding* (2001), Andrew Lloyd Weber's stage production, *Bombay Dreams* (2002), the Chinese film *Perhaps Love* (2005), and Colombian pop star Shakira's performance of her song 'Hips Don't Lie' at the MTV Music Video Awards (2006). Her husband Shirish Kunder frequently collaborates on her films as an editor, while her brother, Sajid Khan, is also a director, as are her cousins,

Farhan and Zoya Akhtar. Khan also frequently appears in brief cameos in several of her films and also recently starred in *Shirin Farhad Ki Toh Nikal Padi* (2012), a romantic comedy directed by Bela Segal, co-starring Boman Irani.

One of Khan's key interventions, first as a choreographer and then as a director, has been to make the Indian hero dance. Prior to the 1990s (the same period which marked Khan's ascent as a choreographer), male stars in Bollywood rarely danced or, if they did, danced poorly (Deshpande 2005). Beginning with her first choreography assignment, for the song 'Pehla Nasha' from the film *Jo Jeeta Wohi Sikandar* (1992), Khan's markedly different approach is vividly on display, as the film star, Aamir Khan, rolls down hills, running his hands through his hair as he is framed in slow motion. Indeed Khan, perhaps more than any other film-maker or choreographer, has increasingly made male stars the key 'items' of song and dance sequences, whereas previously the male figure remained the essentially dormant half of the 'dancing duo' in these interludes. A good example of this can be seen in the reigning male dance star Hrithik Roshan's first film, *Kaho Naa ... Pyaar Hai* (2000), whose smash hit song, 'Ek Pal Ka Jeena', Khan choreographed and in which Roshan, wearing a figure-hugging, mesh see-through top, 'dances like a dream' (Deshpande 2005: 197). Even prior to this, however, Khan's different (gendered) approach to choreography was on display in Mani Ratnam's *Dil Se* (1998), both in the famous first song, 'Chaiyya Chaiyya', featuring Bollywood superstar Shah Rukh Khan (hereafter, SRK) dancing on top of a moving train, and in the film's final song, 'Jiya Jale', in which an oiled and bare-chested SRK dances intensely with Preity Zinta in numerous exotic settings featuring waterfalls, canoes and elephant-enclosed fields.[4] Khan's close working relationship with SRK is well documented and, in her first feature, MHN, which was also the first film to be produced by SRK's company Red Chillies Entertainment, Khan again had SRK give an erotic performance in the song 'Tumhe Jo Maine Dekha', noting, '[O]f course I insisted as a woman director that my hero also wear a white transparent shirt and stand under the waterfall. Just not the girl alone who's going to be doing that.'[5]

Similarly, while there has been a tendency by critics to see the song and dance sequence as one of the 'irrationalities' of the Hindi film form (Gopal and Moorti 2011: 57), in Khan's films 'each song is a set sequence, ... providing a dramatic turn to the story' (Chanda 2011: 150). Along with the attention Khan gives to the choreography of each sequence, she is quite thoughtful about the placement of the songs in her films. Regarding the first song in MHN, 'Chale Jaise Hawaien', for instance, Khan notes:

> I was very clear that twenty minutes into my film, the first song should come. Because I feel, up to eighteen or twenty minutes, the audience is settling in, is watching your film. And twenty minutes later they're ready to get into it, and the *fun* should begin then. And ... that's what I wanted. So exactly I think twenty-one or twenty-two minutes into the film, this first song began.[6]

It is precisely this level of detail that belies claims concerning the random placement of song sequences, at least in Khan's own films. Khan clearly relishes the opportunity to have free rein over both the placement and cinematic style of her songs (as director), as she goes on to note on the director's commentary track of MHN:

> This song ['Chale Jaise Hawaien'] has been a long-time dream of mine, to do a dance number in one shot. And actually do it in one shot, without resorting to invisible cuts or, you know, edits that you can't see, or any kind of computer graphics or special effects. And, finally, since it was *my* film and there was no one questioning me or telling me, 'No no no, you need to have cuts', I could do what I wanted.[7]

Along with directing and choreographing MHN, Khan co-wrote the screenplay with Abbas Tyrewala, which deals with the historically fraught relations between India and Pakistan and features a fictitious programme, 'Project Milaap', in which the two countries orchestrate a civilian prisoner exchange. Describing this aspect of MHN, Khan also illuminates another key component of her approach to film-making, claiming that 'instead of preaching and ... making a really boring film and putting this kind of message in, it would be nice to make a complete entertainer which people would watch again and again, and *then* put a message of peace in it'.[8] Here, we see two key sentiments which continually re-emerge in Khan's oeuvre: First, to make decidedly populist fare and, at the same time, to not forgo certain themes which she feels are important to her. Rather than being diametrically opposed (as some film-makers and critics would frame such aims), the gist of both Khan's approach and her ensuing success has been precisely to proceed in this manner, reflecting a savviness on her part and, simultaneously, a rather level-headed assessment of her audience which, as she notes, 'is far more intelligent than you think'.[9] Khan has similarly been quite straightforward in acknowledging that her films are, in her words, '*filmi* film[s]', adding, 'I never said I was making ... art film[s].'[10]

One witnesses just such a blend of innovation and populist appeal in her second and arguably most successful film, OSO, which again features SRK. In this extremely reflexive production, Khan simultaneously tells a tale of reincarnation within the Hindi film industry and illuminates the inner workings of this industry, both during the 1970s and the contemporary era. In this 'brilliantly orchestrated self-reflexive enactment', she 'certainly takes a risk by incorporating these very formulae and breaking the audience's involvement in the story by showing how it takes to formulae that are clichéd and unvaried' (Chanda 2011: 148; Shastri 2011: 40). It is perhaps for this reason, as Ipshita Chanda notes, that 'Shah Rukh and Farah were so nervous before the film released' and also why, to return to both Khan's previously expressed faith in the audience and her blend of innovation and populist appeal, OSO 'persuades the audience to introspect over cinematic conventions and its own demands in this direction' (Chanda 2011: 148; Shastri 2011: 42). In 'present[ing] a history of the genre by exposing its mechanical workings', Khan again combines two approaches, that is, providing mass entertainment and skewering the very elements informing this mode of entertainment, and thus, 'expos[es] to the gaze of the audience what is generally kept beyond the camera's gaze' (Chanda 2011: 157, 162). As film critic Baradwaj Rangan has noted, 'Farah knows her Bollywood', and it is precisely this knowingness, this familiarity with the inner workings of the industry, that allows her to 'break new ground' (Golani 2014: 35; Rangan 2014: 382). In other words Khan, an industry insider, innovates from within, which may also be one of the key reasons for her success, paradoxically breaking new ground by frequently quoting and reformulating past conventions.

Such quoting and reformulating is, unsurprisingly, nowhere more on display than in the song and dance sequences of Khan's films. OSO, in particular, features numerous innovations at both the technical and stylistic levels. As the film's screenwriter, Mushtaq Sheikh, notes in his book on the making of the film, several of the video effects (VFX) and digital technologies on display in the film—most vividly in certain song sequences, including 'Dhoom Tana' and 'Main Agar Kahoon'—were used in India 'for the first time' (Sheikh 2008: 87).[11] The first song from MHN, 'Chale Jaise Hawaien', similarly made use of technologies such as digital compositing, even as these were combined with the innovative, hands-on approach of Khan's choreographic and cinematographic styles, with the director orchestrating a mass dance sequence employing a Steadicam operator whom she literally pushed and pulled amidst the scores of moving bodies, in order to achieve her long sought after dream of shooting a dance number in one shot. It should come as no surprise that such innovations emerge most vividly in Khan's song and dance sequences, given her background as a choreographer and how this training has crucially informed her vision as a director. As Vishal Dadlani of the popular music duo Vishal–Shekhar notes, 'Working with Farah is a breeze because she comes in as a director, she comes in as a choreographer, she comes in with, like, a full idea of *exactly* what she wants to shoot.'[12]

Interestingly enough, according to Khan, it was her success as a choreographer that delayed her directorial debut (Golani 2014: 34). Yet in the process of choreographing song sequences for other people's films, Khan perfected the style which came to define her own work, creating condensed narratives out of song sequences, even as she drew upon older motifs to do so. A particularly illustrative example of this approach on display throughout the songs in her own films is in the sequence 'Woh Ladki Hai Kahan?' from Farhan Akhtar's *Dil Chahta Hai* (2001, hereafter DCH). Employing a high degree of reflexivity and an equal level of familiarity with the Bollywood canon, Khan choreographs this song as a simultaneous tongue-in-cheek homage to older Hindi film numbers and as a vehicle through which the couple in the film, Sameer (Saif Ali Khan) and Pooja (Sonali Kulkarni), falls in love. It is no coincidence that such a coming together is mediated through films and the film-viewing experience; indeed, the sequence begins and ends with Sameer and Pooja watching a film in a theatre, into which they are subsequently enfolded. In such a way, Khan's song sequence in DCH creates 'a complex negotiation between homage and parody' (Iyer 2016), using earlier cinematic motifs to create a mini-narrative which is simultaneously critiqued through her reflexive treatment. One witnesses a similarly complex negotiation in Khan's later films, particularly in OSO. Along with the 'Dhoom Tana' sequence's digital insertions of Padukone's character into several earlier Bollywood films, the ensuing sequence 'Main Agar Kahoon' engages in a form of backstage musical reflexivity regarding the filming of song sequences in Bollywood, showing all that typically remains outside the camera's purview, for example, blowing fans, levers operating descending cut-out moons and rear projection of background scenery — in other words, laying bare all of the devices at work in constructing the film (song)'s 'fantasy', itself now presented as the orchestrated fantasy of its junior artist protagonist, played again by SRK.

Several critics have commented on the tongue-in-cheek nature of Khan's songs, particularly those featuring SRK. M.K. Raghavendra, for instance, claims that there is 'little doubt that this [reflexivity] is deliberate', arguing that SRK's character in OSO, Om, is 'less a character inhabiting a story than Shah Rukh Khan doing a turn' (Raghavendra 2014: 87). Yet in subsequently stating that 'the film's sole message' is 'SRK and Bollywood', Raghavendra seems to miss a key element of such sequences in Khan's films, even as this places him squarely in the company of other critics who similarly remain sceptical about the possibility that Khan's reflexive song sequences are 'innovative in the

Brechtian sense' (Sarkar 2013: 225).[13] In a similar vein Raghavendra describes OSO as 'the extreme case of the brand becoming the content', claiming that performances such as those by SRK and other stars in Khan's films are 'redolent of the commercials in which they appear' (Raghavendra 2014: 92). It is in such a manner that one can correspondingly read OSO as 'more intent on fortifying the Bollywood firmament than taking it apart' (Sarkar 2013: 225). Yet at least one of these critics simultaneously wonders 'why [he] was feeling so distanced from the proceedings' (Rangan 2014: 379). An initial response may be that, rather than merely 'fortifying the Bollywood firmament', Khan simultaneously transforms 'the means of pleasure into objects of instruction' (Brecht quoted in Sarkar 2013: 225). Such a transformation is achieved precisely through Khan exposing the 'mechanical workings' of her films (and, more broadly, of the Bollywood form). Rather than seeing Khan as 'only' interested in celebrating Bollywood, one must also take into account her crucial spoofing of Bollywood and its myriad conventions, which arguably undercuts rather than fortifies this cinema's form and content.[14]

However, as a further testament to Khan's innovativeness as a film-maker, one can argue that she simultaneously achieves both of the objectives of undercutting and celebrating or, to paraphrase Jean Baudrillard (1987), transcending and dissolving Bollywood and its myriad pleasures in a manner that itself becomes pleasurable.[15] Such an approach — assembling and disassembling the Bollywood form — is eminently on display in Khan's most recent film, HNY (2014), which *The New York Times* described as a combination of '*Strictly Ballroom*-era Baz Luhrmann' with *Ocean's 11*, and 'a pinch of *The Full Monty*' liberally tossed with 'the gaudy excesses of the Eurovision song contest' (Webster 2014). Along with such Western samplings, Khan's film serves as a mashup of multiple genres utilized in her previous films, including the action, comedy, musical, dramatic and caper film formats. Additionally, Khan continues spoofing and paying homage to several earlier Bollywood films with HNY — one of SRK's first lines in this film, for instance, is a paraphrase of one of his most famous lines from DDLJ ('*Bade bade fights mein aisi chhoti chhoti maar to lagti rehti hai'* — in very big fights such small beatings continue to be inflicted), a line that even the US president Barack Obama tried to spoof in his recent 2015 visit to India. Similarly, Khan inflects all of the generic elements listed above with additional twists — interlacing fight sequences, for instance, with homoerotic humor — and, in the process, reformulates these components of the Bollywood 'masala', highlighting what may have previously only been a latent subtext. Such an approach could again be seen in a Brechtian vein, engaging as it does in a series of gestures and quotations of Bollywood that result in a simultaneous celebration and deconstruction of this latter film form. After SRK's character, here named Charlie, assembles his team of accomplices (named Charlie's Angels) he begins training with them under the tute-lage of Mohini (Deepika Padukone), a dance instructor, in order to compete in the World Dance Championships in Dubai which, in turn, will allow him to accomplish his ultimate goal of stealing precious diamonds from the venue's hotel safe (and thus vindi-cating his deceased father). In the process, as Sarkar notes, 'Farah Khan does not spare herself either' (2013: 216), as the series of dance competitions and performances allow her to parody pre-cisely the dance conventions that she herself has played a large role in promulgating. In the dance number titled 'Nonsense Ki Night', for instance, one of the team's members, Tammy (Boman Irani), has an epileptic seizure in the middle of the performance. When members of the jury (including actual Bollywood choreog-raphers such as Khan's assistant Geeta Kapoor) notice this and express concern about Tammy's condition, the other members of Charlie's Angels surround Tammy and began impersonating his seizure as a choreographed dance move, thus simultaneously paying homage to one of Khan's earliest influences, Michael Jackson, and spoofing the dance competition venue at the same time.[16]

Such a parodic approach aligns itself with precisely the spirit of Brecht's own populist aspirations, imploding in the process the (false) dichotomy of instruction versus pleasure. Brecht himself noted, in discussing one of his several plays, the importance of pleasure in the process of estrangement. To read Khan's approach

in a Brechtian vein, one could claim that it is precisely by criti-
quing 'from a position of complicity' that her films 'show up the
commercial character both of the entertainment and of the persons entertained' (Brecht 1957: 41; Feuer 1993: 137). The end credits song sequences of Khan's films are a good example of this,
and a fitting way of concluding this essay. Arguably innovations
in themselves, Khan's end credits sequences, starting with MHN
and appearing in all of her subsequent films, feature members
of the cast and crew (including Khan herself) in a reflexive coda
that the director describes as 'a curtain call where everyone comes
and takes a bow'.[17] Khan goes on to note that 'it would be nice to
have on screen all the people who had worked on our film, not
only the actors but all the unit members, because they were as
much a part of the film as the people who were onscreen'.[18] Yet
occasionally, in an echo of my earlier critique of the binary which
can only frame Khan's films as reflexive or celebratory, these 'curtain calls' go beyond mere homage, including at times what could
be seen as scathing critiques, all the more so for the humorous,
tongue-in-cheek way in which they are deployed. TMK's end
credits sequence, for instance, titled 'Happy Ending', spoofs the
aspirations of its Bollywood hero, Akshaye Khanna, to become a
Hollywood sensation in a clever send-up of the previous year's
Oscar awards ceremony, featuring Anil Kapoor as the master of
ceremonies (MC), re-enacting his own and other Indians' reactions
to the success of *Slumdog Millionaire* (2008), exhorting Khanna to
come to the stage to claim his award, shouting, 'Come on, India!
Come on, my boy!' before proceeding to dance ecstatically with
Khanna, who literally stumbles over himself in joy. The sequence
then cuts to the film's fair-skinned actress, Katrina Kaif, running
her hand up one bare arm, in a faux-ad for 'Veet Hair Removal
Cream', whose tube Kaif then holds up while grinning and wink-
ing at the camera. It is precisely in such sly jabs not only at the
conventions of Bollywood but at those surrounding and informing its discourse (including awards ceremonies, dance competitions and hair removal creams) that Khan deftly employs even
the end credits song sequences in her films as forms of critique,
in which brand images, rather than dominating, are undercut,

and whose brand spokesmen and women, rather than 'redolent of the commercials in which they appear' (Raghavendra 2014: 92), become spoofs of them(selves). Perhaps this is why critics find themselves so 'distanced' at times from the events in Khan's films, even as they acknowledge that 'Farah Khan makes me laugh' (Rangan 2014: 379).

Notes

1   Khan is one of a handful of influential choreographers, including Shiamak Davar, Saroj Khan, Prabhu Deva and Vaibhavi Merchant, whose contributions have helped make Bollywood a cinema of spectacle and dance. However, other than Prabhu Deva, Khan is the only choreographer in the contemporary era who has gone on to direct her own films.

2   As Sangita Gopal and Sujata Moorti have noted, 'To talk of Bollywood is inevitably to talk of the song and dance sequence. [...] Frequently remarked upon by insiders and always remarkable to outsiders, song-dance occupies the constitutive limit of Bollywood cinema' and 'determines ... the form itself' (Gopal and Moorti 2008: 1).

3   The auteur, as David Bordwell and Kristin Thompson note, 'usually did not literally write scripts but managed nonetheless to stamp his or her personality on genre and studio products' (Bordwell and Thompson 2003: 487). This has emphatically been the case with Khan, both in her work as a choreographer and a director, as we shall see in the ensuing discussion.

4   Khan won the Filmfare Award for her choreography of 'Chaiyya Chaiyya', which SRK himself performed on top of a moving train. As Khan recounts, SRK 'wanted to make sure that "Chaiyya Chaiyya" was so spectacular that no actor after would attempt a train dance (nobody has)' (Chopra 2007: 191).

5   See *Main Hoon Na* (MHN) DVD Director Commentary Track (2005). As Anupama Chopra notes, Khan is SRK's favourite choreographer and she has worked with him since the beginning of his career, 'even design[ing] the signature Shah Rukh Khan move (sweeping his hand through his hair) which had the ladies swooning in the aisles' (Chopra 2007: 185).

6   MHN DVD Director Commentary Track (2005).

7   See Note 6.

8   See Note 6.

9   See Note 6.

10   *Om Shanti Om* (OSO) DVD Director Commentary Track (2008).
11   'Dhoom Tana', for instance, which was produced by the special effects division of Red Chillies Entertainment, digitally inserts Deepika Padukone as the character Shantipriya into footage from a series of older films, where her image replaces those of the original actresses (Sarkar 2013: 218).
12   'Making of the Songs' featurette, *Tees Maar Khan* (TMK) DVD (2011).
13   Sarkar, for instance, claims that 'Brecht would be stunned by such a claim' and would 'probably place [OSO's] narrative and formal refurbishments in the same league as fin de siècle opera's "desperate attempts" to provide itself with…a "new" sense' (Sarkar 2013: 225).
14   A number of scholars have recently invoked Brecht in their discussions of Farah Khan, including Sarkar and Chanda, who describes one of the song sequences in OSO, 'Main Agar Kahoon', as engaging in 'almost Brechtian style' (Chanda 2011: 162). For more on the use of Brecht as a way of coming to terms with the internal dynamics of the Bollywood film, see Gehlawat (2010, especially Chapter 2).
15   This is what Baudrillard called 'ecstasy', namely, the simultaneous transcendence and dissolution of a form (Baudrillard 1987: 68).
16   Charlie's Angels reference a character in Jackson's *Beat It* music video who briefly performs a breakdance motion which approximates a seizure and his *Thriller* video with their red jumpsuits. Along with Geeta Kapoor, Khan herself frequently appears as a judge on Indian dance shows.
17   See Note 6.
18   See Note 6.

References

Baudrillard. J. 1987. *Forget Foucault*. New York: Semiotext(e).
Bordwell, D. and K. Thompson. 2003. *Film Art: An Introduction*. New York: McGraw-Hill.
Brecht, B. 1957. *Brecht on Theatre*. London: Methuen.
Chanda, I. 2011. '*Kya Hum Pehle Kabhi Yahan Aye Hain*: Re-turning to Look at the "Indian" in Indian Cinema through Farah Khan's *Om Shanti Om*.' In *Locating Cultural Change: Theory, Method, Process*, edited by P.P. Basu and I. Chanda, 146–72. New Delhi: SAGE Publications.
Chopra, A. 2007. *King of Bollywood: Shah Rukh Khan and the Seductive World of Indian Cinema*. New York: Warner Books.
Deshpande, S. 2005. 'The Consumable Hero of Globalised India.' In *Bollyworld: Popular Indian Cinema Through a Transnational Lens*, edited by R. Kaur and A. Sinha, 186–203. New Delhi: SAGE Publications.

Feuer, J. 1993. *The Hollywood Musical*, 2nd ed. Bloomington, IL: Indiana University Press.

Ganti, T. 2013. *Bollywood: A Guidebook to Popular Hindi Cinema*, 2nd ed. New York: Routledge.

Gehlawat, A. 2010. *Reframing Bollywood: Theories of Popular Hindi Cinema*. New Delhi: SAGE Publications.

Golani, S. 2014. *Decoding Bollywood: Stories of 15 Film Directors*. New Delhi: Westland Ltd.

Gopal, S. and S. Moorti. 2008. 'Introduction: Travels of Hindi Song and Dance.' In *Global Bollywood: Travels of Hindi Song and Dance*, edited by S. Gopal and S. Moorti, 1–60. Minneapolis, MN: University of Minnesota Press.

———. 2011. 'Bollywood in Drag: *Moulin Rouge!* and the Aesthetics of Global Cinema.' *Camera Obscura* 25 (3): 29–67.

Iyer, U. 2016. 'Looking for the Past in Pastiche: Intertexuality in Bollywood Song-and-Dance Sequences.' In *Movies, Moves and Music: The Sonic World of Dance Films*, edited by M. Fogarty and M. Evans. London: Equinox.

Raghavendra, M.K. 2014. *The Politics of Hindi Cinema in the New Millennium: Bollywood and the Anglophone Indian Nation*. New Delhi: Oxford University Press.

Rangan, B. 2014. *Dispatches from the Wall Corner: A Journey Through Indian Cinema*. New Delhi: Tranquebar Press.

Sarkar, B. 2013. 'Metafiguring Bollywood: Brecht after *Om Shanti Om*.' In *Figurations in Indian Film* edited by M. Sen and A. Basu, 205–35. New York: Palgrave Macmillan.

Shastri, S. 2011. '"The Play's the Thing, Wherein I'll Catch the Conscience of the King": Intertexuality in *Om Shanti Om*.' *Journal of Film and Video* 63 (1): 32–43.

Sheikh, M. 2008. *The Making of Om Shanti Om*. New Delhi: Om Books.

Shresthova, S. 2011. *Is It All About Hips? Around the World with Bollywood Dance*. New Delhi: SAGE Publications.

Webster, A. 2014. 'A Bollywood Specialty: Caper Movie, With Extras.' *The New York Times*, C2, 26 October.

Film References

Advani, N. 2003. *Kal Ho Naa Ho*. Dharma Productions.

Akhtar, F. 2001. *Dil Chahta Hai*. Excel Entertainment.

Boyle, Danny. 2008. *Slumdog Millionaire*. Fox Searchlight.

Chan, P. 2005. *Perhaps Love*. Peter Chan.

Chopra, A. 1995. *Dilwale Dulhania Le Jayenge*. Yash Raj Films.

Johar, K. 2001. *Kabhi Khushi Kabhie Gham*. Dharma Productions.

Khan, F. 2004. Main Hoon Na. Eros International.
———. 2007. *Om Shanti Om*. Eros International.
———. 2010. *Tees Maar Khan*. UTV.
———. 2014. *Happy New Year*. Yash Raj Films.
Khan, M. 1992. *Jo Jeeta Wohi Sikandar*. Nasir Hussain Films.
Nair, M. 2001. *Monsoon Wedding*. IFC Productions.
Ratnam, M. 1998. *Dil Se ...* Eros International.
Roshan, R. 2000. *Kaho Naa ... Pyaar Hai*. Film Kraft.
Segal, B. 2012. *Shirin Farhad Ki Toh Nikal Padi*. Eros Entertainment.

2

Mansoor Khan: Narrative and Aesthetic Impulses of a Director in 'Self-exile'

Aysha Iqbal Viswamohan

The Journey Begins

Mansoor Khan's last film as a director was in 2000. *Josh* was a moderate success and since then he has gone into a state of 'self-exile'. Though one does get an occasional glimpse of him at film or social events, by and large he has voluntarily stayed away from the film industry, a place with which several members of his family have been associated. All the interviews that the reluctant Khan has chosen to give in recent times are self-effacing to the point of embarrassment, particularly where he labels himself a 'professional dropout'.

This chapter focuses on Khan's scant yet significant output and analyses how within the framework of escapist cinema, Khan's films redefined the genre of youth films, and how his cinema, popular and also populist to an extent, reworked certain features of popular Hindi cinema for more liberalized[1] times.

When Mansoor Khan made his first venture *Qayamat Se Qayamat Tak* (QSQT, 1988), Hindi cinema was in a state of flux. With the charisma of Amitabh Bachchan waning fast with films like *Shahenshah* (Tinu Anand, 1988), and with a spate of revenge sagas on the one hand and family dramas on the other, the 1980s are often called the 'lost decade' of Hindi cinema. The debacles of his father[2] producer/director Nasir Hussain's *Zamane Ko Dikhana Hai* (1981), *Manzil Manzil* (1984) and *Zabardast* (1985), all starring top actors of the time, and with Husain's regular crew (music director R.D. Burman, lyricist Majrooh Sultanpuri, choreographer Suresh Bhatt, cinematographer Munir Khan), categorically proved that the maestro had lost touch with the changing times. Such was the landscape of commercial Hindi cinema when QSQT was released on 1 March 1988.

Though the basic premises and aspects remained the same as Nasir Husain's films, including fondness for glamorous faces, music, romance and melodrama, it was evident that Mansoor Khan had reinvented the romantic musical genre and added a new idiom to the tired formulas of the decade.

The odds against QSQT (this is the film that started the trend of films with long titles and fashionable abbreviations) were too many to count. Nasir Husain's story about two warring Rajput families seemed out of sync with times where action–disco films were in vogue. Added to this were an unknown leading man whose looks were far removed from the then existing concept of a Hindi film 'hero'; a written off leading lady who had made her debut in a resounding flop *Sultanat* (Mukul Anand, 1986); new music directors, Anand–Milind; and also relatively new lead singers, Udit Narayan and Alka Yagnik. Indeed the only factor that worked was the 'United Producers/Nasir Hussain Films' banner that had the credentials, but a declining success ratio during the entire decade.

QSQT is a simple story about star-crossed lovers from two warring feudal families. Raj (Aamir Khan) and Rashmi (Juhi Chawla) fall in love in spite of the brutal history of their hostile families. Drawing on the premise of Shakespeare's *Romeo and Juliet*, the story is set in contemporary north India. Like Romeo, Raj gatecrashes Rashmi's party and is almost caught by the girl's family. Though instantly attracted towards Rashmi, Raj tries to get over her because of their family history. The couple fatefully meets again in Mount Abu, Rajasthan, where Rashmi is vacationing with her family. Unaware of Raj's family background, she initiates their relationship, though Raj tries for a while to resist her. The lovers are caught between the feudal principles of patriarchy and masculine honour.

The film marked a shift from Nasir Husain's brand of musical romances. The lovers defy their parents and meet clandestinely, yet Raj consistently resorts to lying to his family that he has stopped meeting Rashmi. The lovers elopement and Raj's act of self-stabbing at the end, after Rashmi is killed, is the final act of rebellion against their warring families. This despairing finale and an arguably defeated hero are a far cry from the days of Shammi Kapoor of *Dil Deke Dekho* and *Teesri Manzil*.

The success of QSQT propelled several careers. The film industry was quick to appropriate the formula of young love rebelling against the patriarchal establishment, and a romantic wave ensued resulting in *Maine Pyar Kiya* (Sooraj Barjatya, 1989), *Chandni* (Yash Chopra, 1989), *Love Love Love* (B. Subhash, 1989), *Aashiqui* (Mahesh Bhatt, 1990), *Dil* (Indra Kumar, 1990), *Dil Hai Ke Manta Nahin* (Mahesh Bhatt, 1991). A common feature of all these films was their music. The emphasis was on soft and romantic melodies, and most of them used fresh playback singers and music directors. Soon music became the new hero as films succeeded on the basis of the sale of their music cassettes. Musical romances set the tone for the 1990s where two of Hindi cinemas greatest hits were round the corner: *Hum Aapke Hain Koun...!* (Sooraj Barjatya, 1994) and *Dilwale Dulhania Le Jayenge* (Aditya Chopra, 1995).

Despite (re)inventing a successful formula, Khan's next venture was going to be a stark departure.

Changing to the Top Gear: Family, Relationships and Patriarchy

Father–son relationship has been a focal point of many Hindi films. From *Awaara* (Raj Kapoor, 1951) and *Waqt* (Yash Chopra, 1965) to *Parichay* (Gulzar, 1972), *Trishul* (Yash Chopra, 1978) and *Shakti* (Ramesh Sippy, 1982) commercial Hindi cinema has explored several facets of the bond between fathers and sons. Sons in popular Hindi films sacrifice their lives, fight for their love, avenge family honour or redeem themselves in their fathers' eyes. However, QSQT was instrumental in renegotiating the relationship between father and son. As Dhanraj (Dalip Tahil) serves time in prison for killing Ranbir Singh's (Goga Kapoor) brother Ratan, Dhanraj's family, led by his older brother Jaswant (Alok Nath), migrates from their ancestral village Dhanakpur to Delhi, where Jaswant expands their Delhi-based brother's business. Raj and his cousin (Rajendranath Zutshi) are raised by Jaswant, who chooses to remain unmarried throughout his life and devotes himself to raise Dhanraj's son. Raj grows under the benign influence of Jaswant (who is almost the hero's surrogate father), who is a pacifist unlike the more volatile Dhanraj. Raj's Westernized education and lifestyle is a world apart from his feudal background; likewise, Dhanraj, when he readjusts to a regular family life is, suave, urbane and a liberal father. In this form of contemporary melodrama, therefore,

> the global frame is crucial: for the contemporary family film is distinguished from its earlier avatars in its bid to reconcile the division between the West and the East such that a Western upbringing does not make a protagonist ineligible for the national project in a globalizing era. (Vasudevan 2010: 367)

Mansoor Khan's films have lent themselves to this aspect from the moment Aamir Khan burst on the screen with the song 'Papa Kehte Hain', which became an instant youth anthem. Raj's father, Dhanraj, who is released after 14 years of imprisonment, sees his son performing at his college farewell function. Significantly,

Dhanraj is framed from within the iron bars of a window as he watches his son on stage. The mise en scène is replicated when Dhanraj keeps a watch on his son in the office, ensuring that Raj severs all emotional ties with Rashmi. Again we see him through the window bars while Raj is free from all shackles. This unfettered projection of the hero finds manifestation in Raj's face-off with Ranbir when he declares, '*Hum aapki nafrat ke waris banne ko taiyyar nahin*' (We are not willing to inherit your legacy of hatred). Thus, as a key text of the 1980s that challenges feudalistic patriarchy, the film suggests that 'love constitutes the only transgression against absolute paternal authority' (Thoraval, 2000: 129). Like *Bobby* (Raj Kapoor, 1973) and *Love Story* (Rahul Rawail, 1981), films that provided templates for countless teen romances, Mansoor Khan too followed this pattern of lovers eloping and building an idyllic house in a forest, symbolic of return to nature and innocence.

We might notice that Mansoor Khan's hero was not cast in the mould of the popular leading men of the times, who were tough and macho in the tradition of Sunny Deol–Jackie Shroff–Sanjay Dutt, but was rather close to the teen-romantic heroes such as Rishi Kapoor and Kumar Gaurav. This is the kind of hero who could not single-handedly take on an army of villains and their sidekicks. Scholars also commented on the subtle manner in which Mansoor reversed the gender dynamics: while Aamir was introduced strumming a guitar, Juhi was first seen riding a horse. Again going against the then prevalent grain, it is the hero who is presented as an object of desire[3] (Sooraj Barjatya later followed the trend in *Maine Pyar Kiya*, where it is Salman Khan's body on display rather than the heroine's). In this connection, Jyotika Virdi observes how '[i]n their first encounter Rashmi gazes voyeuristically at Raj's athletic body running toward her against the setting sun' (Virdi, 2004: 184). The traditional 'hunted' becomes the 'hunter' with the girl making the moves with cutely flirtatious lines such as '*Hum par aapka bahut achha impression pada hai*' (I'm very impressed by you). And the constant refrain '*Aa jaaien aap ke paas?*' (May I come closer to you?) brought a new kind of a heroine into focus: a girl who was innocent, yet playful and quite unlike the blatantly sexual and sexualized concept of heroines that was in fashion during that period.

As in QSQT, Mansoor's next *Jo Jeeta Wohi Sikandar* or JJWS (1992) foregrounds relationship between father and son, along with the relationship between siblings. Mansoor reminisces, 'My relations with my father were similar to Sanjay Lal Sharma/Sanju (Aamir Khan's character) in *Jo Jeeta Wohi Sikandar*' (Dedhia, 2013).

Set against the public school backdrop in Dehradun, a north Indian hill station, the film sets the tone as a voice-over narration informs us, '[T]he richest Indians send their children here for higher education ... some are the children of steel mill owners, while some own tea estates.' The 'locals' with their middle-class way of lives and values are disparagingly referred to as *pyjamachhaps* by the elitists. The poor and the lower middle-class send their children to the modest Model School, home to the upright sports coach Ramlal Sharma (Kulbhushan Kharbanda) and his two sons, Ratan (Mamik Singh) and Sanjay. None of Mansoor Khan's films work the class dynamic as potently as JJWS. The prologue of the film sets the tone of class conflict as the binaries between the rich ('Every child is an heir to billions of rupees', the narrator tells us) and the poor class of school children ('The boys are not only academically poor but excel in bad habits') is established. Not surprisingly, the winners have a motto, '*Sabse aage ladke kaun, Rajput! Rajput!*' (Who are the leaders? Rajput!). The juxtaposition of shots need to be observed as Rajput boys work out at the gym and excel in academics, and on the other hand, Model boys throw paper rockets at their teachers and leer at a bikini-clad starlet on the cover of *Stardust*.

Sanju and his friends appropriate the local space and assert their rights over the town in the same way as Max and his gang would do later in Vasco, Goa, in *Josh*. The rich kids may have music systems, hair gels, designer shades, cars and motor bikes, but Sanju and his friends proclaim in a song, '*Ye Galiyan Apni Ye Raste Apne, Kaun Aayega Apne Aage*' (These are our lanes, our streets, who would dare challenge us?). The conflict here is between the old money and those waiting in the sidelines for their chance to make it big.

The plot, loosely borrowed from *Breaking Away* (Peter Yates, 1979), hinges on competing in and winning the most prestigious sports event, the marathon cycle race. Sports films are rare in Bollywood, and till the early 1990s, one can count the good films of this sub-genre on one's fingers, for example, Prakash Jha's *Hip Hip Hurray* (1984). JJWS traces the relationship between sports and teen masculinity (only boys are shown actively playing, while girls observe and cheer), where a boy's worth is measured by winning, or losing, the toughest sports competition on the annual sports day.

That Mansoor is interested in playing out the class and social hierarchies is evidenced through his framing of shots. Ramlal's cafe is situated opposite the posh ice cream parlour, where the rich kids hang out. For Sanju and his friends, this is a dream world to which they can only aspire to and admire from afar. This is further exemplified in one of the earlier scenes in the cafe as a defiant Sanju watches on while his brother earnestly does tables for the snooty Rajput and Xavier boys. Shekhar Malhotra (Deepak Tijori) and his gang, fresh after former's consecutive victory in the sports competition, rag Ratan and call him 'a stupid hunk'. The camera cuts to the humiliation on Ratan's face and next to Sanju's face, as he simmers with silent rage. The director again shows Sanju's point of view as Shekhar flirts with a Queen's College girl and yet again insults Ratan who waits on him with a snide — 'Brought the bottle, not the straw? Idiot!' — as the Queen's girl giggles. The camera cuts to Sanju's face as he asserts himself by throwing a spitball at the girl. We are, thus, sutured into the scene of class conflict among the teens as the stage is set for the final countdown between Model and Rajput.

JJWS continues the Nasir Hussain tradition of a competition dance sequence,[4] juvenile pranks that hark back to *Yaadon Ki Baaraat* (1973) and *Hum Kisise Kum Nahin* (1977), and of course the device of rich girl meeting poor boy who masquerades as a rich boy to impress her. This was one of the subplots in Nasir Husain's *Teesri Manzil*, *Yaadon Ki Baaraat* and *Hum Kisise Kum Nahin*, but in Mansoor's universe, the rich girl turns out to be 'a bloody gold digger' (as Sanju refers to Devika), who shifts attention to the boy of her social class on discovering Sanju's true identity.

As a product of its day, JJWS resorts to the standard populisms of the early 1990s. The rich guys are the Malhotras, the Wadias and the Thapars who are pitted against humbler folks—Ramlal Sharma, Dubeyji, Girdhari *chacha* and Shakur *miyan*. Devika (Pooja Bedi), Richa and Rukhsana are pretty diversions for the Rajput boys and of aspirational value for the Model boys. Khan's portrayal of these girls is a stereotype representation of rich girls: vain, flirty and flighty; on the other hand, Model High's Anjali (Ayesha Jhulka) and Kalpana are steadfastly loyal. They are also the essential 'good' girls with pigtails and long skirts, whereas the 'hot' girl Devika wears make-up and gets her Marilyn moment as her red dress blows in slow motion. To appreciate the timeless-ness of the film, audiences have to listen to the realistic dialogues (credited to Nasir Husain), soak in the vocabulary (*tunna, paunchy, pyjamachhap*), and even pay attention to the relatable clothes and fashion that do not seem dated.

Christine Gledhill in her discussion of the Hollywood melo-drama of the 1950s observes,

> [The construction of this genre is] in terms of conflict between the generations, in which the son has to accept his symbolic castra-tion by the father before he can take up his place in the patriarchal and bourgeois order, proving himself by becoming both an indi-vidual and like his father, capable of reconstituting the family unit. (Gledhill 2007: 319)

As the son who has never been able to find favour with his father, and who always remains in the shadows of the more responsible Ratan, Sanju has to struggle hard to prove his worth. The narra-tive structure and symmetry of JJWS is worth consideration in this regard. Thus, early on in the film, at the end of the first race, as the Rajput-college champion lifts his trophy, a woeful Ramlal sagely declares his philosophy, '*Jo jeeta wohi sikandar*' (The winner takes all); the film ends with Sanju's frozen image raising the cham-pionship trophy, thus mimicking the earlier scene with Shekhar as the centre of attention. At the same time, Sanju's victory also mirrors the sepia tinted image from the family album of his father holding the same trophy decades ago. This is a son who finally redeems himself in his father's eyes, restores his family pride and brings glory to his community.

One realizes that with QSQT onwards Mansoor Khan kept returning to the boys' world, where male codes of ethics and conduct are diligently observed. Khan suggests that there are certain rites of passage that every adolescent must go through, and developing team spirit and sportsmanship are essential part of growing up. Boys' relationship with fathers is paramount in determining what they are or are about to become. Indeed, much of Ratan's motivation for winning the championship stems from his father's desire to beat Rajput College. Once a cycle race champion himself, Ramlal reminisces upon that one glorious moment when he spearheaded the victory of Model School and College and wishes to relive that victory through his more favoured son, Ratan. Later, for Sanjay, it is less of his personal pride, and more of a matter of salvaging family honour (avenging his father's humiliation and his brother's brutal beatings at the hands of Shekhar and his friends) that eventually spurs him on.

Young adult dramas in Bollywood range between realistic attempts such as *Hip Hip Hurray* and *Rockford* (Nagesh Kukunoor, 1999), and (un)intentionally ridiculous *Always Kabhi Kabhi* (Roshan Abbas, 2011) and *Student of the Year* (Karan Johar, 2012). Amidst these, JJWS retains its relevance. As a critic points out,

> *JJWS* keeps all the ingredients of the formula — hero, heroine, six songs, rivalry, melodrama, family and villains — but treats them realistically and with restraint, and the result is just as believable, entertaining and enchanting. Mansoor Khan transposes the Archie comic ethos to Indian soil, sensibly and inventively Indianising it. (Sebastian 2003)

With *Akele Hum Akele Tum* (AHAT, 1995), produced by Venus films, Mansoor Khan graduated to exploring more mature facets of human relationship. Music brings together Kiran (Manisha Koirala) and Rohit (Aamir Khan). Like its source *Kramer vs. Kramer* (Robert Benton, 1979), with AHAT, Mansoor places a man at the heart of a family melodrama. When Kiran's parents, who are very ambitious for their daughter, oppose the relationship, the couple elopes and gets married. However, seven years and a child later, Kiran realizes that her self-engrossed husband will never support her singing career. While Rohit struggles to gain a foothold in the music industry, Kiran gets increasingly frustrated as she slides uncomfortably in her role as a homemaker and a mother. The day Rohit receives the news of his big break (which turns out to be a false alarm), Kiran decides to walk out on her husband and their six-year-old son, Sunil (Adil Rizvi). Now Rohit tries to take care of Sunil, a child he hardly knows. If JJWS focuses on father–son and communication issues, it is the father–son bonding in AHAT that forms the crux of the film, now made famous by the song 'Daddy I Love You' (belted out by the real-life father–son duo, Udit and Aditya Narayan). Father–son bonding in AHAT is different from QSQT and JJWS. Here, Aamir engenders the role of the post-liberalization 'buddy' father. Though the theme of a father as a homemaker has been dealt with in Hindi films (comparisons can be made between the easy-going relationship in Khan's film and the saccharine sweet relationship in *Pyar Jhukta Nahin*, Vijay Sadanah, 1985), in AHAT, the father and son address each other on equal terms, taking turns in giving care to each other in the absence of a mother-figure.

Commercial Hindi film-makers have always been prudish about discussing divorce on screen and are particularly prejudiced against women characters seeking divorce (notable exceptions Vijay Anand's *Guide* [1965] and Gulzar's *Ijaazat* [1987]).[5] However, Mansoor's Kiran is not the suffering Uma from *Abhimaan* (Hrishikesh Mukherjee, 1973), who willingly lets her career take a backseat to placate her egotistical husband. Though Rohit is inattentive and self-seeking, Kiran never lets go of her aspirations to make it big as a singer. (The director balances Kiran and Rohit's marital discord with Farida, played by Tanvi Azmi, a dignified divorcee, who lives on her own.) Going against all stereotypes, Mansoor Khan's Rohit remains a struggler till the end, while Kiran ends up becoming a superstar in mainstream Bollywood films. With AHAT, Khan also revitalizes the conceit of using film within film in mainstream Hindi films, later used with great panache in Farah Khan's *Om Shanti Om* (2007) and Zoya Akhtar's *Luck By Chance* (2009) where the formula is used in order to parody Bollywood stereotypes. Also, worth considering is Khan's parody of a famous music director duo and a music company owner (signalling the character of the obnoxious music video director in Farhan Akhtar's *Rock On!!* [2008]), all of whom embody the mean-spirited businessmen, the nouveau riches who exploit the powerless hero by manipulating him to sell his tunes to them for a pittance. Again, Mansoor renegotiates the gender dynamics as in spite of Kiran's return to her family there is no hint of her giving up her successful film career. The heroine does not have to resort to self-sacrifice in order to restore order in the family.

Bollywood trends during the late 1990s ranged from candy-floss love stories to action films to David Dhawan's brand of comedies. At the same time there was an influx of cinema concerning the diaspora: *Aa Ab Laut Chalen* (Rishi Kapoor, 1999), *Pardes* (Subhash Ghai, 1997) and *Taal* (Subhash Ghai, 1999); cinema of terrorism where the minorities are suspect: *Sarfarosh* (John Mathew Matthan, 1999), *Badal* (Raj Kanwar, 2000) and *Fiza* (Khalid Mohamed, 2000); and cinema of the underworld *Vaastav: The Reality* (Mahesh Manjrekar, 1999). Though made by directors of varying cinematic sensibilities, these films offered an overview of how men react in the context of certain culturally specified gendered codes.

Mansoor's last film *Josh* was released on 9 June 2000 and was filmed in Goa of the 1980s. *Josh* (literally, energy or frenzy) is an 'inspired' version of Robert Wise's musical *West Side Story* (1961), although the plot of rival street gangs was also a nod at Gulzar's macho melodrama *Mere Apne* (1971). The director employs his favourite device of a voice-over narrating the prologue, and we are informed about Goa's historic past, the Portuguese occupation, Goa's liberation in 1961 and about the richest and most powerful man Vasco, in whose honour the town is named.

The theme of 'father issues' surfaces in *Josh* as Max Dias (Shah Rukh Khan) learns about his illegitimacy. His father, Alberto Vasco's statue looms large all over the town without

Max knowing the truth about his paternity. However, the absence of father (or parents) is not felt much, as the town's police officer (Sharat Saxena) and the priest become Max Dias' surrogate 'fathers'. Interestingly, Mansoor makes the son bear the burden of illegitimacy, not Max's twin, his sister Shirley (Aishwarya Rai).

The two rival gangs are Eagles (led by Shah Rukh/Max) and Bichchoo ('The Scorpions', helmed by Sharad Kapoor/Prakash), who have demarcated their territories in Vasco, and are forbidden to trespass on each other's land. *West Side Story's* Prologue number, with Jets and Sharks, appears here as *'Saileru Sailare'* (What did you say?), the confrontational song between the two gangs as battle lines are drawn.

Max's tomboyish sister is the town beauty who every boy wants to flirt with but fears the wrath of Max. The power equations between the rivals gang shift with the arrival of Prakash's younger brother Rahul (Chandrachur Singh) from Mumbai, who has done a course in catering and plans to open his own restaurant. After a series of misadventures, Rahul and Shirley fall in love, leading to the final showdown between their brothers.

The narrative maps the conflict between the natives, and the 'outsiders'. Prakash and his mother, we are told, are the outsiders who have been in Vasco for the last two years (members of Prakash's gang go by nicknames such as Lafdu, Ganpat, Bheja Fry Gotya, and Pepsi). Max and his gang refer to them as *gaavti* (the rustic types), while the natives are disparagingly called *maca pao* (a kind of bread) by the Bichchoo gang.

City sophisticate in Hindi films is generally represented as a source of corruption and moral decay. Rahul, however, is the voice of reason in *Josh*, who reminds one of Ratan (Mamik's role) in JJWS. Mansoor Khan establishes Rahul's pacifism through a mise en scène as Rahul crosses over to the Eagles' territory and takes a stroll while a guitar gently strums on. Rahul takes in the graffiti ridden world of the Eagles, along with young girls selling flowers, elderly people playing a game of pool and nuns riding bicycles. The director, thus, contrasts the riotousness and exclusiveness of the gangs with Rahul's inclusiveness and pacifism.

Here, as in JJWS, Mansoor's proclivity towards the simpler times of pre-Internet is evident, and the art direction captures Goa of the 1980s, with billboards for Nippon battery and Liberty shoes, while the streets are lined with little cafes and bakeries. Rahul's metrosexuality is contrapuntal to the machismo and false bravado of the Eagles and Bichchoos as Max disparagingly refers to Rahul as a *bawarchi boy* (chef boy), and Prakash's friend Gotya (Sushant Singh) tells Rahul during a bloody fight between the members of the two gangs *'Yeh mardon ka khel hai, munna'* (This is a man's sport, little fellow). While the tough-talking Max pays homage to Travis Bickle with his imitation of 'You talkin to me' (*Taxi Driver*, Martin Scorsese, 1976) and flaunts a gun as an accessory, Rahul wins over the locals with cakes, pastries and fruit salads. The contrast between the two kinds of masculinities comes across through music as well. If Rahul's song is the poetic 'Mere khayalon ki malika' (Queen of my fantasies), Max resorts to macho posturing with 'Apun Bola' (with Shah Rukh's vocals), which is a throwback to classic *tapori* (street smart) songs such as A.R. Rahman composed 'Yaron Sun Lo Zara' (*Rangeela*, Ram Gopal Varma, 1995) and Aamir's 'Aati Kya Khandala' (*Ghulam*, Vikram Bhatt, 1998).

Taking 'The Third Curve'[6]

Within the commercial framework, Mansoor has provided entertainment as well as expressed concerns over vexing issues of feudalism, patriarchy, gender inequality, social and class disparities, and communalism. His films have set trends for the generation of film directors that followed him. For example, QSQT foregrounded families and family relationships, and started a trend that in other hands turned into an 'NRI' pleasing cinema. With its concerns about teen romances, coming of age, male bonding, friendship and conflict between generations, JJWS anticipates *Dil Chahta Hai* (2001). Mansoor Khan's films are also remarkable for marking a change in cinematic sites. Specific about his locations, there are no forced tours of Switzerland and New York via dream

sequences as was (and still is) the practice among Bollywood producers. If QSQT is set in Dhanakpur/Mount Abu/Delhi, then
JJWS is set in Dehradun, though most of it is filmed in Ooty/
Kodaikanal (notice that a commentator during the cycle race even
mentions Kodaikanal) and Mumbai; however, the plot in *Josh* is
set in Vasco, Goa. Again, if there was campfire in QSQT, we have
makeshift cafes, ice cream parlours and sports grounds in JJWS,
and *Josh* had the hero romancing the heroine over 'kokum curry'
in restaurants and beaches, where the local bakery becomes an
important location for the Aishawrya Rai-Chandrachur Singh
love segment.

In retrospect, we may argue that Mansoor's films were too
tidy (even murder and suicide are romanticized, almost bloodless), his *chawls* are a tad too designer and even his lower income
group characters come across as rather elitist (cf. Aamir in
AHAT). Steering clear of the campy entertainers of the 1980s (as
well as campiness of Nasir Husain's films), however, his cinema
was not provocative enough, particularly in the times of Ram
Gopal Varma, Anurag Kashyap and Vishal Bhardwaj, though he
attempted addressing issues of class hierarchies (JJWS), gender
relation (AHAT) and religious strife and land grabbing (*Josh*).
Rather than offering a cynical portrait of contemporary society,
Khan's signature style was nostalgic as well as utopian, looking
for something redeemable in human nature.

The theme that is most conspicuous in Khan's films is what it
is to be a man. His is a boys' world where the protagonists struggle to come to terms with the value system of the grown-ups and go
through trial by fire to earn a place for themselves. Consider how
the fickle-minded Sanju Lal gets his comeuppance as an equally
fickle-minded Devika ditches him for greener pastures, and how,
for all their posturing, Rohit and Max emerge as chauvinistic,
wimpy, swaggering beings with a shallow notion of manhood.

At the same time his films are notable for giving us some of
the most spirited women on Hindi screen. QSQT interrogates
the theme of patriarchy, benign and aggressive, and denies
absolute control to patriarchal forces. Mansoor makes Rashmi's

grandmother as an agent of interrogating the established order, and thus, 'an older woman, made powerless and marginal by Rajput values, is the one to challenge its celebrated chauvinism' (Virdi 2004: 185). Unlike the macho dramas in Bollywood films, the masculine in Mansoor Khan's coexists with a feminine agency that provides an emotional coherence.

After *Josh*, Mansoor Khan 'escaped the clutches of the city and moved to Coonoor' (cf. Khan's website). In an interview, when asked about his comeback plans, he responded, 'If I was (sic) making a film now, it would be great. There's so much structure, a wider audience, receptiveness in people. I wish I was making my films now but that's not enough' (Dhingra 2008).

Although Mansoor Khan did not belong to the distinguished Indian art-house tradition, or fit into the fiercely commercial scene, yet there was a niche for him: a film-maker with a degree of control over his product. Khan's scant body of work serves to enlarge the peculiar story of his acknowledged but unresolved talent.

Notes

1 Liberalization and globalization: At the end of the 1980s, the Indian Government started a process of dismantling a protectionist regime initiated after Independence to step up local industrial growth, in order to invite foreign investments. One of the consequences was to open the Indian market to international products, thereby leading to new markets and overall a more throbbing economy. The opening of malls and multiplexes, and launching of satellite television, foreign media and cable television all led to the emergence of new markets at home and abroad. In this connection, Ravi Vasudevan posits,

> Where do we place the cinema in this firmament? What does an exploration of the cinema offer us in terms of understanding the new relations between the state, corporate enterprise, media, and public life? We have a new context for Indian cinema in the 1990s.... One of the major issues here has been the emergence of a significant market, getting high returns in Indian cinema's export oriented sector.... [W]e witness the emergence of

the global nation, where non-resident Indians come to have an increasingly high profile. (Vasudevan 2011: 4–5)

2   To understand where Mansoor Khan's sensibilities originate from, one must have certain degree of familiarity with the filmography of his father, writer/director/producer Nasir Husain, known for his youthful and breezy musicals. It is instructive to remember that Husain had introduced several major stars of Hindi cinema, along with reinventing the screen images of many, including that of Shammi Kapoor, who was given an image makeover as a 'rebel' star with *Tumsa Nahin Dekha* (1957). His *Dil Deke Dekho* (1959) brought rock and roll music to Hindi cinema, while *Phir Wohi Dil Laya Hoon* (1963), *Teesri Manzil* (produced by Nasir Husain, directed by Vijay Anand, 1966), *Caravan* (1971), *Yaadon Ki Baaraat* (1973) and *Hum Kisise Kum Nahin* (1977) remain as some of the most loved entertainers of all time by Bollywood enthusiasts. Nasir Husain's lost–and-found formula (the formula where members of a family get separated due to natural circumstances or the machinations of villains, but are reunited at the end, remained a recipe for success for the film-makers from the 1960s till the 1980s) had certain constant features that the film-makers used repeatedly with actors such as Shammi Kapoor, Joy Mukherjee, Shashi and Rishi Kapoor. With their scenic locations, flamboyant guitar-strumming heroes, pretty and spunky heroines, wealthy fathers, suave villains, a comedy track and chartbusting music, Husain's films were known for their feel-good factor.

3   Nasir Husain's school of cinema anticipates the 'progressive' representation of the heroine in mainstream Hindi films. Consider, for example, how in *Caravan* (1971) Asha Parekh defies social conventions by escaping her manipulative husband and falling in love with the hero. Also noteworthy are the sexual dynamics between Jeetendra and Aruna Irani in the same film, where the aggressive gypsy girl refers to the hero as *garam masala* (hot spice). Both, the 'good' girl and the 'wild' girl, view the hero voyeuristically. But it is the openly lustful cabaret dance, 'Piya Tu Ab To Aaja', where Helen strips and teases a male dancer who is in a state of bondage and is trapped in a cage, that redefined sexual politics and gender equations.

4   In an interview Mansoor expresses his interest in song picturization, 'I realised that if I wanted the songs to look good, I'd probably need to make a film' (Singh 2012). True to this assertion, Khan's films are notable for their imaginative song sequences. QSQT had *Grease* (Randal Kleiser, 1978) like college setting where young people jive to 'Papa Kehte Hain.' (Later on AHAT's Raju Khan and Saroj Khan choreographed 'Aisa Zakhm Diya Hai' had a distinct hangover of 'Papa

Kehte Hain'.) AHAT's 'Raja Ko Rani Se Pyar Ho Gaya' anticipates *Rockstar*'s (Imtiaz Ali, 2011) 'Hawa Hawa' with its carnivalesque sets, while 'Zinda Hain Hum To' captures the spirit of carnival in Goa, and finds echoes in 'Te Amo' from *Dum Maaro Dum* (Rohan Sippy, 2011).

5   For example, *Do Anjaane* (Dulal Guha, 1976), *Ek Hi Bhool* (T. Rama Rao, 1981), *Souten* (Saawan Kumar Tak, 1983) and *Adhikar* (Vijay Sadanah and Chitrayug, 1986).

6   In 2013, Mansoor Khan released his book *The Third Curve: The End of Growth as We Know It* with appropriate fanfare.

References

Dhingra, D. 2008. 'The Return of Mansoor Khan.' *The Times of India*, 27 May. Retrieved 12 July 2015, from *http://timesofindia.indiatimes.com/entertainment/hindi/bollywood/news/The-return-of-Mansoor-Khan/articleshow/3073973.cms*

Gledhill, Christine. 2007. 'Melodrama.' In *The Cinema Book*, edited by Pam Cook, 3rd ed, 315–32. London: BFI & Palgrave Macmillan.

Sebastian, Pradeep. 2003. 'Racing Climax that Won Laurels.' *The Hindu*, 17 January. Retrieved 25 January 2016, from *http://www.thehindu.com/thehindu/fr/2003/01/17/stories/2003011701230300.htm*

Singh, Harmeet. 2012. 'I Took Up Making Films to Redeem Myself.' *Indian Express*, 22 December. Retrieved 22 January 2016, from http://archive.indianexpress.com/news/-i-took-up-making-films-to-redeem-myself-/1047499/

Thoraval, Yves. 2000. *The Cinemas of India*. New Delhi: Macmillan Publishers.

Vasudevan, Ravi. 2010. *The Melodramatic Public: Film Form and Spectatorship in Indian Cinema*. Ranikhet: Permanent Black.

———. 2011. 'The Meanings of "Bollywood.' In *Beyond the Boundaries of Bollywood: The Many Forms of Hindi Cinema*, edited by Rachel Dwyer and Jerry Pinto, 3–29. New Delhi: Oxford University Press.

Virdi, Jyotika. 2004. *The Cinematic Imagination: Indian Popular Films as Social History*. Ranikhet: Permanent Black.

Film References

Barjatya, Sooraj. 1989. *Maine Pyar Kiya*. Rajshri Productions.

———. 1994. *Hum Aapke Hain Koun...!* Rajshri Productions.

Benton, Robert. 1979. *Kramer vs. Kramer*. Columbia Pictures.

Bhatt, Mahesh. 1990. *Aashiqui*. Super Cassettes Industries Ltd and Vishesh Films.

———. 1991. *Dil Hai Ki Maanta Nahin*. Super Cassettes Industries Ltd and Vishesh Films.

Bhatt, Vikram. 1998. *Ghulam*. Vishesh Films.

Bihari, J.K. 1988. *Biwi Ho To Aisi*. Crystal Films Pvt. Ltd.

Chandra, N. 1988. *Tezaab*. N. Chandra Productions.

Chopra, Aditya. 1995. *Dilwale Dulhania Le Jayenge*. Yash Raj Films.

Chopra, Yash. 1989. *Chandni*. Yash Raj Films.

———. 1978. *Trishul*. Trimurti Films Pvt. Ltd.

Ghai, Subhash. 1997. *Pardes*. Mukta Arts.

———. 1999. *Taal*. Mukta Arts.

Guha, Dulal. 1976. *Do Anjaane*. Navjeevan Productions.

Gulzar. 1971. *Mere Apne*. Uttam Chitra.

———. 1972. *Parichay*. Tirupati Pictures.

Husain, Nasir. 1985. *Zabardast*. M.R. Productions.

———. 1984. *Manzil Manzil*. Nasir Husain Films and United Producers.

———. 1981. *Zamaane Ko Dikhana Hai*. Nasir Husain Films and United Producers.

———. 1977. *Hum Kisise Kum Nahin*. Nasir Husain Films and United Producers.

———. 1973. *Yaadon Ki Baaraat*. Nasir Husain Films and United Producers.

———. 1971. *Caravan*. Nasir Husain Films and T.V. Films.

———. 1966. *Teesri Manzil*. Nasir Husain Films and United Producers.

———. 1967. *Baharon Ke Sapne*. Nasir Husain Films.

———. 1963. *Phir Wohi Dil Laya Hoon*. Nasir Husain Films and United Producers.

———. 1959. *Dil Deke Dekho*. Filmalaya.

———. 1957. *Tumsa Nahin Dekha*. Filmistan.

Jha, Prakash. 1984. *Hip Hip Hurray*. Neo Films Associates.

Johar, Karan. 2012. *Student of the Year*. Dharma Productions.

Kalpataru. *Ghar Ghar Ki Kahani*.

Kanwar, Raj. 2000. *Badal*. Aftab Pictures Pvt. Ltd.

Kapoor, Abhishek. 2008. *Rock On!!* Big Pictures and Excel Entertainment.

Kapoor, Raj. 1951. *Awaara*. R.K. Films Ltd.

———. 1973. *Bobby*. R.K. Films Ltd.

Kapoor, Rishi. 1999. *Aa Ab Laut Chalen*. R.K. Films Ltd.

Kapur, Shekhar. 1987. *Mr. India*. Narsimha Enterprises.

Khan, Mansoor. Retrieved 1 October 2015, from http://mansoorkhan.net/

———. 1988. *Qayamat Se Qayamat Tak*. Nasir Husain Films and United Producers.

———. 1992. *Jo Jeeta Wohi Sikandar*. Nasir Husain Films and United Producers.

Khan, Mansoor. 1995. *Akele Hum Akele Tum*. United Seven Combines and Venus Records & Tapes.

——. 2000. *Josh*. United Seven Combines and Venus Records & Tapes

Kleiser, Randal. 1978. *Grease*. Paramount Pictures.

Kukunoor, Nagesh. 1999. *Rockford*. Padmini Films Pvt. Ltd and SIC Production.

Kumar, Indra. 1990. *Dil*. Maruti International.

Manjrekar, Mahesh. 1999. *Vaastav: The Reality*. Adishakti Films.

Matthan, John Mathew. 1999. *Sarfarosh*. Cinematt Pictures.

Mitra, Shibu. 1988. *Paap Ki Duniya*. Vishaldeep International.

Mohamed, Khalid. 2000. *Fiza*. The Culture Company and UTV Motion Pictures.

Mukherjee, Hrishikesh. 1973. *Abhimaan*. Amiya.

Rama Rao, T. 1981. *Ek Hi Bhool*. Lakshmi Productions.

——. 1988. *Khatron Ke Khiladi*. Jagapathi International.

Rawail, Rahul. 1981. *Love Story*. Aryan Films.

Sadanah, Vijay. 1985. *Pyar Jhukta Nahin*. BMB Productions.

Sadanah, Vijay and Chitryug. 1986. *Adhikar*. Chitrayug.

Scorsese, Martin. 1976. *Taxi Driver*. Columbia Pictures Corporation.

Sippy, Ramesh. 1982. *Shakti*. M.R. Productions.

Sippy, Rohan. 2011. *Dum Maaro Dum*. Fox Star Studios.

Subhash, B. 1989. *Love Love Love*. B. Subhash Movie Unit.

Tak, Sawan Kumar. 1983. *Souten*. Mercury Productions.

Wise, Robert. 1961. *West Side Story*. Mirisch Corporation, The Seven Arts Pictures and Beta Productions.

Yates, Peter. 1979. *Breaking Away*. Twentieth Century Fox Film Corporation.

3

Farhan Akhtar: Stardom of the Poster Boy of 'New' Hindi Cinema

Aysha Iqbal Viswamohan

Farhan Akhtar is a star director. The Renaissance Man, as he is fondly referred to by popular English language press in India, does not shy away from comparisons with the cinematic greats and admits his ambitions,

> When you look back at the work done by say Raj Kapoor, Guru Dutt or Kishore Kumar, do you ever stop to think whether they should have just acted or directed. You don't. Their films entertained you and that's important…. I'd rather be remembered for both. (Choudhary 2010: 56)

However, Farhan's list of achievements go beyond acting–directing–producing,[1] because he is an acknowledged 'actor–director–producer–writer–singer–musician–TV host–activist' (Upadhyay 2015). And there lies the problematic of Farhan Akhtar who resists being an auteur but is privileged as a star–director–performer and, therefore, has to be read as a star and the ways in which his image is (re)produced, extended and circulated.

This chapter focuses on how Akhtar has uniquely positioned himself by creating a distinct image of his own, that of a multi-tasking, cerebral and hyphenated artist, and how he differs from his film-maker contemporaries through self-branding and ability to constantly stay in the limelight. Drawing on the theories of stardom, particularly as articulated by Richard Dyer and Rajinder Dudrah, this chapter explores how star identity and stardom formation projects are often cultivated over the years, how a star's image can be decoded in terms of 'multiplicity of its meanings' (Dyer 1998: 63) and how a star is constructed, among other things, through the 'wider articulations in the cinematic assemblage' (Dudrah 2006: 85).

Akhtar belongs to that breed of popular Hindi film-makers, such as Vishal Bhardwaj, Anurag Kashyap and Dibakar Banerjee, who are media-savvy, urbane and known for their brand of self-conscious cinema. This cinema is in many ways different from the parallel cinema of the 1970s that was defined by forces such as Mrinal Sen, Shyam Benegal, Govind Nihalani and several others, who are credited with NFDC (National Film Development Corporation of India) funded films[2] that strove to 'coexist in a parallel trajectory to popular cinema' (Dutta 2002: 26) and that could 'be located in the context of third cinema, postcolonial hybridity and subaltern studies—intellectual developments that have made their mark worldwide' (p. 27). On the other hand, post-liberalization Hindi cinema is the kind of cinema driven by the desire, as Ravi Vasudevan describes, 'to circulate Indian branded commodities in international markets, to build linkages and seek investment from Indians abroad, and to cultivate foreign investment in domestic production, infrastructure, and markets' (Vasudevan 2010: 2).[3]

Post-liberalization, the 'new type of cinema', however, combines the elements of Vasudevan's description of globally positioned cinema as well as independent cinema, along the lines of 'New Hollywood' of the late 1960s and the early 1970s. While these films positioned themselves to accommodate the tastes of a more global audience, the intention of the film-makers of such films as *Hyderabad Blues* (Nagesh Kukunoor, 1998), the unreleased *Paanch*

(Anurag Kashyap, 2003) and *Satya* (Ram Gopal Varma, 1998) was not to market, distribute and promote their products among the NRI audience. A key difference between this cinema and the parallel cinema of the 1970s is that while the exponents of the 1970s' parallel cinema looked predominantly towards European art-house film-makers, such as Vittorio De Sica, Federico Fellini, Roberto Rossellini, Michelangelo Antonioni, Akira Kurosawa, Jean-Luc Godard and François Truffaut, post-liberalized film-makers are majorly inspired by the 'New Hollywood' movement of the 1970s as well as the Hollywood independent cinema of the 1990s. Thus, the role models for the current generation are Martin Scorsese, Brian De Palma, Steven Soderbergh, Steven Spielberg, Quentin Tarantino, Guy Ritchie and David Fincher, though one does find an occasional nod towards Pedro Almodóvar and Alejandro González Iñárritu, along with some Chinese and Korean masters too. While functioning within the mainstream framework, these film-makers experimented with the idiom of cinema rather than telling the old stories in the old ways. With its proclivity towards fractured narratives, allusiveness, exploration of dark themes, representation of gender and relationships, and portrayal of dysfunctional characters, post-liberalized cinema is an aesthetic phenomenon with global ambitions.

Akhtar, who started his career as a second/assistant director for *Lamhe* (directed by Yash Chopra and screenplay by Farhan's mother Honey Irani, 1991) and *Himalay Putra* (Pankaj Parashar, 1997), arrived on the Hindi film scene with *Dil Chahta Hai* that reinvented urban 'cool' and gave India its premier, authentic youth film. The film, set in Mumbai, had a personal flavour where Farhan explored the lives of three college friends and their journey of self-discovery. The characters played by Aamir Khan, Saif Ali Khan and Akshaye Khanna became the poster boys of modern-day friendship and male bonding. The shot in which the three friends are sitting on a derelict, sea-facing wall remains the iconic buddy frame and is cited as a point of reference by many die-hard fans.

Apart from its panache, what endeared Akhtar's film to the metro audience was his attempt to eschew melodrama. Neither candyfloss in the Karan Johar–Yash/Aditya Chopra mould nor grittily realistic as Ram Gopal Varma–Anurag Kashyap brand of cinema, Farhan chose the middle path. The film was non-formulaic because it was a complete departure from the kind of elements that are generally associated with a typical Bollywood film. The film has no hero, no larger-than-life characters and no contrived plot devices. The cool quotient was further well illustrated through its music (by Shankar–Ehsaan–Loy who soon became a constant of most Excel productions) and dialogues by Farhan: '*Mujhe acchi filmei bilkul pasand nahin*' (I don't like good films); '*Hum cake khane ke liye kahin bhi jaa saktey hai*' (We can go anywhere for eating cake); '*Ya toh yeh dosti gehri hai ya yeh photo 3D hai*' (Either this is a deep friendship or this is a 3D photograph). The film was also noted for its innovative song picturization, particularly 'Woh ladki hai kahan?' (Where's that girl?), a retro style song filmed on Sameer (Saif Ali Khan) and Pooja (Sonali Kulkarni) where the couple goes to a movie and watches itself turn up on the screen singing and dancing to film songs from the 1960s to the 1980s.[4]

Dil Chahta Hai, with its sense of immediacy, was received enthusiastically by critics and was an above-average grosser at the box office. Released alongside two of the biggest money spinners of 2001, *Gadar: Ek Prem Katha* (Anil Sharma; henceforth, *Gadar*) and Aamir Khan's *Lagaan: Once Upon a Time in India* (Ashutosh Gowariker; henceforth, *Lagaan*), the film held its own in metro areas and in multiplexes. Hindi cinema got a new upmarket director, a niche previously occupied by Mansoor Khan to some extent. The film won the National Film Award for Best Feature Film in Hindi, though it lost several awards to the international hit *Lagaan*. Critics and the audience raved about its groundbreaking qualities, such as absence of melodrama, natural performances and styling (Farhan's wife, Adhuna, was credited for giving Aamir Khan an image and style makeover). Indeed, the film has consistently retained its position as one of the most fashion-forward films of all time. Its impact was extraordinary and, not so surprisingly, the film spawned a spate of similar films with thrust on bromance, including *Rang De Basanti* (Rakeysh Omprakash Mehra, 2006), *Rock On!!* (Abhishek Kapoor, 2008),

3 Idiots (Rajkumar Hirani, 2009), *Delhi Belly* (Abhinay Deo, 2011), his sister Zoya Akhtar's *Zindagi Na Milegi Dobara* (2011) and *Kai po che!* (Abhishek Kapoor, 2013).

In *Lakshya*, for which Javed Akhtar wrote the screenplay, Farhan carried the theme of coming of age further with Hrithik Roshan playing an indecisive rich brat without any aim in life. Shot extensively in Ladakh, the film's tagline captured its essence, 'It took him 24 years and 18,000 feet to find himself.' Farhan's choice of war as a subject surprised many as they wondered if the Juhu-born and brought up young man was competent and mature enough to handle a heavy-handed theme such as the Kargil conflict of 1999.

As in his earlier work, *Lakshya* too engages with the theme of generational conflict. Hrithik's father in the movie, played by Boman Irani (an Akhtar regular), is disillusioned with his son for his lack of a goal in life, while his older son leads a successful life in the United States. The hero's subsequent joining the Indian Army and maturation into a responsible man forms the crux of the story.

Though *Lakshya* has a cult status today, it opened to mixed reviews when released. The film was also compared with Shashi Kapoor's *Vijeta* (Govind Nihalani, 1982) where the war scenes were depicted realistically and went easy on jingoism. Again, as in *Vijeta*, the protagonist of *Lakshya* too looks for coming to terms with the demons within himself. Interestingly, *Lakshya* came at a time when war films were underpinned by hypermasculine rhetoric such as *Border* (J.P. Dutta, 1997), *LOC: Kargil* (J.P. Dutta, 2003) and to some extent Sunny Deol starring *Gadar* (Anil Sharma) and *The Hero: Love Story of a Spy* (Anil Sharma, 2003), where the last two are more of a 'patriotic' dramas than war films. The film underscores Akhtar's recurring themes of male bonding and coming of age. As Farhan maintains, '[the film is] about a boy who finds himself. I just chose the army to set him in.' (Ashraf 2004). In spite of its critics, *Lakshya* still stands out amidst the contemporary war films for its breaking away from grandiloquence, its identifiable characters and Akhtar's signature humour that is evident in an otherwise serious film.

Farhan's concept of a 'hero' fits rather well within the defini-tion of 'the good Joe type' as posited by O.E. Klapp and explained by Richard Dyer in the discussion of star types. This kind of a hero is easy-going, fits in and likes people...goes along with the majority (Dyer 1998: 48). The pattern that emerged from his first two directorial ventures clearly illustrated that Farhan's protago-nists were predominantly based on their director's own persona, which is that of a regular young man next door, instead of a larger-than-life hero of, say, *Lagaan* and *Gadar*.

Perhaps it was the mixed response to *Lakshya* that led Farhan to rework *Don* (Chandra Barot, 1978), an Amitabh Bachchan block-buster which his father Javed Akhtar had co-scripted with Salim Khan. He justifies his choice, 'Once when I was listening to the background score of *Don* on my iPod I thought to myself, "some-body should remake this film. It's the best film in the world." *Don* stands out as a solo Bachchan movie of its time' (Ruhani 2009: 88). *Don* (2006) is a homage to the original film. Still, it has Farhan's stylistic markers all over it, though he says, 'I needed to sort of stick to the original story only because I had to have the relat-ability of a remake before turning it around on its head by the end of it' (Siganporia 2011: 32). Moreover, Akhtar's sensibilities are evident through his decision of choosing *Don* to remake: 'It was a very contemporary film because it was rooted in the kind of society that is relevant even today and the characters are very modern' (Kulkarni 2011: 81). It is his lack of familiarity with 'old' cinema that brings Farhan closer to his niche audience and makes him more relatable to the current generation of cine-goers. Consider the way in which Shah Rukh in *Don* clad in black play-fully mimes the ballerinas in pristine white in Paris, highlighting a contrast between evil and innocence, at the same time draw-ing attention to the impishness in Don's character. Indeed, this Don, unlike the earlier one, is our *Eulenspiegal* (German term for a prankster), who can be both lovable and dangerous. Akhtar's reinterpretation of *Don* is relevant as its morally ambivalent pro-tagonist and his noirish universe are closer to the impulses of our times than the good-versus-evil themes of the 1970s cinema. With a now (in)famous twist at the end, *Don* resonates more with the dark cinema of David Fincher than the simplistic morality tale of Salim–Javed.

Becoming an Actor

Though Farhan cites the influence of directors such as Martin Scorsese, Guru Dutt, Steven Soderbergh and Ramesh Sippy, he admits his fascination with star-actors Robert De Niro and Amitabh Bachchan and maintains that his 'biggest idols while growing up were actors and not directors' (Choudhary 2009: 42). The realization was well expressed in an interview:

> In this country if you're successful as an actor then your life is better than anyone else in the movies and if you're not successful then it probably is worse than any other person in films. I struggled as a director and as a writer…. From the time I wrote it, to the time it was cast and ready to be made, it was a very frustrating period. (Choudhary 2009: 42)

Perhaps Farhan's decision to turn to acting is also an instance of right timing. After all, in the early 2000, he would have to compete with the high profile debuts of two star sons, Hrithik Roshan (*Kaho Naa… Pyaar Hai*, 2000) and Abhishek Bachchan (*Refugee*, 2000), not the best of time to launch one's acting career.

Owning a film production company offered the kind of freedom he was looking for. *Rock On!!* bears several trademark features associated with Akhtar. Another buddy-cum-coming-of-age film, it continues Farhan's commitment towards making partially autobiographical films telling stories that he knew about, such as his love for rock music, reliance on friends and a passionate desire to break the rules, social and otherwise. *Rock On!!* is about Magik, a band that comes together, disbands and then comes together again after a decade. In 'The Making of *Rock On!!*' Javed Akhtar talks about the challenges of penning lyrics for a film of that nature. However, the lyrics he came up with were describing Aditya (the character in *Rock On!!*) as much as any urban youngster:

'Meri Laundry Ka Ek Bill/Ek Aadhi Padi Novel/Ek Ladki Ka Phone Number/Mere Kaam Ka Ek Paper ... Pichchle Saat Dinon Meine Khoya/Kabhi Khud Pe Hansa Mein, Kabhi Khud Pe Roya.'

(A laundry bill/a half-read novel/a girl's phone number/a useful paper ... I lost in the last seven days/Sometimes I laugh at myself /Sometimes feel sorry for myself).

Rock On!! contains Farhan's familiar tropes: references to popular culture; music of Bob Dylan, Led Zeppelin, The Beatles and The Stones; and Che Guevara. Instances of pastiche often surface, as in *Dil Chahta Hai*, as *Rock On!!* casts a bemused look at what is typically 'filmy'. Consider, for example, the famous *dandiya* (a form of folk dance from Gujarat) scene where the band, much to their discomfort, plays a remix of old Hindi film songs. The portrayal of a boorish music company head who speaks bad English (a joke repeated in *Zindagi Na Milegi Dobara*, where the boys recall the bad English of their school teacher) and has an equally bad taste in music and clothes, and the music video director, who makes constant references to Hindi film musicals he has worked on, are standard Farhan.

The film opened to rave reviews. The DVD jacket proudly bore the comments of what seems like who's who of the film industry. Film-makers as diverse as Farah Khan, Shyam Benegal, Aparna Sen, Karan Johar and Vidhu Vinod Chopra enthused about the film's music and performances, particularly Farhan's. The debutant who sang all the songs in his own voice (an uncommon practice in Hindi cinema where actors lip sync to songs) was featured on the cover of the August 2008 issue of *Rolling Stone* magazine, thereby augmenting his 'capital possibilities' (Dudrah 2006: 86).

Farhan's next outing as an actor was also his second teaming up with his sister, Zoya. The brother–sister duo who had earlier directed the music video of Shankar Mahadevan's experimental title track from his album *Breathless* (1998, with lyrics by Javed Akhtar) came together for Zoya's directorial debut *Luck by Chance* (2009), an insider's view of Hindi film industry with plenty of in-house jokes and filmy anecdotes. A self-reflexive take on film-making and the film industry, it is an addition to the corpora of films such as *Guddi* (Hrishikesh Mukherjee, 1971), *Bhumika* (Shyam Benegal, 1977), *Om Shanti Om* (Farah Khan, 2007), *I Hate Luv Storys* (Punit Malhotra, 2010) and more recently *Shamitabh* (Balki, 2015). Hindi film industry's interest in self-conscious cinema is explained as, '[S]ymptomatic of a global "postmodern style" with polyvocality, pastiche, simulacrum, and parody as some of its defining constituents.... Bollywood is currently engaged in the consolidation of a "Bollywood model" at the heart of global cinema' (Sarkar 2013: 206). Farhan's depiction of an affluent Delhi boy who struggles in Mumbai before making it big in Bollywood has shades ranging between a lovable go-getter and a two-timing, opportunistic boyfriend. The fact that this smooth-talking, grey, unheroic character was well received lends credence to the belief that stars 'embody that particular conception of what it is to be human that characterizes our culture' (Dyer 1998: 99). Evidently, the post-satellite television and post-MTV generation audience do not look for 'the angry young man', a creation of Javed Akhtar and Salim Khan, an establishment hero. Instead, their acceptance of Farhan's Vikram Jaisingh, who ditches his small-time actor girl-friend to gain a foothold in the film industry, mirrors the ambiguous morals of globalized times.

Farhan's next film *Karthik Calling Karthik* or KCK (Vijay Lalwani, 2010) had him playing a complex role where he had to display a spectrum of change and a range of emotions. Karthik is an odd-ball struggling in a construction company and is surrounded by manipulative people. His boss (Ram Kapoor) is an ogre who delights in humiliating Karthik at every opportunity, while he is practically non-existent for his colleagues. Then one fine day, he receives a mysterious call that changes his life forever. The film meanders between the two genres of a psychological thriller and a supernatural film, and did average business. Critics too were mostly divided on the film, with Anupama Chopra calling it a 'vanity project for Farhan' (Chopra 2010). However, most viewers agreed that Farhan did a remarkable job given the constraints of a weak screenplay and a difficult role.

Zindagi Na Milegi Dobara (2011) is another film that almost mirrors Farhan's real-life persona. A road-cum-buddy film with an ensemble cast, the plot focuses on three bachelors taking a road trip across Spain before one of them ties the knot. Farhan's character Imraan Qureshi plays pranks, wisecracks, flirts with beautiful girls, recites Javed Akhtar's soulful poetry, participates in adventure sports, sings (doing his own playback) at the La Tomatina festival, shimmies with flamenco dancers and runs with Spanish bulls, while searching for and briefly uniting with his biological father.

By this point, the line between Farhan's many designations had decidedly blurred, as he became more confident about his acting career:

> Different parts call for different preparation.... For *KCK*, it was an alien world for me, so I had to learn a lot about schizophrenia and gradually understood the mindset of the character.... With *Rock On!!* ... [we] would go and jam with Ehsan and Loy in the studio. In *Zindagi* ..., I was me, so it was a lot of fun to do. (Punnose 2011: 120)

However, Farhan's casting as the rustic athlete Milkha Singh was a choice that baffled many. As an interviewer comments, 'There's nothing in his filmography to suggest that he understands the villager's or the athlete's perspective in India' (Mohta, 2014). By coming out of his comfort zone (taking on a role against his type and acting in an outside production), the artist took a quantum leap of faith. The film marks a crucial turning point in Akhtar's career, who is now taken seriously as a dramatic actor and can finally look beyond the coming-of-age and buddy films, for example, in his most recent, *Wazir* (Bejoy Nambiar, 2015).

A star's celebrity is constructed through not just the films they appear in but also additional ways, such as 'advertising, the fan industry and personal appearances' (Dyer 1998: 61). An immediate consequence of *Bhaag Milkha Bhaag*'s phenomenal success, and the respectability it bestowed upon the star, was the launch of Farhan's social campaign MARD (Men Against Rape and Discrimination). Farhan, a father of two daughters, has been quite active about spreading the message about violence against women. And it is here when Farhan comes closest to his father, who is known for his outspoken views on several sociopolitical issues (Jan Nisar Akhtar, Farhan's grandfather was a renowned poet–lyricist, associated with the Progressive Writers' Movement). Again, Farhan's music video 'Chulein Aasmaan' (Reach out for the sky, 2014) generated plenty of media attention for its strong message of female emancipation and gender equality. Also notable is his involvement with Sanofi Pasteur India's flu awareness programme and his appointment as the UN Women Goodwill Ambassador for South Asia in 2014, all of which reinforce his upmarket, cosmopolitan image.[5]

Farhan made an extended cameo in Zoya's *Dil Dhadakne Do* (2015) which Farhan co-produced, co-scripted (with Zoya) and also wrote dialogues for. Zoya's tale of a wealthy, dysfunctional business family on a Mediterranean cruise received positive reception, and Farhan, who plays Priyanka Chopra's love interest, again played himself, a suave, easy-going character with a great sense of humour. And this is true of other films, such as *Rock On!!*, *Luck by Chance*, *Zindagi Na Milegi Dobara*, *Shaadi Ke Side Effects*, 'that are very close to home, where the characters are sort of like him anyway, so those don't really need a lot of time spent investing in research' (Besseling 2015: 90).

It must be noted that Akhtar is not the only one from his generation to try his hand at different jobs. Karan Johar who has written, produced and directed blockbusters such as *Kuch Kuch Hota Hai* (1998), *Kabhi Khushi Kabhie Gham* … (2002), *My Name Is Khan* (2010) and *Student of the Year* (2012) hosts an immensely popular chat show *Koffee with Karan*. Johar started his career as an actor in the television series *Indradhanush* (Anand Mahendroo, 1989) and more recently has played a negative role in Anurag Kashyap's *Bombay Velvet* (2015). He is credited for designing costumes for several films with Shah Rukh Khan. That Johar is a star director can be evidenced by the fact that he has approximately seven million followers on twitter, is often seen on the cover of film and lifestyle magazines, a space reserved only for the best-selling film stars, and is the brand ambassador for quite a few products. Similarly, Farhan's stardom in post-satellite television times owes aplenty to his various public appearances, stage shows as a presenter and a performer, a staggering series of endorsements and also his television chat show *Oye It's Friday* (2008–09). If stars are commodities that 'sell newspapers and magazines, and are used to sell toiletries, fashions, cars and almost anything else' (Dyer 1986: 5), then Farhan is a star.

In a 2008 interview, Farhan states, 'Direction is something I'm a lot more comfortable with because as a director you only get excited about films you believe in and know you can direct' (Ruhani 2009: 88). Farhan's most recent directorial venture was as back in time as 2011. *Don 2* was a glossy; *Mission: Impossible* (directed by multiple directors, 1996 – till date) franchise-styled caper that did very well at the box office. Critics, however, remained unmoved. The reviewer of *Hollywood Reporter* was not the only one who felt that 'Akhtar, who proved his skills with the groundbreaking *Dil Chahta Hai* (2001), and has since gone on to a successful career as an actor, falls back on tired action film tropes' (Tsering 2011). Though there are many who expect another *Dil Chahta Hai*, in his own way Farhan's contribution to the world of cinema is rather apparent. The risk he is taking is more with his productions (modestly budgeted, thus minimizing the financial risks) which enables him to give breaks to newer talent such as Reema Kagti, Mrigdeep Singh Lamba, Karan Anshuman, in addition to experimenting with genres as varied as seen in *Honeymoon Travels Pvt. Ltd.*, *Talaash* and *Fukrey*. While talking about exploring various genres as a producer/actor, he admits:

> At the end of the day, as a producer or as an actor, I am still involved with that [referring to the film he has directed, not necessarily produced] film and very intrinsically involved with it. Therefore, the emotional satisfaction of making a film.... I am getting with these movies.... They have kind of substituted for the fact that I am not directing a film like that. (Kulkarni 2011: 80)

In other words, acting in and producing films are as important, if not more, to Farhan as direction.

Though widely accepted as the frontline game-changing director, Farhan today is more of a matinee idol. His once-upon-a-time assertion, 'What I want to contribute to this art form doesn't get bigger than direction. ... to be able to take a story from the germ of an idea and then put it out there ... there is nothing as creatively satisfying as that' (Kulkarni 2008: 100), may now, at least to some, appear out of sync with his current image where he 'looks every inch like the movie star he is' (Upadhyay 2015). Akhtar's forthcoming releases bear testimony to this assertion. His histrionics were further tested in *Wazir* (produced by Vidhu Vinod Chopra and directed by Bejoy Nambiar) he starred opposite Amitabh Bachchan.

As he gets involved with acting–producing–singing for *Rock On!! 2* (Shujaat Saudagar, forthcoming), it would be interesting to observe which route Akhtar is going to take. The man who was once believed to take Hindi cinema forward, now appears more comfortable with his act before rather than behind the camera. The latest in line of public appearances is 'Farhan Live', his band that performs concerts across the country. Whether it is at various institutes or colleges, Akhtar is making his music as well as his presence felt among his core audience, which is the urban youth.

The Identity Project

This brings us to my central thesis of Farhan's stardom- and identity-formation project. As a director, Akhtar may not possess Sanjay Leela Bhansali's sense of detailing, Anurag Kashyap's edginess, Imtiaz Ali's understanding of the human condition or Rajkumar Hirani's feel of the pulse of the masses; however, his facility to multitask places him in a unique niche. His accessibility (relatable characters, endorsing products and causes, guy-next-door persona) may lend him an aura of 'ordinariness', however his multitasking is anything but ordinary. In post-liberalized times, the construction of the self is not just desirable but also essential, and 'selfhood is performed through various roles and functions' (Dudrah 2006, 87). The proliferation of print media, television channels and social networking sites necessitates that celebrities remain constantly in the public eye, and what makes a star interesting is the way in which they 'articulate aspects of living in contemporary society' (Dyer 1986: 7). His projection as a family man and concerned global citizen resonates well with the audiences' expectations of a 'good Joe' star, an extraordinary guy who is ordinary like the rest of us. Farhan's success is symptomatic of the times we live in. And although it is too early in the day to understand his larger impact, the acceptance of non-formulaic *Wake Up Sid* (Ayan Mukherjee, 2009), *Rockstar* (Imtiaz Ali, 2011), *Vicky Donor* (Shoojit Sircar, 2012), *Dum Laga Ke Haisha* (Sharat Katariya, 2015), *Hunterr* (Harshavardhan G. Kulkarni, 2015) can be attributed to a handful of films with their 'new and different' (Dwyer 2005: 72) texts, of which *Dil Chahta Hai* remains an important example.

As an actor–director–producer–writer, Farhan has displayed a range and style, played with aesthetics of narrative and even experimented with stylistic devices such as colour grading (the green/grey/blue palette in *Don*) magic realism (*Honeymoon Travels Pvt. Ltd.*), surrealism (*Don*) and supernaturalism (*Talaash*). Exclusive film projects are planned with him in mind, coupled with this, all his upmarket endorsements, his espousal of social-health-related causes, his rock concerts and his excellent handling of the media have served to ensure his visibility. As his work gets diversified, it is difficult to identify a unifying theme, though friendship between males (or *dosti*) and rebellion against a patriarchal, authoritarian figure is a recurring motif in Farhan's films, both as an actor and a director.

One may argue that Akhtar' positioning of himself as a multifaceted artist resists his assessment as a director; after all, at the time of writing this, Farhan is yet to announce his next film as a director. Rather, his body of work leads us to take into account his interest into various mediums of the entertainment business and in this polysemy nestles the essence of Farhan Akhtar.

Notes

1 Farhan Akhtar has directed four films till date: *Dil Chahta Hai* (2001), *Lakshya* (2004), *Don* (2006) and *Don 2* (2011). He has also acted in

nearly a dozen films, making his debut with *Rock On!!* (Abhishek Kapoor, 2009), which he also co-produced, along with Ritesh Sidhwani, for Excel Entertainment, a production company jointly created by Akhtar and Sidhwani. He has produced (but not starred in) *Honeymoon Travels Pvt. Ltd.* (Reema Kagti, 2007), *Game* (Abhinay Deo, 2011), *Talaash* (Reema Kagti, 2012), *Fukrey* (Mrigdeep Singh Lamba, 2013) and *Bangistan* (Karan Anshuman, 2015).

2   Some of the films of this period are: *Bhuvan Shome* (Mrinal Sen, 1969), *Uski Roti* (Mani Kaul, 1970), *Ankur* (Shyam Benegal, 1974), *Manthan* (Shyam Benegal, 1976), *Aakrosh* (Govind Nihalani, 1980) and *Jaane Bhi Do Yaaro* (Kundan Shah, 1983).

3   Also pertinent are Tejaswini Ganti's remarks on post-satellite cinema, '[A]ll signs of poverty, economic hardship, or struggle have been eliminated…the protagonists are incredibly rich—usually the sons and daughters of millionaires' (Ganti 2004: 40).

4   In an interesting study, Bhaskar Sarkar points out that 'while playing with and recalibrating the form, the song sequence also achieves "something fresh" in terms of an oedipal in-joke' (Sarkar 2013: 212), as Pooja imitates the fashion style and dance moves of Saif Ali Khan's mother, the yesteryear actor Sharmila Tagore.

5   This interest in gender roles and gender politics is foregrounded in *Shaadi Ke Side Effects* (Saket Chaudhary, 2014), a film about contemporary relationships. The poster of the film famously evokes Julia Roberts–Richard Gere starrer romantic drama *Pretty Woman* (Garry Marshall, 1990) where the two stars pose standing back to back looking their glamorous best. The poster of *Shaadi Ke Side Effects* positions a pregnant Vidya Balan matched by Farhan with an equally prominent belly (one can read a radical reinvention of image after the overtly physical Milkha). The actor went on his customary promotional blitzkrieg for the film and in his various interviews talked about the heartwarming Hrishikesh Mukherjee-like quality of the film.

References

Ashraf, Firdaus S. 2004. '*Lakshya* is about Hrithik, about Finding Yourself.' April 8. Retrieved 19 July 2015, from http://www.rediff.com/movies/2004/apr/08farhan.htm

Besseling, D. 2015. 'The Actor's Akhtar.' *GQ*, July, 86–91.

Chopra, A. 2010. 'Anupama Review: *Karthik Calling Karthik*.' 26 February. Retrieved 14 June 2015, from http://movies.ndtv.com/movie-reviews/anupamas-review-karthik-calling-karthik-487

Chopra, Y. 2009, February 4. 'Oye, it's Farhan.' *Filmfare*, 40–45.

Choudhary, A. 2010. 'Rock Around the Clock.' *Filmfare*. March 3, 54–59.

Dudrah, R.K. 2006. *Bollywood: Sociology Goes to the Movies*. New Delhi/ Thousand Oaks/London: SAGE Publications.

Dutta, S. 2002. *Shyam Benegal*. New Delhi: Roli.

Dwyer, R. 2005. *100 Bollywood Films*. New Delhi: Roli.

Dyer, R. 1986. *Heavenly Bodies: Film Stars and Society*. New York: Routledge.

———. 1998. *Stars*. London: BFI & Palgrave Macmillan.

Ganti, T. 2004. *Bollywood: A Guidebook to Popular Hindi Cinema*. New York/London: Routledge.

Punnose, R. 2011. 'The Making of a Road Movie.' *Man's World*. July, 116–23.

Ruhani, F. 2009. 'Roll Baby Role.' *Filmfare*. December 23, 82–88.

Sarkar, B. 2013. 'Metafiguring Bollywood.' In *Figurations in Indian Film* edited by Meheli Sen and Anustup Basu, 205–35. New York: Palgrave-Macmillan.

Siganporia, S. 2011. 'The Year that Was and Is. Farhan Akhtar.' *Platform*. November–December, 30–32.

Tsering, L. 2011. '*Don 2*: Film Review'. *The Hollywood Reporter*. 30 December. Retrieved 12 May 2015, from http://www.hollywoodreporter.com/review/don-2-film-review-shah-rukh-khan-277022

Upadhyay, K. 2015. 'How Farhan Akhtar Made Plan A Work.' *Forbes India*. 1 June. Retrieved 12 July 2015, from http://forbesindia.com/article/think/how-farhan-akhtar-made-plan-a-work/40339/3#ixzz3j6wVfy17

Vasudevan, R. 2010. *The Melodramatic Public: Film Form and Spectatorship in Indian Cinema*. Ranikhet: Permanent Black.

Film References

Akhtar, F. 2001. *Dil Chahta Hai*. Excel Entertainment.

———. 2004. *Lakshya*. Excel Entertainment.

———. 2006. *Don*. Excel Entertainment.

———. 2011. *Don 2*. Excel Entertainment and Red Chilies Entertainment.

Akhtar, Z. 2009. *Luck by Chance*. Excel Entertainment and Reliance Big Pictures.

———. 2011. *Zindagi Na Milegi Dobara*. Eros International and Excel Entertainment.

———. 2015. *Dil Dhadakne Do*. Excel Entertainment.

Ali, I. 2011. *Rockstar*. Eros International, Prague-Punk Films and Reel India Pictures.

Anshuman, K. 2015. *Bangistan*. Excel Entertainment.

Barot, C. 1978. *Don*. Nariman Films.

Balki, R. 2015. *Shamitabh*. Hope Productions and ABCL.

Choudhary, S. 2014. *Shaadi Ke Side Effects*. Balaji Motion Pictures and Pritish Nandy Communications.

Benegal, S. 1974. *Ankur*. Blaze Film Enterprises.

———. 1976. *Manthan*. Gujarat Milk Co-op Marketing Federation Ltd.

———. 1977. *Bhumika*. Blaze Film Enterprises.

Chopra, Y. 1991. *Lamhe*. Yash Raj Films.

Deo, A. 2011. *Game*. Eros International and Excel Entertainment.

———. 2011. *Delhi Belly*. Aamir Khan Productions and UTV Motion Pictures.

De Palma, B., J. Woo, J.J. Abrams, B. Bird, C. McQuarrie. 1996. *Mission Impossible*. Paramount.

Dutta, J.P. 1997. *Border*. JP Films.

———. 2000. *Refugee*. JP Films.

———. 2003. *LOC: Kargil*. JP Films.

Gowariker, A. 2001. *Lagaan: Once Upon a Time in India*. Aamir Khan Productions.

Hirani, R. 2009. *3 Idiots*. Vinod Chopra Productions.

Johar, K. 2001. *Kabhi Khushi Kabhie Gham…*. Dharma Productions.

———. 2010. *My Name Is Khan*. Dharma Productions and Fox Searchlight Pictures.

———. 2012. *Student of the Year*. Dharma Productions and Red Chilies Entertainment.

Kagti, R. 2007. *Honeymoon Travels Pvt. Ltd*. Excel Entertainment.

———. 2012. *Talaash*. Aamir Khan Productions and Excel Entertainment.

Kapoor, A. 2008. *Rock On!!* Big Pictures and Excel Entertainment.

———. 2013. *Kai po che!* UTV Motion Pictures.

Kashyap, A. 2003. *Paanch*. Padmini Tele media and Star Talaash Promotions.

———. 2015. *Bombay Velvet*. Fox Star Studios and Phantom Films.

Kataria, S. 2015. *Dum Laga Ke Haisha*. Yash Raj Films.

Kaul, M. 1970. *Uski Roti*. NFDC.

Khan, F. 2007. *Om Shanti Om*. Red Chilies Entertainment.

Kukunoor, N. 1998. *Hyderabad Blues*. Kukunoor Films.

Kulkarni, H. 2015. *Hunterr*. Phantom Films.

Lalwani, V. 2010. *Kartik Calling Kartik*. Eros International and Excel Entertainment.

Lamba, M.S. 2013. *Fukrey*. Excel Entertainment.

Mahendroo, Anand. 1989. *Indradhanush*. Nimbus.

Malhotra, P. 2010. *I Hate Luv Storys*. Dharma Productions and UTV Motion Pictures.

Mehra, Omprakash, R. 2006. *Rang De Basanti*. UTV Motion Pictures.

Mehra, Omprakash, R. 2013. *Bhaag Milkha Bhaag*. Rakeysh Omprakash Mehra Pictures and Viacom 18 Motion Pictures.

Mukherjee, A. 2009. *Wake Up Sid*. Dharma Productions.

Mukherjee, H. 1971. *Guddi*. Rupam Chitra.

Nambiar, B. 2015. *Wazir*. Gateway Films and Vinod Chopra Productions.

Nihalani, G. 1980. *Aakrosh*. Krsna Movies Enterprises.

———. 1982. *Vijeta*. Film-valas.

Parashar, P. 1997. *Himalay Putra*. Vinod Khanna Productions.

Roshan, R. 2000. *Kaho Naa… Pyaar Hai*. Film Kraft.

Sarcar, S. 2012. *Vicky Donor*. Eros International, J.A. Entertainment and Rampage Motion Pictures.

Saudagar, S. (forthcoming). *Rock On!! 2*. Excel Entertainment.

Scorsese, M. 1980. *Raging Bull*. United Artists.

Sen, M. 1969. *Bhuvan Shome*. Mrinal Sen Productions.

———. 2001. *Gadar: Ek Prem Katha*. Zee Telefilms.

Sharma, A. 2003. *The Hero: Love Story of a Spy*. Time Movies.

Shah, K. 1983. *Jaane Bhi Do Yaaro*. NFDC.

Surapur, A. 2016. *Fakir of Venice*. October Films.

Varma, R.G. 1998. *Satya*. Varma Corporation Ltd.

CHAPTER 4

Aditya Chopra's 'Glamorous Realism'

Manjunath Pendakur

Introduction

Aditya Chopra wrote his first feature film story and script when he turned 23. His father, Yash Chopra, a highly regarded Bombay film-maker was well established with a record of a quarter century of Hindi films produced and directed by him. With his parents' support — both financial and emotional — Aditya Chopra directed his first film,

Dilwale Dulhania Le Jayenge (DDLJ) at the age of 24, which, subsequently, became a box office hit in 1995. The film had a continuous run for almost 20 years at Maratha Mandir, a single screen in Bombay, albeit one show per day. No other Indian film has earned that distinction.[1] With such a fantastic launch of his film career that most people dream about but never attain in this unpredictable industry, Aditya has established himself as a writer, producer and director. Although he has directed only three feature films to this day — DDLJ (1995), *Mohabbatein* (2000), *Rab Ne Bana Di Jodi* (2008) — his filmography as a writer and producer is impressive.

Equally importantly, Yash Raj Films (YRF) under Aditya's leadership has grown in size and importance to become a cultural conglomerate with global operations. This phenomenon of corporatization and internationalization of a company can be observed in the case of UTV Movies, Eros and Reliance Big Media Works that clearly are symptomatic of the integration of India into the Western economies. We will return to this matter later in this chapter.

Aditya's aesthetic influence is widespread in the Bombay film industry where other directors such as Karan Johar have emulated him and are hugely successful. Positioning the film to please the South Asian diaspora, more than 25 million in all, and to cash in on the growing urban audience within India are the two strategies common to these followers of Chopra.

Aditya Chopra emerged as a director in the mid-1990s when Indian policymakers were setting the country on a neoliberal path of abandoning Nehruvian socialism and pursuing capitalist development, a model that was crafted in the West during the Margaret Thatcher–Ronald Reagan period. Those two politicians were the torchbearers of market fundamentalism in economics that was given intellectual 'credibility' by Friedrich Hayek, an Austrian economist. Thatcher and Reagan used those ideas to delegitimize the role of government in protecting vulnerable populations in their countries and, when possible, eliminate all 'safety net' policies that had been implemented in the aftermath of the Second World War. Public funding for education and the arts, among other things, began to shrink rapidly while the military spending swelled exponentially. Trade unions were undermined at the same time to beef up corporate profits. The collapse of the Soviet Union in 1989 gave the much-needed fillip for the US government to push this agenda on a global scale by opening up countries for foreign direct investment and bolster capitalist economies around the world. The Indian economic policy shifts starting in 1991 reflect these global tendencies spearheaded by the United States and big capitalist elements within the country. Bollywood, as a term to describe Bombay cinema begins to get used in this period of capitalist expansion and becomes a marketing tool to spread this cinema around the world.

While such changes in the economic policy have complex and sometimes conflicting consequences,[2] the elimination of foreign exchange regulations for imports and travel—allowing 100 percent foreign direct investment[3] and nationalized banks to provide loans for film-making, just to mention a few—did augur changes in Bollywood's mode of production, financing and style. Leading producers abandoned the gritty 'realism' of Manmohan Desai, Ramesh Sippy or Prakash Mehra that dominated Bombay cinema from 1975 to 1985. Love stories that dealt with class or caste conflict rose to prominence with the success of *Qayamat Se Qayamat Tak* (Mansoor Khan, 1988) and even the city of Bombay, the locus of most Hindi films for their stories and characters disappeared (Kapur and Pendakur 2007) for a few years. In the neoliberal phase, melodramatic but still star-studded entertainers, such as *Hum Aapke Hain Koun…!* (Sooraj Barjayta, 1994), became hugely successful with their focus shifting from the conflicts that arose from poverty and degradation to the joys, tensions and conflicts within large, extended families.

While the heroes of Manmohan Desai may have come from the poorest of the poor, often from the villages, Aditya's protagonists are urbanized. Poor people and their problems disappeared from these films, just as their protagonists fighting corruption or injustice vanished. The conflicts dealt within the narrative are covered in glamour and glitz. Yash Chopra refers to this style as 'glamorous realism', a sheen that entertains with familial conflicts and tensions while taking the audience along a three-hour journey of pleasure.

Aditya also began a new trend by setting DDLJ in London and in some gorgeous locations in Switzerland and connecting the characters and the story with Punjab in India. This approach to creating and coaxing an audience at home and abroad to visualize themselves as global citizens continues with Aditya's collaboration with his father in *Jab Tak Hai Jaan* (2012). If DDLJ had not been such a huge success inside and outside the country, this historical twist in creating love stories on film may have gone another way.

This chapter will explore the various elements of Aditya's glamorous realism, beginning with his DDLJ, as a particular contribution to the masala film-making tradition that Indian cinema is known for (Pendakur 2003: 95–107). We will also consider Aditya's leadership of YRF in making it one of the most prominent production and distribution houses and internationalizing it. Masala films are not only a pastiche of 'ingredients' that offer pleasure to the mass audience but are also used in a style unique to each individual director. By examining published materials, YouTube videos and YRF' company documents, we will evaluate Aditya Chopra's magic in creating big box office hits that have become quintessential Bollywood films that circulate all over the world.

Auteur Theory or Authorial Authority

According to Robert P. Kolker:

> French critics began noting similarities across American films that had nothing to do with the studio in which they were made or who produced or wrote them, but by the director. They noted stylistic and thematic coherences that seemed to belong to the person directing the film because they could be perceived and tracked from film to film directed by the same person. From this they developed, what has come to be called the auteur theory, the idea that no matter else is involved in the creation of a film, it is the director who is responsible for the overall design, the visual structure, the vision of the film or a body of films. (Kolker 2015: 5–6)

Kolker further states that

> [the auteur theory, in regard to American film, and especially during the studio period], roughly between 1915 through the early 1950s, is really something of a convenient fiction. More often than not, the director was only one person in the production line through which a film passed from inception to writing to filming to editing to previews to reediting and finally to release. But the director was and is an important figure at the crucial moment of

translating the words of the script into the acting and action on the screen, and often creating the film's visual structure.

Cinema has always been a collaborative art form. Irrespective where films are made, the very nature of putting together a film, its highly technical nature, and with hundreds of people working in a crew—from sets, lighting, camera movement, editing and all other post-production processes involved—cinema has remained not just labour intensive but highly synergetic. Even in the somewhat chaotic conditions of Bombay productions, the director remains staunchly the key creative figure with the vision and skill to piece all of the elements that would make a film narrative come alive on the big screen. In the films written and directed by Aditya, although the choreographer assumes a lot of control over the mise en scène of the song and dance numbers, the overall responsibility of getting the principal photography done on location or sets, having the actors deliver their performances effectively and supervising the editing process belongs to the director. In other words, the supremacy of the director is unquestioned in the Bollywood mode of production. As we will see soon, the collaboration between the father and son gains primacy in the making of Aditya's films, even when he is not the director, the story and the script are his creations.

Father–Son Duo: Learning from the Master

Anupama Chopra, in her book, *King of Bollywood* (2007: 121), points to the closeness in style between Aditya and his father, Yash Chopra. Although she is exaggerating it, she makes a good point about the fact that Aditya grew up in a film culture in the Chopra family:

> Aditya, Yash's elder son, imbibed his father's style from the time he could see and listen. As a four-year old, he wandered around the shoot of *Kabhie Kabhie* with a viewfinder hung around his neck. The heavy instrument occasionally strained his neck, but Aditya refused to let go of it. The monotony of film production did not

bore him. His parents have to drag him away from the set. Until he was six years old, Aditya assumed that everyone worked in the movies. Famous actors, directors, music composers were guests at his sprawling house. Cinema was the world. Aditya did not make a conscious decision to become a filmmaker. It was ordained.

This phenomenon is not new in the typical, family-owned companies that have dominated the Bombay film industry. They launch their own sons and daughters into stardom or into producing/directing because they have the social and economic capital to do so. While Aditya may have learned the tools of film trade from his father, he has kept the young, urban audience in mind as he developed his own aesthetic. The appeal to the young is both domestic as well as global. These are the audiences that fill the multiplexes in Bombay, Toronto, London, New York, Chicago and Los Angeles, let alone the multiplexes located in the gigantic malls in Dubai and other Arab countries.[4] Aditya's films tapped into the emotional need and desires of that audience and their conservative values regarding their female children in terms of marriage, love, piety and domesticity.

Growing up in the shadow of a successful film-maker, who had so many hits to his credit, must have been a difficult one for Aditya Chopra. He had to grow within certain parameters but also establish his own directorial style. The differences between the father and son in making these films could be brought into sharp focus, especially when Aditya wrote the story and script for several of the films directed by his father or in the cases where Aditya was the writer and director, but his father was the producer.

In March 2015, at an event held to celebrate 1,000 weeks of continuous run of DDLJ at Maratha Mandir in Mumbai, Shah Rukh Khan, who played the lead role, spoke about such differences between the father and son, 'Adi's ideas are different from Yashji's…. Yeah! I have worked with both of them. I have worked with Adi when he was an assistant director also' (Khan and Kajol 2014). Then he began to talk about the barn scene in DDLJ where Simran and Raj spend a night together. She refuses to drink some brandy to stay warm and then succumbs to it. She guzzles it down, totally out of character for a 'good girl' brought up in a traditional family. After that 'shocking' act to 'traditional Hindu values', she starts to sing the song, 'Zara Sa Jhoom ...' and runs around with Raj in a Swiss town, half drunk. According to Shah Rukh, Yash Chopra objected to this 'good' girl character drinking and dancing. Aditya then asked Shah Rukh to negotiate with his father and tell him that he wanted to try out his own ideas in the film and to put his point, then, Aditya, reportedly, said:

> Yaar, what dad is saying is correct. Because the kind of director that he is, his ideas and thoughts-modern thoughts-no other director possesses. But with regarding these thoughts, once the film is made and released, I will not come to know if my ideas were good or bad.... I understand what dad is going through but let me make my own mistakes in Dilwale Dulhania Le Jayenge so that I know I can make a better film after this one. (Khan and Kajol 2014).

Shah Rukh Khan further goes on to say:

> So this is the kind of belief that Adi had at that point. I could not go and explain this to Yashji ... but the belief that Adi had then carried him through the next twenty years. But that belief is working under the shadow of the greatest director that the Indian film industry has ever seen and still holding on to his own. (Khan and Kajol 2014)

The proof that Aditya won the argument with his producer–father is in the film was that the shots of Kajol running around drunk and doing stupid things, including breaking a shop window to steal a beautiful dress, remained. The father–son collaboration continued through the years after DDLJ's success in 1995. Aditya wrote many stories and scripts that were directed by his father including Dil To Pagal Hai (Yash Chopra, 1997), Veer-Zaara (Yash Chopra, 2004) and the last film of Yash Chopra—Jab Tak Hai Jaan (2012)[5] that was also set in London and India, just as DDLJ. All these have much in common in the sense that they are all highly romanticized depictions of heterosexual love, dripping with sentimentality, familial loyalty, conflicts created sometimes by unsure feelings, politics, patriarchy, tradition versus modernity and sacrifice for each other or the nation.

In the online version of '*Jab Tak Hai Jaan*: Making of the Film' (Yash Raj Films 2012), some of the key personalities who contributed to the film speak highly of the productive relationship between father and son. These interviews with luminaries such as Gulzar, the lyricist; A.R. Rahman, the music director; and Anil Mehta, the director of photography shed light on the creative engagement between two collaborative individuals who entertained mass audiences globally.

Rahman, one of the top music composers, is a man of few words, but he is all praise for Yash and Aditya Chopra's demands for music in their films, 'Music has to be traditional, yet get young audiences to listen to it; yet serving a compliment to the script.' It is not so unusual in the Bombay film industry where the director looks for songs and dances to complement the script. What is not common is the marriage between traditional sounding melodies that have to have an appeal to the young audiences.

Gulzar goes even further to describe how that combination of talents worked beautifully for *Jab Tak Hai Jaan* while he wrote the lyrics for the film: 'Melody is somewhere in the head…. It is in Yashji's temperament or musical style…. He loves Urdu poetry; remembers a lot of Urdu poetry; and he reads Urdu poetry' (Yash Raj Films 2012).

Even if one takes these accolades with a grain of salt, the memorable lyrics and the musical tunes speak to the mass appeal of these films. This knowledge and expertise of Yash Chopra combined with Aditya Chopra's keen awareness of what the young audience finds pleasurable was a formidable combination for box office success. Films such as *Dil to Pagal Hai* (Yash Chopra, 1997), *Veer-Zaara* (Yash Chopra, 2004), which were written by Aditya and also produced by him, stand out in that regard.

Aditya Chopra comes out shining in the comments made by the leading actors in *Jab Tak Hai Jaan* (Yash Chopra, 2012) for his uniqueness in convincing them to play the lead roles and also in getting them to believe in the characters that they thought were too good to be true. Katrina Kaif, who plays one of the two female leads in the film, explains how Aditya Chopra convinced her to play the role:

> A lot of times you end up imagining the film in your own mind ...
> or you get a general gist of it. But when Adi narrated it, I actually
> saw each scene as though I was watching a movie.... It was what I
> wanted out of a Yash Chopra film. (Yash Raj Films 2012)

Then Katrina reveals that she could not identify with the character and had difficulty in agreeing to play such a role:

> For me, Meera's character I play in Yashji's film, it was very tricky.
> Because there is a major point in Meera's character or in her actions,
> which to me as a person, I would never do. The first thing I said to
> Adi, 'Adi, I wouldn't do it!' He replied, 'I know you wouldn't do
> it, but this is a movie. And you have to find a way to connect to it.

> To me, it was the biggest thing in the film. You have to somehow
> understand what the character is doing; you must believe in it,
> even if the character is not like you. Of course, Adi is a person who
> really guides you as an actor. Shah Rukh was there, you know,
> every one there I had all the help I could get. But honestly for me,
> I started to get more comfortable with it was when I started inter-
> acting a little more deeper, little more personal, with Yashji. (Yash
> Raj Films 2012)

Even if one takes these comments as mutual admiration in an
industry tightly controlled by powerful families, Aditya, as a
writer and director, had gained tremendous clout with DDLJ's
worldwide success. However, each film is a completely new thing
from start to finish. With every film, the director has to convince
the actors to believe in the script and the characters they are sup-
posed to portray.

Extending 'Glamorous Realism':
Reality and Fantasy

In this section, we will consider Aditya Chopra's directorial style
within the 'masala film' tradition that is too central to Bombay
cinema. I have noted elsewhere that 'masala' is an appropriate
metaphor to analyse India's popular cinema because it draws

attention to the variety of ingredients that make up the basic narrative structure of a popular film (Pendakur 2003: 95). In the use of colour, costumes and make-up, elements such as movement, dialogue and its delivery, acting, music and others tend to be boisterous. Their cultural origins and deep influences come from professional and folk cinema and other art forms. These 'masala elements', however, are developed visually in extravagant ways and the best of that can be observed in how the song and dance numbers are created for the big screen. As stated elsewhere, 'A distinguishing characteristic of Indian masala film is that it uses song and dance as a narrative device to enhance the plot line, exposition of character, discussion of moral dilemma, and in effect, the story' (Pendakur 2003: 107). Aditya Chopra toys with reality and fantasy in the three films that he has directed — all set within the masala film-making tradition. In his very first film, DDLJ, he uses songs as fantasy devices where reality and the imagined worlds are seamlessly interwoven to enhance drama.[6] He also borrows from the treasure trove of melodramatic techniques of other filmmakers to tug at the hearts of his viewers and make them cry and laugh. We will look at these aspects of his directorial style in the analysis further.

Songs are the heart and soul of the masala film tradition. The Bollywood narrative form that has evolved in India's 100-year-old film industry gives primacy to music and songs as narrative devices. Top directors craft song picturization carefully and typically with great care and big money to capture all the necessary elements on the screen to not only please the audience but also advance the narrative.[7] Characters are often shown to be imagining an escape from their actual spaces that they inhabit to other exotic locations within and outside India. The audience, thereby, is transported to beautiful spots from Kashmir or Kullu Manali to Shimla or Darjeeling. While the mass audience was exposed to those spectacular areas of India ever since the 1960s, all in colour, the Chopras, however, featured snow-capped mountains and valleys of Switzerland in their films and put stories in the heart of London.

Aditya Chopra's style includes not only placing his characters in gorgeous locations abroad, which is part of the conventions of glamorizing the situation by famous directors such as Raj Kapoor in the 1960s, but also cutting between the 'real' and 'imaginary' in a scene. The characters in certain scenes may be caught in a web of family relations or conflicting emotions that forbid them to engage in a love relationship and the director uses that emotion to bind them together in an imagined world by mixing shots from the characters' reality with their fantasy. Time actually freezes for the characters as well as the audience in a theatre. This narrative technique worked well in DDLJ but not so well in *Mohabbatein* because the latter film ends up in a melodramatic mess with its unbelievable premise of a dead woman showing up in songs. In other words, the reality and fantasy idiom does not work all the time, and when it crosses the boundaries of believability, the narrative loses its hold on the audience.

Further, by way of close analysis of two songs from DDLJ, we will examine how Aditya weaves reality and fantasy in his picturization of songs.

1. 'Na Jaane Mere'

The two protagonists in the film—Raj and Simran—are both Londoners with dissimilar backgrounds. Raj is rich and carefree with a doting father. Simran is the elder daughter of a small shopkeeper who is a traditional Hindu patriarch. He rules the household with an iron fist and believes that Western culture is corrupt and his daughter is better off marrying someone from his village in Punjab. In fact, Simran is betrothed at a young age to her father's friend's son in India. The narrative, however, creates an accidental encounter first between Raj and Simran's father and then with her and Raj as they accidentally become fellow travellers on a Eurail tour. The song, 'Na Jane Mere', is positioned to capture Simran's hidden romantic feelings for Raj after their trip ends.

Simran and Raj say goodbye to each other at the train station in London after their adventure in Europe. Simran invites him to her wedding in India and in an over-the-shoulder close shot, Raj says, 'No, I won't come to the wedding!', and Simran appears bewildered. He turns to walk away leaving her in that location. As the background score starts up, the camera cuts to a wide shot of Simran frozen in one place, clutching the cow bell that she bought in Switzerland and her suitcase next to her. We see passengers moving around her while she remains still. The song, 'Na Jaane Mere', begins while Simran turns around to look for Raj who is not around anymore. The song goes on to say, 'I don't know what has happened to my heart. It was here and now seems lost!' It is a duet that connects these two characters walking through different spaces. The camera cuts from the train station to Raj driving a fancy, red car on a rural road in what seems like a location shot from Switzerland and not England. He is wearing different clothes and is surrounded by greenery, cows in their pastures and snow-capped mountains. His car comes to an abrupt halt as there is a woman on the road dressed in beautiful, long flowing clothes and a hat. She sings, 'You have fallen in love and don't fail to acknowledge it.' The camera then cuts to a shot of Simran walking with her suitcase in a park, lost in thought. Someone grabs her hand and she turns to realize that it is Raj, who now sings, 'You have fallen in love…', the same refrain that Simran sings. She is lost in thought as Raj magically disappears. We then see her going down an escalator to get on to a subway train. Raj is shown going up the escalator as a counter to her movement of going down. She walks down the hallway and finds a man playing a saxophone, and as she looks again, it is Raj who is playing the instrument. A train arrives, the doors open and she sees Raj standing there. The song continues and the shots reveal that they are in two different locations while they are thinking about each other and they experience the new turbulent emotions of love and separation. That reality turns again into a dream-like situation where Simran is sitting atop a tour bus and Raj shows up to continue the singing. From that scene, the director cuts to a long shot of Raj and Simran with a snow-capped mountain in their background where she declares to him, 'You are in love….' The camera cuts to a shot of Simran walking again in a park as it rains and she hears the mandolin that Raj uses to play their signature tune. When she turns to look for him, he is sitting atop a carriage wearing a hat. He comes down playing his mandolin and Simran runs to hug him. Raj and Simran are now dancing in the rain.

The next stanza begins with Raj alone in his red car when he sings, 'Hey, time; stop moving. And go back a bit'. Using parallel cutting, Aditya establishes them in two different locations but joined by the song they are singing. Raj imagines her standing in his car and they are singing the duet in the beautiful countryside. As she continues to walk in London, Raj shows up on a bicycle in a different hat and sings to her. The song ends with Raj arriving in his car at his father's mansion and Simran at her parent's door with her mom welcoming her with a big hug. As she returns to the door to get her suitcase, she sees Raj again in a different set of clothes. As they smile and wave to each other, the director cuts to a shot from the back of Simran, and Raj has disappeared. She is shown to be standing at the door waving to the imagined handsome Raj with a smile.

As we can see, Aditya's deft blending of reality and fantasy works beautifully to convey how the two characters are feeling in that moment and the realization that they are in love.[8] It draws the audience effectively into the characters' interior world while the audience knows all too well that their bleak reality will set up obstacles given their families and patriarchy.

2. 'Tujhe Dekha To Ye Jaana Sanam'

Simran is in the middle of a mustard field in her father's village in Punjab that is filled with yellow flowers, and a cow stands in the foreground with a Swiss bell tied around its neck. The wind blows Simran's hair as the camera mounted on a boom comes down. The director cuts to a very long shot of the field and Raj is positioned at the distance by a tree. The camera now rises up to re-emphasize the beautiful setting in Punjab. The camera then reveals a close shot of Simran who looks like she is wondering if Raj is really there. As he turns to her and opens his arms to her, she is sure now it is Raj and runs to embrace him. The music picks up and the lovers are lost in their embrace. Simran realizes that she is in his arms and turns away to separate herself from him; that is when Raj looks at her and starts to sing, 'Tujhe Dekha To …' in a two shot. The song declares his love for her and then says, 'Where do we go from here? I will simply die in your arms.' She repeats the same refrain and holds his hands and hugs him. The next shot is a wide shot in a church and we see Raj carrying Simran who is dressed as a bride in a red sari. They are in the same church that they encountered on their trip in Europe. The whole song jumps around between real events and imagined ones set in different locations — trains, mountains, green meadows, snow-filled slopes, a lake and a river.

On an idyllic mountain slope, Simran is in a beautiful blue sari and a sleeveless blouse — all contrasted against the snowy white background. Raj is wearing a red shirt. The song continues in that setting and they embrace in a medium long shot. As the song concludes, we are back in the mustard field again with the couple in an embrace and Simran wakes up from that dream-like sequence. Her eyes open and her expression suggests that she knows that her reality is not that pretty with family, tradition and her role as a woman in that patriarchal culture.

Melodrama in DDLJ

Rosie Thomas (1995) offers the following proposition about melodrama in Hindi language films that fits Aditya Chopra's use of it:

> [T]he films are centrally structured around contradictions, conflicts, and tensions primarily within the domains of kinship and sexuality, and that it is an expectation of Hindi film as a genre — in accordance with the conventions of melodrama — that these are resolved within the parameters of an ideal moral universe. This defines, some what rigidly, paradigms of 'good' and 'bad' (or expected and unacceptable) forms of behavior and requires that the forces of good triumph over evil.

Melodrama is not a new way of representing emotions in Indian cinema. It is as old as Indian cinema itself. In fact, it is derided by critics at home and abroad, but remains a powerful story-telling tool in the hands of Bollywood film-makers. Well-handled melo-dramatic scenes can enhance the narrative—be they family conflicts, moral dilemmas of the characters, love–hate relationships, jealousy, envy or other real-life material. When that fails, the scenes or characters may lose their credibility with its audience and become laughable.

Here, we turn to two scenes in DDLJ to analyse Aditya's craft in delivering melodrama.

Simran has returned from her Europe trip and the family rejoices her arrival. The scene opens on a close shot of the fire-place and dollies back to reveal Simran and her mother, Lajjo, sitting opposite each other.

The director cuts to an over the shoulder close shot of Simran who is glowing in that light. Simran says to her mother, 'Remember that I wrote about a man of my dreams in my dairy? He has come in front me.' The reverse over the shoulder shot shows Lajjo's face and she says, 'Uh!', and the background score picks up to add drama.

Several cuts back and forth follow where this interesting conversation about love develops, all seemingly innocent enough. Simran in a close up continues that before going on the trip all she had planned was to enjoy the trip, come home and then go to India to marry the man chosen for her: 'I had reconciled with my destiny, ma. But, how would I know that this would happen to me. He came like a storm and I like a fallen leaf kept flying with him.' Lajjo is intrigued, not worried. Simran goes on,

> I had read and heard that love is like this and that. I never ever understood it. I didn't get it when he helped me the first time by extending his hand. We spent many days together; even then I didn't understand it all. But today, when we separated at the station, I realized for the first time that after this moment I will never see him again.

At that precise moment, the camera begins to track to the right with Lajjo in the foreground, Simran continues, 'I wanted to stop him; wanted to say something to him; wanted to hear him say some-thing. Then I realized that this is what love is all about.... I don't know whether he loves me or not, but I do know this much.' At that moment, the camera has completed the encircling movement around the two characters, and the audience sees *Babuji*, Simran's father, standing in the back. The string instruments in the background pick up to an ominous tone. Simran has not yet seen her father and she declares, 'I can't live with anyone else. I love him, ma. I really do'; then as she raises her eyes, she notices her father. Both mother and daughter raise their heads as the camera cuts to a mid-shot of Babuji towering over them. His eyes are enlarged revealing his anger. The camera zooms to his close-up. Lajjo tries to cover up what had transpired by saying something about girl talk, and Babuji waves his right hand to stop her. As Babuji walks up to Simran slowly, the audience expects violence, but in several shots back and forth the director builds the tension to suggest that patriarchal violence lurks in the shadow. In an over-the-shoulder shot, Babuji says, 'I told you, not to embarrass me…. You had promised me; yet, you betrayed me.' To smooth out the situation, Lajjo tries to intervene by saying, 'Please listen to me,' and Babuji angrily replies, 'I don't want to hear anything!' An over the shoulder close shot of Simran shows how terrified she is. Babuji tells her, 'Pack your things. We will leave for India tomorrow.' Simran whimpers. Babuji continues to order, 'Permanently.' Lajjo moves to console Simran as she begins to cry. Babuji declares, 'Let her cry. She wrote her own future with tears…. She will have to learn to stop crying herself. Let her cry.' The director cuts to Simran's medium shot with the fireplace to the right as her parents move away. She starts to cry and the camera dollies to her close-up. Then, the director cuts to a top angle shot where we see Simran left alone in the living room, crying and collapsing with grief. The scene ends there.

Another critical scene in the film occurs when Lajjo discovers Raj's identity. Lajjo walks into her bedroom and sees Raj and Simran through the window, sitting on the terrace and feeding each other. The young lovers are totally absorbed in themselves and Simran looks very happy. Lajjo loses herself in this delightful moment and, quickly, Babuji's non-diagetic voice rings in her ear. He sternly warns her that it is better for Simran to remember her promise; otherwise, the voice says, 'She will suffer a lot.'

Tears start rolling down Lajjo's face. Her own off-screen voice now speaks to her, 'What happened to me cannot happen to my daughter. By becoming a daughter, wife and sister, she won't continue to sacrifice herself every step of the way. She will live her life as she pleases.' The director now cuts away to a shot of a fountain where a lamp is floating. In the next shot, Lajjo opens the door and lets Raj and Simran come in. She walks to the cupboard and grabs a bundle of jewellery. She quickly takes out her bangles and adds them to the collection. The director cuts to the young couple and Raj looks to Simran with a question mark on his face. As the background music starts up, Lajjo walks up to them and says, 'Take this!' and pushes the bundle into Simran's hands. In an over-the-shoulder shot, Lajjo says to Simran and Raj, 'I don't want to know anything. I know Raj is the same man you met in Europe. I also know that you both love each other very much.' As Simran and Raj continue to stare at her, Lajjo says, 'I was wrong Simran. My daughter will not sacrifice her happiness. She will not sacrifice her love.' Then Lajjo turns to Raj and says, 'I know you will keep my daughter very happy. Take her away from here. Go away. There is no one here who would understand your love. Take her from here. I will manage everything here.' Raj replies to her saying, 'No, maji.' Camera now cuts to Lajjo who replies, 'Before I become weak from my position, please go away with her. I beg of you, son.' The camera now cuts to a three shot. Raj says, 'OK, ma. I will take her away.' He walks Lajjo to the sofa and sits her down and puts the bundle of jewellery back in her hands. Then he tells her a story that his mother used to tell him when he was a kid about choosing the right path, not the easy one. Further, he asks, 'Tell me, maji, is my road the correct one or the wrong one?' Lajjo agrees that his is the correct path and says, 'But you don't know my husband.' To which Raj replies, 'Your husband does not know me.' Raj tells Lajjo that he won't steal Simran but will win her, and then says, 'I will go only when Babuji puts her hand into mine.' Lajjo hugs Simran. Both begin to sob. Raj says, 'Excuse me. This disease of crying, is it genetic in this family?' They all laugh. He puts his head on Lajjo's lap. A serious scene ends in comedy and all around warmth.

While Aditya Chopra excels in using melodrama to heighten the emotions in many scenes in DDLJ, he is less successful in doing the same in his later two films. The crucial weakness in both *Mohabbatein* and *Rab Ne Bana Di Jodi* is that the plot in both films hangs on a slim thread of credibility. Trying to weave five love stories in one film is excessive for any director and Aditya fails to deliver a credible film in *Mohabbatein*. Over the top dialogue between the hero and the principal about romantic love and traditional marriage is unconvincing. In *Rab Ne Bana Di Jodi*, the transformation of the hero from a naive, middle-class clerk to a dancing champion is caught in its own bind. The narrative cannot mask the identity of the hero to the extent where the audience cannot recognize him. That in itself strains the credibility of the narrative because the viewer wonders why his own wife cannot recognize her husband just because his costume and mannerisms are different. Both the films, however, were box office successes at home and abroad, and that is certainly mindboggling. Aditya Chopra appears to have given up directing films after *Rab Ne Bana Di Jodi* and turned to being a producer as well as the CEO of a cultural conglomerate to which we will now turn.

Yash Raj Films: A Cultural Conglomerate

DDLJ's phenomenal success at home and abroad set the stage for Aditya Chopra and his father to embark on a new path to build a vertically integrated company in Bombay. Although YRF was founded in 1970, it grew to great prominence as a conglomerate in the fast-changing entertainment industry in India since the 1990s. A decade after the release of DDLJ, YRF built a state-of-the-art studio with air-conditioned sound stages and advanced digital post-production facilities in Bombay. Shedding the old, grungy image of the Bombay studios, YRF Studios looks more like a high-tech college campus.[9] It embarked on producing family entertainment for television in 2010 and distributes its shows through Sony Entertainment Television. Their other ventures include video on demand, Yash Raj Music and YouTube Channels (YRF Television 2015).

This private corporation's steady ascent to a position of dominance may be seen in the broader, complex neoliberal policy framework of India's economic development, its closer integration with the world capitalist economy after the collapse of the Soviet Union, the growth of cities in India and the rising tide of middle-class families, and the realization on the part of the Bombay film industry that there was a sizeable market abroad for filmed entertainment. In a recent special report on India, *The Economist* pointed out:

> Over 27 million people of Indian origin, including some temporary migrants, live overseas, many of them in the Gulf. They remit $70 billion a year to their home country, more than any other group of expats. That adds up to 3.5% of India's GDP, outstripping foreign direct investment. (*The Economist* 2015: 15)

Their desire to consume home-made cinema and all its other cultural products — the DVDs, star studded, live musical extravaganzas, designer clothes featured in movies and other consumer commodities hawked by the major stars — is a heady mix of opportunities for Bollywood corporations. YRF, under Aditya Chopra, pivoted to globalize its operations successfully to capitalize on these potential opportunities worldwide for Bollywood entertainment.

This development of a film company diversifying and internationalizing is also emblematic of a family-owned firm, typical structure in which Bombay cinema flourished for nearly 100 years, assuming a modern, corporate identity, although tightly controlled by Yash Chopra's family. Aditya, at the helm of this corporation, has expanded its activities to include new avenues for creative work and profits. It has a vertical organizational structure of production and distribution of films and other entertainment commodities that are marketed on a worldwide basis. To date, YRF has 65 feature films to its credit and under a new banner called Y-Films, established in 2011, Aditya Chopra has also produced three films aimed at the youth market (Yash Raj Films 2015).

YRF now has a global presence. It boasts of having offices in 12 distribution territories of India and also in the United Kingdom, United States and UAE, which are the key markets abroad for Bollywood films. YRF was the first company from Bombay to set up direct distribution in the United Kingdom and the United States right after DDLJ. This was a strategically critical action because the prior practice of simply leasing exhibition or video rights to local distributors did not yield significant revenues. By their presence in New York City, for example, YRF gained local market practices, audience taste culture and also stem video piracy. YRF seems to have a direct pipeline to not only the dominant theatrical chains in the United States but also Netflix, the biggest streaming service with a subscriber base of 45 million. Simultaneous release of Hindi films in the nearly 1,000 multiplex screens in India and hundreds of screens in certain US markets where there is a considerable density of South Asian population became possible.

In addition to theatrical and home entertainment markets for releasing their films, YRF has ambitious plans to grow its production operations in the United States. The risky path for Bombay producers, however, is not always paved with gold. Its subsidiary, YRF Entertainment, started co-ventures with US companies by optioning novels and partnering to make feature films for Hollywood film audiences worldwide. *Grace of Monaco* (Olivier Dahan, 2014) is the first such co-venture for YRF Entertainment with 10 Hollywood companies. The film had an estimated budget of $30 million starring Nicole Kidman and a host of 28 distributors bought its rights in different markets around the world because it is a biopic of a major Hollywood star, Grace Kelly. Critics panned the film and it appears not to have gotten a US theatrical release yet. Yash Raj's experience with Walt Disney Pictures in coproducing *Roadside Romeo* (Jugal Hansraj, 2008) was also not a successful venture. An animated feature with an estimated budget of $1.7 million, the picture reportedly grossed $55,000 in the US box office and almost $2 million from international markets (Boxofficemojo. com 2015). With the kind of market clout that Disney has in the United States, the picture was screened in only 29 theatres and then flopped.

The Hollywood majors, in particular, 21st Century Fox, Walt Disney Pictures, Viacom and Sony Pictures have expanded their operations in distribution and production of Bollywood films in recent years. Their strategic move was to buy up major Bollywood companies to gain access to talent, market knowledge and profits from a high-growth industry. This is unlike in the 1940s when Hollywood companies actively discouraged national cinema from developing on its own terms because they simply wanted to sell their built-up inventory of films all over the world. In the current phase of globalization, however, the strategy that is being pursued by the Hollywood's dominant corporations is to acquire local companies to make films in local languages, which has been dubbed as 'glocalization'. To his credit, Aditya turned down an acquisition offer by Walt Disney Pictures in 2008 to become equity partners in YRF. Subsequently, Disney bought 49 per cent of UTV Movies, another conglomerate, and when India eliminated ownership restrictions, Disney gobbled up UTV Movies. As India's economy has continued to open up for foreign capital in various sectors, this integration and internationalization of successful Indian companies will only intensify. YRF, as a privately held company by the Chopra family, continues to operate independently of such pressures, at least at the present time.

Conclusions

Aditya Chopra grew up in privilege with great social capital that his parents had accumulated. The family's financial and emotional support as well as its close connections to talented stars and others in the industry, let alone his father's great reputation as a leading producer–director of family entertainers clearly helped Aditya's launch into the film industry. What he has done with that high level of social capital is quite impressive from several perspectives.

Aditya Chopra's 'glamorous realism' flourishes in many films that come out of Bombay in the midst of a wider variety of films that cater to the ever-changing tastes of South Asian audiences worldwide. Aditya's huge success with DDLJ paved the way for other Bombay film producers to reach the global markets and exploit the need and desire for entertainment from India. Aditya's films idealize romanticism and wrap the contradictions and conflicts of society in sentimental portrayals of characters and the visual pleasure of exotic locations, songs and dances. In essence, Aditya Chopra does not alter the masala film-making tradition in India but strengthens it.

DDLJ's financial success placed the family-owned YRF in the top tier of Bombay film production–distribution houses. YRF grew exponentially as a vertically integrated corporation with global distribution of their films, which has been a winning strategy. Aditya appears to have successfully internationalized the company by not just building a state-of-the-art studio in Bombay but also producing films that bank upon the home audience as well as the South Asian diaspora.

In the short run, the company's collaborations with Hollywood film-makers did not yield financial or artistic success. What is noteworthy is that Aditya has guided the company well, fended off takeover attempts by Walt Disney Pictures and given many younger, talented actors as well as directors the opportunities to make films under the YRF banner. That is praiseworthy in a fickle industry where financing and distribution are not only risky but also often impossible to attain or under the control of mafia dons (Pendakur 2003: 51–55; Srivastava 2003). Not all of the films made under Aditya Chopra's supervision have reached the same level of box office success that was enjoyed by DDLJ, but his leadership in producing diverse content—romantic comedies, action thrillers and period films—and nurturing new talent continues. That contribution as a whole is remarkable because it keeps Bollywood as an industry and a cultural form vital for the future, let alone entertaining its audiences worldwide.

Notes

1   One account places DDLJ in the top 11 all-time hits of Bollywood, and its revenues in India are estimated to be ₹ 10.065 billion and from the overseas markets around ₹ 12.22 billion. See BoxofficeIndia.com (2015). US$1 equaled approximately ₹ 66 in 2015.
2   For detailed analysis pertaining to telecommunications and media in India, see Pendakur (2013).
3   Between 2000 and 2008, approximately $50 billion flowed into India's economy in private equity funds (Raghavan 2015: B4).
4   The rise and significance of multiplexes in India's malls as indicators of neoliberal policies and their effect on the structure and functioning of the film industry have been researched well. See Pendakur (2012).
5   Many of his films show up on lists of global box office success compiled by Indian media. See Hooli (2014) and Chand-Suhas (2012).
6   The artistry involved in creating song sequences — particularly lyrics and picturization — has been analysed thoroughly. See Kabir (2005) and also Pendakur (2003: 119–43).
7   In Hindi language cinema, many contemporary directors stand out in how they painstakingly create song–dance numbers. Important among them is Sanjay Leela Bhansali who has several big-budget extravaganzas to his credit. See *Devdas* (2002), *Goliyon Ki Rasleela Ram-Leela* (2013) and *Bajirao Mastani* (2015).
8   In *Rab Ne Bana Di Jodi*, Aditya creates a similar scene where events in reality contrasted with the things in the characters' imagination.
9   See http://yrfstudios.com (accessed on 28 February 2015).

References

BoxofficeIndia.com. 2015. 'Top Lifetime Grossers Worldwide.' Retrieved 8 April 2015, from http://wayback.archive.org/web/2013102120272

Boxofficemojo.com. 2015. *Roadside Romeo*. Retrieved 4 April 2015, from http://www.boxofficemojo.com/movies/?id=roadsideromeo.htm

Chand-Suhas. 2012. 'Top Bollywood Hits Down The Years (1940–2014).' IMDb, 16 July. Retrieved 11 April 2015, from http://www.imdb.com/list/ls009418032/

Chopra, A. 2007. *King of Bollywood: Shah Rukh Khan and the Seductive World of Indian Cinema*. New York: Warner Books.

Hooli, S.H. 2014. 'Top 20 All Time Highest Grossing Bollywood Movies,' December 30. Retrieved 11 April 2015, from http://www.ibtimes.

co.in/pk-happy-new-year-kick-bang-bang-enter-list-top-20-all-time-highest-grossing-bollywood-618734

Kabir, N.M. 2005. *Talking Songs: Javed Akhtar in Conversation with Nasreen Munni Kabir*. New Delhi: Oxford University Press.

Kapur, J. and M. Pendakur. 2007. 'The Strange Disappearance of Bombay from its Own Cinema: A Case of Imperialism or Globalization.' *Democratic Communiqué* 21 (1, Spring): 43–59.

Kapur, V. 2012. 'Escapist Fantasy: Why should Anyone Pickup a Novel to See How Faithfully It Depicts Real Life?' Retrieved 21 March 2015, from http://www.thehindu.com/opinion/columns/vikram-kapur/escapist-fantasy/article3967883.ece

Khan, Shah Rukh and Kajol. 2014. 'Shah Rukh Khan and Kajol at Maratha Mandir to Celebrate DDLJ 1000 Week.' Retrieved 30 March 2015, from https://www.youtube.com/watch?v=yimO1nd2xsU

Kolker, R.P. 2015. *The Cultures of American Film*. New York: Oxford University Press.

Pendakur, M. 2003. *Indian Popular Cinema: Industry, Ideology and Consciousness*. Creskill, NJ: Hampton Press.

———. 2012. 'Digital Pleasure Palaces.' *JumpCut* 54 (Fall). Retrieved from http://www.ejumpcut.org/archive/jc54.2012/PendakurIndiaMultiplex/index.html (accessed on 30 March 2015).

———. 2013. 'Twisting and Turning: India's Telecommunications and Media Industries Under the Neo-liberal Regime.' *International Journal of Media & Cultural Politics* 9 (2): 107–31.

Raghavan, A. 2015. 'Global Private Equity Firms, Having Lost Once in India, Are Back in Force.' *The New York Times*, B4, 7 April.

Srivastava, S. 2003. 'Analysis: Bollywood and the Mafia.' *BBC News*. Retrieved 12 Feb 2015, from http://news.bbc.co.uk/2/hi/south_asia/3152662.stm

The Economist. 2015. 'The Diaspora. The Worldwide Web: India Should Make more of a Valuable Asset Abroad.' Special Report, 23 May.

Thomas, R. 1995. 'Melodrama and the Negotiation of Morality.' In *Consuming Modernity: Public Culture in a South Asian World*, edited by Carol Appadurai Breckenridge, 157–82. Minneapolis, MN: University of Minnesota Press.

Yash Raj Films. 2012. '*Jab Tak Hai Jaan*: Making of the Film.' Retrieved 28 March 2015, from https://www.youtube.com/watch?v=1KDl8hc6CB0

———. 2015. 'Company Info.' Retrieved 4 April 2015, from http://yashrajfilms.com/AboutUs/CompanyInfo.aspx?SectionCode=PRO001a1

YRF Television. 2015. 'Archive.' Retrieved 28 February 2015, from http://yashrajfilms.com/Television/Television.aspx?SectionCode=TV0001

Film References

Chopra, A. 1995. *Dilwale Dulhania Le Jayenge*. Yash Raj Films.

——. 2000. *Mohabbatein*. Yash Raj Films.

——. 2008. *Rab Ne Bana Di Jodi*. Yash Raj Films.

Chopra, Y. 1976. *Kabhie Kabhie*. Yash Raj Films.

——. 1997. *Dil To Pagal Hai*. Yash Raj Films.

——. 2004. *Veer-Zaara*. Yash Raj Films.

——. 2012. *Jab Tak Hai Jaan*. First Step Productions and Yash Raj Films.

Dahan, O. 2014. *Grace of Monaco*. Stone Angels, YRF Entertainment and Umedia.

Hansraj, J. 2008. *Roadside Romeo*. Yash Raj Films and Walt Disney Co.

Khan, M. 1988. *Qayamat Se Qayamat Tak*. Nasir Husain Films.

CHAPTER 5

Authorship, Industry and the Intermedial Relay: The Films of Vidhu Vinod Chopra

Sudhir Mahadevan

This chapter offers a broad survey of film-maker Vidhu Vinod Chopra's work with an emphasis on his early films. As one of a third generation of 'art' film-makers (and only the second generation of those graduating out of the Film and Television Institute of India [FTII]), Chopra's career evinces a number of different strands. While his student film *Murder at Monkey Hill* (1975) and the films that followed up to *Parinda* (1989) suggest a fascination with the mechanics of Hitchcockian suspense and the tonal ranges of film noir, his subsequent directorial ventures include romances set against the epic backdrop of historical events and war films. These are *1942: A Love Story* (1994), *Kareeb* (1998), *Mission Kashmir* (2000) and *Eklavya: The Royal Guard* (2007; henceforth, *Eklavya*). More recently, he has co-written and produced a number of hugely successful dramatic comedies starting with *Munna Bhai M.B.B.S.* (2003).

I shall begin with a broad survey of his career because such a survey has implications for the relationship between authorship and industrial practice in Indian cinema. From there, I would want to proceed to a closer look at certain stylistic tendencies that are noteworthy.

A key argument that I want to make here is that the desire to engage with commercial melodrama is already evident in his early murder mysteries. Conversely, the psychological realism of the murder mysteries and the psychosexual inclinations of the family melodrama have continued to inform the more commercial fare directed by him. Furthermore, as a director, his more recent works suggest an aspiration towards Hollywood, not the contemporary Bollywood star vehicle, or for that sake, the multiplex film. As a producer, I shall argue that, he likewise eschews both the aforementioned in favour of a commitment to the more long-lasting genre of the social and the all-India family film. I shall conclude with a brief reflection on how we might map Chopra (and his FTII generation) within a broader atlas of film history that includes Hollywood as well as the French New Wave.

Authorship and Industry

Authorship in Bombay cinema is not a topic that has received considerable scholarly attention, if one discounts biographies of particular iconic directors such as Guru Dutt, Raj Kapoor or even the pioneering D.G. Phalke. In Chopra's case, the overall body of work 'produced' by him poses multiple challenges. I placed the word produced in quotes because the production process, the division of labour, creative and otherwise, and the roles of a writer, a producer and a director are not so clear cut in Bombay cinema. Chopra's career is in effect a demonstration of the fluid borderlines of professional expertise, as he has worn several hats in his career.

If I were to restrict my consideration simply to the movies Chopra has directed, it would appear that he has had a steady cinematic output as a director (roughly one film every four years), starting from 1978 when he made a documentary film, *An Encounter With Faces* for Films Division (India's government-run documentary films unit). This steady pace continued till *Mission*

Kashmir (2000). Post-2000, however, Chopra directed only two films, *Eklavya* (2007) and *Broken Horses* (2015). (I shall not be discussing the latter since I did not have access to the movie [theatrical or otherwise] at the time of this writing.)[1]

However, considering the totality of his work reveals a career that far exceeds the directorial role. He has served as a writer (or a 'screenplay associate') in 15 of a total of 17 films (including *Broken Horses* and *Wazir*). Writing, however, is a collaborative and even frequently uncredited enterprise in the film industry. Suketu Mehta's memoir of life in Mumbai, *Maximum City* (2004), offers a glimpse into how *Mission Kashmir* (2000) developed from the script to the finished product as the result of a series of contingencies and collaborations. Mehta, a writer, initially invited by Vikram Chandra (Chopra's brother-in-law) to observe the brainstorming session for *Mission Kashmir* at Chopra's house was roped in to participate in the process and finally became an active and credited collaborator in the development of the storyline. Indeed, five people share writing and screenplay credits for the movie: Vidhu Vinod Chopra, Suketu Mehta, Vikram Chandra, Abhijat Joshi and Atul Tiwari (the latter for dialogue).

Mehta offers a vivid account of the changes films undergo as a film-maker ropes in stars and music directors, convinces distributors to advance funds for the production on the basis of the star and the music, negotiates with government censors and petitions politicians to relax censorship requirements. A combination of kinship relations, political and extra-political pressure, demands by stars and the imperatives of the state shape the script which at any rate is not a bound, material entity: directors pitch stories orally to stars. Writers themselves tend to be seriously underpaid with little control over the work once it has become the basis for a movie. As other scholars have noted, the paradigm of creative authorship in the Bombay film industry sees ideas as not being subject to ownership. That, in addition to 'Indianization' (or the transformation of a storyline into an Indian film palatable for Indian audiences and replete with song–dance sequences), undermines charges of plagiarism that are often directed at the industry (Ganti 2012, 2013).

Given the aforementioned points about industrial practice, I would caution against any stable definitions of creative roles. That said, I do think it might be useful to distinguish the two phases to his career as a director: the suspense/thriller/noir phase that ended with *Parinda* (1989) and the historical epic phase that ended with *Eklavya* (2007). One could identify a third phase: the socially conscious dramatic comedy phase, one in which Chopra has served as a co-writer and a sole producer but not a director. This phase would range from *Munna Bhai M.B.B.S.* (2003) to *PK* (2014). Here again, the writing was collaborative in all of these films and has often involved the same figures from one film to another: Chopra, Rajkumar Hirani, who also directed the last four films produced by Chopra, and Abhijat Joshi, who has been involved in almost all of Chopra's films as a screenwriter starting with Chopra's box office dud *Kareeb* (1998).

At the very least, the third phase of his career in which he has served as a producer and a co-writer seems to demand its own consideration given the stability of collaborators in the writing process and given that most of these Chopra-produced films have been directed by the same director, Rajkumar Hirani. To search for a Chopra stamp in this third phase would capitulate to a more restrictive understanding of authorship (Chaudhary 2014). The third phase certainly reveals a unity of genre and a scale of production (big budget, major stars and socially conscious comedy-driven narratives) that do indicate a consistency of approach in Chopra's production house, Vinod Chopra Films. Both the *Munna Bhai* films (*Munna Bhai M.B.B.S.* [2003] and *Lage Raho Munna Bhai* [2006]) insert the eponymous gangster in ethically challenging situations that ultimately result in the resurgence, in Munna Bhai and through him in the world around him, of fundamental humanist values that oppose mercenary practices as well as overly professionalized and specialized approaches to problems. *3 Idiots* (2009) is a movie about the stultifying rote pedagogy in institutions of higher education that make real innovation and excellence difficult to achieve while also putting immense pressure on the younger generation to produce academic success. *PK* (2014) offers a surprisingly astute and comical look to religion through the eyes of an alien whose total ignorance becomes a rich optic for exposing the arbitrary beliefs and often duplicitous practices that constitute institutionalized religion. In all these films, satire becomes central to social critique.

We need to situate these very recent comedies in a changed landscape that includes at least two other tendencies. The first is the 'multiplex cinema' of the last 15 years which has been characterized by an attention to surface detail in setting and character that hearkens back to the middle-cinema of the 1970s and 1980s of Sai Paranjpye, Basu Chatterjee or Hrishikesh Mukherjee. This is an ethnographically acute satire of the contemporary middle class. It offers a sometimes dystopian focus on the atavisms that continue to haunt small towns' and middle-class neighbourhoods' encounter with the modernity of globalization. The scales of production are modest, and films are addressed to an urban (and perhaps urbane) audience that can afford and wants to watch movies in multiplex theatres. There is also the other, more visible, conspicuous strand, the exorbitant and often spectacular star vehicles that are more consonant with 'Bollywood' (as is the case with Shah Rukh Khan or Salman Khan movies).

Seen against both of these film-making practices, what becomes clear is Chopra's desire as producer to stick to a certain tradition of the 'social', the genre that has dominated the history of Indian commercial cinema and is defined by stories set in contemporary society (as opposed to the 'period', the historical epic or the devotional film). In some Chopra-produced films, this genre retains its core attributes, albeit with a lightly ironic sensibility: an attempt to integrate melodrama, action and spectacle, including song–dance sequences, into family-friendly entertainment. In others, such as *PK* (2014), some key ingredients are missing (the hyperbolic pathos of melodrama and song-dance sequences). But all the recent films he has produced clearly aim to reach as wide an audience as possible via socially relevant entertainment.

I find this a particularly interesting trajectory for a director who began with an investment in suspense, noir and murder mysteries. Chopra has situated himself and his creative and commercial interests in that strand of Bombay cinema with the longest and most stable history, even as the landscape of film-making around him introduces new genres and new conceptions of what constitutes a commercial film.

It might be worth noting here that Chopra's most acclaimed film, the noir city film *Parinda*, was released in 1989, on the cusp of the decade that witnessed changes in the Indian economy and in the film industry whose ramifications are still unfolding.[2] It is not, however, till *Satya* (1998), Ram Gopal Varma's violent and superbly kinetic vision of Bombay and its underworld nearly a decade later, that one sees a reprise that is aesthetically reminiscent of *Parinda*'s investment in noir as well as garnering the sort of attention and iconicity that *Parinda* gained.

I raise the issue of style here at this juncture because in the interim, an early indication of things to come in that decade of transformation was Mani Ratnam's *Roja* (1992). *Roja*'s production values, style, subject matter and music signalled a profound shift in the sensory experience of the cinema.[3] We might say then that the 1990s and beyond (Ratnam, then the Barjatyas, then the diaspora film, then multiplex cinema) 'interrupted' *Parinda*'s noir tendencies, leaving it as the notable instance of cinephiliac work by a generation of FTII-trained film-makers (Chopra, Saeed Mirza, Kundan Shah and Sudhir Mishra) whose careers were bracketed on one side by the realist art cinema of the 1950s to the 1970s, and on the other, by the dramatic 1990s (I will have more to say about this particular generation and its influences in the last section of this chapter). Put another way, *Parinda* is also the first instance in which that very generation would make the transition to commercial cinema and television, utilizing bankable stars and storylines. There is one last point to integrate in this section. Interestingly, both Ratnam and Chopra have conformed to the commercial film format (ingredients of comedy, melodrama, action, song and dance) even as newer forms of films have emerged since the 1990s. Their work suggests that a version of the 'formula film' in the post-1990s era continues to be a viable proposition.

In Chopra's case, perhaps this gravitation towards and investment in the commercial melodrama and the social is already in evidence early in his career in movies like the murder mystery

Khamosh (1985), albeit as ambivalent satire. For in that movie, the murder occurs on the set of a film shoot of a run-of the-mill melodrama. It is, therefore, to this film and his other films that I now turn to consider the permutations of suspense, spectacle and melodrama that have shaped Chopra's most significant work.

From Suspense to Melodrama

Let us begin with Chopra's student short thesis film made at the FTII, *Murder at Monkey Hill* (1975). The dual impulse of formalism and a desire to deviate from and yet acknowledge the dictates of commercial viability is evident in this film about an unusual and dread-imbued romance between a young heiress, Prabhi, and the young man, Akhtar, hired by her uncle to murder her. As the killer, Akhtar is a conflicted man with flashes of empathy; Prabhi for her part endures humiliation to prove her love for him. The plot is mostly a series of conversations between the two. Gestures towards popular cinema include the very brief use of a commercial hit song, 'Ruk Jaana Mere Jaana', to notate budding romance. The rest of the music is mostly *Shadows*-style instrumental rock music with a surf guitar sound. However, the sudden flashes of Akhtar's humanity motivate the strains of the sitar. This is a textbook aural delineation of a sentimental Indian cultural world in Bombay commercial cinema. It abruptly transports us, as far as this movie is concerned, from Westernized psychosexual crime to Indian sociocultural comfort zone. Intimate conversation heard from up close accompanies extreme long shots of the couple. As for the formalism, split screens, Vertovian montages involving trains and a credit sequence of black and white images of the crew shooting *Murder at Monkey Hill* reveal a highly self-conscious approach.

Murder at Monkey Hill is a polemic. The first title of the movie reads: 'An attempt at communicating with the Bombay financier. PS Mr Financier: Finance us!' Then the credits follow. Then the screen reads: 'An attempt to brutally assault the senses of a Bombay financier.' And, finally, then the movie begins. As for the ending, it is abrupt, arrested at a heightened moment of suspense as the young heiress is running for her life. The film-maker has exhausted his film stock. The following lines appear on titles, and are also spoken aloud by the film-maker:

> Well, what do you know? We're out of stock. No more shooting. But Mr Financer what more could you expect in only 4000 feet and 4 days to shoot it? Now if you buy us sufficient facilities don't you think we could make you a jubilee? It is a business proposition. Do consider it! Yes we're trained in to fine soldiers and expected to fight battles without any weapons. To fight you in the nude is not heroic. It is suicide!! But where do we go from here? To you or to FFC? P.S Mr Financier/Finance us!

The National Film Finance Corporation (FFC), later to become the National Film Development Corporation (NFDC), and the FTII had both been established in 1960 by the Government of India. A third institution, the Films Division, the government-run (and by some accounts, the world's largest) documentary films unit, had been established much earlier in 1948. Chopra's early career involved all three institutions. While the FFC's initial mandate had been to support films with prospects for some commercial success, by the late 1960s, the FFC had decided to support low-budget 'experimental' films, which resulted in films such as Mrinal Sen's *Bhuvan Shome* (1969) and more notoriously, Mani Kaul's *Uski Roti* (1970). However, in 1975, the government censured the FFC for its reckless support of experimental cinema and the entire board resigned in protest (Amladi 2000; Krishen 1991). Chopra graduated from the FTII in 1975 and perhaps the reference to the FFC in his film is an index of these tempestuous times. While one can speculate on where Chopra stood on the government's censure of the FFC, *Murder at Monkey Hill* clearly hedges its bets by framing the FFC as inadequate, while seeking to attract the attention of a financier it finds unresponsive.

Chopra's first film as a professional film-maker was a documentary film he made for Films Division, *An Encounter with Faces* (1978). The movie, about delinquent children (mostly boys) in children's homes in Mumbai and the circumstances that led them to these homes, is narrated by the children themselves in a series of testimonies that comprise the film. With its frontal focus on the speaking face, its vernacular settings, a linear, additive structure that mostly abjures dramatic development or temporal specificity (although the testimonies of some of the children are impassioned protest), and relatively simple single takes for each child, this movie emerges as a quintessential portrait film. Chopra alternates each frontal still-camera interview with a handheld camera's forward passage through the hallways of these juvenile homes, their classrooms and vocational training facilities, the narrow by-lanes and dusty grounds of the city's slums. A motif is established of a contrast between the two-dimensional 'still' image of the rigid and self-consciously immobile poses of the children speaking to the camera, and the mobile camera that vectors through space, the latter a departure from and perhaps response to the legacy of state-sponsored ethnographic portraiture and its static views.

Within the Films Division itself, the Griersonian documentary was under a vibrant and creative attack by the 1960s with film-makers such as Pramod Pati, K.S. Chary, S. Sukhdev and V.K. Murthy who produced movies of extraordinary innovation in form as well as treatment of established subject matter. Chopra was only one of many of the film-makers emerging from the FTII who gravitated towards the Films Division (Garga 2007).[4]

After the documentary, Chopra remade *Murder at Monkey Hill* as *Sazaye Maut* (Death Sentence, 1981). *Khamosh* (Silence, 1985), a whodunnit, followed *Sazaye Maut* and it is to this movie that I now turn.[5] A film crew is in Pahalgam, a town in Kashmir, shooting a melodrama sensationally titled *Aakhri Khoon* (The Last Murder). The shoot is disrupted when one of the actresses is found dead hanging from a tree. The role being played by the actress in the movie also entails her death by murder. As it turns out, this is no simple case of suicide. The rest of the movie is given over to the investigation as more murders ensue. A series of repetitive scenarios, and repetitions within scenes, mark this film as a conspicuously structured narrative. The movie withholds information on the real killer till the very end, building a plot full of false leads, red herrings and characters with shady motivations and mysterious and damaging habits (drug addiction and somnam-bulism). Then the real killer turns out to be none other than the main male lead of *Aakhri Khoon*, killed at the nick of time as he tries to kill his female co-star, the actress playing the female lead in the fictional movie.

Aakhri Khoon is itself a hackneyed commercial melodrama: a hapless Kashmiri village belle, Niloufer (Shabana Azmi), a marauding villain Dilawar Khan (Avtar Gill), the heroine's younger sister (Soni Razdan) and the urban hero (Amol Palekar) who will fight Dilawar Khan ('*Main uska khoon pee jaoonga*' [I will drink his blood], he exclaims to Niloufer, reciting one of the big-gest clichés of Hindi commercial cinema's action sequences). The plot of *Khamosh* is essentially a behind-the-scenes glimpse into the shooting of a movie. The world of the movie set and crew, with its tangled set of obsessions and pathologies, is as high strung as the plot of the movie being shot, *Aakhri Khoon*, and even echoes the latter in the murderer's motivations. Soni Razdan's murder is prefaced by her rehearsal of her murder scene and her pleas to be spared, rehearsed 'ad nauseam', so that when she is actu-ally murdered, her scream is ignored. The characters' indifference to Razdan's scream is counter-balanced by our full awareness of both the cliché of the female body in distress, the 'screaming point' in Michel Chion and Claudia Gorbman's words (1999), warranted by a veritable body genre, melodrama (Williams 1999) and its renewal now as a plot device in a different genre (the who-dunnit). Put another way, melodrama is at once backstory and desired effect in the world of a whodunnit.

Binod Pradhan's brilliant camerawork (to be repeated in other Chopra films such as *Parinda* and *1942: A Love* Story) and Renu Saluja's editing (Saluja was Chopra's spouse and worked on a number of other films of his as well) include the full panoply of psychological effects, menacing following shots alternated with the unknown killer's point of view from a distance to a score that is part *Jaws* and part *Rosemary's Baby*. When the crew discovers the body, a long take in the form of a 90-second slow circular pan rotates in close-up across the downcast faces of the crew standing in a circle, while the voice of an off-screen and unknown crew member grieves aloud about the tragedy of Soni's sudden death. Knowing as we do by now, the dynamics of romance, intrigue and jealousy between the various crew members, the free-floating, untethered grieving voice sounds phony, enacted and indeed overly melodramatic. A combination of sensation and ratiocination, therefore, effectuates the more dramatic plot twists of *Khamosh*.

Chopra's next film, *Parinda* (1989) is now justifiably iconic in the history of Indian cinema and more specifically in the vicissitudes of noir in Hindi cinema. Unrelentingly dark and pessimistic, the movie presents us with two brothers, and the failure of the older criminal one in keeping his sibling from being pulled into the same deadly vortex. The movie's song-sequences are repeatedly interrupted by the menace of the city that threatens to destroy any possibility of carving out a peaceful domestic space, hearkening back to the innovative use of song sequences by Guru Dutt in the 1950s. (The soundtrack makes use of Aaron Copeland's *Fanfare for the Common Man* as well as Modest Mussorgsky's tone poem, *Night on Bald Mountain*.) The movie has attracted two superb discussions that are difficult to surpass in their attention and insight. Lalitha Gopalan offers a close reading of the film's style, its debts to the genres of noir and gangster films, its Hitchcockian building of anticipation, its repeated use of flashbacks as 'an economy of circulating memories' belonging to all and yet none of the characters (Gopalan 2002: 154) and the movie's place in the history of the cinematic city. Ranjani Mazumdar (2002, 2007) hones in on the latter and the movie's construction of the city as a site of terror, despair and catastrophe. In addition, the sudden shifts in tone characteristic of melodrama are intercalated with the 'exhilaration of dread' (Vasudevan 2007) characteristic of the city film. This occurs notably I think in the scene in which Karan (Anil Kapoor) rushes to meet his police officer friend Prakash (Anupam Kher), his drive through the city interspersed as a song sequence with happy childhood memories, culminating in Prakash's assassination and death in Karan's arms. We of course know all along that Karan is going to be a witness to his best friend's murder by ruthless assassins, producing suspense and pathos at one and the same time.

Gopalan notices Chopra's self-referential tendency in a scene in the movie, wherein as Karan enters a hotel room to murder Moosa and avenge Prakash's death, the movie playing on television in that room is a scene from Chopra's earlier film *Khamosh* in which Shabana Azmi is in the shower, while on the television in her hotel room, we see the famous shower sequence from Hitchcock's *Psycho* (1960). Thus, we see a TV playing a scene from an earlier movie in which the TV plays a familiar scene from a still earlier movie. Adding to this self-referencing, the omniscient knowledge provided to us throughout *Parinda* as a route to building suspense, the use of the 'vertigo' shot (when Kishan's on the phone with his boss, Anna, early in the film) and the shock of seeing the romantic duo gunned down at the conclusion of the film, *Parinda* sets up a remarkably allusive intertextual relay, to borrow Gopalan's words. One could add that this is also an intermedial relay that documents the media ecology that informed Chopra's generation (the advent of television in the 1980s and the migration of his contemporaries such as Saeed Mirza to that medium). *Parinda* echoes *Murder at Monkey Hill* in at least two other ways. One is that the psychotic killer Akhtar in *Murder at Monkey Hill* anticipates in a much milder form the cruelty of Anna, the gangster (played by Nana Patekar; his name is the word for elder brother) in *Parinda*. Another perhaps less ambiguous echo occurs in Paro's line, 'I'm frightened, Karan' during the song 'Tumse Milke', a line also spoken by Prabhi to Akhtar in *Murder at Monkey Hill* (and in both instances to sudden occurrences).

As far as tone is concerned, *Parinda* is closer to the 2007 film *Eklavya* directed by Chopra, far more so than the historical and war epics that immediately followed *Parinda* and preceded *Eklavya*. So I want to set aside the war epics for now and leapfrog to *Eklavya*. On the one hand, *Eklavya* is nothing like *Parinda* in its look (mostly sweeping daylight shots of the majestic royal palace and its game of succession being played out inside) or sound (Vedic chants to drum beats and strains of Hindustani classical music vocals). Yet, *Eklavya* is a strikingly sombre film that opens at a point when all the major characters seem to have exhausted their will to live. There is only one song in the movie, a lullaby that affords at best sad memories for the character listening and an unspoken desire in the character singing; in other words, sentiments with no meeting ground, as it were, are entombed in the psychologies of their bearers. The movie seems to have been made for an international audience (and was presented as India's entry to the Academy Awards) and, hence, the strangely depopulated nature of the diegetic world, focusing almost entirely on the core characters and an occasional glimpse at villagers persecuted by the king's landlordism. One wonders if Hollywood could have come up with such existential angst in a royal period drama. Harshvardhan, the character played by Saif Ali Khan, explains to Rajjo (his betrothed, Vidya Balan) that he remains silent about his feelings for her: 'I can't express myself…. You know … this fort. It does terrible things to people. This citadel of customs, traditions, rites and rituals is driving me insane. Rajjo … I'm no longer the Harsh of your dreams.' He never conclusively becomes the Harsh of her dreams by the movie's end, even if the ending is the unusually subdued marriage of Harsh and Rajjo.

The movie is nominally based around a story from Mahabharata of Eklavya, the outcaste boy who sacrifices his thumb, and his excellence in archery, at the demand of the Brahmin sage Drona. Caste critique, however, is not the movie's aim. Instead, loyalty to one's employer at all cost is put to risk and justified through retroactively discovered blood ties. Eklavya (Amitabh Bachchan) is a royal guard in charge of protecting the royal family of Devigarh, a former princely state with no political power in post-colonial India, corrupted from within by secrets. The movie pits competing understandings of dharma or duty. When the effete and impotent, Shakespeare-spouting king (Boman Irani) is murdered by his own brother and nephew, Eklavya resolves to avenge their death. But the killing was ordered by Harshwardhan (Saif Ali Khan), the royal heir, because he learns that his terminally ill mother, the queen, was actually strangled to death on her deathbed by the king in a jealous rage because she kept calling out to Eklavya as she lay dying. Harshwardhan has also discovered that his real father is not the impotent king, but Eklavya, a secret his mother reveals to him only in her posthumously read letter. Thus,

Eklavya is left with the difficult task of killing his own son, the royal prince, for having killed the king in whose service Eklavya has served as a royal guard.

In the ethical conundrums at work, the movie vaguely echoes the dilemma of Kishen, the criminal brother in *Parinda* (loyalty to his boss competing with his need to protect his younger brother Karan). If *Parinda* references *Khamosh* which in turn references *Psycho*, *Eklavya* cites *Parinda* in a crucial scene in which Eklavya (Bachchan) murders the king's nephew, Udaywardhan (Jimmy Shergill) to avenge the king's death. The scene begins not with an establishing shot but with the scene from *Parinda* when Anna's killers drive up behind tinted windows to the circle where Karan's happy reunion with Prakash is underway. Udaywardhan is watching *Parinda*, when Eklavya enters the room; his figure blocks the blinding beam of the light from the projector behind Udaywardhan. Two subsequent shots depict Eklavya in front of the screen, transforming his face into a surface of projection for *Parinda*. The first is a three-quarters view of Eklavya facing us with the screen behind him. The next is a dramatic close-up of Eklavya's weathered face looking up and off-screen as the pigeons on the screen behind him rise up in flight. When Udaywardhan points the barrel of his gun (a shallow focus wide angle image) at Eklavya, we see in the reverse shot that the killing of Prakash from *Parinda* is underway on the screen. Eklavya gets up and turns off the lights in the room, silencing the film and plunging the room into darkness. A series of shots ring out, but we have been told earlier in the film that while Eklavya's sight may be failing his ability to follow sound is exemplary. And so, when the lights come back on, we see the back of Udaywardhan's head, his neck impaled with a knife. A rack focus shifts our attention to the screen where, for the first time in sharp focus, we see from *Parinda*, Karan clutching Prakash's bloodied body in his arms.

With this citation, we are reminded of Chopra's roots in a radically different universe: that of the urban, noir gangster film, a far cry from the dunes of Rajasthan and its majestic palaces where *Eklavya* is set. It may well be that Bachchan's stardom is being appropriated; his iconicity embossed on *Parinda* even as he too absorbs *Parinda*'s iconicity into his image.[6]

Given that his new film *Broken Horses* (2015) is apparently unlike the commercial fare from the Hindi film industry, I wonder if Chopra's aspiration is for narratives striving for some compromise between his art–cinema roots and more commercial forms, including Hollywood. Melodrama occupies an ambiguous position in this equation. *Eklavya* eschews the exteriorization of emotion characteristic of melodrama and signals the most pronounced move towards psychologized interiority in its characters.

From this perspective, *1942: A Love Story* (1994), the film he directed after *Parinda*, and, to a lesser extent, *Mission Kashmir* (2000) are transitional spectacles. *1942: A Love Story* braids the Quit India Movement with the budding love affair between the son of a wealthy landlord sympathetic to the British rule and the daughter of a freedom fighter/revolutionary. Compared to Mani Ratnam's *Roja* that preceded it in 1992, let alone Chopra's earlier films, the movie's execution feels unremarkable, with none of the polish of *Roja*. Chopra has stated in interviews that his main impulse for making the movie was to present audiences with mellifluous film songs that he believed were sorely lacking in commercial cinema by then (Chopra and Dwyer 2015). At any rate, the movie depicts a snarling British general so exaggerated as to be unintentionally comic and ridiculous. The flat lighting makes the excessive bloodletting in the final scenes grisly. As such, *1942: A Love Story*'s look seems uninformed by the advertising-influenced polish of Ratnam's films. It does not seem an early example of post-liberalization new-media savvy patriotism of the kind witnessed in *Rang De Basanti* (2006). Neither does *Mission Kashmir* (2000), Chopra's other film. But *Mission Kashmir* returns to *Parinda* territory in exploring the traumatic, multigenerational, cyclical and psychosexual underpinnings of political violence.

In this, the movie returns us as well to melodrama's privileged locus of social conflict, the family. One example will clarify the importance of the family and, therefore, the melodrama in this movie. After the heroine Sufiya (Preity Zinta) has learned that the hero Altaaf (Hrithik Roshan) is in fact a terrorist and forbids him from seeking to establish contact with her, we return to the sets of 'Bumro', a song that had occurred earlier in the plot. This return to the sets of a happy song is now actually Altaaf's sleeping nightmare. This time, the song plays faintly and the background dancers perform the steps silently as if they were automatons. The entire setting is now darker, turning the pretty hues of the Indo-Persian style setting into sombre expressionism. Altaaf is arguing with Sufiya over the justness of his violence. Sufiya turns to Altaaf, smiling as if possessed, in a moment with distinct horror film undertones. She whispers that his political crusade against the Indian state is nothing but a revenge fantasy to avenge the 'collateral damage' of the death of his parents at the hands of the Indian Army. As she walks away, the younger childhood version of Altaaf walks up to the older one and hands him a pistol. Altaaf shoots Sufiya. Turning Sufiya's lifeless body towards him, he finds instead, his adoptive mother (Sonali Kulkarni), wife to the army man (his adoptive father) who Altaaf knows had killed his parents and whom he has set his mind to kill in return.

Mission Kashmir begins with an iconoclastic gesture. Its opening image, of a houseboat in a beautiful lake, an iconic image of Kashmir, gives way to the houseboat's explosion into a ball of fire, initiating the movie's narrative on displacement and terror. Unlike *Roja*, for instance, Chopra's portrayal of the terrorists manages to present enough characters among the terrorists with sympathetic or at least everyday qualities to offset the starker portrayal of the main terrorist Hilal (Jackie Shroff), who is Altaaf's mentor. Rather than pitting a Hindu civilian against Muslim terrorists, as *Roja* does, the movie pits one traumatized Muslim against his Muslim adoptive father, his Hindu adoptive mother and the Muslim woman of his childhood. Chopra's ethos remains secularist and humanist first, and only after, an expression of patriotism and nationalism, anticipating perhaps his commitment to the broad address of the social film genre as a producer.

In addition to this commitment, here again, Chopra seems to have not bought into the neoliberal ethos or the sensorium of globalized cultures or the pleasures of multiplex cinema. Instead, his two war and historical epics seem anchored in the cusp of the industry's transformations in the 1990s and yet at a remove from it. They index a partial move from the suspense/mystery mode to the commercial melodrama mode, but with no indication of a desire to venture into the post-1990s Bollywood blockbusters or the sardonic and realist humour of the multiplex film that one finds in the films of, say, Dibakar Banerjee. If anything, the ambiguous combination of the psychological realism of murder mystery and noir with elements of commercial melodrama in Chopra's directorial ventures has yielded a desire to move towards Hollywood as a director and a commitment to the older genre of the social as a producer.

An Atlas of Influences

Chopra and his contemporaries at the FTII drew on Hindi movie classics as well as the iconic works of Hollywood directors such as Coppola, Scorsese and Spike Lee. His references to Hollywood in interviews as well as in his movies compel a parallax view of the film school generation of Indian cinema. A triangulation of this second generation with the French New Wave, as well as all the varying facets of New American Cinema, may be worthwhile if not possible here in any detail.

Chopra's first film *Murder at Monkey Hill* (1976) was made a year after *Jaws* (1975), four years after *The Godfather* (1972) and three years after *Mean Streets* (1973), all movies made by Hollywood's film school generation (Spielberg, Coppola and Scorsese, respectively). These are all directors he has referenced in interviews, and I assume, given that Chopra was in film school in the 1970s, that he may have also watched the movies of the French New Wave from more than a decade earlier that influenced Hollywood's film school generation. He was likely familiar with the iconic films that are now considered hallmarks of a New American Cinema and all of its attendant stages: surprise 'counter culture' hits like *The Graduate* and *Bonnie and Clyde* (both 1967), the blockbuster mentality put in place by *Jaws* (and *The Godfather* before it) and the rise of independent cinema with Spike Lee, Steven Soderbergh and

David Lynch in the late 1980s. His peers, such as Kundan Shah and Saeed Mirza, have alluded to other movies and directors of the period. Antonioni's *Blow-Up* (1966) as allusion in Kundan Shah's *Jaane Bhi Do Yaaro* (1983) is well known. But even a movie like Saeed Mirza's *Salim Langde Pe Mat Ro* (1989), made the same year as *Parinda*, opens as a surprising distillation of Scorsese's *Mean Streets* (1973), which too opens with a voice-over narration. As Salim walks through the streets of Bombay early in the morning as the city is just about to come to life, his figure is superimposed over shots of the city itself. Additionally, one cannot help but think of the iconic images from Melvin Van Peebles' *Sweet Sweetback's Baadasssss Song* (1971) of Sweetback rendered spectral and de-substantialized through superimpositions, montage, split screens, as he too walks through urban landscapes while being marginalized within them like Salim. All of which is a roundabout way of saying that triangulating the French New Wave and New American Cinema with Chopra's FTII generation might yield unexpected results, echoes perhaps of a shared syntax that, in the Indian context, went well beyond the 'developmental realism' of Benegal or the lyrical realism of Ray. It may also allow for a comparative study of cinematic modernisms and their engagement with youth culture, subaltern identities and cinephilia. That remains a pending task for a history of the poetics and politics of Indian cinema.[7]

Notes

1   Going by press coverage, *Broken Horses* seems to be a fulfilment of a longtime desire on Chopra's part to write and direct a movie in Hollywood. It is being presented in India and by Chopra himself, as an instance of Indian success in conquering a new frontier (Hollywood) that serves somewhat more complexly than the press coverage would acknowledge; as vague aspiration of true quality, source of ideas and impetus for restructuring Indian film industrial practice along more rationalized lines since the emergence of Bollywood in the 1990s as a culture industry with global aspirations, and as a 'crossover' success.

2 I am referring to the opening up of the Indian economy to the vagaries of world markets, the emergence of India as a significant location in the networks of information technology, the end to the monopoly on television by India's state-run Doordarshan and the seemingly overnight influx of satellite and cable TV, the emergence of the Bollywood 'diaspora' film and its brand of cultural nationalism with lucrative markets in the global North, the synergizing tendencies of TV companies entering film production, the discourse of a new film industry that has left its chaotically produced, speculatively financed, underworld-linked days behind (in fact, that is far from the case), the more recent entry of Hollywood into Bollywood film production, the attempts to bring India more in line with global intellectual property regimes (with significant stakes for Hollywood) and the emergence of multiplex theaters and attendant genres catering to more selective audiences. For a comprehensive overview of these developments, see Athique 2012.

3 Recall the (at the time) still very new stereo surround sound (and the Asian pop styles of some of the songs) or the realism and directness of the handheld camera movements that escaped the frontality of composition and view that had by and large marked the Indian commercial film, or for that matter, the very subject of terrorism in Kashmir.

4 *Encounter* was presumably nominated for an Academy Award in the short film category but I have found no record of this in the listings of winning and nominated films in that decade.

5 The movie was, as with so many Chopra films, co-written and in this instance, the writers included Saeed Mirza, Sudhir Mishra and Kundan Shah, all Chopra's classmates from film school and all crucial filmmakers at this moment. As is well known, Vinod Chopra and Sudhir Mishra were the names of the two main characters in Kundan Shah's cult classic and comic masterpiece *Jaane Bhi Do Yaaro* (1983). Sudhir Mishra and film editor Renu Saluja were the assistant directors for Shah's film, suggesting a close-knit community and the exchange of expertise and creative labor within its ranks.

6 Bachchan's 1970s films such as *Deewaar* and *Zanjeer* do after all belong to the pre-history of *Parinda*. Ranjani Mazumdar tracks the journey from the angry young man of Bachchan in the 1970s and 1980s to the psychotic hero of Shah Rukh Khan in *Baazigar* (1993) and *Darr* (1993). *Parinda's* psychotic villain recalls Bachchan's tragically scarred hero from films like *Deewaar* (1975), and presages the psychotic hero played by Shah Rukh Khan.

7 I am thinking here of James Tweedie's (2013) recent work on the relation between the French, Chinese and Taiwanese New Waves.

References

Amladi, Parag. 2000. 'The Rule and the Exception: Good offices and Bad in Bhuvan Shome.' In *The Enemy within: The Films of Mrinal Sen*, edited by S. Chakravarty, 22–36. Trowbridge, Wiltshire: Flicks Books.

Athique, Adrian. 2012. *Indian Media: Global Approaches*. Cambridge, UK; Malden, MA: Polity Press.

Chaudhary, Bodrul. 2014. '"We've already hit gold with *PK*," says Vidhu Vinod Chopra in an exclusive interview.' *Bollyspice*. Retrieved 14 May 2015, from http://bollyspice.com/94764/weve-already-hit-gold-pk-says-vidhu-vinod-chopra-exclusive-interview

Chion, Michel and Claudia Gorbman. 1999. *The Voice in Cinema*. New York: Columbia University Press.

Chopra, Vidhu Vinod and Rachel Dwyer. 2015. 'In conversation with Vidhu Vinod Chopra.' Retrieved 15 April 2015, from http://www.soas.ac.uk/south-asia-institute/events/27mar2015-in-conversation-with-vidhu-vinod-chopra.html

Ganti, Tejaswini. 2012. *Producing Bollywood: Inside the Contemporary Hindi Film Industry*. Durham: Duke University Press.

Ganti, Tejaswini. 2013. *Bollywood: A Guidebook to Popular Hindi Cinema*. London; New York: Routledge.

Garga, B.D. 2007. *From Raj to Swaraj: The Non-fiction Film in India*. New Delhi; New York: Viking.

Gopalan, Lalitha. 2002. *Cinema of Interruptions: Action Genres in Contemporary Indian Cinema*. London: BFI Pub.

Krishen, P. 1991. 'Knocking at the Doors of Public Culture: India's Parallel Cinema.' *Public Culture* 4 (1): 25–42.

Mazumdar, Ranjani. 2002. 'Ruin and the Uncanny City: Memory. Despair and Death in Parinda.' In *Sarai Reader* 2, edited by Ravi S. Vasudevan, Jeebesh Bagchi, Ravi Sundaram, Monica Narula, Geert Lovink and Shuddhabrata Sengupta, 68–77. New Delhi: Sarai.

Mazumdar, Ranjani. 2007. *Bombay Cinema an Archive of the City*. Minneapolis: University of Minnesota Press.

Mehta, Suketu. 2004. *Maximum City*. New York: Alfred A. Knopf.

Tweedie, James. 2013. *The Age of New Waves: Art Cinema and the Staging of Globalization*. New York: Oxford University Press.

Vasudevan, Ravi. 2002. 'The Exhilaration of Dread: Genre, Narrative Form and Film Style in Contemporary Urban Action Films' in Ravi S Vasudevan, Jeebesh Bagchi, Ravi Sundaram, Monica Narula, Geert Lovink & Shuddhabrata Sengupta (eds) *Sarai Reader* 2. 59–67. New Delhi: Sarai.

Williams, L. 1999. 'Hard Bodies: Gender, Genre and Excess.' In *Feminist Film Theory: A Reader*, edited by Sue Thornham, 267–281. New York: New York University Press.

6

Rajkumar Hirani: The Outsider

Baradwaj Rangan

Rajkumar Hirani has made only four films — *Munna Bhai M.B.B.S.* (2003; henceforth, *Munna Bhai*), *Lage Raho Munna Bhai* (2006; henceforth, *Lage Raho*), *3 Idiots* (2009) and *PK* (2014) — and yet, his work has the appearance of an oeuvre. You can talk about his films the way you talk about the films of more established auteurs, primarily because of the elements that keep appearing in one film after another. This is not to say that his films are rehashes. They're clever re-imaginings of core conceits and ideas, and one way to talk about Hirani's career is to examine these 'repetitions' more closely.

The Hat Tip to Hrishikesh Mukherjee

You can talk about the homage to Hrishikesh Mukherjee. Hirani has often spoken about his admiration for Mukherjee's films and it comes as no surprise. Hirani's films, from the two *Munna Bhai* entries to *3 Idiots*, are essentially reworkings of Mukherjee's films such as *Anand* (1971), *Bawarchi* (1972) and *Khubsoorat* (1980), where a free-spirited outsider breezed through stuffy surroundings and made people rediscover what they'd lost. In *Munna Bhai*, the *bhai*-turned-doctor protagonist Munna looks at an X-ray of the skull and pronounces his verdict: 'lymphosarcoma of the intestines'. This was Rajesh Khanna's condition in *Anand*. The name of the film (and its protagonist) is evoked in the character of Anand bhai, a patient in the hospital where Munna works. In the charming *Ferrari Ki Sawaari* (Rajesh Mapuskar, 2012), which Hirani co-wrote, there was an echo of the scene in *Guddi* (Hrishikesh Mukherjee, 1971) where a student is late to school and ends up leading the choir in prayer. In the quirkily named *PK*, the narrator (Jaggu) writes a book on the titular character—and that's what the Amitabh Bachchan character did in *Anand*. (His book was named *Anand*, Jaggu's book is named PK.) But consider the title itself. It goes back to the joke in *Chupke Chupke* (Hrishikesh Mukherjee, 1975) that transformed the initials of a character (PK) into the Hindi word for 'intoxicated'.

You can talk about the 'narrator', which is a favourite Hirani trope—*Munna Bhai* is narrated by Anand Bhai, *Lage Raho* by Mahatma Gandhi, *3 Idiots* by Farhan Qureshi and *PK* by Jaggu. This lends his stories the warm, 'once upon a time' quality of a fable while also elevating the protagonist as someone whose story is worthy of being told.

Fathers, Sons and Daughters

You can talk about the father–son (or daughter) bond, very important in Hirani's world. It keeps showing up repeatedly, even amongst the supporting characters—the Parsi father and son in *Munna Bhai*; Khurana Uncle and Sunny (the Dia Mirza character's fiancé) in *Lage Raho*, which also featured the heartless son who drops his father off at the senior citizens' home; the real Rancho and his father in *3 Idiots*; Sharman Joshi and his eczema-afflicted father in *3 Idiots*; the robot-copter-making Joy Lobo and his father in *3 Idiots*; 'Virus' and his unseen son in *3 Idiots*. In *3 Idiots*, Farhan is born at 5:15 pm; at 5:16, his father looks into crib and says, 'My son will be an engineer.' Sahni plays Anushka Sharma's father in *PK* and asks her not to marry a Muslim/Pakistani. Hirani's fathers get the stories going by putting pressure on their children. The reason Munna became a 'doctor' is due to his father's pressure. He ran away from home, and after many years, when he summoned up the courage to call his father, he thought he'd get a 'How are you?' at the other end. Instead, the father asked, 'What do you do in Mumbai? I hope you aren't a no-good ruffian or crook'. A terrified Munna blurts out that he is a doctor, which is what his father wanted him to become.

You can talk about Hirani's love for the word 'Imperial' — which is the name of both the medical institute in *Munna Bhai* (Imperial Institute of Medical Studies) and the engineering college in *3 Idiots* (Imperial College of Engineering).

You can talk about the innocents. In *Munna Bhai*, Munna wonders aloud, like a child, 'There are 206 types of bones! Never thought of that while breaking them, did we?' In *Lage Raho*, Munna has no qualms telling a gathering that he can see Gandhi and that he can talk to him. There's not a trace of cynicism in him. And the perennially wide-eyed PK is the most innocent of all, full of questions and incapable of lies. He even comes into this world naked, like a child.

Indian Values, Western Winks

You can talk about the Indian values in Hirani's films, a kind of *desi-ghee* wholesomeness. September 5, our Teacher's Day, is a crucial component of *3 Idiots*. In *Lage Raho*, when Circuit tells the builder Lucky Singh that Munna is in love, the latter says he has some empty flats that can be 'used' — Circuit blushes and says it's not *that* kind of love. And in *Munna Bhai*, when Munna tells Chinki that he wants to meet her, she calls him to a club. There he sees a most un-Indian girl dressed in a revealing 'Western' outfit, surrounded by men and 'Western' music, and doing 'Western' things like drinking. He rejects her instantly — and we might add, rather hypocritically, for someone whose favourite pastime is to hit the bottle in Circuit's company. To know why, we just have to think back to the 'M Bole To' song, where, during the celebrations in his neighbourhood, he chases off a Michael Jackson wannabe and sways to the strains of the very Indian *Bholi Surat Dil Ke Khote* (innocent face, deceptive heart); he also performs the famous 'Bhagwan step'.[1] That he's rooted in a romantic notion of India is evident from the presence of dancers from all parts of the country — a Punjabi, a Bengali, a Tamilian, a Maharashtrian and a Gujarati.

You can talk about how, despite Hirani's commitment to the notion of Indianness, his films flirt with 'Western' aspects like sex. Sometimes, this is done for fun, as with the 'dancing cars' in *PK* and the old man from *Lage Raho* admitting to 'net practice' when his friends ask him if he can 'bat' after getting married at this age. And sometimes, this is done in all seriousness. When Zaheer in *Munna Bhai* is told he won't live much longer, Munna arranges for a performance by a dancer. Zaheer falls for her. There are hints that she did more than just dance with him. And yet, this doesn't feel like Hirani is violating the 'wholesome' code, because Zaheer doesn't smoke or drink. He is devout and wants to take his mother on the Haj pilgrimage. He's also never touched a woman. The Haj dream will never come true. So, Munna is just ensuring that Zaheer experiences something of life before embracing death.

Hirani's Cinema, Hindi Cinema

You can also talk about how Hirani's cinema owes so much to 'Indian cinema', and not just because his films feature a mix of all ingredients — humour, pathos, drama and romance, the broad mix of which today's major film-makers (Dibakar Banerjee, Farhan Akhtar or even Anurag Kashyap) seem to have little use for. The broad outlines of Hirani's films are essentially hero-versus-villain showdowns — Munna versus Dr Asthana, Munna versus Lucky Singh, Rancho versus 'Virus', PK versus Tapasvi Maharaj. (Munna says, in the first film, 'Do you know why God sent me to this particular college? God said, 'Go, settle the score with the man who made your father cry.') And in true Indian-film fashion, the heroine is often the villain's daughter (Chinki in *Munna Bhai* and Pia in *3 Idiots*). The great Indian tradition of the 'interval twist' is also something we find in Hirani's films, most notably in *3 Idiots*, when we find out that Rancho wasn't...Rancho. Bollywood is known for willing suspension of disbelief; this is reflected in *Munna Bhai* series as well. At the end of the first film, Munna marries Chinki. At the beginning of the second, he's single. In Munna and Circuit as well as in the three idiots of *3 Idiots*, we find the bromance that's such a part of Indian cinema. (Raju Rastogi would rather jump to his death than snitch on Rancho.) There's drama, there's melodrama — when Simran runs away in *Lage Raho*, it's exactly on the day of her marriage; when the two remaining idiots find Pia, it's exactly the day of her marriage. There's the instant change of tone we find in our films — slapstick to sentiment in the scene in *3 Idiots* when Farhan and Raju land up in the real Rancho's house. One minute, Raju is threatening to empty an urn of ashes into a Western closet, the next they're listening to an emotional flashback. Or take Raju Rastogi's flashback, it's even presented like an Indian film from the 1950s — scene after scene of tragedy on a screen that becomes comedy for the viewer. Like a lot of Indian cinema, especially Hrishikesh Mukherjee's cinema, there's playacting. When, in *Munna Bhai*, Munna's father says he's coming to Mumbai, Munna's friends pretend to be doctors and patients to complete the illusion that Munna is running a clinic. In *Lage Raho*, Munna and his friends pretend to be professors and students in a college. And like many Indian films from a particular era, nature cues us to the emotions being played out. During the childbirth scene in *3 Idiots*, it's pouring when the pregnancy drama is taking place; once the baby is born, the sun is out again.

The Old Guard, the New Way Forward

You can talk about the traditionalists in Hirani's cinema. The old guard (or the establishment) — Dr Asthana, Virus and the professors in *3 Idiots* — goes by the book. Dr Asthana believes that doctors cannot have emotions: 'In my 25-year career, I have never befriended a patient. I have not felt their pain, just cured it. Friendship, empathy, attachment—these are weaknesses for a doctor.' In 3 *Idiots*, the professors *literally* go by the book—they want just the definitions in the book, nothing else. When a professor asks for the definition of a machine, Rancho explains it the easy way—anything that reduces human effort, like a fan or a telephone. But what the professor wants is what Chatur breathlessly recites,

> Sir, machines are any combination of bodies so connected that their relative motions are constrained and by which means, force and motion may be transmitted and modified as a screw and its nut, or a lever arranged to turn about a fulcrum or a pulley about its pivot....

And the Hirani protagonist goes for a more instinctual, even folksy approach—he's the anti-traditionalist, who doesn't go by the book. Rancho illustrates this in 3 *Idiots* when he assumes the role of a teacher and asks the class a question. The students scramble for the answer in the given time. Then, Rancho says,

> Now rewind your life by a minute. When I asked this question, were you excited? Curious? Thrilled that you'd learn something new? Anyone? No. You all got into a frantic race. What's the use of such methods. Even if you come first, will your knowledge increase? No, just the pressure. This is a college, not a pressure cooker. Even a circus lion learns to sit on a chair in fear of the whip. But you call such a lion 'well-trained', not 'well-educated'.

He goes further and adds, later, that grades create a divide, like the caste system. Rancho may be talking about engineering school, but he, like Hirani's other protagonists, is a practitioner of an alternative system of medicine, one that can cure an ailing society.

A traditionalist doctor in *Munna Bhai* refuses to treat a dying patient because he's off duty—Munna roughs him up and makes him do his duty. Then there's the cure he patents—the *jadoo ki jhappi* (a magic hug). It's the antithesis of everything Dr Asthana believes in—it suggests that friendship, empathy and attachment are needed. (Dr Asthana's distance from concepts like hugging is demonstrated in the scene where he meets Munna's father. They are old acquaintances and he nears Munna's father, as if to embrace him, but opts to clutch his arm instead. There's — literally and figuratively — an arm's length between them.) Other 'cures' by Munna involve a positive-thinking song (for a suicidal youth) and a favourite game (for the carom-loving Parsi elder) — these may not pass the 'rational logic' test, but then Indian cinema has always relied on emotional logic. Munna may not be a doctor in *Lage Raho*, but his 'cures' continue here too — only, instead of medicine, he uses Gandhi's principles like *satyagraha*, that is, truth-telling, and turning the other cheek. In *3 Idiots*, the medicine — or mantra, depending on how you look at it — is the everything-will-be-okay exhortation 'all is well'. It's borderline-magical — a still-born child begins to kick when the mantra is uttered. (Munna's efforts, too, are deemed magical by Chinki — she uses the word *chamatkaar*.) And in *PK*, the mantra is 'wrong number'. Do not trust god-men. Instead, trust your own instincts and obtain the 'right number' to reach God.

Ethical Rascals

You can talk about how Hirani's heroes are usually rascals, and yet, they aren't without ethics. In *Munna Bhai*, Munna kidnaps a loan-defaulting rich man for ransom, but when he finds out the man has already paid the loan shark's brother, he lets him go. Now Munna turns to the loan shark, who's commissioned this kidnapping and demands money from 'him'. '*Kyonki tune apun se* wrong *kaam karaaya. Apne babuji kehte hain: Beimaani karne ka nahin aur sehne ka nahin.*' (You made me do something wrong. My father says, don't be dishonest and don't tolerate it either). Later, when Dr Asthana refuses to continue with class until Munna gets out, he leaves — not because he's scared of Asthana but because he doesn't want the other students to miss a class on his account. And yet, Munna has no qualms about cheating on his exams (with the help of the hapless Rustom) in *Munna Bhai* or cheating on the radio quiz (with the help of a posse of kidnapped 'Bapu experts').

What explains this? Perhaps the fact that this cheating is done in jest, in order to get the plot moving, and it shouldn't be examined too closely. This cheating-in-exams trope finds its way into *3 Idiots* too—the real Rancho asks the man we know as Rancho to write exams in his name.

You can talk about Hirani's tendency to fill his films with well-meaning advice. Follow your passion (*3 Idiots*). It doesn't mean you're a success if you have a $3.5 million mansion, with a heated pool and a Lamborghini in garage (*3 Idiots*). It doesn't matter whether it's India or Pakistan, Hindu or Muslim (*PK*). Here's Jahnavi, the RJ from *Lage Raho*:

> For all those rushing around this crazy city…. Is this the way we mean to live? Is this the way we wish to die? Has the monsoon delayed your train? When was the last time you walked in the rain? You know your favourite soap's twists-n-turns, but have no time for your mother's concerns. Why don't we stop to feel the sand between our toes? Why don't those 108 channels wipe away our woes? You, who connects at the click of a mouse, do you know who lives in the neighbouring house? In this era of emails and mobiles, when did you last see your best friend's smile? When did you see your last sunset? When did you see the stars come out at night? For all those rushing around in this crazy city…. Is this the way we mean to live? Is this the way we wish to die?

More advice from this film: '*Satya ki raah par chalo*' (Be truthful). And don't just mouth it. *Do* it! That's why Munna has to tell Jahnavi the truth about who he is, because she fell for him thinking he's a professor.

In Good Faith

Hirani's films are specifically concerned with debunking blind faith, whether it is the faith you put in your college professor or in God. The alien protagonist of *PK* labels religion as '*dar ka* business', the business of fear. He makes the case for a more merciful God, who'd say, 'There are millions of hungry children in Delhi. Give them the milk you offer me.' *3 Idiots* gives us this advice:

There's no use 'bribing' gods to get what you want—say, clearing an exam. The malaise is deep-rooted. Virus may be the head of an engineering college, a man of science, but yet he asks an astrologer whether his daughter is going to have a baby girl or boy. In *Lage Raho*, we have the numerologist Batuk Maharaj who is proved to be a fake. The man is played by Saurabh Shukla, who also plays the fake god-man in *PK*. Actors keep recurring in Hirani's cinema. Parikshat Sahni plays Jimmy Shergill's father in *Lage Raho*, Madhavan's father in *3 Idiots* and Anushka Sharma's father in *PK*.

You can talk about how it isn't just the actors who keep reappearing in Hirani's cinema—it is also the writer (Abhijat Joshi), the situations and the plot points. There are threats—in *Lage Raho*, Munna dangles Hari from the latter's top-storey office and orders him to attend his father's birthday; in *Munna Bhai*, Munna holds Rustom's father 'hostage' so that Rustom will write exams for him. There's the humiliation scene—in *Munna Bhai*, Munna and his family are humiliated by Dr Asthana; in *Lage Raho*, Munna is exposed as a thug when Circuit takes over the old age home. (The cause for both these events is played by the same actor: Boman Irani.) There's the testing scene—in *Munna Bhai*, Dr Asthana asks three professors to determine Munna's worthiness as a doctor; in *Lage Raho*, a psychiatrist is asked to determine Munna's sanity. There's the get-out-of-class moment—the order is issued to Munna in *Munna Bhai* as well as to Rancho in *3 Idiots*. There's the ragging moment in *Munna Bhai* and *3 Idiots*, where freshers are asked to parade in their underwear. There's the scenario about exposing unworthy romantic candidates—in *Lage Raho*, a man is exposed by the way he treats a waiter; in *3 Idiots*, Pia's fiancé is exposed as a man obsessed with price tags. Then there is the situation of Munna not having seen Chinki in *Munna Bhai*, not having seen Jahnavi in *Lage Raho*. Falling in love, in Hirani's world, isn't as important as the other things, the more message-oriented things. In *Munna Bhai*, the love song unfolds well into the second half. So too in *PK*. Even the love song in *Lage Raho* is staged not like the usual duet but like a surreal circus, which harks back to Hirani's mentor Vidhu Vinod Chopra, who has produced all of Hirani's films so far.

The Outsider

And above all, you can talk about Hirani's outsider–protagonist. Each of his films features something seen through new eyes, the eyes of an outsider. In *Munna Bhai*, the medical profession is seen through the eyes of a goon. In *Lage Raho*, Gandhi-ism is seen through the eyes of a goon. In *3 Idiots*, the factory-like education system is seen through the eyes of someone who actually wants to learn rather than make marks, pass exams. And in *PK*, we have the ultimate outsider, an alien, through whose eyes we see man-made religions.

We, here, first meet this outsider in *Munna Bhai*. Munna is a ruffian—so he's an outsider in terms of normal society. He ran away from home—so he's an outsider in Mumbai. When he walks into the hospital and says he's going to become a doctor, the orderly laughs and says, 'And I'm going to be Health Minister'—he knows Munna is an outsider in these hallowed portals, which have devices like entrance exams to keep outsiders out. We think he'll become an insider when he becomes a student, but when he enters the class the first time, all other students rise and say, 'Good morning, sir'—age-wise, too, he's an outsider. And language-wise too—he speaks a *tapori* slang, while the 'insiders', the people to whom things come easily, speak a more refined Hindi. The film's most ironic moment is that this outsider is outed by another outsider, one of his own—the domestic help who sees his picture and tells Dr Asthana that Munna isn't who Dr Asthana thinks he is.

In *Lage Raho*, Munna is an outsider to Gandhian values. In *3 Idiots*, Rancho is an outsider by social rank, a gardener's son. And the protagonist of *PK* is the ultimate outsider—he's an alien, an outsider to the planet. The difference between this alien and the other Hirani outsiders is that he did not consciously enter this world, but as with the others, his 'outsider eyes' help us look at an institution (medicine, Gandhian values, engineering and religion) from a distance.

There are other outsiders too—most famously, Chatur Ramalingam in *3 Idiots*. He's doing everything by the book, he's being a classic 'insider'—and yet, when he delivers that *chamatkaar/balaatkaar* speech, he's mocked as an outsider. He doesn't know the language, he doesn't know the culture. He was born in Uganda, studied in Puducherry and is mocked as 'angrez' during ragging when he speaks in English, especially as he's wearing angrez underwear, with a stars-and-stripes design. But, we feel for Chatur after his fiasco at the speech because we feel Rancho, of all people, should know better about being an outsider. For the first time, Hirani punishes the very outsider and, yet, his cinema celebrates.

Note

1 Actor Bhagwan had a distinctive style of dancing. For details, see Gangadhar (2002).

Reference

Gangadhar, V. 2002. 'Immortalised by His Dance.' *The Hindu*, 8 February. Retrieved 11 June 2015, from http://www.thehindu.com/thehindu/fr/2002/02/08/stories/2002020801240300.htm

Film References

Hirani, Rajkumar. 2003. *Munna Bhai M.B.B.S.* Vinod Chopra Productions.
———. 2006. *Lage Raho Munna Bhai*. Vinod Chopra Productions.
———. 2008. *3 Idiots*. Vinod Chopra Productions.
———. 2014. *PK*. Vinod Chopra Productions.
Mapuskar, Rajesh. 2012. *Ferrari Ki Sawaari*. Vinod Chopra Productions.
Mukherjee, Hrishikesh. 1971. *Guddi*. Rupam Chitra.
———. 1971. *Anand*. Rupam Chitra.
———. 1972. *Bawarchi*. Rupam Chitra.
———. 1975. *Chupke Chupke*. NC Sippy Films.
———. 1980. *Khubsoorat*. Roopam Pictures.

CHAPTER 7

Sanjay Leela Bhansali: In the Realm of Innovative Cinematic Experiences

Varsha Panjwani

Sanjay Leela Bhansali has directed seven films: *Khamoshi: The Musical* (1996), *Hum Dil De Chuke Sanam* (1999), *Devdas* (2002), *Black* (2005), *Saawariya* (2007), *Guzaarish* (2010) and *Goliyon Ki Rasleela Ram-Leela* (2013). His movies are in direct contrast to his personality; whereas Bhansali is far from imposing, his films are grand and epic in scale. Producer and director Karan Johar (2004) has said, '[H]is films are not films, they are experiences; experiences of opulence, of beauty, of sheer cinema. His every frame is a painting on celluloid.' A review of Bhansali's *Guzaarish* in *The Times of India* echoes Johar's words: '[F]ilm maker, Sanjay Leela Bhansali and his cinematographer (Sudeep Chatterjee) have created a collage of riveting paintings on screen, where both the interiors of a crumbling mansion and the outsides of an incandescent Goa landscape literally transport you to an art gallery' (Kazmi 2010). *Time* magazine voted Bhansali's *Devdas* as one of the 10 greatest films of the millennium not least because it 'is a visual ravishment, with sumptuous sets, fabulous frocks and beautiful people to fill them; it has a grandeur the old Hollywood moguls would have loved' (Corliss 2012).

If there are admirers of Bhansali's style, there are detractors too. His movie, *Saawariya*, was the target of an affectionate tongue-in-cheek lampoon at the 2008 Filmfare Awards where the hosts, Shah Rukh Khan and Saif Ali Khan (2008), danced to a made-up song about the fact that the dominant colour palette of Bhansali's *Saawariya* was an unremitting blue. Meanwhile, Bhansali's *Devdas* was accused of 'obscuring the story's emotional core by plastering the surface of the film with gorgeous yet distracting details to create opulent, extravagant spectacle, filled to the brim with vast sets and stunning costumes' (Creekmur 2007: 186).

Whether Bhansali's films are being parodied, praised or ridiculed, they have been recognized for their unique visual styles. There is no doubt that Bhansali works through excess and one may be tempted to relate this to post-liberalization Bollywood's propensity for celebration of consumerism and affluent lifestyles. However, any such linkages will be thwarted by the fact that Bhansali's films contain no product placements at all. Rather, his style mixes fantasy, indigenous theatre forms, and paintings, and thus, demands to be studied as apart from Bollywood's glorification of consumption. This essay, therefore, offers a sustained critical engagement with the visual style of Bhansali's films because such analysis is essential to understanding his movies and assessing their impact. It stresses that style is not separate from content but rather a part of it. In this, the essay follows the theorist Bazin (1967: 30), who argues that to concentrate on style is

> not to preach the glory of form over content. Art for art's sake is just as heretical in cinema as elsewhere, probably more so. On the other hand, a new subject matter demands new form, and as good a way as any towards understanding what a film is trying to say to us is to know how it is saying it.

The study of visual style is usually divided into three major components: mise en scène, cinematography, and editing (Bordwell and Thompson 2004). This essay does not aim to offer a comprehensive coverage of all these elements of style in Bhansali's work.

Rather, the methodology of zooming in on different stylistic features of selected movies is aimed at demonstrating how elements of film style (such as shot composition, mise en scène, editing and use of colour) become potent ideological tools in the hands of Bhansali and his creative team.[1] As such, the essay offers a fresh critical lens for reading Bhansali's visual style.

It is difficult to do justice to all of Bhansali's complex and differently styled movies individually within the confines of an essay so the analysis will be limited to *Black*, *Guzaarish* and *Goliyon Ki Rasleela Ram-Leela* as they are illustrative of two broad themes in Bhansali's oeuvre—disability and literary adaptation. *Black* is about a deaf-blind girl's quest for knowledge and *Guzaarish* revolves around a quadriplegic man's appeal for euthanasia. An examination of the style of these movies facilitates our understanding of how Bhansali has found new ways of telling stories about disability. *Goliyon Ki Rasleela Ram-Leela* relates to the second theme as it is based on William Shakespeare's *Romeo and Juliet*. Through an analysis of its stylistic features, this essay demonstrates the way in which Bhansali does not simply adapt a play into a film but creates new styles and hybrid forms of cinema in the process.[2]

Black and *Guzaarish*: Forging an Innovative Cinematic Style

Black was an important milestone in bringing disability cinema to mainstream Bollywood. The movie features superstars Amitabh Bachchan and Rani Mukherjee and was a critical and commercial success. The movie is based on Helen Keller's autobiography *The Story of My Life* (1996), which was first published in book form in 1903, in which she immerses the reader into her world and her experience of acquiring language as a deaf-blind girl. She writes about the way in which she understood that water 'meant the wonderful cool something flowing over my hand', about the 'odour of the mimosa blossoms' which encouraged her to climb a tree and about her first 'conscious perception of an abstract idea' when her teacher 'touched [her] forehead' and spelled the word 'think' as she was concentrating on a lesson (Keller 1996: 12, 14, 15). In adapting this work, Bhansali set himself a challenge as he would have to find a 'cinematic grammar' to pull the audience into Keller's world as effectively as she had done in her autobiography.

Black begins with a darkened screen which cuts to deaf-blind Michelle McNally (Rani Mukherjee) typing out her life story in Braille. As she types, the screen once more fades to a completely black. This shot lasts for nearly 45 seconds (quite a long time in terms of a static shot length). This opening establishes the style of the film in which, at a number of times, instead of jump cuts or seamless fades, the screen is black for a few seconds. This technique has close links to a scene in the film in which Michelle is blatantly disobeying her teacher, Debraj Sahai (Amitabh Bachchan). They are in the middle of their lesson when the lights in the house go out leading Debraj to panic. While Michelle steals past him to enjoy the cake she was being denied, Debraj stumbles and is found lying on the floor by the time Michelle's mother brings him a candle. It is then that Debraj has an insight and registers that *'andhere me aakhen bhi kisi kaam ki nahi hoti'* ('in the darkness, we have no use for our eyes'). His comment relates to one of the important tenets of disability studies. Scholars upholding the social model of disability have sought hard to preserve a difference between 'impairment' and 'disability'. As Marja Evelyn Mogk (2013: 4) explains,

> [T]hink of impairment as a physiological feature *of a body*, such as vision loss or paralysis. Think of disability on the other hand as a dynamic resulting from one or more features *of an environment*…. Thus disability is not a characteristic of an individual, but of a *social reality*.

Debraj's fall and Michelle's victory resulted from the fact that, in that moment, the environment around them changed. When the lights were out, it is Debraj who felt disabled. However, before the audience learn all of this narratively, they have already experienced it in the form of the black screen. These shots plunge the audience into complete darkness (which would happen when the movie audience is watching the film in a cinema rather than on a DVD). In producing a dark auditorium, all the cinema-goers with eyesight would have been disabled in that they would not be able to see the film or their surroundings. This editing technique, or *Black's* cinematic grammar, ties in with its narrative and makes its audience experience and absorb the constructed nature of disability.[3]

The mise en scène of the film points to another way in which disability is socially generated. Art director Omung Kumar (2005) explains how snow provided the crew with a major production challenge. In a booklet which accompanies the DVD, he relates an interesting anecdote:

> For the very first schedule of 'Black' the entire unit went to Simla in mid-January. It was cold but there was no sign of snow. Since the unit could not wait around indefinitely for the weather gods to oblige, kilos of salt bags bought from the local market and snow making machines from Bombay helped complete that schedule. The shooting would be done early at 4 am. And when the locals emerged they'd be amazed to see so much snow! It looked so authentic that they would touch it to check whether it was real.

Kumar points to an important quality of snow—the fact that it is tactile. People wanted to feel it either because they could not rely on their eyes alone and wanted their other senses to confirm what they were seeing or because snow invites touch. One of the most sensuous images created by this movie is the feel of snow on skin. Following the black screen of the opening sequence, we see Michelle's outstretched hand and, one by one, the flakes of snow fall on her skin. She feels them on her palms and her face and the camera registers these actions at leisure. The scene is calculated to create a desire to reach out and touch the snow. This shot resonates with a scene mid-way through the movie where Michelle and Debraj are sitting on a bench in Shimla. The pupil shows signs of distraction and Michelle holds out her palm which signifies that she is expecting snow. Debraj, however, tells her, '[I]t is not going to snow; please concentrate on your studies.' Michelle then starts reaching for her umbrella and again Debraj rebuffs her. Just seconds later, however, it starts to snow and Debraj instantly tries to grab the umbrella but it is now Michelle's turn to snub him. She does not let him have the umbrella and teases him mercilessly. When he finally does get hold of the umbrella, she does a little dance which she always does when she is feeling happy. This moment destabilizes Debraj's smugness; he might be able to see and hear but he is not able to feel the crispness in the air which to Michelle signals the onset of snow. The movie subtly indicates that deaf-blind Michelle is not disabled but differently abled. Yet the movie does not contribute to what Mitchell and Snyder would call the 'supercrip' stereotype where, for instance, a blind person would be shown to acquire a sonar-like ability to sense objects (Mitchell and Snyder 2000). The scene demonstrating Michelle's abilities, instead, questions the hierarchy or hegemony of senses where vision and hearing are valued more than touch, taste and smell.[4] Kumar insists that they went to such lengths to manufacture snow because snow was essential for the story and the shots containing snow do go beyond the narrative in revealing how much disability is generated by environmental factors and arbitrary value systems. The filmic vocabulary in *Black* is an important contribution to the disability debate as it generates new ways of engaging with disability through film.

Whereas *Black* opens with a black screen, the opening shot of *Guzaarish* is diametrically opposite. The audience sees black curtains being parted to let in the morning light. These curtains reveal an ornate window with beautiful white shutters. The woman parting these curtains looks longingly and lovingly towards the bed where a man is lying. The bed is surrounded by another set of sheer curtains, chandeliers, gilt-edged picture frames and fresh flowers. The colour palette is comprised of soft blues and muted greens, with a hint of hot pink. The light is soft. Thus, the movie opens with a set which invites the audience to read the genre as 'romance' or 'love story'. Music starts playing in the background as the woman moves with mesmerizing grace. The sequence which follows is akin to a dance. There are no awkward, jerky movements but a fluidity to the routine in which this woman with red lipstick takes off the man's blanket, brushes his teeth, takes off his clothes, and then washes his curly hair. The skylight lets in just the right amount of top light and we see pictures and mirrors everywhere. Again, the lighting is soft and the hues are romantic. In the foreground, the man is on a purpose-designed hoist as the woman washes his hair. We see her fingers run through his beautiful hair and their faces are so close that one expects that they will lean in for a kiss but it does not happen and the air crackles with sexual tension. It is only then that the man is put in a wheelchair. By this time, it is of course clear that the man has lost the use of his limbs but what is interesting is that the mise en scène establishes the genre as romance before the first word is uttered or the first clue to the man's history is given. Moreover, the couple shares an easy intimacy as we see the woman putting on her big glasses and reading a newspaper as the pair laugh about something she has presumably read. This, at least at first, looks as though it is going to be a love story where one of the partners just happens to be a wheelchair user, thereby mainstreaming or 'normalizing' this couple.

The statement above probably raises the question of why this couple needs mainstreaming at all, but such romantic pairings are extremely rare in mainstream Hindi cinema. 'One of the most important mainstream films on disability, and perhaps among the first that combined a narrative interspersed with some basic discussion of sign language and independent living for the Deaf [sic] was Gulzar's 1972 film *Koshish*' (Pal 2013: 111), but in this movie both the husband and the wife are deaf. Bhansali's own debut *Khamoshi: The Musical* featured a couple wherein both partners were deaf and mute. The Hindi film model reflects the prevalent social perception in India too. In a special episode on love, sex and disability on *We the People*, anchored by Barkha Dutt on NDTV, one of the participants mourns that 'there is this whole idea about matching not the compatibility but the disability when you're disabled in partnership' (Goyal 2015). In a society and film industry where such narratives find mutual reinforcement, a mainstream Bollywood film of a couple wherein one of the partners does not have any physical impairment and the other is a quadriplegic is a refreshing change.

A counter argument might posit that despite the mise en scène, the narrative of the movie is concerned with euthanasia, not with romance. After all, in the movie, the quadriplegic Ethan Mascarenhas (played by Hrithik Roshan) files an appeal for euthanasia, and when the court denies his appeal, his nurse Sofia D'Souza (played by Aishwariya Rai) promises to assist him in his suicide. While the premise seems to suggest that it rehearses the stereotype of the disabled as despondent, the screenplay and cinematography continue to focus on the romance and love story between the couple. The editing of the movie buttresses this argument. In the climactic scene of the movie, Ethan announces his marriage to Sophia. He requests her to walk towards him not as his nurse but as his wife. When Sophia hugs him on his bed, Ethan starts singing joyously. All of Ethan's friends join him on his bed for a group hug as a final farewell. This, however, was not the original ending scene. As shot, the movie continued with a scene in which Sofia visits Ethan's grave. The audience is then shown a reporter standing outside Ethan's house and reporting 'live' from this location. She explains that it would be difficult for the court to reach a decision or give a verdict on Ethan's case as all his fans claim that they assisted in the 'murder'. If this were the ending scene, then the film would have begun with the expectation of a romance but would have ended by debating euthanasia. However, by deleting this scene and ending the film with Sophia in Ethan's arms, the movie emphasises a love story and matrimony. Thus, the mise en scène, the set and the editing all contribute to mainstreaming a powerful love story between an able bodied and a quadriplegic person, and challenge the common assumption in media and in society that if you are disabled and 'if you are going to be with someone romantically, then you have to be with someone who is also differently abled' (Dutt 2015).

Pal (2013: 109) surveys more than 200 films and concludes that Indian cinema offers its consumers a full range of 'globally prevalent disability stereotypes'. He adds that the narrative of recent films (especially Bhansali's) 'strongly reinforces an othering view of disability in India' (Pal 2013: 124). While there is no dearth of Indian movies which peddle and produce disability stereotypes, this essay demonstrates that we should look at style as well as narrative in discussing a film's engagement with disability. Bhansali did marry the disability narratives on the one hand and the cinematic style on the other to raise provocative questions about the perception of disability on Bollywood screens.

Goliyon Ki Rasleela Ram-Leela: Experiment in Adaptation

Bhansali often combines high literature with Bollywood; his *Devdas* is a remediation of Sarat Chandra Chatterjee's story of the same name, *Saawariya* is a take on Fyodor Dostoyevsky's *White Nights* and *Goliyon Ki Rasleela Ram-Leela*, as mentioned earlier, is a remake of *Romeo and Juliet* (Shakespeare). Bhansali's treatment of *Devdas* enraged columnist Shobha De who described it as a 'monstrosity'. She deemed the movie a 'disco-Disney, desi-chutney version' of Chatterjee's 'epic'/'classic'/'timeless' tragedy (she uses all these words interchangeably). While she reserves most of her criticism for Bhansali's version, it seems that she is uncomfortable with adaptation more generally when she says that 'there have been other Devdases—some flawed, some passable, some bad' (De 2002). De is not alone in bringing up what is known in adaptation studies as 'fidelity criticism' (a consideration of questions such as, 'Is the film better than the book or play?'). This line of enquiry still enjoys cultural currency among audiences but has been rigorously questioned by film adaptation theorists who point out that such criticism often overlooks the range of differences between the media. To elaborate, we must take into consideration the fundamental differences between the factors (technology, casting, designing, director's interpretation, camera angles and budget) involved in making and enjoying a film, and writing and reading a novel or staging and attending a play. Even if we move away from questions of fidelity and acknowledge that different forms of narrative are enabled through each media, Fredric

Jameson asks us to put more pressure on difference as a critical category. He asserts that 'the universal repudiation of "fidelity"… certainly constitutes some initial commitment to Difference', but '[W]hy stop with this weak and purely logical category? Difference is also opposition, antagonism, struggle, and it seems possible that the difference between novel and film versions also harbour some more-active tension between word and image, if not litera-ture and film themselves' (Jameson 2011: 230). His observations for a novel and a film also hold true for other media conversions and encourage us to see adaptations as different versions which may be in opposition with the source text. There are, however, alternatives to this model and films can 'develop and enhance' as well as 'discard and contradict' (MacCabe 2011: 23). It is not a big leap, then, to argue that the same film adaptation can develop and enhance some elements whilst discarding, contradicting and competing against other elements of the source text. It is in the realm of this messy critical dialogue that Bhansali's films reside and it is to an examination of these adaptive ventures that the essay now turns.

Bhansali sets his adaptation of *Romeo and Juliet* in an Indian town where the powerful Saneda (Capulet) and Rajadi (Montague) families have established criminal empires. Before acquiring this long-winded, tongue-twister of a name, Bhansali's latest movie, *Goliyon Ki Rasleela Ram-Leela*, was simply called, *Ramleela*. Ramleela (or Ramlila) is also the name of a folk dramatic art form based on the central Hindu text, *Ramcharitamanasa*. This enraged some Hindu communities and they claimed that the director and performers had hurt their religious sentiments by using *Ramleela* as a title for a movie containing scenes of sex and violence. Bhansali responded by issuing a statement in which he qualified that his film was inspired by and based on William Shakespeare's *Romeo and Juliet* and that it has nothing to do with Indian folk-lore Ramleela (Bhansali 2013). Despite his claims, as the essay will now point out, Bhansali's movie is in every way related to this tra-ditional Hindu play. Abandoning any attempt at a slavish fidelity to Shakespeare's text, the film blends *Romeo and Juliet* with tropes from the Ramleela to create a unique film experience.[5]

Ramleela (literally Ram's play), is performed according to the annual Hindu calendar around the festival of Dussehra and as such is both a religious and a theatrical performance; it is also very much a part of the visual storytelling of Bhansali's film. To take two of the most obvious examples, when the movie's Romeo, tellingly named Ram, bursts upon the screen for the first time, he sings a song and launches into a ludicrous (but rivetingly so) dance number with hundreds of extras. Some of these extras are dressed as monkeys. According to Hindu mythology, an army of monkeys led by the powerful monkey god, Hanuman, were ardent devotees of the Hindu god, Ram. As such, the Ramleela contains many episodes that demonstrate Hanuman's devotion. By referencing Hanuman in this song, Bhansali invites us to make links between the Hindu god Ram, the peace-loving ruler and his namesake in the movie who seems to be the only one interested in following an actively pacifist agenda in this violent town. In another scene, when a villainous plotter in the movie, a character with no parallel in Shakespeare's play, reveals his schemes, we see a giant effigy in the background. This, too, comes from the Ramleela. The Ramleela performances traditionally culminate by burning an effigy of the corrupt and tyrant demon king, Ravana. An effigy of Ravana in the background here encourages the audience to transfer the negative associations of Ravana onto this plotter. In both these instances, therefore, references from the Ramleela function as codes to read the characters in the movie.

Ramleela is not only used to impart deeper characterization but is also a way through which the film is experienced. Bhansali uses the Ramleela to give his audience an experience that is close to attending a Shakespeare performance. An overview of the performance conventions of Ramleela is in order. While each Ramleela troupe adapts, cuts and embellishes the text freely, it follows a series of loosely based performance conventions. Crucially, the audience is made aware of the artifice and the improvised nature of the performance. For instance, through the course of the plot, the monkey god, Hanuman, performs the following actions: he carries a doctor with his entire house and furniture to the place where Ram lies wounded, transports an entire mountain to this patient's bedside and crosses the entire breadth of an ocean in a single leap by increasing in size and flying on the wind. Instead of trying to render these wondrous feats as naturalistic, the Ramleela performances embrace this theatricality. Such 'non-naturalistic' forms 'by convention acknowledge the audience; in doing so they emphasize the fact that meaning in theatre is created by the actors and spectators together'; more significantly, 'such forms require a *collaboration* between the actors and the spectators for the meaning to emerge' (Kapur 1990: 3, 4). Sometimes, the greater the degree of collaboration required, the more the audience enjoys the play because of their increased imaginative investment in it. For the devout Hindus in the audience, this is of further significance. The belief in the theatrical illusion despite objective evidence is roughly equivalent to believing in the powers of the gods, sometimes despite the reality of their world. The theatrical leap of faith then becomes a religious leap of faith. The Ramleela encourages this audience stance and has moments that work only by rupturing the illusion. This theatre, therefore, works by baring its apparatus instead of trying to find sophisticated ways to disguise it.

These performance conventions are not unfamiliar to audiences of Shakespearean drama. Sixteenth- and seventeenth-century English plays are full of meta-theatrical moments that include asides, soliloquies, epilogues and prologues that address the audience directly to the play-within-the-play, and such fantastic stage directions as the famous '*Jupiter descends in thunder and lightning, sitting upon an eagle: he throws a thunderbolt*' (Shakespeare 2005: *Cymbeline* 5.4.93–94) force the audience to acknowledge the artifice of a performance. Concomitantly, it is commonplace to register that Shakespearean drama relies on and rejoices in the imaginative responses required by its partially non-naturalistic mode of performance.[6] The fact that Ramleela and Shakespearean drama share these similarities allows Bhansali to provide a very Shakespearean and yet a very Indian experience to his audiences.

Consider the particular set of scenes in *Ram-Leela* which opens with sounds of thumping drums and dazzling light, and we see a Ramleela procession passing through the town. Crowds throng the streets and shower down flower petals as the procession progresses. The core of this pageant is a lavish wagon on which we see Ram and Hanuman. This Ram is different from the Ram (or Romeo) of the movie (to avoid confusion, the essay will refer to this Ram as Ramleela's Ram). Ramleela's Ram stands on the wagon, blessing his gazers, while Hanuman is on a swing hanging from an arch on the wagon. The crowd seems to be enjoying the spectacle when Hanuman gestures to one of them that he is thirsty. His audience within the film immediately grasps that the actor is not in character here. In other words, they understand that it is not Hanuman but the actor playing him who is thirsty. Yet, they are happy to continue to indulge the illusion. By introducing a discerning audience within the movie, and ushering in the gap between 'actor' and 'character' in the Ramleela within the movie, Bhansali reminds us how much the Ramleela depends upon the 'imagination' and cooperation of the audience.

Then, Bhansali parallels the movie's Ram with Ramleela's Ram because the former is also included in the Ramleela procession. Although the movie's Ram does not have an acting part in the Ramleela, he holds a loudspeaker and playfully shouts, '*Ramji ki chal dekho/aakhon ki mazaal dekho*' ('Look at the way Ram moves/ note the audacity of his eyes') to introduce Ramleela's Ram to the crowd. This couplet—and this is important—comes from the song that was used to introduce the movie's Ram near the beginning of the film. Here, Bhansali is adapting the well-known Shakespearean trope of multiplying frames. To clarify further, when we first see the movie's Ram, he sings this song to introduce himself. Towards the end of the movie, he takes part in a procession and uses this song to introduce Ramleela's Ram, parodying his own first entry. The movie here indulges in a meta-cinematic gesture where we begin to see that the film's Ram is as much an actor in costume as Ramleela's Ram. By revealing its own artifice, Bhansali playfully replicates the meta-theatrical qualities of Shakespearean drama and similarly suggests that film too depends on the imaginative collaboration of the audience.

Bhansali then pulls off a final coup de théâtre (or a final coup-de-film) by blurring lines between the Ramleela and the movie still further. The Ramleela tableau is not a mere spectacle in the midst of the film but actively advances the plot by ushering in multiple casualties. It is worth detailing exactly what happens. As mentioned before, the actor playing Hanuman is parched and he signals this to his audience. On cue, one of the onlookers within the movie throws bottled water towards him. The actor playing Hanuman takes the first sip and immediately spurts the water out. While it is not clear whether he has been poisoned or simply shot in the act of taking his first gulp, it is established that death has claimed a victim.

By this point, the film's Ram has left the procession to attend to other business, and another murder takes place. Again, the actual killing is not shown. Instead, we see a close-up of Ramleela's Ram as his expression changes from serenity to fear, and we are left to imagine the brutal and public nature of his murder. Although these are very cinematic shots, it is exceedingly difficult to separate which action belongs to the Ramleela and which does not, and which characters belong to the Ramleela and which ones are outside it. The victims, for instance, are both within the Ramleela as Hanuman and Ram, and outside it as innocent Rajadi civilians who get murdered. These killings within the inset performance are particularly apt in the context of Renaissance drama which often employs the 'convention of representing stylized but excessive retributions through the expedient device of court entertainments' (Jowett 2007: 1488). In both cases, that is, in the case of Renaissance drama and this film, the inset performance spills out into the main play/film. Thus, it becomes impossible to decide whether the Ramleela performance is framed within the film or the film is framed within the Ramleela.

Thus, Bhansali utilizes standard conventions and tropes of Renaissance drama, but he employs the Ramleela to do so. This is a savvy move as the majority of Indian audiences watching this movie would have had some experience of viewing or participating in a Ramleela. Although the most lavish Ramleelas are generally performed only in a few places in India, smaller scale Ramleelas are performed in thousands of places during Dussehra. The performance of the Ramleela within the movie would act as a shorthand for the Indian viewer and cue them to the ways of seeing demanded by this non-naturalistic form. Thus, for this

Shakespeare adaptation, Bhansali experiments with generating layers of spectatorship and then plays with complex slippage between these layers in the way Shakespearean plays demand.

Conclusion

In *Goliyon Ki Rasleela Ram-Leela*, Bhansali imaginatively recreates not only the parent text and its narrative mode but uses indigenous theatrical art forms for the purpose. This is a strand of his work that he is keen to promote. Defending his loud, extravagant, melodramatic movies, he tells Chopra (2013), 'I like it Tamasha style.' He further stresses:

> I feel that that's our tradition. That's what we should be very proud of. Italian cinema is very proud of the way it does its films.... In Japanese cinema, if you look at Kurosawa's films, it's folk theatre and they express it in a certain way. We get a little apologetic about it [the Indian Tamasha style] and I don't want to be apologetic about it.

Style, clearly, is very important to Bhansali. Whether he is promoting indigenous folk theatre in *Goliyon Ki Rasleela: Ram-Leela*, using colour and editing shots to force his audience to focus on the constructed nature of disability in *Black*, or employing mise en scène to destabilize generic expectations and by extension assumptions about love and disability in *Guzaarish*, his film grammar raises provocative sociopolitical questions. With such visual and narrative experiments, Bhansali deserves a place in world cinema alongside extraordinarily talented directors such as Baz Luhrmann, Peter Greenaway and Christopher Nolan who push the boundaries of the filmic medium to generate new cinematic experiences.[7]

Notes

1   For a general discussion of film style in Bollywood, see Dwyer and Patel (2002).

2   In doing so, this chapter argues that we should see Bhansali in the light of an auteur. The essay embraces auteurship because Bollywood films are often dismissed as 'masala movies' containing a highly formulaic pattern which is incompatible with original artistic expression. While there is no dearth of such formulaic movies (important subjects for study in their own right), Bhansali's movies should be seen as works of cinematic art. Also, studying a set of films as the work of an auteur is a useful critical tool in comprehending style, technique and expression or stylistic and thematic markers which are common to a particular director's films. However, the concept of a director as an auteur cannot be accepted uncritically. In her immensely valuable book of interviews with Indian film directors, Tula Goenka (2014: 31) states that

> although the *auteur* theory has had waxing and waning popularity in Western cinema studies and criticism, it is clearly the term that best describes most of the Indian filmmakers I met. They often write, direct, produce, shoot and edit their own films…and their singular artistic vision is what appears up on the screen.

This work proceeds more cautiously and does not subscribe to the idea that a film is a director's 'singular' artistic vision. Rather, it must be recognized that the artistic vision is always a collaborative venture in which all creative personnel (including the director) are involved. For this reason, wherever possible, set designers, editors and script writers are identified and credited with the creation of the movie's style in collaboration with the director.

3   Documentary film-maker Shweta Ghosh provided an interesting angle to this technique. In her documentary film *Accsex* (which explores ideas of disability and sexuality), she experimented with using blurred images for parts of the movie so that non-disabled viewers could momentarily experience disability. She told me that some of the viewers were made uncomfortable and expressed annoyance at this technique (private communication with the author, discussing the documentary film, *Accsex*).

4   For a detailed discussion of the anthropology of senses and how the hierarchy of senses is culturally constructed, see Classen (1997). It is ironic that Bhansali uses films, an audio-visual medium, to question the privileged status of sight and hearing.

5   Bhansali is evoking a long theatrical tradition of employing indigenous theatre forms for Shakespeare productions in India. For examples of such performances, see Trivedi (2010). Also, see *The Magic*

Hour performed by Arjun Raina in which he mixes Shakespeare with Kathakali. For details of this production, see Loomba (2005). For the use of Ramleela in a recent Indian film, adaptation of *A Midsummer Night's Dream* (*10ml Love*, directed by Sharat Katariya [2012]), see Panjwani (2016).

6   For a discussion on how Shakespeare's plays operate as non-naturalistic performances, see Dessen (1984).

7   Christopher Nolan's style is amply discussed in Furby and Joy (2015). Gras and Gras (2000: vii) explain in the introduction to their collection of interviews with Peter Greenaway how the director is intent upon 'using the potential of cinema as an image based medium' and the way in which he 'wishes above all to bring the aesthetics of painting to filmmaking and to diminish the influence of narrative'. Lawrence (1997: 1) stresses that 'Greenaway's films are marked by an astonishing proliferation of detail and a remarkable breadth of reference.' Cartelli and Rowe (2007: ix) discuss Lurhmann and Greenaway in the context of their Shakespeare adaptations and note how these directors 'share a propensity for visual and narrative experiments that conspicuously diverge from more classical modes of adaptation'. Together, these studies point to numerous ways in which Bhansali's style is similar to theirs and shares a propensity for experimentation.

References

Bazin, A. 1967. 'The Evolution of the Language of Cinema.' In *What is Cinéma?* translated by H. Gray, 23–40. London: University of California Press.

Bhansali, S.L. 2013. '"Ram-Leela" Not Related to Lord Ram or Krishna: Makers.' *The Indian Express*, Chennai, 13 November.

Bordwell, D. and K. Thompson. 2004. *Film Art: An Introduction*. New York: McGraw-Hill.

Cartelli, T. and K. Rowe. 2007. *New Wave Shakespeare on Screen*. Cambridge: Polity Press.

Chatterjee, S.C. 2005. 'Devdas.' In *Devdas and Other Stories*, translated by V.S. Naravane. New Delhi: Roli Books.

Chopra, A. 2013. Interview with Sanjay Leela Bhansali. *The Front Row with Anupama Chopra*. Star World India.

Classen, C. 1997. 'Foundations for an Anthropology of the Senses.' *International Social Science Journal* 49 (153): 401–12.

Corliss, R. 2012. 'The 10 Greatest Movies of the Millennium (Thus Far).' *Time*, 15 May. Retrieved 11 June 2015, from http://entertainment.time.com/2012/05/17/top-10-movies-of-the-millennium/

Creekmur, Corey K. 2007. 'Remembering, Repeating, and Working Through *Devdas.*' In *Indian Literature and Popular Cinema: Recasting Classics*, edited by Heidi R.M. Pauwels, 173–90. London: Routledge.

De, S. 2002. 'Whose Devdas is it?' *The Times of India: The Sunday Times*, 21 July.

Dessen, Alan C. 1984. *Elizabethan Stage Conventions and Modern Interpreters.* Cambridge: Cambridge University Press.

Dostoevsky, F. 2009. 'White Nights.' In *A Gentle Creature and Other Stories*, translated by Alan Myers, 1–56. Oxford: Oxford University Press.

Dutt, B. 2015. 'Special Episode on Love, Sex and Disability'. *We the People.* NDTV.

Dwyer, R. and D. Patel. 2002. *Cinema India: The Visual Culture of Hindi Film.* New Jersey: Rutgers University Press.

Furby, J. and S. Joy. (eds.). 2015. *The Cinema of Christopher Nolan: Imagining the Impossible.* New York: Columbia University Press.

Goenka, Tula. 2014. *Not Just Bollywood: Indian Directors Speak.* Noida: Om Books International.

Goyal, Nidhi G. 2015. 'Special Episode on Love, Sex and Disability.' *We the People.* NDTV.

Gras, Vernon W. and M. Gras. (eds.). 2000. *Peter Greenaway: Interviews.* USA: University Press of Mississippi.

Jameson, F. 2011. 'Adaptation as a Philosophical Problem.' In *True to the Spirit: Film Adaptation and the Question of Fidelity*, edited by C. MacCabe, R. Warner and K. Murray, 215–34. Oxford: Oxford University Press.

Johar, K. 2004. Interview with Aishwarya Rai and Sanjay Leela Bhansali. *Koffee with Karan* (Season 1: Episode 4). Star World India.

Kapur, A. 1990. *Actors, Pilgrims, Kings and Gods: The Ramlila at Ramnagar.* Calcutta: Seagull Books.

Kazmi, N. 2010. 'Movie Review: *Guzaarish.*' *The Economic Times*, 19 November.

Keller, H. 1996. *The Story of My Life*, edited by Candace Ward. New York: Dover Publications.

Khan, Shah Rukh and Saif Ali Khan. 2008. *Saawariya.* Filmfare Awards. Retrieved 26 May 2015, from https://www.youtube.com/watch?v=nO_Oaz7v2Ss

Kumar, O. 2005. 'On Production, DVD Booklet.' *Black.* Directed by Sanjay Leela Bhansali. Mumbai: Yash Raj Films.

Lawrence, A. 1997. *The Films of Peter Greenaway.* Cambridge: Cambridge University Archive.

Loomba, A. 2005. 'Shakespeare and the Possibilities of Postcolonial Performance.' In *A Companion to Shakespeare and Performance*, edited by B. Hodgdon and W.B. Worthen, 121–37. Oxford: Blackwell Publishing.

MacCabe, C. 2011. 'Introduction: Bazinian Adaptation: *The Butcher Boy* as Example.' In *True to The Spirit: Film Adaptation and the Question of Fidelity*, edited by C. MacCabe, R. Warner and K. Murray, 3–26. Oxford: Oxford University Press.

Mitchell, David T. and Sharon L. Snyder (eds.). 2000. *Narrative Prosthesis: Disability and the Dependencies of Discourse*. Michigan: University of Michigan Press.

Mogk, Marja E. (ed.) 2013. 'Introduction: An Invitation to Disability.' In *Different Bodies: Essays on Disability in Film and Television*, 1–16. North Carolina: McFarland & Company.

Pal, J. 2013. 'Physical Disability and Indian Cinema.' In *Different Bodies: Essays on Disability in Film and Television*, edited by M.E. Mogk, 109–30. McFarland & Company.

Panjwani, V. 2016 (forthcoming). 'Shakespeare in Indian Independent Cinema.' In *Shakespeare in Indian Cinemas*, edited by P. Trivedi and P. Chakravarti. New York: Routledge.

Shakespeare, W. 2005. *Cymbeline*, edited by M. Butler. Cambridge: Cambridge University Press.

———. 2009. *Romeo and Juliet*, edited by J. Bate and E. Rasmussen, Hampshire: Macmillan.

Trivedi, P. 2010. 'Shakespeare and the Indian Image(nary): Embod(y)ment in Versions of A Midsummer Night's Dream.' In *Re-playing Shakespeare in Asia*, edited by P. Trivedi and M. Ryuta, 54–75. New York: Routledge.

Film References

Bhansali, Sanjay Leela. 1996. *Khamoshi: The Musical*. Polygram Films Entertainment.

———. 1999. *Hum Dil De Chuke Sanam*. Bhansali Films and Jhamu Sugandh Productions.

———. 2002. *Devdas*. Mega Bollywood Pvt. Ltd.

———. 2005. *Black*. SLB Films and Applause Entertainment Ltd.

———. 2007. *Saawariya*. SPE Films, SLB Films.

———. 2010. *Guzaarish*. SLB Films.

———. 2013. *Goliyon Ki Rasleela Ram-Leela*. Eros International and SLB Films.

Gulzar. 1972. *Koshish*. N.C. Sippy.

Part II

**Cinema of Commentaries and Interventions:
History, Politics and Society in Bollywood**

In the Morbid Interregnum: Vishal Bhardwaj's Realist Aesthetic and the Neoliberal Imaginary

Jyotsna Kapur and Soumik Pal

The crisis consists precisely in the fact that the old is dying and the new cannot be born; in this interregnum a great variety of morbid symptoms appear.

— Antonio Gramsci (1935)

Gramsci wrote those lines in prison as Italy advanced towards fascism, and he noted a fundamentally contradictory feature of capitalism come alive. As the liberal State turned increasingly authoritarian, suspending the constitution it also lost its legitimacy, that is, the 'consensus' (which, as a Marxist, Gramsci understood was already contingent upon force) that it embodied the 'rule of law'. As Gramsci (1935: 450) explained that when a bourgeois state forswears the constitution, it essentially declares lawlessness as the governing principle in life, producing an 'organic' crisis in which violent, spectacular solutions and 'charismatic men of destiny' take a powerful hold of society and the imaginary. This is the morbid interregnum, between a past that is over and a new yet to be born, in which the stakes are high, literally hanging between death and survival. The tendency of the bourgeoisie to betray its own liberalism, that is, civil rights or free speech, and dissolve it in favour of dictatorial regimes that could guarantee the value of its investments had been noted earlier by Marx (1852) with regard to Napoléon Bonaparte and his coup in 1852.

As an unqualified return to the principles of the free market since the 1970s worldwide, neoliberalism has brought the authoritarian lawlessness of the liberal state to the surface once again. As State apparatuses have become mechanisms for deregulating constraints on capital and crushing its opposition, a morbid alliance of politicians, police and the so-called 'criminal underground' has come above the ground. What is 'real' and 'realistic' takes on a new palpable urgency in this scenario as the dissolution of the consensus/rule of law makes life increasingly unpredictable, and consequently, seems unreal and without meaning.

In this chapter, we take up the work of Vishal Bhardwaj as a key to unlocking the nature and experience of neoliberalism. And, what makes Bhardwaj an auteur, that is, someone recording the register of these times, is his inquiry into the intense tensions that surround what it means to be 'realistic' in everyday life today. If there is one feature that marks Vishal Bhardwaj's oeuvre, it is his commitment to realism, defined not as a convention or style but as close attention to particularity, to the fixity of people's locations in specific places and times. Thus, the struggles of his characters are grounded in their locations, histories and the world they occupy, and are not merely psychological or internal. In other words, the realism offered in the film follows Brecht's dictum that 'the picture given of life' must be compared 'not with another picture, but with the actual life portrayed' (Brecht 1957: 112).

As someone who was born in the small town of Bijnor and grew up in Meerut (both in Uttar Pradesh [UP]), Bhardwaj brings to the screen a marked sensitivity to the textures of the small and provincial towns, especially the Hindi heartland. From locations etched in minute detail to characters whose lives and expressions stem from precise geographical locations and times, his films present a world grounded in its specificity, against the boundary-less, generic world of a big budget Bollywood film whose protagonists take their lavish, portable, traditionally ritualistic-yet globally savvy lifestyles all over the globe.

Bhardwaj's fidelity to locality, that we hope to show, is an extraordinarily astute aesthetic choice in revealing the particular distortions of realism as an overarching principle in the culture and politics of neoliberalism. Bhardwaj's oeuvre then allows us to reflect on the nature of the real in neoliberalism and to ask what kind of radical aesthetic would be capable of countering the dissolution of reality that has accompanied the neoliberal turn.

Gramsci had turned to Machiavelli — to the violent conflicts that marked the birth of the bourgeoisie in the sixteenth century as the landed bourgeois 'princes' fought to acquire power from a dissolving aristocracy — to elaborate on the true nature of capitalistic antagonism. Bhardwaj does something equally inspired. He turns to the renaissance theatre of Shakespeare, in particular the trilogy of tragedies, *Maqbool/Macbeth* (2003), *Omkara/Othello* (2006) and *Haider/Hamlet* (2014) to reflect on India today. In other words, Bhardwaj (like Gramsci) returns to the birth of capitalism to trace its inner logic so as to understand its second coming as neoliberalism. The only difference is that while Gramsci turned to a political writer, that is, Machiavelli, Bhardwaj, as a film-maker, turns to a storyteller and dramatist, that is, Shakespeare.

There is, by now, a well-established critical theory that Shakespeare set his plots against the broader sociopolitical and economic contexts of his time and the plays reveal the inherent contradictions of capitalism during its birth pangs (Dollimore 1984). For instance, in Hamlet we learn that '[t]here is something rotten in the state of Denmark (Act 1) indicating hostility and suspicion from the top to the bottom as what is known by the authorities, what is not and on what basis the State acts is uncertain. Similarly, in *Macbeth*, as Malcom and Macduff plan their attack on Macbeth, they mourn the condition of their motherland, Scotland (Act 4, Scene 3, see Miola 2004: 66), thus saying:

Alas, poor country
Almost afraid to know itself. It cannot
Be called our mother, but our grave; where nothing
But who knows nothing is once seen to smile
Where sighs and groans and shrieks that rend the air
Are made, not marked.

It is difficult to deny that there is a remarkable resonance between this 'description' and the 'disappearances', 'encounter killings' and 'interrogation centres', characteristic of the dismissal of the process of law in favour of swift sentences against the so-called terrorists, militants and dissidents. Or take the suspension of the country's laws, pertaining to trade and labour, in special economic zones (SEZs) that are marked off territorially from the country for the purpose of enhancing trade with global capital. In this situation, death and torture are not marked, they simply happen. To paraphrase Shakespeare in Macbeth, it's a place '[w]here sighs and groans and shrieks are made not marked'. And, what does it feel like to live in such a world?

Realism and Capitalism

Machiavelli had defined 'realism' as a clear-eyed commitment to self-interest ready to turn to sheer force, if necessary. As Machiavelli (1505, p. 81) never tired of repeating the warning to the princes (it is not clear if he was disclosing the system to the people or advising the princes), it is 'fear that preserves you by a dread of punishment which never fails'. Realism, in this instance, requires strong arming and cheating as a way of transforming reality for self-advantage.[1] We can describe this attitude as ruthless–pragmatic.

There is another commonplace use of the term 'realistic', which is to accept the limits of a situation, as in, 'be practical', that is, do not dream the impossible, to change the situation. This is the other side of the active 'do or die' ruthless–pragmatism — an attitude that we describe as the 'practical pragmatic'. It calls for a type who can fluidly and flexibly accommodate wheeling and dealing at a smaller scale with a focus on survival. Both versions of pragmatism, however, have one paradoxical assumption in common: Reality is antagonistic and constantly changing, yet this is also what is constant about it. The demand to constantly adjust to a 'new normal' beautifully unites this paradox. Our point so far is that this is a fundamentally violent situation because it erodes any taken-for-granted notions about reality itself.

These two versions of pragmatism under neoliberalism, that is, the ruthless and the practical, are also thoroughly gendered. Falling back on patriarchal tradition, the pragmatic–ruthless merges with masculinity and the practical pragmatic is cast as feminine. Thus, the anxieties borne of capital are displaced onto gender and normalized. For instance, if a woman were to act ruthlessly pragmatic in her career, she would be seen as acting like a man and, thus, invite appropriation and punishment. The gender-appropriate way for women is the realistic pragmatic, where they are called upon to 'adjust' and 'accommodate' to the reality, whether through sublimation as in sacrifice or through a knowing practical resignation.[2] Meanwhile, the overall conditions which produce pragmatic ruthlessness as a way of life are made invisible.

Reading Bhardwaj and Shakespeare from the vantage point of their women protagonists can help us understand the gendered culture of capitalism, in particular the dominant logic that the individual is pitted in a relentless death battle against antagonistic others. In this regard, we find *Maqbool* to be the most prescient of Bhardwaj's Shakespearean trilogy. Subsequently, we begin our analysis with *Maqbool* and conclude with some thoughts on why *Omkara* and *Haider* are somewhat inadequate in grasping the tenor of our times.

Reading the Neoliberal Imaginary Through *Maqbool*

Spread apart by almost five centuries and halfway across the globe, Shakespeare's Lady Macbeth (early 1600s) and Vishal Bhardwaj's Nimmi (played by Tabu in his remake of Macbeth,

Maqbool) echo the same anguished cry of despair. In her restlessness after Duncan's murder, Lady Macbeth bemoans (Act 3, Scene 2 in Miola 2004: 40):

> Nought's had, all's spent, where our desire is got without content.
> 'Tis safer to be that which we destroy
> Than by destruction dwell in doubtful joy.

And, in the last moments of her life, Nimmi pleads with Maqbool, *'Hamara ishq to pak tha na miya? Pak tha na hamara ishq to pak tha na? Bolo, na bolo na'* (Tell me, Miyan, our passion was pure! Tell me, our passion was pure!). Desire, both find out, is not the route to freedom, but rather it is what betrays them, making them thoroughly complicit with the very world they had hoped to escape. Both women descend into a nightmarish sleep from which they are literally unable to awaken, metaphorically representing a state akin to losing the will to live. And, it is in their inability to continue to go on living after such knowledge that we may find the key to why we experience these narratives as tragic.

In Bhardwaj's retelling, Duncan appears as Abbaji (played by Pankaj Kapoor), the head of a gang in the Bombay underworld at the fin de siècle of the twentieth century. Maqbool/Macbeth (played by Irrfan Khan) and Kaka/Banquo (played by Piyush Mishra) are his seconds-in-command. In a major departure from Shakespeare's plot, Bhardwaj casts Lady Macbeth/Nimmi as Abbaji's mistress. Consequently, Abbaji's murder becomes even more essential for Maqbool and Nimmi since he stands in the way of the consummation of both their political ambition and sexual passion.

Furthermore, by casting Nimmi as Abbaji's wife, Bhardwaj deepens Shakespeare's characterization of Macbeth as a man who is paralyzed by intense self-doubt regarding his ability to be a lover and then a father. We are introduced to this lack in the opening scenes of the film itself. Having disposed of Abbaji's gang rival, Mughal (played by Gyanchand Rikki), Maqbool, Banquo and the policemen are sitting around celebrating their victory. As the men banter about their sexual exploits, Maqbool gets a call from Nimmi asking if he is safe. As Maqbool moves away to take the call, the men make wisecracks at the remote possibility that Maqbool may have, after all, found himself a lover! Nimmi, of course, later mocks Maqbool for his passivity. She taunts him, saying that he would die for her, but dare not act on his desire so long as Abbaji is alive.

Macbeth, in Shakespeare's construction, was either childless or had lost a child (Lady Macbeth avers that she had, perhaps once, nursed a child). But, even before Shakespeare reveals this to us, he hints, right at the start of the play itself that Macbeth's deepest fear is that he will disappear into history with no trace or heirs. The witches stoke this fearful anxiety, predicting that while Macbeth will be the king, Banquo will be the father of kings. Astutely, Bhardwaj casts Kaka's (Ajay Gehi) son, Guddu as Maqbool's true rival. Maqbool is intensely aware that Guddu can obliterate him and emerge as Abbaji's heir, especially since he is involved with Abbaji's daughter Sameera (Masumeh Makhija). Meanwhile, both the play and the film aver that Kaka is a happier, more contented man than Macbeth, perhaps because he is a father. The father–son bond is also shown as going the other way around as those who have fathers are portrayed as happier than the fatherless. While Guddu enjoys the playful protection of his father, Maqbool is somewhat desperate to earn Abbaji's affections and trust. Even Boti whose father Abbaji has been murdered is better off than Maqbool because he can eventually avenge the murder of his father. Maqbool meanwhile will always remain an orphan.

Even as he murders Abbaji and takes up with Nimmi, Maqbool's first thought upon hearing about her pregnancy is if the child is his. 'When was the last time you slept with Abbaji?' he asks as soon as Nimmi shares the news of her pregnancy. The seed once sown, takes a deeper hold over Nimmi, driving her insane. Bhardwaj turns Lady Macbeth's hallucinations about the blood she cannot clean off her hands into an even more abysmal terror. Nimmi is tormented by the inconsolable cries of the baby in her womb, who cries, as she tells Maqbool, because 'they had killed the child's father'. Maqbool, by this point, desperate and sinking into his own hell hits her, crying out, 'I am his father'.

There is a powerful metaphor here of the tragic outcome of the severing of continuity between generations. While the father sees himself disappeared in the future, the yet-to-be-born is already in despair about the murder of its father. What could be a more powerful rendering of Gramsci's notion of the morbid interregnum than this?

Bhardwaj also underlines the passing of the old into an uncertain new by darkening Abbaji's power and cruelty with his vulnerability as an aging Muslim don in post-1993 Bombay, who is also the father of a daughter. Abbaji is beholden to Kaka and Guddu as the father of the bride. As Nimmi never fails to taunt Maqbool, Guddu will inherit Abbaji's empire as his son-in-law, leaving Maqbool in the same place he has always been, a slave or pet dog serving his master.

At the film's denouement, Guddu replaces Abbaji after a bloody victory over Maqbool and his associates. Maqbool, now on the run for his life, leaves Nimmi's dead body to try to reclaim his child. But, he can only watch from behind a glass window as Sameera and Guddu adopt Nimmi's child. The utter sense of futility and loss is magnified as Maqbool, now unafraid and unmindful of the enemy who stalks him, staggers out of the hospital and is shot in the back. The camera takes on his point of view as he reels to the floor, the sky turning red for a fleeting moment and then back to blue again. A bird flies across suggesting the complete emptiness or release brought by death to a man who has found himself to be ultimately disposable. The scene is a visual simile of Macbeth's existential cry:

> Out, out brief candle!
> Life's but a walking shadow, a poor player
> That struts and frets his hour upon the stage
> And then is heard no more. It is a tale
> Told by an idiot, full of sound and fury
> Signifying nothing. (Act 5, Scene 6, see Miola 2004: 77)

These lines are twofold in enunciation. At one level, it is Macbeth reflecting on the utter meaninglessness of his life now that Lady Macbeth is dead, and all that killing and dying appears to have been for nothing. Simultaneously, Shakespeare speaks in these lines as a playwright reflecting on the nature of life itself as a performance and, thus, gives voice to the subjectivity of the modern self, the simultaneous conviction and doubt in the ability to act and make one's destiny. At the end of his life, Macbeth questions if there is no more to life than merely playing out a role and that too as a 'walking shadow', that is, secondary character in a script written by someone else. Was all the passion and fury a foolish delusion, a mere act that had signified nothing?

Maqbool too makes a desperate last attempt to write his life's script. He retrieves the sick Nimmi from the hospital, hoping to escape from Bombay with her and their child. But when they arrive home, Nimmi starts to hallucinate about blood on the sheets and walls and Maqbool realizes the impossibility of their future together. He drops their passports from his hand and sinks to the ground, his face registering the resignation of a man now reconciled to a future he cannot change. Technically, the passports represent escape, but Maqbool faces the meaninglessness of such an 'escape' without Nimmi. Even though Nimmi is physically alive, she is already an apparition, a shadow. Bhardwaj frames this realization against a mirror relying on the enlightenment trope of a play within a play or a mirror within an image; a gesture of self-reflexivity which expressed both the characters' desire for free will and a protest against its impossibility, calling upon audiences to think about the stage as a metaphor for life.

The Self as Protagonist and the Struggle with Mortality

Such bleak despair and the realization that one has merely played a role arises in history and, as we learn from Lefebvre (1958), can only come from a belief in the possibility of freedom, self-knowledge and acting upon that knowledge. For instance, Lefebvre explains, the pre-modern king was not playing at being a king. In contrast, Machiavelli's writings were, like self-help manuals these days, advice for 'princes' on how to act convincingly like princes. Pre-modern subjects were, Lefebvre explains, one with their social roles, and the notion of an authentic self emerged only with the production of private life as distinct from public life. The claim over personal freedom and privacy was revolutionary and made possible by the outright challenge thrown to kingly divine rights and the Church in early modernity.

Simultaneously, the modern secularization of life was accompanied by the loss of belief in the after-life, giving death a finality it had earlier lacked and making life seem ever more transient and, therefore, all the more precious. 'Out, out brief candle' is the dark realization borne out of the knowledge that although it is impossible to believe in destiny anymore, one's life is still not for one's making. Rather, the idea of destiny is now replaced by the diminutive but no less potent notion of luck. Maqbool is not fated to die like Oedipus who was destined to kill his father and sleep with his mother. Rather, Maqbool simply runs out of luck and has the stomach for more killing as Nimmi descends into madness. Ultimately, responsible for his own fate he finds life without Nimmi meaningless.

Such loss of faith in any essential value of life has only magnified in our century. In a deeply moving and incisive account, Hans Jonas (1966) has written that the modern temper (and he is referring to the twentieth century) is incapable of conceiving of immortality. The reasons he cites are attributable to the war-torn genocidal century. These include the loss of faith in justice and the enlightened nature of humanity, the failure and distortions of public memory and, finally, a certain foreboding that we, as a civilization, are faced with extinction. In other words, we no longer believe that justice will be done or that people will remember injustice, and haunted by the sense of our historicity as a species, we are drawn to nihilistic questions about the meaning of human life itself.

To this, we may add Marx's insistence that capitalism is the regime of death over the living, of abstraction and alienation of such high order that life is literally sucked out of the living (labour) and that our relationship to others and the world is totally subjected to the vampire-like logic of capital accumulation. Without money, one can disappear entirely, even from one's own life as in people driven to suicide because they lose their jobs. In an incisive account, David McNally (2011) describes the ever-so-popular zombie and vampire myths as the unconscious of capitalism, especially the bizarre and mysterious nature of the twenty-first century finance capital which has reduced entire populations to experience life as mere flesh, as the living dead.

Death hovers over *Maqbool* and its characters are soaked in the knowledge of the accidental nature of their life. A dark bitter humour about death is woven throughout the film, its characters continuing a pragmatic assessment of their chances at beating it or even articulating an erotic investment in death over life. The film begins with two policemen, a pandit (played by Om Puri) and a purohit (played by Naseeruddin Shah) in a police van with a gang member they have nabbed from Abbaji's rival gang. The irony in the choice of their names is that the lowest functionaries of religion (pandits and purohits are Brahminical priests) are conflated with the lowest ranks in the police, thus indicating that the connection between Hindutva and the neoliberal state.

While one of them is drawing a horoscope of Mumbai on the glass window, the other cleans his gun getting ready to shoot the hapless criminal, who is hoping against hope that he may escape alive after he divulges information about the traitor in Abbaji's gang. The policeman with the gun comments that it is very difficult to shoot someone who is already terrified and sadistically goads his captive to laugh. 'One arrives laughing and bids adieu laughing', he chastises the poor man. As they get him drunk and build his hopes that he may escape with his life, they are in fact cynically waiting for it to strike midnight to finish him off. Their ritualistic prepping of him like a sacrificial lamb, after he has served his purpose, makes a complete mockery of the worth of human life. Blood splatters on the horoscope drawn on the glass and the policeman complains, '*Dekh ke mara kar yaar saari Mumbai khoon se bhar di*' (Buddy, you should take care when you shoot. You have splashed the whole of Mumbai with blood). The death of a man is nothing but a blot, but it foretells in Shakespearean vein the violent tale that is yet to come.

Maqbool's tragedy lies in the fact that he dares to defy death by attempting to make his own destiny. At one point in the film, Abbaji is arrested and Maqbool wants to revenge on the police officer who had arrested Abbaji and slapped Maqbool in the process. Abbaji, astutely reading the times, understands that his arrest was a bitter pill that he must swallow and dissuades Maqbool. Abbaji reckons that his allies in the state machinery, that is, the chief minister, Bhonsle (played by Shammi Narang) and the police, need to make a show of their independence of the underground and simultaneously nod in favour of the Hindutva turn by arresting him. Knowing the pattern of attacks on Muslims during religious festivals, Abbaji plead with Maqbool to vent his anger on Abbaji and spare the community for, as he says, 'any action now will engulf them all in flames of destruction'.

Finally, in what is the deepest marker of the eroticization of death in this milieu, Nimmi demands of Maqbool at gunpoint that he proclaims his love for her. Staged on a pier-like rock formation jutting out into the water, she steals his gun and turns it upon him. Their meeting place, at a far distance from the mainland, highlights the illegitimacy and isolation of their encounter. In any event, of all the characters in the film, it is Nimmi who risks death for pursuing her desires. Plotting Abbaji's death while under his roof, she puts her life in immediate danger. Subsequently, it rings true when she asks Maqbool to choose her life or Abbaji's, thus breaking him out of his indecision. Nimmi, thus, breaks the boundaries of the practical–pragmatism expected of women—a transgression for which she pays with her life.

Capitalist Realism: From Elizabethan England to Bombay

Bhardwaj constructs his portrayal of the Bombay underworld with astute realism. Realism is an integral part of the film's narrative and Bhardwaj's camera inhabits the space with his characters. In a scene where Palekar (played by Jaywant Wadkar), a politician from the opposition in Maharashtra politics, tries to cozy up to Abbaji by using the occasion of Eid al-Fitr to get himself invited to his house, Abbaji teaches him a lesson using those very cultural conventions that he had hoped to exploit. Palekar wants to form an alliance with Abbaji, hoping to supersede the alliance Abbaji already has with Bhonsle, the current chief minister. He requests to have *daalgosht* (a traditional dish in which meat is cooked with lentils with concoction of spices) at Abbaji's house, and once he is there, Abbaji starts by mentioning with a studied politeness that the daalgosht he had requested for is served on a different Eid. Thus, he shows up the out of place and unwanted nature of Palekar's proposed alliance. He later offers a 'paan' to Palekar. When Paekar refuses, Abbaji forces it in his mouth, literally shutting him up and insulting him in front of his court. Palekar using Eid as a way to propose an alliance and Abbaji's rebuttal firmly embed the story post-1990s Bombay.

In another pivotal scene later in the film, Abbaji refuses to contract with a businessman referred to as 'Professor sahib'. Professor is proposing a business deal for smuggling weapons into India through the sea route. The businessman offers an astronomical sum of ₹ 3 billion to be delivered even before the job is done. Abbaji refuses this apparently lucrative deal, stating '*Humari kabiliyat, humara karobaar aur humare pair zameen par hai … tayrna bhi nahin jaante*' (My expertise, my business and my feet are on the ground … I don't even know how to swim). Then, as Professor suggests that Abbaji could take his business empire across the world, Abbaji replies that Mumbai is his 'beloved' and he has no desire to relocate to Karachi or Dubai.

This scene makes a very conscious reference to the history of the Mumbai mafia and invokes the character of the infamous real-life mafia don, Dawood Ibrahim. A history of the Mumbai underworld (Zaidi 2012) shows that Dawood was the first Mumbai don to become globalized, first leaving for Dubai and then, later, settling in Karachi. What set Dawood apart from his predecessors was that he was able to anticipate and ride the oncoming neoliberal transformation of India. He shifted base to Dubai at a time when the ruling class of Dubai was looking to convert it into a business hub by offering massive tax concessions and welcoming any sort of investment globally. Subsequently, Dawood moved to Karachi, riding on the back of money he had been funnelling into the emerging network of terrorist outfits linked with religious fundamentalism.

Although Dawood's links with Pakistan and Dubai had some basis in his religious identity as a Muslim, he nevertheless represented a new kind of globalized don—one who knew how to exploit neoliberal forces, such as tax concessions, dismantling of entire economies, deregulation of labour laws and assassinations, to the fullest. Dawood represents the criminal underside of the legitimized, free-floating, globalized strategist, called the EHM (economic hit man) by John Perkins (2004), who travels around the world on behalf of corporate capital with the objective of securing profit accumulation by exploiting or dismantling existing relations, including national governments that may stand in the way.

Even though *Maqbool* is presumably set in the time it was released (around 2003), and as the aforementioned rise of Dawood to power happened before that, Abbaji's mention of Karachi and Dubai and his refusal to get involved in weapon smuggling can well be read as a historical counterpoint to Dawood.[3] In an earlier scene, Abbaji is described as having started with gold smuggling and then moving on to contract killings and forced land acquisitions—in line with the historical trajectory of the underworld in the shift to the neoliberal economy.

Bhardwaj casts Abbaji as an aging don, now simply unable to swim, both literally and metaphorically, in the ocean that is spreading beyond the shores of Bombay, turning Bombay into one node in this expanded network. Abbaji says as much announcing that he is simply too old to be running around, whether from the law or after Nimmi, 'the scrap of a woman' he can no longer control. Thus, in the post-Dawood era, the very existence of Abbaji is an anachronism.

Abbaji's excessively slow gait, grotesque body, gruff voice and attire and demeanour evoke someone who is out of time, yet desperately clinging on. Moinak Biswas (2006) has noted that Abbaji appears already dead. This is viscerally palpable in his fascination with and parasitical grip on younger women. Bhardwaj shows the embarrassment with which his daughter sees Abbaji kiss Nimmi's foot, Maqbool's feverish visions of Abbaji in bed with Nimmi and a wooden, doddering Abbaji dance with his new mistress, Mohini (Shweta Menon), at his daughter's wedding.

Macbeth too was set in a time of transition, in the midst of a collapsing feudal order. As churches began to sell off their lands to landlords, who now aspired to the status of nobility, the period unleashed among these 'princes', as Machiavelli noted so brilliantly, a profound crisis regarding legitimacy. The princes needed the law to assert their rights on a kingdom they had acquired, but they needed to break that very law to acquire the kingdom from its incumbent. What Machiavelli (1505: 84) disclosed was a greed for power and indifference towards morality, prescribing the princely personality as half beast–half man:

> You must know there are two ways of contesting, the one by the law, the other by force; the first method is proper to men, the second to beasts; but because the first is frequently not sufficient, it is necessary to have recourse to the second. Therefore it is necessary for a prince to understand how to avail himself of the beast and the man.

As Stephen Orgel (2004) has noted, Duncan was a usurper. The play begins with Duncan repressing a rebellion in which Macbeth plays a significant role. Duncan and Macbeth were cousins and Duncan's murder may well be seen as a political assassination to ensure the kingdom of Scotland for Lady Macbeth and Macbeth. According to Orgel, Macbeth's defeat essentially constituted Britain's invasion of Scotland and the effective victory over what had so far been a battle between Scottish Celts and Anglo-Norman invaders.

In shifting the ground to Bombay in the midst of India's transition to neoliberalism, Bhardwaj projects the underworld as a mirror and accomplice of the essentially autocratic and amoral neoliberal state now courting global capital. For instance, Abbaji is protected by the chief minister, Bhonsle, who in turn depends on Abbaji for the 'minority vote' and unspecified underworld dealings. The Inspector General of Police, who we only know of but do not see, is the third element in this triad. He manages Bhonsle's relations with the underworld by manoeuvring its various factions to strengthen arm business deals, acquire property and dispose of dissidents.

Bhardwaj's most brilliant insight into the similarity between the Machiavellian and neoliberal state is his choice of the 'encounter killing' as the epitome of a system in which the institutions of law are themselves the instruments of lawlessness. The film begins inside a van, with the two policemen holding one of Mughal's men as hostage who they will soon kill in an 'encounter'. Later in the film they allow Boti (played by Ankur Vikal), Mughal's son, to escape from, what he fears will be, an encounter killing. They 'stage' these murders with consummate ease, joking and making wisecracks as if these are the most natural part of their jobs as policemen. To stage an 'encounter', that is, to kill a prisoner in police custody, while brazenly fabricating a cynically thin plot that the killing took place because the prisoner was trying to escape the police, has become painfully a fact of life in these times. What would be a murder is no longer a murder, and the constitutional rights of the prisoner count for nothing because the police are itself the murderer.

The encounter killing teaches the most direct lesson about the terrifying truth of the neoliberal state, which is that the rule of law has been entirely abandoned and replaced, as Machiavelli (1505) had explained all those centuries ago, by the rule of force which had to be carried out by the 'cunning of the fox' and the 'strength of the lion'. Giorgio Agamben (2005) has characterized this as the 'state of exception', a perpetual state of emergency in which the constitution — which stands for citizens consensus for the rule of law — is discarded. And once you discard the constitution, there is no basis for the rule of law and, hence, the indifference to questions of morality.[4] In neoliberalism, the contradictions of liberal democracy, that is, between a political system that favours the equality of its citizens (the principle of one person–one vote) and an economic system that undermines that equality, are resolved in favour of autocracy. The agencies of law enforcement turn into systems of autocratic force with the power of life and death over people — with no consequences or punishment for arbitrary exercise of power. The result is impunity with immunity.

In a clear-headed account of the systemic nature and the hierarchy of 'encounter killing', Vernon Gonsalves and ArunFerreira (2015) explain that at the bottom of this system are 'encounter specialists' and 'executioner teams'. Bhardwaj dramatizes this hierarchy through the persona of ACP Devsare (played by Murli Sharma) who is higher on the rung and swoops in the end to finish off Maqbool, now that he has lost all political patronage. At the very bottom are the police teams who follow orders, stage the encounters and must take the blame in the rare circumstance that the encounter is exposed as a murder.

In an inspired move, Bhardwaj casts the two lowly police officers, Pandit and Purohit, as the witches of Macbeth. They are invariably in uniform, other than once when they come to Sameera's wedding in the most outlandish outfits, which appear all the more so because this is the only time they are out of uniform. Of all the characters in the film, the two policemen are given no back story or psychological depth. Consequently, they can simultaneously be participants as well as narrators who comment on the strange and unnatural world that they inhabit. The strange night of Abbaji's murder is built up with the two policemen predicting an unlikely rain and the ominous gathering of clouds of rain and foreboding. As day turns to night, the policemen are still sitting at the horoscope in the rain, with hoods over their head and the fortune teller's tongue sticking out, as though indicating the inevitability of the impending crime.

As the foot soldiers of the neoliberal regime, the lowly policemen are the embodiment of the neoliberal state, for it is in them that the apparent paradox of the legal but illegal regime is unified. Grotesque, slimy and oddly asexual, they are the epitome of the practical pragmatic — scavengers who feast on death and get what they can as scraps thrown at them. Their fortune-readings are utterly banal. Their predictions do not call upon any supernatural powers. Instead, they are straight up machinations to influence actions in the present to produce desired outcomes, which essentially is to keep the antagonism going, in their words maintain a 'balance between fire and water'. Throughout the film, Pandit and Purohit construct horoscopes on the most ordinary of places. For instance, Pandit draws the *janampatri* of Bombay on the steamed window of the police van, frosted by the fear and hope of the prisoner who is to be encountered. Towards the end of the film, they use kebabs to draw a horoscope on the hood of the police van. These horoscopes resemble chessboards, suggesting that fortunes are not being deciphered in the stars but written by powers that be and advanced by their foot soldiers. What is Shakespearean is that all of nature appears to rise in rebellion against such a world. The cyclical nature of seasons and of day and night is shattered, portending the disaster humans have wrought upon themselves.

Life as Theatre/Movie

Shakespeare had referred to theatre as a metaphor for life itself, using devices such as a play within a play (Hamlet) or, in the case of Macbeth, a reflection on life as a role. Bhardwaj invokes Bollywood similarly. On the one hand, the link between the underworld and Bollywood is grounded in history. The Bombay dons have had a special relationship with Bollywood, from fascination with Bollywood stars and celebrities to money laundering in the film business and the lucrative video piracy business of Bollywood films. So, it is entirely appropriate that Abbaji confers the management of Bollywood as an award/promotion to Maqbool (equivalent to Duncan granting Macbeth the title Thane of Cawdor) for his part in killing a rival. On the other hand, the connection with Bollywood also avers the metaphorical consideration of the cinematic nature of neoliberal life and politics. Pandit tells Maqbool that Abbaji would have been a great actor had he been in Bollywood. Political crises are media-managed. In one plot twist, we learn that Bhonsle's rival Palekar had bought 15 members of Bhonsle's party. Yet, in a brief scene, we see Bhonsle's spokesperson feed the media the story that the party members are happily taking a break while Maqbool and Bhonsle watch this on TV.

Again, Machiavelli's (1505: 85) advice comes to mind: '[A]ppear merciful, faithful, humane, religious, upright, and to be so, but with a mind so framed that should you require not to be so, you may be able and know how to change to the opposite'.

When the police say, '[S]omeone is going to get lucky today,' they mean the very opposite which the poor prisoner they hold in their grip soon learns at the cost of his life. Deceit and the resulting confusion between appearances and reality mark *Maqbool's* world. Survival depends upon speed as a split second can mean the difference between life and death.

In *Maqbool's* world, all victories are merely temporary. Thus, Bhardwaj traces a ruthless–pragmatic and nihilistic masculinity at the core of its antagonistic world. Maqbool hesitates before killing Abbaji, telling Nimmi that he *is* her father. But, once he has murdered Abbaji, he must live by the sword or die. Maqbool literally stares death in the face when he first sees Abbaji's dead body and hallucinates that the dead man is looking at him directly in the eye. Similarly, when Kaka's dead body is brought to the compound in the midst of the funeral prayers for Abbaji's murder, Maqbool breaks into a hysterical panic that the man is alive. However, had he not killed Kaka, he could have been killed himself. The police/witches lay out this path for him right in the beginning, predicting either Abbaji's empire or death at the hands of Guddu.

Sleepwalking, the Living Dead and Desire

What we find compelling about Bhardwaj's remake is how he foregrounds Nimmi's desire (and the impossibility of its fulfilment) as a critique of the world she finds herself in. In Macbeth and Lady Macbeth, Shakespeare had brought to the stage a couple whose passionate bond drove its electric charge from the complete intertwining of sexual and political passion. Their political desire to dethrone Duncan was inseparable from the passion they shared as lovers and comrades-in-arms.

In *Maqbool*, Abbaji physically stands in between the consummation of Maqbool and Nimmi's passion, and the time they spend together is fraught with danger, stolen from the certain punishment of death if their desire for each other was to be discovered. What unites Nimmi and Maqbool is also an intense awareness of their declining significance in the world they occupy. Nimmi, the film affirms, is from the declining courtesan culture of Lucknow whose charms cannot stand up to the Americanized-English-speaking Bollywood starlet, Dolly. Maqbool is losing out to Banquo/Kaka's son, an ambitious jeans-clad, Hindu youngster more in line with a dominant Hindutva order.

Going farther than Shakespeare, Bhardwaj crystallizes Nimmi and Maqbool's desire for an alternative future, both literally and metaphorically, in the form of the child she carries to birth. Nimmi's final descent into death coincides with the birth of her child, and she dies sickened with the dreadful doubt that the child was conceived not of her desire but bondage, and that it is the father is Abbaji. From a woman bold enough to risk death for her desire, Nimmi ends up simply as a body who is kept alive only to give birth to a child who is ultimately claimed as Abbaji's. When Guddu arrives at Abbaji's mansion to rescue Sameera at the start of his final ascent to power, he could have killed Nimmi but elects not to, claiming that she is pregnant and, thus, a mother. Once, however, they acquire the child there is no need for Nimmi. Nimmi, who had aspired to autonomy, to rid herself of the title of Abbaji's mistress now dies as his whore.

As both seller and commodity, the figure of the whore blurs into the neoliberal construction of the self as a commodity to be packaged and sold in constant completion with others. Self-consciousness about playing roles has reached new heights with the language of marketing, that is, positioning, branding and packaging, seeping into self-definition as a commodity. It finds expression in postmodern non-essentialism and irony for which the self is only a performance. Yet, Bhardwaj refuses such cynical pragmatism in favour of tragedy. We see Nimmi suffer, not because she feels guilty of Abbaji's murder as a conventional interpretation of Macbeth would have suggested, but rather because of the anxiety that the unborn child is Abbaji's and that the passion she had shared with Maqbool has sunk her deeper into the world she hoped to escape. Thus, the anguish of her last words to Maqbool, stated as a question: '*Hamara ishq to pak tha na miya? Pak tha na hamara ishq to pak tha na? Bolo, na bolo na*' (Tell me, Miyan, our passion was pure!). Maqbool shakes his head, but the answer is unconvincing, more a wish than a denial. Being unable to awaken into this world then is Nimmi's tragic refusal to live in it.

In a historicist reading, Stephen Greenblatt (1980) has asked if the desire for self-fashioning is itself not a mere delusion, a social construct that emerged in history as a way to regulate human behaviour rather than free us. The problem with such a historicist reading is that, in its non-essentialism, it throws out any notion of human nature, including the desire for autonomy, altogether. If free will is, as historicists insist, merely a social construct then it may well be claimed that different cultures will have a different relationship to it, with some having no value. In other words, there will be no political position from where we may object to the suppression of free will. No perspective from where we would view Nimmi's end as tragic.

Yet, *Maqbool* will only work as tragedy if we understand Nimmi's failure as the awful recognition of being trapped in a life where acting on one's dreams does not change reality but only reinforces it and where trying to create a new future only brings back the power of the past. At the core of the tragedy is her failure to act upon the future, represented in the child she carries. Outside the symbolic order in which it was conceived, the child lacks the language to speak of an alternative future. Consequently, *Maqbool* plays itself out as a darkly absurd lament on life, which grieves not the death of the old, but rather the failure of the new to be born.

The power of death over the living and of the past over the future runs through the film as a sound motif that recurs with every prophecy that Maqbool takes towards his death, already predicted at the start of the film. Nimmi implodes from within, underlining the deeply disturbing underside of neoliberal subjectivity and the revulsion at prostituting oneself. The problem with the historicist position is that in deconstructing free will as merely a social construct, it naturalizes a world that makes self-determination impossible. Certainly, the ability to exercise control over life arises in history, but what brings it about is the abundance generated by human labour and ingenuity which make it possible to imagine and desire freedom over one's life. Once arisen, the desire for autonomy is not easily forgotten as a mere construct.

Bhardwaj's Other Shakespearean Interventions and an Unanchored Masculinity

In his subsequent Shakespearean adaptations, Bhardwaj has continued to stage the lawless–autocratic state, but now the state functions more as a background rather than the constitutive element of drama. The drama is largely displaced on to gender, as a kind of inner struggle over masculinity. For instance, *Omkara/Othello* is located in the nexus of caste, crime and politics of UP. Omkara (Ajay Devgan) is the deputy of the Party chief, a half-Brahmin who has risen to power by the sheer dint of his grit. Dolly/Desdemona, the daughter of another high-ranking official, falls in love with Omkara, a choice that alienates her from her father. Omkara's energetic, clever and ruthless deputy, Langda Tyagi/Iago, who is superseded by him, sows the seeds of jealousy in Omkara's mind, leading ultimately to a blood bath in which Omkara murders Dolly, Tyagi and himself.

Like Nimmi, Bhardwaj casts Dolly too as a small-town girl who dares to assert her desire. Dolly initiates the relationship, expressing her passion for Omkara. Going against her father, she defends her choice to the elders. With his usual attention to small-town India, Bhardwaj presents in Dolly a woman who is better educated than Omkara, has gone to college and is touched by a certain modern language of romance. All three main women characters in *Omkara*—Dolly/Desdemona, Billo Chamanbahar/Bianca and Indu/Emily—break lines of sexual propriety. Billo is a whore; Tyagi succeeds in playing on Omkara's fears that Dolly is carrying on an affair with Kesu/Cassius; and Indu is the village 'shrew' who uninhibitedly presents wifedom as a form of sexual exchange requiring the wiles of prostitutes. All three women have one time or the other broken the pragmatic–practical mould to make their own destinies.

Bhardwaj, yet, loses the sight of the significance of caste in the midst of the violent politics that wreaks havoc on the world of *Omkara*. Ania Loomba (2002) has pointed out in relation to *Othello* that what is transgressive about Desdemona's desire is not only the gender dimension that it is the woman who articulates it but that she desires a black man. It is because she desires a black man, Loomba explains, that Desdemona doubly violates the norms of her times. Bhardwaj simply indicates but fails to deepen the anomalous presence of Omkara in UP's caste-based politics. Omkara is, after all, a half-caste who supersedes Tyagi, a Brahmin. Tyagi finds himself routed by both globalized Kesu and half-caste Omkara, and sets out to seek revenge. The entire narrative of *Maqbool* was premised on the simultaneous escalation of the lumpen state and Hindu fundamentalism, that is, the *Jaya Maharashtra* campaign. It was only within this larger frame that Abbaji could appear as emblematic of a passing age and Maqbool's ambition to replace him, over the bid made by Guddu, so bound for failure. Similarly, as the rule of law embedded in the constitution dissolves, caste has become an even more brutal factor in life as may be witnessed in the reign of terror embodied in honour killings and outright battles over land and resources.

Omkara retreats into the relationship between Dolly and Omkara and comes to fixate on Omkara's insecure masculinity, attributing his feelings of inferiority to Dolly's beauty, youth and education. Caste simply disappears in this narrative and the film focusses on a traditional suspicion and hierarchy between men and women, carried down from the ancient scriptures and shared here between father and husband. Dolly's father's words that women are deceitful come to echo in Omkara's ears and become more significant to the narrative than the taunt half-caste. Because, the film moves so far from the politics of state and caste and devolves into an ahistorical exploration of masculinity, it ends up in the most stereotypical casting of Dolly as a docile, submissive and innocent victim. It rids Dolly of the epithet of a whore only to cast her as its opposite, a dutiful wife, thus a projection against which masculinity writes itself. In contrast to the insightful way in which Bhardwaj had used the 'encounter killing' as a key to the lawlessness of the state in *Maqbool*, he fails here to develop the institutionalizing of *bahubali*, the strong man of action, as an indicator of the final dissolution of electoral democracy. The story then takes an ahistorical turn, presenting an India that has not become 'modern enough' rather than one where the modern signals a violent return of the old.

Haider/Hamlet (2014) is set in Kashmir in the 1990s, with Haider/Hamlet as a young Kashmiri student who returns upon the news of his father's disappearance only to find himself caught up in a war zone where one's complicity with the terror state is essential for survival. Haider's father, Dr Meer was a liberal doctor who dispensed medical care to anyone who sought it without discriminating against 'militants' and is, thus, disappeared in a 'crackdown'. Haider's mother, Ghazala/Gertrude then takes up with her brother-in-law, Hussain Meer, who we learn had identified and betrayed his own brother.

Here again, we find the trope of the whore haunting the woman protagonist, this time in the role of Ghazala, the mother. Caring only for her survival and her son's, she marries her husband's brother only to blow herself in the end in a suicide bomb. In *Haider*, Kashmir turns almost entirely into a background set against which the drama unfolds between a mother, son and her lover. Other than a few pointed references to the 'rotten state' of Denmark — as in the crackdown by the police in the beginning of the film and Haider's speech in the bazaar where in a mad delirium he reads out the provisions of the Armed Forces Special Powers Act (AFSPA) — the complete dissolution of the constitution is scarcely touched. AFSPA is the most direct illustration of the declaration of the state of emergency that Gramsci and Agamben speak of. A handover from colonial rule, AFSPA gives the army complete control over civilian life and grants it immunity with impunity. If the encounter killing is a symptom of the neoliberal state as the state of emergency, AFSPA is its direct declaration; the subjugation of citizens by outright declaration of war against them by the state.

In this situation, the difference between silence and complicity is completely obliterated, as to be silent is to comply with the reign of terror and, thus, betray. But, the price of speaking is death and disappearance without a trace. 'Kante se kanta nikalna' (Taking out the thorn with the thorn) is how Manohar Parrikar (Patel 2015), India's Defence Minister, recently described the Machiavellian principle by which the Indian State deals with terrorism. Basically, the State arms 'terrorists' against 'terrorists' and you have a war zone where deceit, cunning and force blur the lines between enemies and allies.

Even then, Bhardwaj fails to weave that overwhelming reality into his narrative. After all, complicity with the military occupation against others, including lovers, friends and family, is a way of survival. Ultimately, therefore, betrayal to oneself and one's loved ones is written into this culture of fear. Ghazala betrays her husband to survive. Haider's inability to kill his uncle would have stemmed, in this case, from the subconscious knowledge of his own complicity with the terror regime. He keeps getting distracted from finding his father because to uncover the workings of a state, for example, is to invite the fate of his own father, that is, disappearance.

Finally, Ghazala's death by suicide bombing at the end appears forced because of the sanctimonious advice she gives her son to disavow violence because, as she tells him, revenge only begets revenge. This advice is an abrupt turn-around in the narrative and finally cuts off any connections it had made with Kashmir as the birth-spring of Haider's indecision or Ghazala's own guilt as a coping mechanism in a state where survival comes at the cost of betrayal. Instead, Ghazala's advice suggests that the conflict in Kashmir is between equals, and that Haider can simply 'forgive' and move on. The mother is restored to the role of the nurturer as she takes her own life, punishing herself for her transgressive desires, and the Kashmir conflict is resolved. The final credits roll and they thank the Indian Army and Police for help with the earthquake and remark on the subsequent increase in tourism in Kashmir, thus concluding with a happy ending that is eons away from the disturbing picture of Demark that Shakespeare had constructed in *Hamlet*.

Conclusion

Jonathan Dollimore (1984) has described Shakespearean tragedy as radical for the reason that the agony, psychological torment and violence wrought and encountered by its characters are shown as a product of intensifying social contradictions. In *Maqbool*, Bhardwaj indicates not the timelessness of Shakespeare, but rather his timeliness in telling us that little has changed. *Maqbool* leaves us sickened, as if, to paraphrase R.H. Tawney (1926: 235), with 'the taste as of ashes on the lips of a civilization which has bought to the conquest of its material environment resources unknown in earlier ages, but which has not yet learned to master itself'. The narratives of *Omkara* and *Haider*, in comparison, inadequately embody the social contradictions of neoliberalism and instead displace the conflicts onto familiar patriarchal stereotypes of masculine anxieties against desiring women. Nevertheless, Bhardwaj's decision to locate Shakespeare in contemporary India is prescient.

In revisiting texts from the founding moments of capitalism, Bhardwaj draws out the seductions of an amoral and ruthless kind of destructive and self-destructive pragmatism that underlies the capitalistic imagery and its disregard for the rule of law embedded in its liberal constitutions. Perhaps, the ruthless-pragmatic or practical–realist common sense of total capitalism can only be shaken by the scale and drama of Shakespearean tragedy and its warnings of unnatural and unseasonal catastrophes that lay in store for a world that is at such odds with humanity itself.

For concluding a few thoughts on our approach to the discussion of auteurs and neoliberalism, which is the subject of this book, we may well be asked, for example, why we have placed such heavy emphasis on *Maqbool* in a discussion of Bhardwaj as an auteur. The answer lies in our consideration of films as historical artefacts and the film author as both a subject and object of history, that is, made by and acting upon history through her art. This approach relies on setting up a dialogue between historical enquiry and cinema studies in which the latter expands the archive and, thus, challenges official history while the former enriches cinema studies, contextualizing cinematic experience and language in broader historical contexts. Accordingly, the text is neither reduced to illustrate a historical context nor read formalistically as independent of history. Nor is it simply a point of reference to rest the claims of grand theory. Consequently, auteurs/ artists are considered agents whose uniqueness lies in the depth with which their art resonates with their times. It is this resonance with his times that makes Shakespeare still open to interpretation today. *Maqbool* is, as we have tried to suggest here, the most resonant with the subjectivities and experience of neoliberalism and at the same time a text marked by its director Vishal Bhardwaj's particular performance of realism in cinema.

Notes

1   See Kapur (2011, 2013) for a detailed discussion of lumpen subjectivities and neoliberalism.
2   See Kapur (2011) for the feminization of the pragmatic realistic.
3   Dawood was involved in getting explosives into Bombay that led to the 1993 series of bomb blasts in Bombay.
4   This is, of course, not limited to India alone but is part of a worldwide shift. John Perkins (2004: 26) finds out through his participation in driving the US foreign policy and financial interests around the world that 'promoting capitalism often results in a system that resembles medieval feudal societies.'

References

Agamben, G. 2005. *State of Exception*. Chicago: University of Chicago Press.
Biswas, M. 2006. 'Mourning and Blood-ties: Macbeth in Mumbai.' *Journal of the Moving Image*. Retrieved 15 May 2015, from http://www.jmionline.org/article/mourning_and_blood_ties_macbeth_in_mumbai

Dollimore, J. 1984. *Radical Tragedy: Religion, Ideology and Power in the Drama of Shakespeare and His Contemporaries*. Revised edition, 2004). Durham: Duke University Press.

Ferreira, V.G. 2015, April 29. 'Andhra and Telangana Encounters: How Police Gets Away with Murder.' Colours of the Cage: All the World's a Cage. Retrieved 17 September 2016, from https://arunferreira.word-press.com/author/arunferreira/page/4/

Gramsci, A. 1935. *Selections from the Prison Notebooks of Antonio Gramschi*. Revised edition 1971, edited by Q.H. Smith. London: Lawrence and Wishart.

Greenblatt, S. 1980. *Renaissance Self-fashioning: From More to Shakespeare*. Revised edition 2005. Chicago, CA: University of Chicago.

Jonas, H. 1966. *The Phenomenon of Life: Towards a Philosophical Biology*. New York: Harper & Row.

Kapur, J. 2011. *Neoliberalism and Global Cinema: Capital, Culture, and Marxist Critique*, edited by J. Kapur and K. Wagner, 197–216. New York: Routledge.

———. 2013. *The Politics of Time and Youth in Brand India*. London: Anthem Press.

Lefebvre, H. 1958. *Critique of Everyday Life*, Volume I. Revised edition 1991, translated by J. Mooreith. London: Verso.

Loomba, A. 2002. *Shakespeare, Race, and Colonialism*. Oxford: Oxford University Press.

Machiavelli, N. 1505. 'The Prince.' Translated by W.K. Marriott. Constitution Society. Retrieved 15 May 2015, from http://www.con-stitution.org/mac/prince00.htm

Marx, K. 1852, December–March. 'The Eighteenth Brumaire of Louis Bonaparte.' Marxist Internet Archive. Retrieved 5 June 2015, from https://www.marxists.org/archive/marx/works/1852/18th-brumaire/

McNally, D. 2011. *Monsters of the Market: Zombies, Vampires and Global Capitalism*. Chicago, CA: Haymarket Book.

Miola, R.S. 2004. *Macbeth: William Shakespeare*. New York: Norton.

Orgel, S. 2004. 'Macbeth and the Antic Round.' *Macbeth: William Shakespeare*, edited by R.S. Miola, 342–56). New York: Norton.

Patel, A. 2015, June 1. 'Instead of Resorting to Bluster, Manohar Parrikar Should Get Indian Military a Big Stick.' Scroll In. Retrieved 5 June 2015, from http://scroll.in/article/731396/instead-of-shooting-off-his-big-mouth-manohar-parrikar-should-get-indian-military-a-big-stick

Perkins, J. 2004. *Confessions of an Economic Hitman*. New York: Plume.

Tawney, R.H. 1926. *Religion and the Rise of Capitalism*. New York: Mentor Books.

Zaidi, S.H. 2012. *Dongri to Dubai: Six Decades of the Mafia*. New Delhi: Roli Books.

Film References

Bhardwaj, V. *Maqbool*. 2003. Kaleidoscope Entertainment and Vishal Bhardwaj Pictures.

———. *Omkara*. 2006. Big Screen Entertainment, Panorama Studios and Shemaroo Videos Pvt. Ltd.

———. *Haider*. 2014. UTV Motion Pictures and Vishal Bhardwaj Pictures.

CHAPTER 9

Post-colonial Transgression in Deepa Mehta's Feminist Quartet

Alka Kurian

In this chapter, I propose to critically evaluate some of the key films of the Indo-Canadian film-maker Deepa Mehta, whose work explores the lives of the marginal and the subaltern, in particular gendered subaltern, whether in India, the country of her birth, or Canada, her adoptive home. In particular, I will be looking at four of her women-centred films that I refer to as her post-colonial 'Feminist Quartet'. Known internationally as one of the leading female film directors of the Indian diaspora, with 12 feature films to her credit, Mehta first rose to worldwide prominence with her elements trilogy: *Fire* (1996), *Earth* (1998) and *Water* (2005). While *Fire* focuses on patriarchal demonization and invisiblization of female sexual desire, *Earth's* narrative looks into women's sexual brutalization during 1947 Partition and *Water* explores the socially sanctioned Hindu widow oppression. Mehta garnered a polarized reception among national and international audiences for the trilogy: some singularly celebrated the representation of subversive post-colonial Indian femininity in her films and others appeared to be deeply offended by what they saw as a defilement of traditional Indian values. The portrayal of lesbian love and the ridiculing of traditional Hindu rituals in *Fire* so scandalized the right-wing Hindu fundamentalists that theatres screening the film were attacked. The controversy generated by *Fire* came back to haunt Mehta when she was forbidden in 2000 from making *Water* in India. Branding Mehta as an outsider intent on tarnishing India's image, protesters rampaged and put the film sets on fire. Mehta had to wait another five years to make the film at a secret location in Sri Lanka and with an entirely new set of crew and actors. Her 2009 diasporic film *Heaven on Earth*, which centres on the reality of domestic abuse among the Canadian Punjabi diaspora, completes her feminist quartet. Despite its powerful feminist politics and its scathing critique of Punjabi diasporic hetero-normativity, the film, surprisingly, did not generate much controversy.

Critics have often accused Mehta of commodifying and exoticizing India for Western viewers interested only in 'snake charmers and child brides' (Chaudhury 2009), and of combining themes and aesthetics with the deliberate purpose of causing controversy as a publicity stunt. While her Canadian critics have regarded the diasporic film-maker's obsession with India as cultural imposition, her detractors in India are suspicious of this fixation; they accuse Mehta of perverting her authentic culture, being out of touch with India, making money overseas by selling the country's negative images and showcasing its 'shame' (e.g., same-sex love, widow oppression and women's sexual brutalization) and undermining in the process the triumphant images — such as 'India Shining' — of a country poised to become the next global economic giant. Readers will recall how Satyajit Ray's *Pather Panchali* (1995) too had become equally controversial for contradicting Nehruvian ideology of industrial modernization through the representation of its poverty. Moreover, Mehta's cinematic representation of powerful and agentic female characters, and not merely ideological nationalistic fabrications, constitutes yet another sore point among the conservative sections of her originary home.

In defence of Mehta's work, though, Chaudhury wonders whether more than anything else is it 'Mehta's status as an immigrant woman film-maker, her export success, and competing vision of a globalized "India" [that] have been the key factors in the antagonism against her' (2009: 8). The author also justifies self-exoticization and commoditization of the Third World — usually the preserve of the colonial masters — as a deliberate strategy for success for diasporic film-makers in the realm of global cinema. The diaspora cannot help but cleave to its authentic ethnic and distinctive culture, perpetuating it through a continuously circular reference to it (Naficy 2001). Driven 'by the aesthetics of juxtaposition and the binary structures that nostalgically repress, fetishize, and favourably compare there with here, then and now, home and exile, [diasporic] films in general derive their power not from purity and refusal but impurity and refusion' (Naficy 2001: 6). And it is this willingness for difference, claims the author, which helps film-makers to locate themselves in an essentially dislocated world and become authors of their films, gaining a modicum of control over their lives.

Since making Canada her home at the age of 23 in 1973, Mehta has defined herself as a 'hybrid person who can move from continent to continent' (Levitin et al. 2003: 277) feeling at home in a multiplicity of economic, political or cultural backgrounds in both North America and India. While accepting the appellation of a transnational film-maker, she is conscious of her location within the realm of uncertainty and transition, hovering within the interstices of her identities that are neither fully Canadian nor completely Indian (Levitin 2001).

I draw on Naficy (2001) to qualify Mehta's work as 'accented' or 'interstitial', that is, the cinematic style, technique, ideology and aesthetics that she shares with other diasporic and exilic film-makers, offering a 'dialogue between the home and host societies of the film-maker (Naficy cited in Moodley 2003: 67) as well as with her audience — many of whom are transitional or exilic — who resonate with the films' characters. Stemming from the geographical, temporal, emotional and psychological displacement from her originary home, and unlike the universalistic and monolithic nature of mainstream cinema, Mehta's cinema represents identities in ways that are unconventional and controversial. Mehta wilfully embraces the borders/interstices/margins of her home/host nations for, while margins can be awkward and unsafe, they are nevertheless an important 'profound edge', 'a site of radical possibility' or 'a space of resistance' that helps 'produce counter-hegemonic discourse' and 'offers to one the possibility of radical perspective from which to see and create, to imagine alternatives, new worlds' (Hooks 1990: 149–50).

Mehta's quartet challenges women's representation as metonymy for national culture and portrays instead women's rebellion against their oppression and hetero-normative nationalist commodification. Her films explore women undertaking 'journeys of identity' (Naficy 2001: 6) that are not just physical or spatial in nature but are profoundly philosophical and psychological, that is, journeys that help discard old identities and embrace new ones. Stuart Hall's definition of identity formation comes in handy in understanding Deepa Mehta's feminist project:

> Identity is not as transparent or unproblematic as we think. Perhaps instead of thinking of identity as an already accomplished fact, which the new cultural practices then represent, we should think, instead, of identity as a 'production', which is never complete, always in process, and always constituted within, not outside, representation. (1990: 222)

Following this insight, one could claim that rather than being predetermined, essential, fixed or immutable, identities in Mehta's films are in the process of coming into being, identities that are performative, that cross borders — both internal and external — and that make choices, dissent or give in to the desire and gratification of the self. Being in essence, therefore, fluid and mobile, Mehta's female identities meditate over the politics of subordination, submission, identity politics and agency of the self. They undergo a process of transformation which necessitates transitioning from a state of reflection, introspection and rejection to a proactive construction of identities that enable them to become 'subjects of their own lives' (Moodley 2003: 68).

Central to Naficy's 'accented' cinema is the idea that an authentic representation of the self can only be realized by members of one's own community who alone can truly capture the nuanced nature of their own stories and experiences. Western cinematic practice, consequently, can only allude to but not fully apprehend the Third World lives, culture and people. Borrowing from Mohanty et al.'s (1991) contention, who find fault with Western feminism's inability to shed light on Third World experience, could one attribute these representational gaps and fissures in Western cinema to its assumptions about the Third World identity as singular, undifferentiated and homogeneous. Inherent within Mohanty's claim that the 'Third World woman is not a monolith' is her critique of the practices of colonization which produce the image of an average Third World woman who, unlike her educated, modern and agentic Western female counterparts, is portrayed as 'ignorant, poor, uneducated, tradition-bound, religious, domesticated, family-oriented and victimized' (Moodley 2003: 70). Since this truncated representation of the Third World would not do, claims Mohanty, it needs changing so as to situate her within the specificity of the material, social, political and historical conditions within which she is located. It is only through Western feminists acknowledging how class, ethnicity and race intersect the lives of Third World women or, importantly, through Third World women proactively engaging in the politics of self-representation that this work can be carried out. Similarly, an authentic 'accented' filmmaker too would need to clarify the ideological positionality of her film-making practice and take into account race, ethnicity, gender, class, politics and nationalism with the view to understand and realistically represent Third World women's experiences in her cinema. As a post-colonial feminist film-maker, Mehta's cinematic oeuvre underlines her consciousness of her women characters undertaking the 'journeys of identity' to comprehend and break free from the constructed nature of their identities based on predetermined notions of Indian femininity that is bound to hetero-patriarchal nationalism.

Through an investigation of Mehta's feminist quartet, I will explore the ways in which, as a post-colonial women director, Mehta overturns traditional gender roles expressed in dominant nationalist stories by offering radical and alternative stories of love, belonging, sexuality, gender and political participation. The four cinematic texts offer a close exploration of the challenges and dilemmas confronted by women (and men) who are denied self-determination and equal citizenship to the idea of nation (or imagined nation) due to their identification as a metonymy of nation. These post-colonial films are embedded within narratives of sexual desire, violence (both private and public), religious bigotry, class and caste persecution, movement, travel and exile.

Masculinist understandings of nation and nationalism(s) have tended to perceive the concept of gender as supplementary to the process of nation formation. 'Colonial' and 'post-colonial' nation-formation, in my view, has always been a bourgeois patriarchal prerogative. In her incisive study on the link between gender and nation, Yuval-Davis (1997: 2) argues that a predominantly large number of hypotheses on nations and nationalism (Gellner 1983; Hobsbawm 1990; Kedourie 1993; Smith 1986, 1995) have tended to view the notion of gender as a supplementary departure from the main argument. Operating from the position of an essentialist binary understanding of gender differential, the so-called national fathers view women as biological reproducers and nurturers, and as bearers of the nation's culture and honour. The resulting symbolic weight carried by women relegates them to the private realm of home and hearth to be, in turn, controlled and guarded by the nation's virile, hetero-patriarchy.

Moreover, these hetero-patriarchal control mechanisms, which draw the lines of difference between the genders and reinforce men's traditional roles within the family, community and nation, end up silencing women's voice. The narrative tension in the textual narratives under examination in this chapter is built precisely around this loss of gendered agency through women's physical, mental and sexual control; their abduction and sexual brutalization; their physical and social ostracization and exploitation; and their battering within the domestic sphere. Feminist fictional writing and other discursive practices, on the other hand, conceive of the nation on the basis of a different set of gendered (feminine as well as masculine) conceptions of the world. The four texts under investigation are significant in the way they creatively trace the genealogies of both female and male protagonists in the British and post-colonial Indian subcontinent as well as within its diaspora, and explore the sociopolitical dilemmas they face along a multiplicity of vectors. To start with, my analysis builds on the commonly promoted notion of women's predicament and their resultant vulnerabilities associated with their appropriation by the nation as private and collective cultural symbols. Despite the validity of this critique, I find it somewhat limited in that it does not fully account for the predicaments faced by non-bourgeois subaltern masculinities whose subject positions are compromised in the 'post-colonial' state due to the 'minoritization' of the nation's majority ethnic and sectarian communities. Included also in my conversation is an investigation of the anxieties around alternative forms of masculinities challenged by the more aggressive and virile masculine normativities that are constructed along the lines of traditional notions of sexual difference. I propose thereby that rather than being temporally or historically fixed and unchanging the categories of gender and nationality are traded in a constant process of metamorphosis and, through the act of cultural or discursive representation, acquire stability, consolidation or transformation. This, in my opinion, is reminiscent of Hall's notion of identity as not being fixed but coming into existence through representation (1990). It is only thus, I believe, that we will be able to trace the gradual formation, shifting, erasure or reformation of masculine and feminine subject positions and agencies and understand the unravelling of their success (or failure) in subverting perceptions of the Third World gendered subjectivities as ahistorical, monolithic and singular.

Textual Analyses

Fire

Released in 1996, and as the first of Mehta's elements trilogy, *Fire* represents social transformations in contemporary India from a gendered perspective. Set in a cramped and overcrowded South Delhi middle-class Hindu home, the narrative in *Fire* is structured around two sisters-in-law Radha (Shabana Azmi) and Sita (Nandita Das) married in a socially dysfunctional Hindu family. Ashok (Kulbhushan Kharbanda) penalizes his childless wife Radha's barrenness by dedicating his time, money and resources to a Hindu guru, an advocate and proponent of celibacy. Ashok's younger brother Jatin (Javed Jaffrey) chooses to spend his nights with his girlfriend instead of his new bride Sita. Mundu (Ranjit Chowdhry) doubles up as a family servant, errand boy to the take-away business run by Radha and Sita, and a personal helper to the stroke-ridden mother-in-law, in whose presence he masturbates as he watches porn on the only VHS player in the house, kept in her room. Emotionally starved and marginalized Radha and Sita fall in love with each other and, shunned by all members of their family, flee from home. This, I claim is not a simplistic rejection of an unsuccessful heterosexual marriage. I draw on Ferguson (1981) to interpret the film from a sociopolitical definition of lesbianism that identifies the weakening of the heterosexist bourgeois family as offering the 'material conditions that were vital for the growth of lesbianism as a self-conscious cultural choice for women' (p. 168) and which freed them from masculine dependence. The film depicts the gradual masculine loss of control on the household whereby both Ashok and Jatin are relegated to the margins of the family as Radha and Sita asset their voice and agency. I further draw on Gopinath (1988) to maintain that Mehta offers the emergence of lesbian desire from within the gaps and fissures of uncompromising urban Indian middle-class hetero-normative conservatism. The film charts the ways in which it is precisely the legitimate hetero-normative homosocial practices and rituals that facilitate the

articulation of homosexual attraction. By disrupting socially sanctioned homosocial spaces and rituals — such as *karva chauth* (where
Hindu wives fast for their husband's long life) or massaging each
other's feet and hair — into sites of homoerotic desire and pleasure,
Radha and Sita appropriate 'permeable relation and the slippages
between female homosociality and female homoeroticism' (p. 634).
Not only did this shift legitimize their assertion for sexual egalitari-
anism but also enabled them to 'add another dimension of joy to
their already emotionally intense friendship' (Ferguson 1981: 168)
with each other. Also, the fact of Radha and Sita not being mothers
offers further insights into their political disruption: Radha cannot
conceive and Sita chooses not to have a child. I read this as the
film's inherent critique of the regularization of women's eroticism
as only being realized and fulfilled through motherhood.

Three weeks after its successful screening to full houses in
major theatres in India, the showing of Mehta's film *Fire* (1996)
was interrupted by a small group of protesters (Moorti 2000: 1).
Wearing saffron coloured scarves to indicate membership to the
right-wing Hindutva party, they began raising slogans and breaking furniture in theatres in Mumbai and Delhi, prompting other
theatres across the country to withdraw the film. The fact that
it took that long for the film to be attacked and that the attacks
happened only in the presence of the media signal the orchestrated nature of the attacks. They denounced the film's representation of lesbian sex, which, they maintained, was an affront
to traditional Indian values and national purity. Homosexuality,
they claimed, was unnatural, unpatriotic, vulgar and evidently
irrelevant in India. Further, why should one corrupt innocent
female minds by telling them about things they did not know?
Hindu women satisfying each other through lesbian love would
jeopardize the institution of marriage, family and patriarchy,
and decimate the Hindu population, making it vulnerable to
being overrun by the minorities. Mehta, they said, was striking
at the heart of the chaste and pristine 'Indian' culture through
her imperialistic gaze that had been clouded by the decadent,
immoral, corrupt, materialistic and hedonistic West. Clearly, it
would seem that the nation's safety depended on the welfare of

patriarchal families and for which individual rights must be sacrificed. The film's condemnation reached across national borders so that in some of the countries with substantial Indian diaspora (Singapore and Kenya), the film was officially banned. Speaking out in favour of the film's screening, various organizations and women's and civil rights' groups challenged the attacks on the freedom of expression, the representation of feminine sexual desire and the rigid definitions of national culture. Members of the press and mass media offered a variety of responses to the film, with some focusing on the film's critics and others speaking in favour of the film's representation of gender and sexuality. Some of the questions that rose to the surface are as follows (Hobsbawm and Ranger 1983): What is the relationship between national identity, gender, sexuality, religion and globalization? What kind of a golden age of Indian culture does the Hindu right refer to, demonizing the legacy of Western imperialism, when women were freer in pre-colonial times? What chance does it stand when traditions themselves are modern inventions, facilitated through rituals and repetitions?

At the core of the controversy within which the film was mired are the ways in which femininity was mobilized by right-wingers in often competing definitions of Indian identity, in particular given the general sense of anxieties attendant upon the substantial economic and social changes stemming from global flows of people, labour, ideas and money. An assertion in *Fire* of women's sexual desire and lesbian love came, therefore, to be interpreted by the right-wing as a threat to a hetero-normative homogenous and pristine culture of the nation. The truth is that a rising number of women in contemporary India are no longer bound to domesticity: they work, earn money and are increasingly making independent decisions. It is important to note that the film's release coincided with the rise of the right-wing movement, which as an exceptionally powerful force in the 1990s offered a deeply incongruous attempt to combine modernity and tradition by empowering women through affirmative action plans as it relocated them within patriarchal domesticity and through enforced heterosexuality (Moorty 2000).

While Radha in *Fire* represents traditional femininity and subservience, Sita, on the other hand, is modern, suspicious of tradition and open-minded. Hurt by anxious masculinity that is incapable of making sense of a quickly transforming globalized society, they are trapped between repressive customs, traditions and desires. What *Fire* offers is narrative possibilities: that women don't need to martyr themselves to marriage, family or tradition; they can imagine and live a life outside marriage and oppressive rituals and customs; female sexual desire is not necessarily realized within hetero-normative marriages and that sexuality can help navigate out of oppressive hetero-normativity. It is in this manner that *Fire* is subversive. It upends a Bollywoodesque melodramatic plot to subvert expectations mobilizing the trope of post-colonial female sexuality: A deromanticized family is represented as a site of oppression, loneliness and inequality; feminine rituals (e.g., karva chauth) are rendered satirically to illustrate how tradition and religion manipulate and control women's lives; personal relationships are prioritized over the communal good and, finally, women are represented as courageous and fearless instead of scheming and manipulative, the usual trope of Bollywood cinema and many mainstream television dramas.

Earth

Based on Pakistani writer Bapsi Sidhwa's novel *Cracking India* (1991), *Earth* offers a concurrent representation of the end of the British colonialism, the 1947 holocaustic Partition of the Indian subcontinent and minority women's subjugation. The 1947 Partition of the Indian subcontinent into India and Pakistan resulted in widespread sectarian violence and an unprecedented mass exodus of people across the country's newly created eastern and western borders. The distressing loss of person, property and home that ensued soured forever the hard-won freedom that came with the nation's decolonization. Around one million Hindus, Muslims and Sikhs were killed, more than 18 million became homeless and approximately a hundred thousand women from either community were abducted.

Set in the 1940s Lahore, the narrative in *Earth* (released in India as *1947: Earth*) is built around the lives of the central protagonists Lenny (Maia Sethna), an 8-year-old Parsi girl afflicted with polio, and her Hindu nanny, Ayah/Shanta (Nandita Das), a feisty young woman who uses her beauty to her advantage. The narrative conflict is located in the relationship between Ayah and two of her Muslim admirers—the ice-candy man, Dil Navaz (Aamir Khan), and the masseur, Hassan (Rahul Khanna). On discovering Ayah's preference for the masseur, a jealous ice-candy man kills his rival while Ayah takes refuge in Lenny's house. The plot climaxes when he coaxes Lenny into divulging Ayah's whereabouts so that Ayah's screen of protection, acquired through her association with the apparently religiously neutral Parsi family, is slashed and drawn away as she is abducted, sexually abused and exploited by her most trustworthy friends. Ice-candy man marries her and lives off her income by forcing her into prostitution. The resolution to this highly fraught drama takes place with Lenny's mother (Kittu Gidwani) and godmother helping Ayah escape from ice-candy man and from there on to her family in India. It must be noted here, however, that Mehta chooses to not include Ayah's post-abduction narrative in her film.

The diegesis begins and ends with the adult Lenny as she conjures the memories of joy and horror of her childhood and which are offered to the reader in the form of a 'linear' flashback. The simplicity of Lenny's syntax and diction and the earnestness and sincerity of her tone, together, underline the unpremeditated, child-like innocence of her voice. However, along with Lenny's polio-afflicted leg, I see this as yet another creative strategy that heightens the narrative's dramatic irony. Almost from the start of the narrative, we become aware of the manner in which the film-maker uses Lenny's questioning gaze and tone to unravel and challenge the hegemonic patriarchal and majoritarian foundations of Indian society. Lenny's reaction to abducted women (temporarily sheltered behind Lenny's house) as 'fallen women' foreshadows the eventual loss of Ayah's agency and subject position. Further, Lenny's pessimistic and questioning tone interrupts the narrative as well as problematizes the connection between discourse and truth. We can gauge the level of her confusion as she wonders about the meaning of partition. Going by Ray's description of partition as a 'neat cartographic creation of a new geographic entity' (2000: 131), Lenny's repetitious inquiring gaze signals the human cost extracted by the cold rationality of the country's political slicing which fractures this very 'neatness' of the process. Moreover, the naivety of her tone and actions dramatizes the narrative in the way that it lends itself to a multiplicity of interpretations. Lenny's articulations in the novel of her fears about the country's division ('India is going to be broken. Can one break a country?') are represented in the film by her smashing a ceramic plate on the floor and then examining its resultant 'jagged' shards. Lenny's visual language (announced in the novel by words such as cracking, sundering, breaking, tearing and digging) performs a dislocation between the signified and its signifier, which underlines the epistemic violence that is central to the masculinist, nationalistic ideology.

It would be useful to look at the themes of gender and nation that are mobilized in *Earth* to underline the bourgeois patriarchal nation-construction as well as the gradual shifting and transformation of gendered agency both in the 'colonial' and the 'post-colonial' nations. The transformation of Ayah's relationships across class and sectarian divisions problematizes Benedict Anderson's depiction of the modern nation as a deep 'horizontal comradeship' (1991: 6–7) and highlights the complex interaction of gender, sexuality, nationalism and sectarian belonging. The narrative conflict is located in Ayah's relationship with the Muslim ice-candy-man Dil Navaz and the masseur Hassan, the Sikh businessman and the Hindu moneylender. Their opposing ideological positions on nationalism complicate their competing affection towards Ayah. Left out of the romantic triangle (Ayah chooses Hassan over him) and enraged by his sisters' brutalization and murder at the hands of the Hindus, Dil Navaz opts for a radical Islamist position. Hassan, on the other hand, chooses love over nationalism and decides to convert to Hinduism, a decision for which he along with Ayah is penalized. Hassan is killed (most likely at the behest of Dil Navaz). His gentler masculinity appears to come in the way of a more aggressive and virile masculinity and is, hence, sacrificed in the name of nation-construction based on unified notions of male virility and sexual purity. Ayah is abducted, sexually brutalized and sold into prostitution by Dil Navaz, reinforcing, in my view, patriarchy's bestial struggle over land, property and women. Ownership of women in this case surprisingly reverses notions of pollution and purity.

Earth offers detailed documenting of the gruesome killings during the sectarian civil war that ensued at the time of the country's partition: Men are dismembered or burned and houses are set ablaze. Caught up in the madness of ethnic purging that results from 'the identification of politics with the *self* of a community' (Ranciere cited in Ray 2000: 133), it is the women who are doubly victimized: They get singled out in the 'generic killings orchestrated by various religious denominations...in the name of the pure nation' (Ray 2000: 133). Men at least had escape routes through voluntary or forced institutionally sanctioned religious-conversion procedures of Islamic circumcision or Hindu shuddhi (purity). For women there was no such salvation.

Such an idea is conveyed in *Earth* through the vivid representation of Ayah's brutal abduction. This underlines the male anxiety with regard to women who lose their value as mothers or nurturers, or as embodiments of the nation. In failing to become, in this manner, metaphoric and symbolic icons for the nation, women become objects of hatred; in the process they invite their self-annihilation and are ruthlessly wiped out. Ray argues that because national identity depends 'constitutively on difference [it] means that nations are forever haunted by their very definitional others.... Hence [we witness] the nations' insatiable need to administer difference through violent acts of segregation, censorship, economic coercion, physical torture, and police brutality' (2000: 135).

Water

Set in the holy city of Varanasi in 1938, the third film of Mehta's elements trilogy, *Water* offers a scathing critique of the socially sanctioned deprivation of Hindu widows. Based on the tenets of *Manu Smriti*, a 2000-year-old Hindu book of law, the widows live a life of renunciation, poverty and chastity as an expression of their dharma towards their dead husbands. In a patriarchal society where female identity is shaped by male members of her family, for a widow, the death of her husband signals the cessation of her own life: Not only does she reach a stage of 'social death', but being identified only as a 'vessel of reproduction', her social death leads her to the 'sexual death' (Mukherjee 2008: 36). Considered inauspicious, and an economic burden on the society, widows are abandoned by their families in impoverished widows' homes where their lives are strictly regulated through culinary, sexual, sartorial and social restrictions. They renounce all sources of joy and happiness, eat only one meal a day, keep regular fasts, wear only white clothes (the colour of mourning), sleep on the floor and shave their heads. Despite intervention by several Hindu reformers (e.g., Ishwar Chandra Vidyasagar) advocating for widows' right to normal, happy and fulfilling lives, for example, through remarriage, many widows even today lead a life of destitution. *Water* could be seen as an expression of Mehta's contribution to this reformist tradition where she calls out Hindu hetero-patriarchal widow oppression and denial of their human rights through religious manipulation, social ostracization, economic dispossession, deprivation and sexual exploitation. Mehta's inspiration to make this film happened during a visit to Varanasi where she was struck by the image of a Hindu widow who was 'bent like a shrimp, her body wizened with age, white hair shaved close to her scalp' (Chaudhury 2009: 10).

Water was screened at the Toronto Film Festival as a world premiere, was Canada's entry for Best Foreign Language Film and received a nomination at the 2007 Oscar awards. The film unravels the lives of the following key characters living in a widow's ashram situated on the banks of the sacred river Ganga: a recently widowed 8-year-old playful and rebellious Chuyia (Sarala Kariyawasam) who brings energy, life and colour to the dull and mournful widows' ashram; the young and beautiful Kalyani (Lisa Ray) who is prostituted for the ashram's upkeep; the middle-aged, caring and questioning Shakuntala (Seema Biswas) and Madhumati (Manorama), the shrewd and gluttonous matron of the ashram. The film's narrative unfolds against the backdrop of Gandhi's campaign for self-determination, a progressive non-violent, anti-colonial movement, offering a sharp juxtaposition to the regressive social conditions within which the widows are mired. Narayan (John Abraham), a high-caste liberal and reformist Brahmin, falls in love with Kalyani and offers to marry her. He debunks social taboos and religious bigotry around widowhood, a social practice, which in fact, is maintained to keep widows from accessing their dead husband's property and wealth, and to control their sexuality. Incensed by the prospect of loss of income for the ashram, Madhumati imprisons Kalyani in her room, shears her hair and presses Chuyia into prostitution. However, horrified by the knowledge that she had been offering her sexual services to Narayan's father, Kalyani takes her life in the Ganges. A grief-stricken Narayan abandons his family and the city to go join the anti-colonial nationalist movement, taking Chuyia along with him.

The Ganges in the film is symbolic in the way it represents life, purification sanctification, pollution and death. While it cleanses dirt, pollution and sins, it also becomes a channel along which first Kalyani and then Chuyia are taken for sexual service to upper class men. And while it is life giving to those that swarm to the holy city for salvation and deliverance, the Ganges, just like institutionalized religion (Caldwell 2011: 3), also swallows up Kalyani, offering her no resistance, leaving not a trace of its complicity in destroying the body of a woman that it thought was far too audacious and adventurous for her own good. So, is it symbolic too that the train that brings Gandhi to the city, is the very train on which Narayan escapes to a modern nation, leaving behind the old nation stultified by religion, custom, ritual, taboo, deceit and treachery?

Who then is the final protagonist in the film when all have gone away? Truly devoted to her faith, Shakuntala is caring and nurturing and despite being marginal within the larger narrative ends up becoming the force of change. She challenges the priest Sadananda (Kulbhushan Kharbanda) on the ethics of widow oppression and learns from him about the recent legal provision for widow remarriage, a provision opposed and disregarded by religious groups. It is through Shakuntala's character that Mehta offers her critique of the ways in which men in positions of power can manipulate religion, overlook the law simply because it comes in the way of their lives and perpetuate women's exploitation. Armed, therefore, with the knowledge of this legal provision and strengthened by the awareness of a way out of oppressive tradition, Shakuntala grabs Chuyia away from Madhumati's clutches and thrusts her into Narayan's arms, as he is taking off on the train to join Gandhi, the final harbinger for progress and change.

Heaven on Earth

Set in Canada, *Heaven on Earth* (released in India as *Videsh*) centres on the theme of spousal abuse faced by a young Punjabi woman, Chand (Preity Zinta), who has recently arrived from India through arranged marriage to Rocky (Vansh Bhardwaj), a man she has never met before. In a cramped home located in the working class city Brampton near Toronto, she lives with her husband's extended family: his parents, his sister, his unemployed brother-in-law and his niece and nephew. Burdened by the enormous financial pressure placed upon him, and harassed by his possessive mother (Balinder Johal) who fears losing him through marriage, Rocky takes out his frustration, often on his mother's behest, on Chand through psychological and physical battering. Chand tries everything to woo her husband, including enticing him with a magical root given to her by a Jamaican co-worker Rosa (Yanna McIntosh). However, the magical root ends up tempting a cobra snake in the backyard who, disguised as her husband, visits her when she is alone. Accused of infidelity, she opts to prove her innocence by putting her hand inside the cobra's pit, risking death by snakebite. While she comes out victor, she decides to leave the abusive marriage and goes back to India to take a chance with her family even though it does not appear to be very sympathetic to her plight in Canada.

While there exists considerable research on the topic of domestic violence, there is little scholarship on its intersection with immigration. Inadequate too are cinematic representations of this theme despite the scale of its prevalence among South Asian immigrant families. Apart from Gurinder Chadha's *Bhaji on the Beach* (1993), Jag Mundhra's *Provoked* (2006) and to some extent Rensil D'Silva's *Kurbaan* (2009), diaspora films tend to offer romanticized narratives of raced and nationalistic accounts of us versus them, papering over the reality of internal gendered cracks within South Asian immigrant families. In the process, they recreate falsified narratives of immigrant struggles and predicaments within which the reality of partner abuse experienced by women behind closed doors of culture, tradition, honour, family and values never comes out. Partially based on Girish Karnad's short play *Nagamandala* (1999), *Heaven on Earth* centres the issue of spousal abuse in a Punjabi family in Canada, offering an unsentimental account of the fear, battering and trauma experienced by immigrant women. What sets Mehta apart is that unlike Chadha and Mundhra, she refuses to offer a one-sided single story of abuse through essentialist representations of the abuser. Instead, she locates her narrative within what Razak refers to as a 'violent space' (2003, quoted in George and Rashidi 2014) marked simultaneously by the patriarchal nature of Indian families and culture, the absence of institutional or informal support structures as well as the experience of structural and institutional violence faced by South Asian families as raced immigrant subjectivities. Her film is unique in that it offers a meditation on the circumstances and conditions that turn spaces of shelter, protection and identity into violent spaces of abuse, alienation, fear and illness. In an interview with Sukhmani Khorana, Mehta states that living in Toronto, she had always being intrigued by the rampant culture of domestic violence within the Indian diaspora, one of the fastest growing ethnic groups in Canada. Without finding fault only within Punjabi patriarchal culture, she understands domestic abuse as stemming from the process of immigration itself. The shifting nature of family dynamics caused by migrating to the West and the pressure to maintain the old order that can no longer be brought back together put enormous strains on both men and women (Khorana 2009). The resulting tension and anxieties combined with structural and institutional processes of discrimination and marginalization lead to a vicious cycle of violence and abuse perpetrated against women.

Many scholars regard domestic violence as a primarily gender-based oppression performed within essentially patriarchal South Asian families with clearly defined roles of submission, subservience, silence and an unwavering commitment to the age and gender hierarchy within a joint family whose members collectively hold the woman to account were she to stray from her boundaries and penalize her through physical battering and moral and communal censure (Agnew 2009; Dasgupta 2000; Goel 2005). However, this cultural explanation of domestic violence is inadequate as it essentializes cultures as ahistorical, universal and forever frozen in time and space. An intersection between power and culture reveals the ways in which the two can be mutually exclusive. The more powerful a community, the more liberal it tends to be; the less powerful a community, the more it holds onto its cultural exactitude (Volpp cited in George and Rashidi 2014). As a result, spousal abuse in immigrant communities needs to be understood from the matrix of socio-economic disempowerment embedded in racism rather than simply an attribute of male dominance. It is, therefore, important to regard the situation of domestic violence from a structural and intersectional perspective that brings together institutional and individual reasons for gendered violence. Crenshaw (1991) too connects racism and patriarchy to explain the ways in which they 'deny men of colour, the power and privilege that dominant men enjoy' and which manifests itself in the form of domestic violence in families of colour (George and Rashidi 2014: 69).

It is this intersectional and multi-layered portrayal of the immigrant spousal abuse in a working-class Punjabi immigrant family which is at the heart of Mehta's *Heaven on Earth*, which she does through projecting a complex set of masculinities and femininities located along generational and gendered differentials. Afraid of losing her status in the family to a young and beautiful Chand, Rocky's domineering mother plays the victim card with her son, making him feel guilty for wanting to be with his wife. Checking her husband constantly, she takes away his voice. She does this both at home and outside, for example in the shopping malls, where they seek temporary refuge during the day whilst their bedrooms are rented out to day-tenants. While the film does not allude to it, the mother's aggression is embedded within the patriarchal system where she has had to learn to fight her way to survive. The disappearance of her husband's dentures reflects the loss of his voice/agency. The mother showers a litany of invectives on her unemployed son-in-law who skulks around in the house, potentially dispirited by not being able to put his education to use in a racist and xenophobic labour market. His wife chides Chand for showing off her BA degree, for education never really rescued working-class immigrants. Chand should feel lucky, she says, to have found work in the factory washing and ironing dirty hotel towels even though the former never gets to see the money she earns. Clearly, the sister-in-law has internalized racist stereotypes of working-class immigrant women being economically unproductive, accepting the marginalization and, hence, vulnerability of her subject position. As well as being the sole male breadwinner in the family, Rocky has the added burden to finance his brother's immigration from India. While the narrative exclusively centres the immigrant community, occasional images of a depressed and dejected Rocky stepping out of posh offices located in tall and imposing high-rise buildings indicate his exclusion from white professional spaces of wealth, power and privilege. I draw on critical race feminism (Mohanty et al.1991; Narayan 1997) to make the point that Rocky is a victim of white patriarchal culture where all social relations of his ethnic group are subordinated in the interest of the dominant culture.

Chand's battering by Rocky is embedded, therefore, in the coming together of multi-layered, intersecting and interlocking forms of structural and institutional oppression, that is, patriarchy and the racist, sexist and xenophobic wider community. Together, they generate the conditions for abuse to take place in the 'violent space' within immigrant families where men get away by controlling and coercing their wives, who having just travelled transnationally have little knowledge of or access to private or public structures of support. Drawing on Narayan (1995), Chand could be seen as a 'mail-order-bride' who unwittingly makes herself vulnerable to spousal abuse by agreeing to marry a perfect stranger for reasons of socio-economic prestige that comes with the move to the developed West. It is the breakdown of this dream—of success, comfort, glamor and privilege—that the film takes pain to elucidate. Chand's physical battering leads to the loss of self-respect and dignity, causing acute mental agony and depression. Whilst alone, she indulges in self-talk, comforting herself by reciting poetry learnt from her mother (Gick Grewal). This along with the narrative of the cobra snake is symptomatic of Chand's mental breakdown. In a study on the psychological and emotional wounds of immigrant South Asian women in the United States, Diya Kallilvayalil comments on the paucity of research on the long-lasting and severe emotional ramifications of domestic violence that include anxiety, depression, post-traumatic stress disorder and suicide (2014: 81). The silence domestic violence owing to notions of family honour and tradition is exacerbated by the shame and stigma associated with the question of mental health. Together they encourage the culture of 'double silence' on these issues so that neither do the victims seek help from social services (Ahmad et al. 2009; Narayan 1995) nor do they reach out to psychological counselling services. Drawing, however, on Kallilvayalil (p. 88) who gestures towards the use of cultural discourse as a means for coping with domestic abuse, I contend that faced with recurring psychological humiliation and physical trauma, and after the initial emotions of shock, fear, denial and helplessness, Chand undergoes psychological distancing from reality. She lapses into a dream world, an imaginary space, which she fills up with her mother's poetry and fairy tales about the mythic snake coming to her rescue.

Conclusion

In this chapter I have investigated post-colonial diasporic cinematic representations of subversive Indian femininity through an analysis of Deepa Mehta's feminist quartet. The attempt has been to cleave apart conventional constructions of Indian women to make the point that traditional hetero-normative familial and societal structures are at the root of women's subjugation. Through a close reading of *Fire, Earth, Water* and *Heaven on Earth*, I have examined transgressive Indian women's decolonizing of their bodies, minds, sexualities and labour. I regard Mehta's films as brilliant pieces of cinematic work, which shed light on the complex and multi-layered ways in which human relations undergo profound transformation as people shift identities and acquire new subject positions through a process of introspection, transgression and movement across borders—be they psychological, temporal or geographic. Mehta's films are anti-colonial in the way they probe gendered, classed, raced and sexual power relations within both the centre–periphery binary and internal relations of domination and subordination. They are anti-oppression in the ways they illuminate the multiple interlocking structures of oppression lived by people regardless of whether they belong to dominant or subordinate positions. It is thus that I understand Mehta's use of cinema as a tool for articulating her post-colonial dissidence and resistance which she does from her interstitial, exilic and diasporic location.

References

Agnew, V. 2009. 'Immigrant Women and Violence.' In *Racialized Migrant Women in Canada: Essays on Health, Violence and Equity*, edited by Vijay Agnew. Toronto, Canada: University of Toronto Press.

Ahmad, F. et al. 2009. '"Why Doesn't She Seek Help for Partner Abuse?" An Exploratory Study with South Asian Immigrant Women.' *Social Science and Medicine* 69 (4): 613–22.

Anderson, B. 1991. *Imagined Communities: Reflections on the Origin and the Spread of Nationalism*. London: Verso.

Burton, D.F. 2013. 'Fire, Water and the Goddess: The Films of Deepa Mehta and Satyajit Ray as Critiques of Hindu Patriarchy.' *Journal of Religion & Film* 17 (2).

Caldwell, T. 2011. 'River of Life and Death: Women, Religion, Power, and Purity in "Water".' *Screen Education* (64): 115–20.

Chaudhury, S. 2009. 'Snake Charmers and Child Brides: Deepa Mehta's *Water*, Exotic Representation, and the Cross-cultural Spectatorship of South Asian Migrant Cinema.' *South Asian Popular Culture* 7 (1), 7–20.

Crenshaw, K. 1991. 'Mapping the Margins: Intersectionality, Identity Politics, and Violence against Women of Color'. *Stanford Law Review* 43 (6): 1241–99.

Dasgupta, S. 2000. 'Charting the Course: An Overview of Domestic Violence in the South Asian Community in the United States.' *Journal of Social Distress and the Homeless* 9 (3): 173–85.

Ferguson, A. 1981. 'Patriarchy, Sexual Identity, and the Sexual Revolution.' *Signs* 7 (1): 158–72.

Fernandez, M. 1997. 'Domestic Violence by Extended Family Members in India: Interplay of Gender and Generation.' *Journal of Interpersonal Violence* 12 (3): 433–55.

Gangoli, G. and M. Rew. 2011. 'Mothers-in-law Against Daughters-in-law: Domestic Violence and Legal Discourse Around Mother-in-law Violence Against Daughters-in-law in India.' *Women's Studies International Forum* 34 (5): 420–29.

Gellner, E. 1983. *Nations and Nationalisms*. Oxford: Blackwell.

George, P. and M. Rashidi. 2014. 'Domestic Violence in South Asian Communities in the GTA: Critical Perspectives of Community Activists and Service Providers.' *The Journal of Critical Anti-Oppressive Social Inquiry* (1): 67–78.

Goel, R. 2005. 'Sita's Trousseau: Restorative Justice, Domestic Violence and South Asian Culture.' *Violence Against Women* 11 (5): 639–65.

Gopinath, G. 1988. 'On Fire', *GLQ: A Journal of Lesbian and Gay Studies* 4 (4): 631–36.

Hall, S. 1990. 'Cultural Identity and Diaspora.' In *Identity, Community, Culture, Difference*, edited by Jonathan Rutherford. London: Lawrence and Wishart.

Hobsbawm, E. 1990. *Nations and Nationalism Since 1780: Programme, Myth, Reality*. Cambridge: Cambridge UniversityPress.

Hobsbawm E. and T. Ranger. 1983. *The Invention of Tradition*. Cambridge: Cambridge University Press.

hooks, b. 1990. *Yearning: Race, Gender, and Cultural Politics*. Boston, MA: South End Press.

Kallivayalil, D. 2007. 'Mental and Emotional Wounds of South Asian Women.' In *Body Evidence: Intimate Violence Against South Asian Women in America*, edited by Shamita Das Gupta. New Jersey: Rutgers University Press.

———. 2010. 'Narratives of Suffering of South Asian Immigrant Survivors of Domestic Violence.' *Violence Against Women* 16 (7): 789–811.

Kedourie, E. 1993. *Nationalism*. Massachusetts: Blackwell.

Khorana, S. 2009. 'Maps and Movies: Talking with Deepa Mehta.' *Bright Lights Film Journal* 63 (February).

Levitin, J. 2001. 'Deepa Mehta as Transnational Filmmaker, or You Can't Go Home Again.' In *North of Everything: English-Canadian Cinema Since*

1980, edited by William Beard and Jerry White. Edmonton: University of Alberta.

Levitin, J. et al. 2003. *Women Filmmakers: Refocusing*. Vancouver: University of British Columbia.

Liao, M.S. 2006. 'Domestic Violence Among Asian India Immigrant Women: Risk Factors, Acculturation, and Intervention.' *Women and Therapy* 29 (1–2).

Majithia, S. 2009. 'Melodrama and the Secular Subject.' Dissertation presented to the Faculty of the Graduate School of Cornell University.

Menjivar, C. and O. Salcido. 2002. 'Immigrant Women and Domestic Violence: Common Experiences in Different Countries.' *Gender and Society* 16 (6): 898–920.

Mohanty, C.T., A. Russo and L. Torres (eds.). 1991. *Third World Feminism and the Politics of Feminism*. Bloomington & Indianapolis: Indiana University Press.

Moodley, S. 2003. 'Postcolonial Feminisms Speaking Through an "Accented" Cinema: The Construction of Indian Women in Films of Mira Nair and Deepa Mehta.' *Agenda: Empowering Women for Gender Equity*, 58 (African Feminism Three): 66–75.

Moorti, S. 2000. 'Inflamed Passions: Fire, the Woman Question, and the Policing of Cultural Borders.' *Genders* (32): 1–58.

Mukherjee, T. 2008. 'Deepa Mehta's Film Water: The Power of the Dialectical Image.' *Canadian Journal of Film Studies* 17 (2): 35–47.

Narayan, U. 1995. 'Male Order Brides: Immigrant Women, Domestic Violence and Immigration Law.' *Hypatia: Feminist Ethics and Social Policy* 10 (1, Part 1): 104–19.

———. 1997. *Dislocating Cultures: Identities, Traditions, and Third World Feminism*. New York: Routledge.

Naficy, H. 2001. *An Accented Cinema: Exilic and Diasporic Filmmaking*. Princeton, NJ: Princeton University Press.

Ray, S. 2000. *En-gendering India: Women and Nation in Colonial and Postcolonial Narratives*. Durham and London: Duke University Press.

Razak, S. 2003. 'A Violent Culture or Culturalized Violence? Feminist Narratives of Sexual Violence Against South Asian Women.' *Studies in Practical Philosophy* 3 (1): 80–104.

Sidhwa, B. 1991. *Cracking India*. Minneapolis, MN: Milkweed Editions.

Smith, A.D. 1986. *The Ethnic Origin of Nationalism*. Oxford: Blackwell.

———. 1995. 'Gastronomy or Geology? The Role of Nationalism in the Reconstruction of Nations'. *Nations and Nationalism* 1 (1), 3–23.

William, P. and L. Chrisman (eds.). 1994. *Colonial Discourse and Post-colonial Theory*. New York: Columbia University Press.

Yuval-Davis, N. 1997. *Gender and Nation*. London: SAGE Publications.

Film References

Mehta, D. 1996. *Fire*. Trial by Fire Films Inc. and Kaleidoscope Entertainment.

———. 1998. *Earth*. Cracking the Earth Films Inc. and Jhamu Sugandh Productions.

———. 2005. *Water*. Deepa Mehta Films, Flagship International and David Hamilton Productions.

———. 2008. *Heaven on Earth*. Astral Media, Canadian Broadcasting Corporation (CBC) and Hamilton Mehta Productions.

CHAPTER 10

Sounding Dystopia: Anurag Kashyap's Films and Relocation of Popular Tropes

Madhuja Mukherjee

This chapter studies Anurag Kashyap's films as interplay of many cross-references. It shows how Kashyap produces a complicated narrative about social degeneration by locating his films in both suburban Mumbai and in the suburbs (and small towns) of India, which is intensified through his aural and visual designs. While films such as *Dev.D* (2009) and *No Smoking* (2007) have generated scholarly debates, this chapter focuses on his style, which may be described as 'neo-noir', and illustrates in what way it develops through a range of films. It especially discusses *Paanch* (unreleased), *No Smoking* and *Ugly* (2014) to illustrate how conflicting zones (such as gritty outdoors and fantastic interiors) produce narratives about dystopian cities (like Mumbai), which are marked by discontents, despair and dread. This chapter proposes that with Kashyap (and his associates) the focus of the 'cinematic city' shifts from the town to suburban Mumbai. In addition, through a close-reading of *Dev.D* and *Gangs of Wasseypur* (GoW) Part 1 and 2 (2012), it draws attention to Kashyap's method of bringing together paradoxical sounds and situations, themes, spaces and characters and the manner in which cinephila fabricates a network of reflective images and sound tropes. Briefly, this chapter considers Kashyap's emergent style and its import in relation to 'mainstream Bollywood'.

Film-maker Anurag Kashyap became part of public debates at the time when *Paanch* (unreleased), made during 2000, was not handed Film Certification by the (Indian) Censor Board for six reasons.[1] Apparently, the film celebrated violence, produced a blueprint for criminal activities (especially depicted killing of the police) and presented a group of alienated youth who unapologetically did drugs and sex. In fact, the film seemed to have no positive characters; moreover, it used double meaning words (which had sexual connotations) and, more importantly, it carried no 'social message'. While, *Paanch* was viewed and reviewed by the Censor Board, it was eventually not released in the theatres since Kashyap and his team disregarded board's advice to re-edit and re-shoot certain sections of the film. With regard to this controversy veteran ad film-maker Prahlad Kakkar said the following (in 2001): '[I]t's the way half the world is. If the censors ban it, it's going to be the biggest Indian underground cult film.'[2] Indeed, *Paanch* (besides the other unreleased film *Gandu*, Qaushiq Mukherjee [popularly known as Q]) attained a cult status in time; furthermore, it has circulated (amongst the youth particularly) through piracy and other forms of unauthorized transactions.[3] In retrospect, *Paanch* seems particularly significant because of the ways in which it introduced a definite and recognizable 'Anurag Kashyap style' in terms of its mise en scène (including the use of the light, camera movement and performance), situations (unpredictable and realistic events), spaces (e.g., the city underbelly/police station and extensive night shots), characterization (or exploration of a number of social outsiders and the 'femme fatale') and a remarkably different world view compared to contemporary Bollywood.[4]

The creation of conflicting interior spaces (e.g., the high rise apartment and the garage space that appears like 'underground' in *Paanch*) indicates Kashyap's deep-seated concerns; in addition, such zones are often juxtaposed with (exterior) shots of the city. For instance, *Black Friday* (2007, in India), one of Kashyap's most controversial films, explored such multiplicity with great virtuosity.[5] Likewise, in one of the early sequences of *Paanch*—in which the out of work band members decide take up a job in a local cafe—the following scene crops up. In the foreground there is a table and behind it doors and windows which present a slice of the different registers that make a dense cityscape. An office staff (wearing a blue shirt) enters the cafe/frame, cut to a shot (close-up) of glasses (being lifted by Pondy) and then cut to a (composite) shot of the client and Pondy; the client orders an 'egg, half-fried', which is followed by a tête-à-tête.

Client:	'One egg half-fried. Listen! The yellow part should not be broken.'
Pondy:	'Yes sir.'
Client:	'Listen! The white part should not be brown [deep fried].'
	[Pondy nods, and is about to leave. Camera remains stationary, we see them in low light, and against a sharp backlight].
Client:	'Okay Listen! When you put salt, put on the white part, not on the yellow.
	Hey listen! The egg should not become hard.
	And, Listen! It should be freshly hatched by the chicken.'
Pondy:	'Sir, the chicken is called Champa, is it okay with you?'
	[The man slaps him.]

While the main plot of the film is intensely dark and portrays the impossible aspirations of a band, as well as focuses on their gradual involvement with crime, the braiding of such comic moments (which are spontaneous and deploy deliriously repetitive dialogues or gestures to provoke comic intensities) that create narrative pauses has become part of Kashyap's style of writing and shot taking. The stretching of time, which holds back the narrative tension in order to draw attention to the everyday city, is evident in *Black Friday* and *Ugly* (2014) as well. In fact, while commenting on the (now well-known) interrogation scene from *Ugly*, Kashyap clarified that it was 'improvised ... to show police apathy and the power trip';[6] furthermore, he elaborated on his style of shooting by suggesting:

> I'm more excited about working on location. I decide my shots when I'm on location. I even change things against the plan. I adapt my whole shooting style based on the area I'm shooting in. For me the geography of the location matters, mannerism of actors matters.
>
> I like to observe people. I like to understand where they're coming from. The whole idea behind the *chase scene in Black Friday was to show where these people came from. You see their lifestyle, you see where they live, at the edge of a bloody nallah, at the edge of economic progress.* [italics added] They don't have place to walk, they're crammed together. That's where they come from and that explains their frustration, and discontent.[7]

In fact, issues of 'discontent' and 'dread' are curiously perceptible in the scene in which Luke (Kay Kay Menon) and his group decide loot Nikhil's father. Meanwhile, Nikhil (at whose garage the group would rehearse and also the person who had agreed to be in hiding in order to be part of their [fake] kidnapping plan) has been killed by Luke, in his rage. Thus, they enter Nikhil's (father's) house and begin to vandalize the place. Then, unexpectedly, each member vanishes into the dark interiors, individually. After this tension is built, it is revealed that Joy has taken out food from the freezer, and everyone else has joined him. This comic interjection, however, is fiercely unsettled as Nikhil's father returns home. First, Luke tells him that Nikhil is back, then they tickle him and ask him to dance; finally, at the point when the old and weak man cries out (in protest), they strangulate him with a telephone wire. Set in the dark interiors, this feverish reversal of the feast into a murderous carrousel highlighted the grotesqueness of the everyday.

City of Discontents: Contemporary Worlds, Smut and Noise

I

Paanch presented a dystopian world that was inspired by the Joshi-Abhyankar murders that happened in Pune 25 years earlier.[8] The case involved the killing of nine people strangulated by five 'normal' college-going students. The film highlighted the involvement of the middle-class and the aspiring youth, in abysmal crime and violence, which emerged out of a wide range of wants and desperation. Additionally, while the accounts of the Joshi-Abhyankar murder cases are incorporated in the film, these are presented as ordinary and accidental incidents.[9] The film opens with the story of five young people who belong to a rock band called 'Parasites', and thereafter, it portrays their gradual descent into criminal activities beginning with the first killing of Nikhil, which, eventually, snowballs into a series of dreadful murders. More important, in the context of cinematic explorations, are the two indoor locations—a Mumbai apartment and a garage space—which become crucial in the manner in which these 'reintroduce' the 'noir' style.[10] For instance, while Luke, Murgi, Joy, Pondy and Shiuli endure a nightlife in a claustrophobic Mumbai apartment and jam in a garage space, an expressive set design, hand-held camera movements, swish pans, use of blue filter and reflective performances craft an environment of deep anxiety and fear; in addition, these effectively produce certain recognizable (narrative) patterns and (audio-visual) motifs which have become powerful aspects of what may be described as the 'Anurag Kashyap style'.

As a matter of fact, at that time *Indian Today* (2001) published an article regarding the *Paanch* controversy; it compared the film with the 'Bollywood' blockbuster *Dil Chahta Hai* (DCH; Farhan Akhtar, 2001) and underlined the differences.[11] While

DCH entails the story of three young men, the film's first half is shot in Mumbai and in the exotic landscape of Goa, and the second half shows the urban and metallic cityscape of Sydney. A lifestyle film of sorts, it presented a new cartography of leisure, which comprised music, dance, fashion, travel and romance (Mazumdar 2007). After its release DCH became a cult, prefigured specific fashions tendencies and introduced a consumption culture, which was somewhat fanciful at that time. Mazumdar (2007) has categorized such Bollywood films as films with 'panoramic interiors' in relation to the films about 'gangland Bombay'. I have analysed elsewhere, how Mazumdar reworks what M. Madhava Prasad (1998) had described as 'feudal-family romances' and as the 'Amitabh Bachchan movies' (Mukherjee 2009). Furthermore, Prasad's (1998) landmark book-length study of the ideology of Hindi film also examined Hindi middle-class films of the 1970s. Prasad proposed that the 'feudal space' is transferred in these (middle-class) films 'in the space of modernity' at the time during which the class begins to consider itself beyond the 'community grid'. While women's issues became decisive, problems of urban spaces, housing, jobs, etc. or middle-class' encounter with the (expanding) city, along with its ambiguities, became significant subjects of these films. In connection to this, one may suggest that a set of contemporary films deploying realistic aesthetics (in terms of the setting and narrative logic) caters to the neo-middle classes located in the big cities.[12] While Gopal (2011) has elaborated upon the crises of the 'neo-middle classes', the films that address such predicaments are described as 'multiplex films' by the film industry.[13] This renewed category of films, nevertheless, is deeply linked with questions of class, work, leisure and spaces of (rapid) urban developments. This chapter frames the films — with an imagined niche audience — as the 'neo-middle cinema'.

II

The growth of multiplex cinemas is forcefully connected with liberal economic policies that encourage new lifestyles and consumer habits. The neoliberal economic policies of the government become apparent through the growing connections between spatial remodelling, inflow of multinational investments, changes in our everyday living, consumption habits and emergence of media spaces (Appadurai 1995). Therefore, within the setting of urban developments and the growing scale of consumption, new systems for leisure—like the multiplexes within the shopping malls—cater to neo-middle-class needs. Moreover, compared to the previous systems of taxation for the single theatres, the official policies to permit the multiplexes to deploy 'flexible' ticket pricing as well as low or even zero degree of taxation during the first five years posit the multiplexes in an advantageous position compared to the old single theatres located in the older parts of the (big) cities and the suburbs (Mukherjee 2014). Besides, one may argue that the multiplexes have initiated unique demands and neoteric spaces (for consumptions) and invite new generation of viewers who are otherwise exposed to the cinemas of the world/art-house cinemas (through TV networks and easy downloads) and are cinephiles of sorts. Moreover, multiplexes address peoples (educated urban middle classes) who are significant consumers of contemporary Indian-English literature and are inclined to display present-day leisure cultures in spaces of high consumption. Thus, beyond the mainstream blockbusters (popularized by Dharma Productions, Yash Raj Films, etc.) as well as the hard-hitting action flicks (produced by Ram Gopal Varma and company), a new type of cinema, with relatively smaller budgets, produced outside the networks of the large-scale production houses, and involving a 'reality effect', is widely held particularly by the neo-middle classes.

Such neo-middle-class films would tentatively include small-budget, independently produced and intensely debated films, such as *Ek Hasina Thi* (Sriram Raghavan, 2004), *Hazaaron Khwaishein Aisi* (Sudhir Misra, 2005, in India), *Being Cyrus* (Homi Adajania, 2005), *Johnny Gaddaar* (Sriram Raghavan, 2007), *No Smoking* (Anurag Kashyap, 2007), *Miss Lovely* (Ashim Ahluwalia, 2012) and *Ugly* (Anurag Kashyap, 2014), or even more popular films, such as *Bheja Fry* (Sagar Ballary, 2007), *Honeymoon Travels Pvt. Ltd.* (Reema Kagti, 2007), *Aamir* (Raj Kumar Gupta, 2008), *Mumbai Meri Jaan* (Nishikant Kamat, 2008), *A Wednesday* (Neeraj Pandey, 2008), *Delhi Belly* (Abhinay Deo, 2011), *B.A. Pass* (Ajay Bahl, 2013, in India) and so on.

Within this category, one may also consider Dibakar Banerjee's films such as *Khosla Ka Ghosla!* (2006), *Oye Lucky! Lucky Oye!* (2008) and *LSD: Love, Sex Aur Dhokha* (2010); Vishal Bhardwaj's creative transformations of Shakespearean tragedies along with *Kaminey* (2009); Kiran Rao's *Dhobi Ghat* (2011) as well as international successes such as *Udaan* (Vikraditya Motwane, 2010), *Ship of Theseus* (Anand Gandhi, 2013, in India), *The Lunchbox* (Ritesh Batra, 2013) and so on. Such films negotiate emergent production strategies (by imagining a niche audience), international distribution systems and alternative exhibition networks (including film festivals, multiplex releases and TV premieres) and—one may argue—are deeply marked by the ideology of the neo-middle classes.

As mentioned earlier, Sangita Gopal has considered the contemporary middle classes, their consumption cultures and their crises in relation to specific 'horror' flicks (like *Bhoot*, Ram Gopal Varma, 2003), which tackle new 'habitations of fear'. Indeed, a range of films such as *Mumbai Meri Jaan*, *A Wednesday*, *Aamir* and so on (and also political narratives like *Hazaaron Khwaishein Aisi*) present the anxiety and fear about impending (terrorist) attacks. Such films are deemed as successful 'multiplex films' alongside certain chilling neo-noir films and urban-crime thrillers, such as *Ek Chalis Ki Last Local* (Sanjay Khanduri, 2007), *Manorama Six Feet Under* (Navdeep Singh, 2007), *Kaminey* and so on, which present a disintegrating city and explore its nightlife. Moreover, 'puzzle' narratives (or plots with disparate nodal points) like *Ship of Theseus* as well as self-reflective comedies such as *Bheja Fry*, *Honeymoon Travels Pvt. Ltd.*, *Delhi Belly* and so on portray an evolving curve. As a matter of fact, *Rocket Singh: Salesman of the Year* (Shimit Amin, 2009) and a recent film *Piku* (Dibakar Banerjee, 2015) appear like self-conscious revisions of what has been studied as Hrishikesh Mukherjee/Basu Chatterjee's 'middle-class cinema'. Truly, the erstwhile blockbuster frame (of the festival releases and/or single theatre releases that would enjoy a 'silver jubilee') is perhaps only represented by Salman Khan's productions such as *Dabangg* (Abhinav Kashyap, 2010) or perhaps through a film like *Talaash* (Reema Kagti, 2012), and Milan Luthria's *Once Upon a Time in Mumbaai* (2010), which recall both the period and the narrative address of former mainstream Hindi films.

III

Anurag Kashyap's films, one suggests, are both connected and segregated from this contemporary graph in the ways in which he explores darkly noir narratives, set in the dystopian city. While Naremore (2008) discusses how noir has a long-drawn (ambiguous) history and has been popular over a long period of time and across territories, responding to his 'dark' style, Kashyap said the following:[14]

> [T]hat is called the noir kind of cinema. It is a term coined by French critics for dark cinema that comes out of depression — where everything is little heightened, darker, shadowy…. It has alleys, a femme fatale….

Writing about the contemporary 'Bombay noir', Gopalan (2013) argues that these films unsettle established definitions; moreover, she suggests that 'Bombay noir' reinvents film noir by mixing other generic elements (such as urban fringe films, crime-thrillers, cruel and action films) and are possibly part of global cinephilia. While Gopalan discusses *Johnny Gaddaar* in length, this chapter illustrates how Anurag Kashyap's films work within the larger rubric of worldwide cinephila and re-fabricate the noir frame. 'Noir' one may argue is in itself a cinephilic attempt, and contemporary (Bombay) noir reconfirms the relationship between film noir and cinephilia. A thorough study of a set of recent films (mentioned earlier) shows how the noir tendency is linked with cinephilia and that, indeed, 'cinephilia is central to film noir' (Creekmur 2013).

No Smoking, for instance, has been described as 'descent into morality' and becomes a reflection on Kashyap's deteriorating personal relationships.[15] K (K for 'Kashyap' and K for 'Kafka'), the protagonist of the film, is caught in a claustrophobic married life and workspace, which pushes him towards further severities. In order to save his dysfunctional marriage, K eventually decides to give up smoking and agrees to join the 'Prayogshala' (a workshop/programme to quit smoking that is controlled by Baba Bangali), which eventually turns out to be a momentous trap. In the end, thus, the soul and body are separated, while K remains suspended in a state of limbo. Moreover, the dreariness of this plot is presented through an intense exploration of a creative mise en scène and is realized my means of an effective set design as well as the fluid/staccato camera movements and edit effects. With regard to *No Smoking*, Mazumdar (2010: 176) suggests that

> [t]he architectural plan for *No Smoking* was a very important concern for Anurag Kashyap right from the inception of the film. Through surrealist sequences combined with a plethora of electronic, glass, and steel surfaces, *No Smoking* foregrounds the two most important spaces of the film. The first is K's penthouse designed to evoke a cold modernist aesthetic. The second is the world of Baba Bengali, a 'primitive' world of the underground set in the Dharavi slums of Bombay.

In effect, K's home is crafted through a minimalist decor, straight lines, glass, mirrors and other reflective surfaces, along with abstract black and white paintings, and a colour palette that uses black, blue-green and (somewhat sporadically) red to underscore the theme of isolation, (self) obsession and bleakness. Therefore, as K and Anjali discuss divorce in their high-rise apartment, we perceive the alluring and enigmatic city of Mumbai as a backdrop. Eventually, however, as K decides to go the 'Prayogshala', an elaborate play of mise en scène presents 'an other' Mumbai. As K drives through the crowd and slum area, the film presents Mumbai (suburbs) and its overgrowth through K's point of view. K encounters a world comprising soiled material (like jute), paper mashie, parched walls, junk metals, dirt, oil, filth and people (especially Muslims) — a muggy environment, in short — which has remained, by and large, unaddressed in the mainstream blockbusters. K's dark suit and dark glasses, thus, seem gross in comparison to the bare torsos of working people. Furthermore, *No Smoking* thickens a dystopian environment by producing spaces like 'Siberia' in which K plunges through his nightmares as well as the 'real' city that involves extensive location scenes through which K's traverses before he may enter the laboratory (Prayogshala). Kashyap's re-figuration of Mumbai is unique in the way that he first builds a city that has many levels; thereafter, he further divides such multiplicities by way of juxtaposing many (contradictory) places and situations.

The Kafkaesque world, therefore, evolves as K first descends or physically goes down the stairways, and yet again, runs into women (whose faces remain covered) and un-sculpted male bodies, and later, when he tries to escape through the doors (with moss-green glass panes) and eventually returns to Baba's space. Clearly, the narrative of disquiet and gloom is worked out through a massive exploration of mise en scène. Hence, while Mumbai appears alluring and elusive from his apartment, the deployment of an enormous set design reveals the density of (world's 'largest' slum) Dharavi. Consequently, the bird's eye view (or distancing) is reverted into an intense engagement with the city underbelly (through compelling camera movements), which effectually presents Kashyap's imagination of Dharavi just as we perceive faces, people, junk, waste, grime and noises in a manner in which it seems uncannily real and deeply disorienting. Besides, the physical 'descent' — as opposed to the uses of the elevator to K's office — through several levels, for instance, from the carpet factory to K meeting women sitting on the stairs until he finds Baba Bangali, becomes crucial. This zigzag movement stages imageries, which appear like vertically flipped shots of the horizontal growth of Mumbai (see Mehta [2004] and *Jaane Bhi Do Yaaro*, Kundan Shah, 1983). The movement, thus, is disturbing and depicts a world in oppositions and is probably comparably only to Sudhir Patwardhan's paintings.[16] Indeed, the grimness of the plot is impressively presented through the mise en scène and especially through the set design. Kashyap, and the art director Wasiq Khan, produced an outline of unease by creating several layers and surfaces, as well as through objects, textures and faces, which illustrates the murkiness of life.

This world, however, is not a 'real' world. It is a perception of the city that seems to be controlled and policed, yet, constantly threatens to grow out of control. Contradictory themes, which include moral policing/failure of state apparatus, as well as obsession with (new) electronic gadgets/media surveillance, are few of the major concerns of Kashyap. In one of the most engaging sequences in *No Smoking*, therefore, at the point when K refuses to sign the cheque, Baba Bangali brings out a VHS tape that has recorded all his actions until the moment he entered the 'Prayogshala'. Commenting on surveillance, Kashyap underlines the function of media manipulation (especially through TV, tape, mobile phones and CCTV); besides, the scene also portrays Kashyap's obsessions with the medium itself as well as with his cinephilic self-reflections by locating K's tape amongst a range of other tapes (which include those of Kay Kay Menon, K.L. Shaigal, Kunti Shah and so on). Thus, as the anxiety about surveillance continues, and K finally gets out of the ghetto/Dharavi/'Prayogshala', he tries to light a cigarette while driving his car. At this moment, a tremendously powerful bang splits the windscreen and yet, at that point K's hearing abilities become impaired. The 'silent' scene in effect underscores the density of sounds—of cars and crowd moving, glass breaking, people shouting, police talking, lighter clicking—and produces an intense picture of everyday Mumbai. Indeed, *No Smoking* highlights Kashyap's passionate engagements with cinematic narrative and design which include locations, settings, faces, music, sound and noise.

IV

Ugly is a retake on Mumbai's underbelly, involving peoples, places, objects, idiom, gestures and movements which create a thick tapestry of cross-references. The plot of the film revolves around the disappearance of a 10-year-old girl, Kali, whose parents are separated. While both her parents and her stepfather (a police officer) are locked in a long drawn battle concerning egotism, the story of the little girl is seemingly lost as the plot of kidnapping and extortion thickens with other issues. In *Ugly*, the city is organized through many registers, it is under control (through technology and surveillance), visceral and edgy, and, yet, simultaneously remains deceptively outside the controlling power of the gaze and the state machinery. While surveillance, regulation and state mechanism have been critiqued by Kashyap in a range of films, in *Ugly* these subjects are both presented as a part of the harsh routine and elaborated upon through thoughtful and insightful commentary on faith or lack of it, love, jealously, pride, greed, vengeance and hopelessness.

Shot in Andheri East, and concerning a struggling actor Rahul Bhat (also the real name of the actor and Kashyap's 'muse'), the film presents an array of egotist and frustrated characters, who lose the plot as it were (as in the whereabouts of the lost child) and become part of an interlaced kidnapping plan in which stakes become higher at every turn. The issue of the child's disappearance, thus, gradually recedes both from the plot and from the narrative, and by means of disparate technologies (such as land phones, old TV sets, computers, laptops, DVD players, headphones, internet, CCTV and GPS) the film effectively shows the manner in which gadgets (like iPhones) are our new fascinations and the fashion in which these circumscribe our existence. [17] And, thus, in the end, ironically, a police officer finds the clue about the missing child through old paper files; moreover, the climatic sequence foregrounds both the theme (mediated everyday) and the state in which the machinery functions. In last sequence, Shoumik (the police officer) enquires with Shalini (his wife) as to why she had asked for 65 million—from her father—even when the 'kidnapper' had demanded 50 million. 'What were you planning do with it?' enquires Shoumik, and to this Shalini replies, 'I was planning to get everything, which you have failed to give me,' and also asks, 'Why did you marry me?' The intimidating mood of this scene is produced through claustrophobic interiors and overwhelming close-ups. Having lost the key to freedom (since her friend Rakhee eventually betrays her), and out of yawning frustration, Shalini shoots Shoumik as he goes out to trace the (fake) 'kidnapper' (her brother, Siddhant). In the long run, a heavily bleeding Shoumik, held erect by his men (the police force), arrives at the spot (while the entire force awaits him to finally perform vengeance). After Shoumik breaks in, the interior space (lit with yellow and blue tinted lights) shows Siddhant dancing frantically in his (red) underwear, with a string of notes attached to his waist. This scene is further intensified through Siddhant's act of recording 'selfies' (on an iPhone) in frenzy. As time is stretched through slow motion, the hard-hitting music underscores the ugly side of contemporary lives. [18]

City, Cinema and Cinephilia: The Dark Side of Development, Patterns and Motifs

I

The city—beginning with Walter Benjamin's landmark work on Paris as well as Henri Lefebvre's, David Harvey's and Michel de Certeau's seminal methods to reconsider public spaces and cultures—has been the locus of a range of debates and creative engagements. In this chapter, I wish to draw attention to the 'cinematic city' and specifically to 'our experiences' of the city through the screen as well as through the memory of specific cities—such as Paris, Venice, Mumbai, Kolkata and so on—that are produced and evoked through cinematic time-space (AlSayyad 2000; Prakash 2010). In case of mainstream 'Bombay' melodramas, for instance, the city has figured repeatedly and forcefully in a range of films beginning with *Kismet* (Gyan Mukherjee, 1943), *Neecha Nagar* (Chetan Anand, 1946) and so on and then followed by what I have described as a string of 'early noir' films, for example, *Baazi* (Guru Dutt, 1951), *Taxi Driver* (Chetan Anand, 1954), *C.I.D.* (Raj Khosla, 1956) and so on.[19] The noir visual style was, as well, perceptible in certain melodramas including *Shree 420* (Raj Kapoor, 1955), *Pyaasa* (Guru Dutt, 1957), *Kalapani* (Raj Khosla, 1958), *Howrah Bridge* (Shakti Samanta, 1958), etc.[20] Many of these films present a shady city, marked with murk, filth and blood, in which despairing people struggle post-independence bedlams.[21] Indeed, a noir-type mise en scène — for instance, low key lights and long dark shadows, silhouetted figures emerging from nowhere, actors performing scenes totally in the dark as well as unsettling close-ups of their faces, angular shots and unclear reflections — crafted an environment of claustrophobia, disquiet and despair even in romantic situations. Besides, intimidating mood is generated through extensive night shots, through sharp juxtapositioning of visual extremes between night and day, and, additionally, by way of meandering shots through undefined streets and mansions set against the 'black' or 'noir' sky. Therefore, fostering the idea of a cinematic city, one suggests that the 'Indian noir' is the dark side of Indian melodramas.

Prakash (2010: 3) suggests that '[m]odernism was a uniquely metropolitan phenomenon.... But a shadow always hung over the modernist halo'. Moreover, Ranjani Mazumdar (2009) in her article 'Cosmopolitan Dreams' argues:[22]

> It is indeed intriguing that five years before the first film of the French New Wave, Navketan's *Taxi Driver* used the clair camera to affectionately map the city of Bombay in a manner that was quite unusual at that time. Unlike *Baazi's* studio iconography of Bombay, *Taxi Driver* was overwhelmingly shot in the public spaces of the city. The use of the taxi as a mode of vision provided the film with a wanderlust aesthetic that combined the movement of the taxi with the possibilities of new camera technology.... [Moreover] [t]he nightclub is the site where some of the important action sequences unfold and Sylvie is quite central to these sequences....[23]

Such settings of cosmopolitan modernism and the complexities of urban growth, thus, become a powerful backdrop in our attempt to understand contemporary neo-noir films produced by Anurag Kashyap.

II

In relation to issues of early noir and contemporary noir discussed so far, this chapter proposes that the 'Bombay' films (meaning films both produced from and made about Mumbai), which were made post-1990s, reinforce the noir angst by shifting the city centre — and the locus of the narrative — from the town to suburban Mumbai and effectually re-count the history of overgrowth and disquiet. Indeed, one may argue that Anurag Kashyap's imagination and representation of Mumbai suburban life through a particular style of narration (involving locations, milieu, characters, situations, recognizable settings, gestures, sounds, etc.) indicate a decisive shift in the locations of mainstream films. The post-1990s films, including *Dharavi* (Sudhir Mishra, 1992), *Satya* (Ram Gopal Varma, 1998), etc., mark a crucial departure from the pervasive Mumbai iconography, which were produced through plethora of Hindi films since the 1950s (including *Taxi Driver* and *Kaal Bazaar*, for instance), through the 1970s and the 1980s blockbusters, such as *Deewaar* (Yash Chopra, 1975), *Shaan* (Ramesh Sippy, 1980), etc., as well as by means of middle-class films, such as *Rajnigandha* (Basu Chatterjee, 1974), *Gaman* (Muzaffar Ali, 1978), *Ghar* (Manik Chatterjee, 1978), *Gharaonda* (Bhimsain Khurana, 1977), *Manzil* (Basu Chatterjee, 1979) and so on. Thus, for example, the VT station, Marine Drive, Worli Sea Face, the Kaal Ghoda area, the Mumbai Taj hotel, the Fort area, Metro cinema, etc., recede to draw attention to spaces of new habitations (like Andheri East in *Ugly*).[24] Along with this forceful re-figuration of the swelling city, equally significant for this chapter are the ways in which Kashyap recalls the memory of the 'cinematic city' in order to re-frame its alternative images.

In one of his interviews, for instance, Kashyap mentions:[25]

I used to live in PMGP colony in Andheri East, Mumbai. I have seen this world very closely. People such as Imtiaz Ali, Nawazuddin Siddiqui, Ashutosh Rana and Kumud Mishra have all lived there once. I have a lot of friends who are still struggling, they come to Mumbai to make it big in the film industry and when they don't, they refuse to let go. Rahul Bhat, who had led that life, was my muse for Ugly.

Indeed, in *Paanch* as well, Kashyap seemingly 'struggled' with many such thematic and stylistic fascinations, and in retrospect the film helps us locate his later films within a specific aesthetic framework. Moreover, it encourages us to connect his oeuvre with the works of some of his associates and contemporaries (namely Ram Gopal Varma and Vishal Bhardwaj).[26] For instance, the song 'Paka Mat ... Baith ja Yahin Tu ja Maat ... Abey Gheen Aati Hai Khuja Maat' (Sit here, don't get going ... don't scratch is its disgusting) from *Paanch*, composed by Vishal Bhardwaj, evokes the memory of the song 'Kallu Mama' from the momentous film *Satya* and, thereby, underscores Bhardwaj's own musical arrangements, instrumentation, uses of unconventional voices and tonal quality. Furthermore, while Kashyap had written the screenplay of *Satya*, Bhardwaj had composed the music of the film. In fact, while Bhardwaj had also produced *No Smoking*, Kashyap has been unapologetic about the ways in which his own anxieties have produced his stories.[27] Furthermore, there are a range of locations (Dharavi in Mumbai or Paharganj in Delhi, for instance), situations (set in police station, for example), characters (social outsiders) and particular actors that speak to each other and return like motifs. For example, the actor, Tejaswini Kolhapure, who plays the so-called femme fatale in *Paanch* (and eventually gets her partners killed, gets all the money and even becomes a rock star) is brought back by Kashyap in *Ugly*.[28] Therefore, one may suggest that Shiuli of *Paanch* (the enchantress) reappears as the repressed and battered Shalini in *Ugly* (who seduces her husband's friend) and *en fin* betrays her father, husband and daughter, in her desperate attempt to acquire freedom. Indeed, Kashyap's films are intensely intertextual, and intently self-reflexive.[29] Moreover, Kashyap also mentions that[30]

> *Paanch* was a darker version of *Dil Chahta Hai, Gulaal* perhaps was a darker version of *Rang De Basanti*. It couldn't get made. Nobody believed in a subject like that, and the ghost of *Paanch* still hung fresh over me. Another year passed. Then, in 2003, I tried to do

Alvin Kallicharran, a black, mad amalgamation of everything that comprises a Hindi heartland childhood: *Bal Bharati, Champak, Manohar Kahaniyan, Satya Katha*....

Indeed, a media delimited world that may be absorbed my means of comic strip frames has been explored in *No Smoking* (in the opening sequences by way of thought balloons, for example) through spaces and faces (for instance, the figure of Anjali as the secretary), which chalk out dystopia. Likewise, the tragicomic sequences, and the uses of dark humour in relation to the scriptwriter Abbas Tyrewala, become an elaboration of such views. In effect, references of actual persons are a mark of Kashyap's preoccupations. For example, Abbas Tyrewala is the writer of films such as *Main Hoon Na, Maqbool, Munna Bhai M.B.B.S.* and *Salaam Namaste*. Kashyap reintroduces Tyrewala (played by Ranvir Shorey) as K's friend in *No Smoking*, who first introduces cigarette to him and then recommends him to the 'Prayogshala'. Curiously, the sequences in concern open with a large backlit Manga image. The camera tilts down to show the two friends reminiscing their earlier days, cut to an inter-title: '*Kyun ki bachpan bhi kabhie naughty tha*' (Since childhood was naughty too).[31] A sepia tinted comedy sequence (set in a bathroom) in fast pace, intercepted with canned laughter, shows them smoking, which is followed by Abbas' father entering the scene. Suspecting that the two are in a gay relationship, the father is eventually relived to figure out that they were (only) smoking. As the 'problem' is apparently resolved, the scene shifts to a club in which the same programme is playing on TV, just as K tells Abbas, 'You are no longer the same, your tyre has gone flat'. In fact, Kashyap suggests that[32]

I refer to films a lot. Like in *Dev.D*, I make references to *Gulaal*. Nobody has noticed because *Gulaal* hasn't been released yet. The character from *Gulaal* in his costume is sitting next to Abhay after Duniya song. We did it for no reason. Raja just walked in and told me that he has to make an appearance in the film. He has been waiting for *Gulaal* for last seven years, so he just makes an appearance in my every film. He was also there in *No Smoking*.

While Kashyap packs his narratives with many such allusions and personal references, a meaningful framework emerges through *Dev.D* and GoW Part 1 and 2, in which the memory of popular cinema is used as a narrative device and, therefore, relocates his films within a mesh of cross-references and becomes a powerful trope in due course.

III

The last sequence of *Dev.D* highlights the manner in which Kashyap's films may be located in a labyrinth of intertextual references. In addition, what emerges from his interviews is the fact that Kashyap draws heavily from his own life, surroundings and experiences, and has been deeply influenced by the edgy style of international film-makers such as David Fincher, Wong Kar-wai, Fatih Akin and Martin Scorsese.[33] In connection to such authorial overlaps and cross-references the last sections of this chapter illustrate in what way such creative intersections craft dense audio and visual tracks (of films such as *Dev.D* and GoW). Such interplay of (audio-visual) texts, one argues, reinvents existing narrative structures and produces a new stream of reflective stories.

I have discussed elsewhere regarding the multiple adaptations of *Devdas* and the manner in which the ending fabricated by P.C. Barua became influential, particularly the fashion in which specific images/shots (like the face of despairing Paro) from the 1935 film travelled through other adaptations (Mukherjee 2011). Contrarily, during a personal conversation in 2007, Kashyap had suggested that he wanted to make a film that would completely deconstruct the idea of 'Devdas'. While his references are his immediate past (especially Sanjay Leela Bhansali's *Devdas*, 2002), in the process he also pays his seditious tributes to the earlier texts. Furthermore, Kashyap borrows certain fundamental elements from the *Devdas* archetype, in order to quote and subvert it. Therefore, Kashyap makes basic changes to the plot, for instance, the narrative of the *Dev.D* deserts Paro towards the end, and the last journey sequence of the film explores a whitewashed wasteland as opposed to the darkness of the country explored by P.C. Barua, Bimal Roy (1955) and S.L. Bhansali. Intercepted by the enchanting face of Chanda, the landscape dissolves into spaces of suburban underdevelopment and our uneven histories. Likewise, towards the dreary end of his journey, an exhausted Dev is thrown out of a pub. As he befriends a dog, a heavily doped driver speeds in, hits a wall and kills himself. While on the one hand, Kashyap quotes a scene from *Head-On* (Fatih Akin, 2004), on the other, through this return journey of Dev to live with Chanda (like Vijay in *Pyaasa*, who returns to Gulabo, the prostitute), Kashyap somewhat disdainfully presents narratives of our 'schizophrenic' every day. In his interview, Kashyap also states that[34]

That was the mood I wanted to capture. Dev D is a drifter, who doesn't know what he is after. Every time he goes through something, he suffers, he starts walking and a song plays in the background. The song is his state of mind.

Furthermore, he adds:

[W]hen we enter Paharganj, mood changes. When the character starts drifting, my camera drifts along. Our idea was to capture the feel of location and character. [...]

When Abhay told me the concept of *Dev.D*, the first thing that occurred to me was Paharganj. Before I thought of what I'm going to do, I thought of Paharganj because that's the place that really stands for decadence.

In fact, Kashyap's shot taking and the editing style become remarkably different as the narrative shifts to Paharganj, Delhi. The exploration of the nightlife, narrow lanes, cramped houses and the use of blue–yellow–green–red neon signs that are juxtaposed with imaginative interiors (which includes both Chanda's space and hotel rooms) produce a dynamic urban landscape. According to Ramna Walia (2014: 57):

Integrating newspaper headlines with the visual sprawl of urban dystopia, *Dev.D* subverted the templates of sex, sexuality, agency and desire, placing the narrative in the midst of a transforming youth culture (Figure 8). Kashyap composes the mise en scène of the film in a manner that infuses the characters with the kinetic rhythms of the city.

In a similar vein, the well-known 'Emosanal Attyachaar' song, performed by 'Patna ke Presley' (Elvis Presley of Patna, Bihar) in the film, is introduced at the point when Paro is married off to someone else. This becomes a significant departure from the original text and the ways in which the enigmatic *shehnai* has been used in other adaptions. Moreover, Kashyap states:[35]

> Things that you assimilate will come naturally to you. When I look back in *Dev D*, the whole brass band scene is [inspired from] Emir Kusturica, the whole 'emotional atyachaar', where does it comes from, it comes from Om Dar-Badar—'Meri Jaan A A A, B B B' and last scene, it comes from *Head On*. The scene where Chanda says 'what do you know about pain' comes from *Paris Texas*. It's just one frame but from that one frame evolves a whole different language. It's an organic process.

Indeed, while at the plot level it signifies contemporary cultural practices, the treatment of the powerful and sharp sounds of the brass band, along with the somewhat off tune singing performed by Nawazuddin Siddiqui and Kashyap's assistant (heightened by the yellowish lights), unsettle the tragic overtones of the theme and illustrate the manner in which Kashyap calls to mind the memory of a wide range of films.

IV

Kashyap's preference for brass band is also evident in his magnum opus GoW Part 1 and 2. Additionally, in GoW Kashyap evokes the memory of multiple music cultures, especially, the memory of popular film music. For instance, the title song of *Kasam Paida Karne Wale Ki* (Babbar Subhash, 1984) reused at a key moment in GoW—at the point when Sardar Khan decides to directly confront Ramadhir Singh, the person who has killed his father—is crucial. *Kasam Paida Karne Wale Ki* had also featured the song 'Jeena Bhi Kya Jeena' (How do I live) that was apparently modelled on Michael Jackson's music video *Thriller*. Moreover, Mithun Chakraborty's (the actor of the film) star persona, described as 'poor man's Bachchan' by the popular press (and also India's Michael Jackson because of his dark skin and dancing skills), was like that of an underdog who was attempting to disrupt the plot of social injustice through his musical ability.[36] This song, performed in GoW, by a 'Mithun Chakraborty lookalike', therefore, makes the sequence both hugely comic and emotionally tense, since it indicates an impending violence. In order to highlight cinematic tension and suspense, Kashyap intercepts it with Sardar Khan's voice and his brazen warning (he will bomb the area, and will make Ramadhir Singh's entire family dance in public). Repeated applications of conflicting music and sounds vis-à-vis the plot make Kashyap's films a mutated text, which draw attention to larger networks of themes, concerns and styles.

Moreover, while GoW 1 ends with Sardar Khan's brutal killing (which is shot, mostly, in low angle against the sky, and is presented through slow motion), this moment of tremendous loss is reinforced through the application of one of the most memorable songs from the film (i.e., 'Jiya Ho Bihar Ke Lala' [Long live son of Bihar]). And yet, GoW 2, which opens with Sardar's family grieving over his dead body, transforms this situation into a tragicomic one by involving the theatre actor Yashpal Sharma, who performs the popular number 'Yaad Teri Ayegi' (Shall remember you). The use of a popular song from a 1980s unsuccessful film, *Ek Jaan Hain Hum* (Rajiv Mehra, 1983), is intriguing. Similarly, after the tragic killing of Sardar's eldest son, Danish Khan, the song 'Teri Meherbaniyan' (Your kindness) is performed prior to the burial. The film *Teri Meherbaniyan* (K.C. Bokadia, 1985) narrated a revenge story of a dog who waits to hit back following the murder of his master. In the original song ('Teri Meherbaniyan'), the dog appears to be shedding tears silently while the song plays in the background.[37] The recalling of such 'camp' cultures explains Kashyap's schema and the range of experiences he hopes to evoke and comment upon.[38]

V

Regarding reinvention and recalling of existing tropes, one may refer to Walia (2014: 32) from another context and suggest that it

> also establish[es] an archive of cinematic legacy and rescue[s] Bombay film history from the monolithic narrative of plagiarism. Moreover, this resurgence not only draws on the after-life of the old classics [or cults] within popular culture but also reflects on the changing modes of production, circulation and exhibition of films in the contemporary Bombay film industry.

Furthermore, by reclaiming an existing soundtrack, and by mixing it with the sound of brass band, Kashyap thickens the sonic environment of Hindi films, just as he stresses upon contemporary sound cultures and the many passages of musical transactions. Concerning (such) cinephila, Elsaesser (2005: 40) argues:

> Cinephilia take one, I suggested, is a discourse braided around love, in all the richly self-contradictory, narcissistic, altruistic, communicative and autistic forms that this emotion or state of mind afflicts us with. [...] At the forefront of cinephilia, of whatever form, I want to argue, is a crisis of memory: filmic memory in the first instance, but our very idea of memory in the modern sense, as recall mediated by technologies of re-cording, storage, and retrieval. [...]
>
> The new cinephilia of the download, the file swap, the sampling, re-editing and re-mounting of story line, characters, and genre gives a new twist to that anxious love of loss and plenitude, [...] This work of preservation and re-presentation—like all work involving memory and the archive—is marked by the fragment and its fetish-invocations.

A close reading of GoW, however, shows that Kashyap has a far more critical approach than what Elsaesser describes as 'Cinephilia take one and new'; in effect, even when his style is 'richly self-contradictory, [and somewhat] narcissistic', the memory of past events is held together by a complicated frame. For instance, GoW, which received international attention and became a contemporary cult, tackled problems related to coal mining in Bihar, and community conflicts. This is followed by accounts of the growth of coal business during the 1960s, the rise of coal mafias and their gradual entry into politics. The plot is, however, spiked with situations of intense violence and bloodshed, supported by zestful characters and faces, Kashyap's characteristic comic interjections as well as his stylistic diversions and a soundtrack, which was produced through a cogent association with local elements.[39] GoW, thus, does not merely indulge in a recreation of a period vis-à-vis old films; contrarily, Kashyap deploys a range of disconnected elements and fragments of sounds, and thereby, re-fashions a past in order to comment on it through popular tracks. For instance, the settings and interior spaces (which include specific gadgets such as the stove, thereafter, the freezer, vacuum cleaner and other everyday household objects), as well as the exteriors (chalked out by the iconic ambassador cars), and the locations of suburban town complicate the structures of 'period' films.[40] In the song 'Kaala Rey', therefore, Kashyap presents Faizal Khan's growing stature as well as, through the inclusion of the 'pager' as a specific element of the mise en scène, draws attention to a historical shift in media cultures and technologies.

VI

Kashyap is a self-confessed fan of Amitabh Bachchan's on-screen persona (as evident in his short *Bombay Talkies* [2013]). The star persona of Amitabh Bachchan has grown over the years through a series of texts and is recognized through an ambiguous tragic aura (or a man with a haunting past), brooding intensity, forbidding anger, an (oedipal) obsession for the mother and a certain type of compassion, which allows him to shed a tear, as well as a proletariat identity with leadership capabilities (although somewhat detached from his own class, therefore, a loner). Bachchan performed a range of marginalized characters such as small-/big-time smuggler, dock worker, railway porter, wronged police officer, coal mine labourer, religious minority and so on. The figure frequently faced death at the closure, thereby resolving much of the tricky questionings brought forth by the text, though the portrayal of a wounded body and his left arm has been a topic of intense arguments so far. Indeed, the physical bearing of a larger social suffering and trauma as in *Deewaar*, *Trishul* (Yash Chopra, 1978), *Kaala Patthar* (Yash Chopra, 1979) or *Agneepath* (Yash Chopra, 1990) becomes a crucial narrative device in GoW. The memory of the star persona of Bachchan figures as a powerful structural device by means of which the narrative unfolds. Moreover, by weaving a mesh of cross-references, Kashyap crafts a potent story that comments on public cultures and its significance within social histories.

In one of the crucial murder sequences of GoW 2, for example, after Faizal Khan begins to attain public approbation by chopping off the head of his friend Fazlu, the Bachchan framework comes forth as a powerful grid. Thus, at the point when Fazlu celebrates his win at the local elections, Faizal goes to his place and shares a puff. Faizal says, 'I use to think, I am Bachchan [...] but I figured out that I am only a supporting actor.' Yet, to reinstate himself as a masculine figure, Faizal slits Fazlu's throat instantaneously. Through GoW, Kashyap, indeed, makes several remarkable connections between a withering state, masculinity, power, violence, bloodshed, anguish, political history and memory, as well as constructs it through popular tropes. This frame of the towering masculine symbol, around which the narrative develops, is, in fact, introduced at the point when Faizal returns as an adult and has been already interpolated into the star persona. The *Trishul* plot (about estranged father–son), hence, seems to mirror his story and eventually becomes a compelling tool that drives the narrative forward. Thus, at the point when Faizal begins to trade with guns, his return journey from Banaras (by train) is intersected by a chanced encounter with a Bachchan lookalike. Facing each other, Faizal and the unknown character seemingly pause to reflect upon such uncanny cultural phenomenon.

While references to popular films as a historical index are commonplace, explorations of such elements as a narrative strategy are crucial aspects of Kashyap's style. Beginning with his tribute to the Madurai 'triumvirate', and by deploying Yashpal Sharma's performances at key points in the film, Kashyap arranges a rather knotty structure.[41] As a matter of fact, the major characters are modelled—or model themselves—on popular action heroes such as Salman Khan and Sanjay Dutt, just as their star personas provoke a range of events.[42] Such intricate plotting becomes consequential as we reconnect Definite's (Sardar Khan's son, Faizal's stepbrother) story in GoW 2, and his fascination for Salman Khan, with the visual quotations conjured at the point when Sardar is killed in GoW 1. While Durga, Definite's mother, is instrumental in killing Sardar, the poster of *Maine Pyar Kiya* (Sooraj Barjatya, 1989) used at the juncture this news arrives home functions as a visual sign that enables us to read the Salman Khan trope as a useful tool with a narrative import. Indeed, through such evocations, and through Faizal's desperations to perform 'Bachchan', the sociopolitical complexities of the 1980s surface and become meaningful. Furthermore, GoW presents a critique of popular cultures since it ends with Faizal, driven by frenzy, injecting countless bullets into the Ramadhir Singh's dead body. This elaborate sequence (in terms of shot taking and pacing) is intensified by the application of the song 'Kahe Ungli Mein Pakare Rahe Paniya Re Mura' (Why are you trying to hold water in your palm, you fool/[...] any time you get a chance to live, do not refuse, you fool ...) which underlines the futility of such enormous violence, while the voice-over (by Piyush Mishra) later emphasizes the fact that nothing has changed in Wasseypur following the countless deaths. Popular cinema, which is intensely connected with and can also comment on historical changes, becomes a powerful vehicle through which political conflicts are recalled, retold and subverted.

Notes

1   On censorship see Mehta (2012).
2   See http://www.india-today.com/itoday/20011022/cinema.shtml
3   See Liang (2005) on issues of piracy and democracy.
4   See Desai (2003) for a thorough reading of *Bollywood*.

5 See http://www.rediff.com/movies/2005/apr/05anurag.hxxtm/

6 See http://indianexpress.com/article/entertainment/play/anurag-kashyap-says-he-is-bored-with-his-own-ideas/

7 See http://dearcinema.com/author/bikas-mishra

8 The film *Badlapur* (Sriram Raghavan, 2015), set in Pune, also narrates a story about a series of (unintended) murders. The location of a town (and not a metro) becomes an important site in *Being Cyrus* (Homi Adajania, 2006, in India) as well.

9 See http://www.india-today.com/itoday/20011022/cinema.shtml

10 For an interesting study of the reworking of noir see Naremore (2008) and Prakash's (2010) edited volume for an extensive study of the 'noir' and (international) cinema.

11 See http://www.india-today.com/itoday/20011022/cinema.shtml

12 See Fernandes (2000) for a thorough reading of the (new) middle class.

13 See Athique (2011) for a historical study of the development of multiplexes.

14 See http://www.rediff.com/movies/2007/oct/24anurag.htm

15 See http://dearcinema.com/author/bikas-mishra

16 See http://sudhirpatwardhan.com/paintings.htm

17 *Karthik Calling Karthik* (Vijay Lalwani, 2010) also tackles obsession with telephone and aural pleasures.

18 *That Girl in Yellow Boots* (Anurag Kashyap, 2010) also deals with city, dystopia and surveillance.

19 See Madhuja Mukherjee (2016).

20 A number of cinematographers of the period, including V.K. Murthy, have discussed the ways in which they were influenced by Hollywood noir.

21 See Abbas' memoir (1977) about the city, cinema and post-Independence violence.

22 See http://www.india-seminar.com/2009/598/598_ranjani_mazumdar.htm

23 Interestingly, Kashyap's *Bombay Velvet* (2015) includes a song about a certain 'Sylvia'.

24 Such erstwhile spaces are brought back in Kashyap's *Bombay Velvet*.

25 See http://indianexpress.com/article/entertainment/play/anurag-kashyap-says-he-is-bored-with-his-own-ideas/

26 See http://www.rediff.com/entertai/2001/oct/13paanch.htm

27 See http://www.rediff.com/movies/2007/oct/24anurag.htm

28 See Grossman (2009) for a contemporary reading of 'femme fatale'.

29 See Ott and Walter (2000) for an analysis of intertextuality as a stylistic tool. This essay also discusses 'parodic allusion, creative appropriation and self-reflexive references' as three distinct intertextual strategies.

30   See   http://archive.tehelka.com/story_main20.asp?filename=hub
      100706Catcher.asp
31   Note that this is an allusion to the popular TV series *Kyun Ki Saas
      Bhi Kabhi Bahu Thi,* which is also referred in the opening of GoW.
32   See http://dearcinema.com/author/bikas-mishra
33   *Bombay Velvet* opens by acknowledging Martin Scorsese.
34   See http://dearcinema.com/author/bikas-mishra
35   See http://dearcinema.com/author/bikas-mishra
36   See   http://memsaabstory.com/2009/09/02/kasam-paida-karne-
      wale-ki-1984/ for an interesting retake on the film.
37   See https://www.youtube.com/watch?v=8DXl8sFB1AM
38   For an interesting study of 'camp' see Sontag (1999).
39   See https://www.youtube.com/watch?v=SPg5GUpxOKI
40   See Landy (2001) on historical films.
41   Yashpal Sharma is rendered thrice in GoW. He also performs, in
      both male and female voices, for the cult song 'Salame Ishq Meri
      Jaan' from *Muqaddar Ka Sikandar* (Prakash Mehra, 1978) at the point
      Faizal begins to fall in love.
42   Both Salman Khan and Sanjay Dutt have faced trial under the
      Indian Penal Code.

References

Abbas, K.A. 1977. *I Am Not an Island: An Experiment in Autobiography.*
      New Delhi: Vikas Publishing House.
AlSayyad, Nezar. 2000. 'The Cinematic City: Between Modernist Utopia
      and Postmodernist Dystopia.' *Built Environment* 26 (4): 268–81.
Appadurai, Arjun. 1995. 'Disjuncture and Difference in the Global
      Cultural Economy.' In *Global Culture: Nationalism, Globalization, and
      Modernity,* edited by Mike Featherstone, 295–310. London: SAGE
      Publications.
Athique, Adrain. 2011. 'From Cinema Hall to Multiplex: A Public
      History.' *South Asian Popular Culture* 9 (2): 147–60.
Benjamin, Walter. 1969. 'Paris: Capital of the Nineteenth Century.'
      Perspecta, 165–72.
Creekmur, Corey K. 2013. 'Cinephilia and Film Noir.' In *A Companion
      to Film Noir,* edited by Andre Spicer and Helen Hanson, 67–76. John
      Wiley & Sons.
De Certeau, Michel. 1984. *The Practice of Everyday Life.* Berkeley, CA:
      University of California Press.
Desai, Jigna. 2003. *Beyond Bollywood: The Cultural Politics of South Asian
      Diasporic Film.* London: Routledge.

Elsaesser, Thomas. 2005. 'Cinephilia or the Uses of Disenchantment.' In *Cinephilia: Movies, Love and Memory*, edited by Marijke de Valck, and Malte Hagener, 27–43.

Fernandes, Leela. 2000. 'Restructuring the New Middle Class in Liberalizing India.' *Comparative Studies of South Asia, Africa and the Middle East* 20 (1): 88–104.

Gopal, Sangita. 2011. *Conjugations: Marriage and Form in New Bollywood Cinema*. Chicago, IL: University of Chicago Press.

Gopalan, Lalitha. 2013. 'Bombay Noir.' In *A Companion to Film Noir*, edited by Andre Spicer and Helen Hanson, 496–511. John Wiley & Sons.

Grossman, Julie. 2009. *Rethinking the Femme Fatale in Film Noir: Ready for Her Close-up*. Basingstoke: Palgrave Macmillan.

Harvey, David. 1979. *Social Justice and the City*. London: Edward Arnold.

Lefebvre, Henri. 1974. *The Production of Space*, translated by Donald Nicholson-Smith. Blackwell.

Liang, Lawrence. 2005. 'Porous Legalities and Avenues of Participation.' *Bare Acts, Sarai Reader* 6: 7–17.

Mazumdar, Ranjani. 2007. *Bombay Cinema: An Archive of the City*. Ranikhet: Permanent Black.

———. 2010. 'Friction, Collision, and the Grotesque the Dystopic Fragments of Bombay Cinema.' In *Noir Urbanisms: Dystopic Images of the Modern City*, edited by Gyan Prakash, 150–86. Princeton University Press.

Mehta, Monica. 2012. *Censorship and Sexuality in Bombay Cinema*. University of Texas Press.

Mehta, Suketu. 2004. Maximum City: Bombay Lost and Found.

Mukherjee, Madhuja. 2009. 'Photoshop Landscapes: Digital Mediations and Bollywood Cities.' *Journal of the Moving Image* 8 (December): 50–72.

———. 2011. 'Remembering *Devdas*: Travels, Transformations and the Persistence of Images, Bollywood-style.' *Topia, Canadian Journal of Cultural Studies* 26: 69–84.

———. 2014. 'Not So Regal Show-houses of Calcutta: Sub-cinemas, Sub-cultures and Sub-terrains of the City.' In *Strangely Beloved: Writings on Calcutta*, edited by Nilanjana Gupta, 146–54. New Delhi: Rainlight/ Rupa Publications.

———. 2016. 'That figure in the dark: Of melodrama, noir and multiplicity during 1950s.' In *Indian Film Culture/Indian Cinema*, edited by Gautam Kaul, 116–36. Kolkata: Codex (Federation of Film Societies of India).

Naremore, James. 2008. *More than Night: Film Noir in Its Contexts*. University of California Press.

Ott, Brian and Cameron Walter. 2000. 'Intertextuality: Interpretive Practice and Textual Strategy.' *Critical Studies in Media Communication* 17 (4): 429–46.

Prakash, Gyan. 2010. *Mumbai Fables*. Princeton University Press.

———. (ed.) 2010. *Noir Urbanisms: Dystopic Images of the Modern City*. London: Princeton University Press.

Prasad, M. Madhava. 1998. *Ideology of the Hindi Film: A Historical Construction*. New Delhi: Oxford University Press.

Sontag, Susan. 1999. 'Notes on Camp.' *Camp: Queer Aesthetics and the Performing Subject*: 53–65.

Walia, Ramna. 2014. 'Recycle Industry: The Visual Economy of Remakes in Contemporary Bombay Film Culture.' *Synoptique, An Online Journal of Film and Moving Image Studies* 3 (1): 30–66.

11

Globalization, Reflexivity and Genre in Zoya Akhtar's Films

Nandana Bose

This chapter examines the thematic and stylistic tendencies that resonate in the emerging body of work of the new wave Bollywood film-maker and writer, Zoya Akhtar, who has directed three Hindi feature films till date — *Luck by Chance* (2009), *Zindagi Na Milegi Dobara* (You Live Only Once, 2011, henceforth referred to as ZNMD) and *Dil Dhadakne Do* (Let the Heart Beat, 2015). She is a rarity in the Bombay film industry since she is a critically acclaimed and commercially successful female film-maker, although this biased, gendered industrial context is gradually changing. According to noted film critic and writer Anupama Chopra, 'Ms. Akhtar … is among an emerging breed of female directors altering the contours of Bollywood, the Mumbai-based Hindi film industry' (2011). Instead of appraising her work through the somewhat outdated prism of auteurship, I contend that the collaborative nature of film-making significantly underpins any singular directorial vision that one might discern in her corpus of work.

She is the daughter of the legendary scriptwriter, poet and lyricist Javed Akhtar. I would argue that being part of the famed

Akhtar family has given her opportunities, access and support that would be unavailable to a rank outsider. Much like
the other commercially successful female director Farah Khan,
who is also Akhtar's first cousin, the latter uses her status as
a Bollywood 'insider' to great advantage in her ability to cast
superstars and to access a network of material resources and
talent. Besides these two cousins, there is a growing brigade of
female film-makers that include Kiran Rao and Reema Kagti
who have recently made critically acclaimed, offbeat films.
While Rao directed the artsy new wave film *Dhobi Ghat* (2010),
imbued with 'world cinema sensibilities' (Gupta 2011), and
lauded for its 'atmospheric' and 'visceral' portrait of Mumbai
(Shekhar 2011), Kagti, a long-time friend of Akhtar, has directed
Honeymoon Travels Pvt. Ltd. (2007) and *Talaash* (The Search,
2012), starring superstar Aamir Khan in an introspective role of
a troubled policeman haunted by the accidental death of his son,
a prostitute and a broken marriage. Chopra observes that 'these
film-makers haven't exactly come out of nowhere'. Ms Rao is
married to Aamir Khan, while Ms Akhtar is second-generation
Bollywood, daughter of Javed Akhtar. Undeniably, as Ms Kabir
points out, '[T]hese women have had a major leg up thanks to
family and friends' (Chopra 2011).

Reflexivity and (Self) Referentiality

As a child of the industry, Akhtar has been adept at reworking and
redeploying the familial mode of production through creative collaborations with family members and friends, many of whom she
has grown up with and who are currently major stars and established industry personalities. I would argue that Akhtar's body of
work thus far is deeply rooted in the personal and familial, and is,
thus, self-referential in a broad sense—It consistently references
the substantial creative labour invested by her family members
and friends (in the various roles of an actor, a singer, a producer,
a scriptwriter, a lyricist and a dialogue writer), her lifestyle and
the milieu and privileged social circles in which she has grown

up, and reflects her urban sensibility and love of adventure and travel. As she says, 'I am very urban...I think I'm still in that zone where things are personal and where I'm still coming from personal experience. I don't think I've developed to that space yet where I can go elsewhere' (Kumar and Chaturvedi 2015: 126).

First films are often very personal and autobiographical, and this is certainly true of Akhtar. Her debut feature film, *Luck by Chance*, is reflexive of Akhtar's film background and upbringing that enabled her to cast an enviable list of former and current stars (such as Rishi Kapoor, Dimple Kapadia, Juhi Chawla and Hrithik Roshan) and character actors (Boman Irani), and to feature cameos by Aamir Khan, Kareena Kapoor, Abhishek Bachchan, Ranbir Kapoor and Karan Johar, to name just a few high-profile film personalities.

In her words:

> I grew up in the Bombay film industry. As a child I spent a lot of time on movie sets, so making films was a natural progression for me. First films are usually very personal and my story evolved in the world I knew best — Bollywood. Although I am steeped in it, I continue to be fascinated by how this mass producing machine functions.... So I found myself asking, just what makes it tick? (*Luck by Chance*, DVD liner notes)

Luck by Chance is a testimony to the clout, industrial connections and interpersonal contacts that she enjoys by belonging to the 'Akhtar banner'. In the words of Akhtar,

> It [*Luck by Chance*] was also very close to home. I've grown up in the industry.... I just know these people. I know them inside out and I've hung out with them.... I hear how it works and I know the stars. I was privy to all these people. (Kumar and Chaturvedi 2015: 127)

Akhtar has used her family connections and personal networks very well, initially as a casting director in her prodigiously talented brother Farhan Akhtar's debut feature film *Dil Chahta Hai* (What the Heart Desires, 2001) that is hailed as an iconic buddy film. She cast her brother in her debut film and her second feature

ZNMD, where she draws excellent performances from him. 'Well aware of her brother's strengths, she knows how to project him on screen, making him stand out even in the presence of a star-studded ensemble' (Vaishnav 2015). It was also co-produced by her brother's production company, Excel Entertainment, and featured lyrics and poetry by her father. According to film critic and film-maker Khalid Mohamed (2009), '[Although] Akhtar's script [of *Luck by Chance* was] a bit lengthy…it [had] the distinct advantage of her father Javed Akhtar's brilliant dialogue….' It could also be argued that the opportunities that came her way, very early on in the pre-directorial phase of her career, were due to her family connections. Mira Nair approached her and offered her the chance of working as one of the assistants for *Kama Sutra: A Tale of Love* (1996), then she worked with Dev Benegal for *Split Wide Open* (1999) and Kaizad Gustad for *Bombay Boys* (1998), following which she pursued a course in film production at New York University (Kumar and Chaturvedi 2015: 123).

Predictably, her third and most recent film, *Dil Dhadakne Do*, a comedic family drama, has significant contributions from her multitasking brother and father—Farhan's company, Excel Entertainment, once again produces his sister's film; his cameo appearance and scene-stealing entry have fans raving; he is a dialogue writer and duets with Priyanka Chopra on the title song, whilst the first person narrator-dog Pluto Mehra's memorable dialogues are penned by her father, Javed (*Business of Cinema News Network* 2014). I contend that such familial dependence limits the creative vision and artistic range of a young, emerging film-maker who is working very much within her comfort zone and operating within a familial space in which her father, brother, extended family members and childhood friends are the pillars that have supported her burgeoning career.

Generically Diverse

A noteworthy aspect of her film-making is her ability to dabble in diverse genres—*Luck by Chance* was, as discussed earlier, a self-reflexive, satiric meta-film on the chaotic and idiosyncratic Bombay film industry. According to a *The New York Times* review, 'It might seem as if Bollywood couldn't possibly satirize itself … but Zoya Akhtar manage[d] the trick deftly in *Luck by Chance*, an appealing tale of two would-be actors looking for movie stardom …' (Genzlinger 2009). Her next film was the road movie shot in Spain, ZNMD, an unusual genre for Bollywood which did wonders for Spanish tourism. As the trade analyst, Taran Adarsh observes, the film was 'definitely not for ardent fans of kitsch or those with an appetite for typical masala entertainers … [but] … a film for a more evolved, mature and cinema-literate audience that's geared up to embrace and support newer genres of cinema' (Sahni 2011). Unlike her first film which wasn't very successful at the box office, ZNMD was an instant hit. As observed by Chopra (2011):

> It opened in July at No. 1 on the Bollywood box office charts, No. 7 in Britain and No. 15 in the United States. According to boxofficeindia.com, which tracks grosses of Hindi movies, *Zindagi Na Milegi Dobara*, amassed about $19 million in five weeks, making it the third-biggest hit of the year…. Critics swooned over the crackling dialogue, the slow-paced but clever script and the stunning cinematography.

She then co-wrote the screenplay for a psychological thriller *Talaash*, another uncommon genre in the Bombay film industry, which was directed by Kagti, whose debut film *Honeymoon Travels Pvt. Ltd.* showed potential although it failed to stir up the box office, and was produced by Farhan Akhtar's production company. She then followed it up with a didactic social drama, challenging oppressive gender stereotypes in *Sheila Ki Jawaani*, part of an omnibus of four short films titled *Bombay Talkies* (2013), which is a commemoration of a hundred years of Indian cinema. However, in Akhtar's words, since capturing a hundred years of Indian cinema in a short film would be virtually impossible, the film as a whole is in fact an 'ode to the audience' (Sen 2015: 2). In her short film, Vicky (Naman Jain) is a child whose gender identity flowers in a profoundly imaginative exchange with the

star Katrina Kaif, as Sheila, from the item song featured in Farah
Khan's heist comedy *Tees Maar Khan* (2010). Sen (2015) astutely
observes that

> It [*Bombay Talkies*] proffers, as most representative of Bollywood,
> an array of filmmakers who, at least on paper, seem unlikely bed-
> fellows: Karan Johar and Zoya Akhtar are scions of Bollywood
> dynasties — insiders who have come of age very much within the
> feudal-familial dispensation of old Bollywood — and make films
> that remain largely tethered to tried and tested formula of songs,
> stars and melodrama.

The other contributors are established male directors, Karan Johar,
Dibakar Banerjee and Anurag Kashyap. On her co-contributors,
Akhtar, who consistently (and frustratingly) refuses to engage
with, or even acknowledge, gender politics within the film industry, opines:

> They are very competitive, and they are very good filmmakers....
> But at the end of the day you will see four films back to back, and
> you aren't going to care about which one was made by a man and
> which one by a woman. You will just say, this film is good and this
> isn't. (Kumar and Chaturvedi 2015: 137)

Dil Dhadakne Do is a family drama, Akhtar's favourite genre,
imitative of the quirky, comedic style of the reputed auteur Wes
Anderson. In her words, 'I just wanted to do a family story with a
sibling story at the core of it. I think there is nothing more important in forming a human being than your family' (Gupta 2015).
This is particularly true of her since her family has played a pivotal role in the blossoming of her directorial career.

Globalization and Travel

How far are Akhtar's films informed by the forces of liberalization
and globalization? It is difficult to think of any other contemporary film-maker more receptive to representing a certain narrow
strata of Indian society whose lives have been transformed by the

embrace of a neoliberal, capitalist economy in post-1990s India than Akhtar. She appeals to a privileged, urban cultural sensibility that is far removed from the diegetic world of slums, exploitation and deprivation of *Salaam Bombay!* (Mira Nair, 1988), the film responsible for her becoming a director. In her words, 'I saw *Salaam Bombay*. That was it. I just knew I wanted to make movies' (Kumar and Chaturvedi 2015: 122). It is an ironic inspiration considering that some of the recurrent themes resonating in her films are the celebration of affluence and all its attendant materiality — heady consumerism, hedonistic pleasures and indulgences of globe-trotting, super-rich Indians in the post-liberalization era who need to fix their broken relationships or rediscover themselves against the backdrop of exotic locales.

ZNMD is an exercise in cine-tourism, depicting thrill-seeking global Indians in a testosterone-driven buddy film, which is an uncanny replica of her brother's film *Dil Chahta Hai*, made exactly a decade ago. The location has simply changed, from Goa to Spain, but the character goals and motivations remain strikingly similar and repetitive — wealthy Indian youths discovering their identity and the meaning of life, love and relationships whilst vacationing in style. Her second feature film is a paean to consumerism, the ostrich Hermes Kelly bag named 'Bagwati' being a symbol of this excessive consumption, a fetish of capitalism — a material object regarded with extravagant reverence and obsessive devotion by the three friends, Imraan (Farhan Akhtar), Kabir (Abhay Deol), and Arjun (Hrithik Roshan). It is also a reiteration of Western-style individualism, where friendship and male bonding displace the centrality of the Indian family.

ZNMD and *Dil Dhadakne Do* (whose title is the name of the opening credit song in ZNMD) are 'lifestyle' films in which international travel and the ease of transnational mobility become an index of how transformative and beneficial the neoliberal, capitalist economy has been for a few affluent, privileged Indians. Indulging in conspicuous consumption such as buying branded products, travelling first-class, renting luxury, high-end cars, vacationing on luxury cruise-liners and staying in expensive, boutique hotels in foreign countries reflect and affirm the purchasing power and new money now available to a small coterie of people residing in post-liberalized, capitalist India. Although for the majority of Indians, such an excessive lifestyle is still beyond their reach, Akhtar knows her audience very well and her cinematic representations of elitist recreational consumption tap into aspirational and competitive tendencies of middle-class India. This is borne out by the box-office successes of both films, the unprecedented popularity of Spain as a destination for Indian tourists post-ZNMD (Harjani 2011; *Insider* 2014) and the spike in interest in cruise vacations and related advertising after *Dil Dhadakne Do*'s release (*Mumbai Mirror* 2015). Akhtar understands the importance of travel in terms of storytelling and weaving a narrative of the well-heeled, globe-trotting Indian who is at ease in foreign lands, spending money and indulging in consumerism, and imitating the patterns of high-end global tourism such as adventure sports and leisure activities of Western tourists.

Conventional Cinema

Despite her reputation and image as an unconventional film-maker in the Bombay film industry, Akhtar is actually fairly conventional in terms of textual and industrial gender politics, maintaining the patriarchal status quo, film style and aesthetics. As Anupama Chopra observes, '[T]o Ms. Akhtar, discussions about discrimination are largely a waste of time.' 'Of course there is truth in it,' she said, 'but we are big girls. Deal with it. If you can make a movie, you can also tell someone to, ahem, get lost' (2011). Interestingly, unlike earlier female film-makers, this new generation isn't making women-centric cinema since this new breed of women directors 'wear[s] their accomplishments and the gender politics lightly' (Chopra 2011). Akhtar said that she never considered turning the friends in ZNMD into women because that 'would have been a very different journey' (Chopra 2011). In fact, it is noteworthy that a woman directed, what some consider as, the best Bollywood bromance of the last 10 years. ZNMD was also written by women: The story and screenplay were by Kagti and her. Akhtar conveniently submits to (instead of attempting to subvert or challenge) the patriarchal structure of the industry by casting male stars (including her brother) and writing strong male characters. 'She is the only current director in Bollywood who dares to pack in half-a-dozen stars in one frame' (Vaishnav 2015). In her own words:

> We knew it [ZNMD] was a big-budget film, and when you're making a film like this, at least in India, you should have actors if you want your films to see the light of the day (*sic*). Roads trips with men [are] more cinematic.... There's more I could have done as a director. [p. 131] I think it's the emancipation of man. I think it is men freeing themselves ... where ZNMD was concerned ... I just wanted it to be more physical — the adventure, the physicality of it ... it's more interesting because men don't talk that much and they have a level of stupidity they can reach, which women can't reach ever. [p. 132] I feel men are easier to depict than women. Women are way more complicated, more unpredictable and more layered. I find it more difficult to write women.... Also, men don't have hormones that go up and down. (Kumar and Chaturvedi 2015: 136)

Mira Nair, one of the first female Indian directors to achieve international recognition, says that Bollywood's new female directors 'think in a more expansive way.... Their cinema is a reflection of their world, keeping their own tangent, wanting the marketplace and managing' (Chopra 2011).

She also works within the stylistic conventions and limitations of Bollywood by adhering to the formulaic framework of industrial production that mandates the inclusion of elaborate song and dance spectacles (such as 'Senorita' and 'Paint it Red' in ZNMD; and 'Girls like to Swing' and 'Gallan Goodiyaan' in *Dil Dhadakne Do*), multi-stars and melodrama, with the corporate gloss and sheen of new money that funds the Bollywood new wave. She might appear to be novel and innovative, but I would argue that her marketing strategies, branding and shrewd deployment of the publicity machinery impart an illusory perception of originality and unconventionality. As Vaishnav (2015) observes,

> [I]n spite of having all the qualities of a new-age, unconventional filmmaker, Zoya's directorial voice remains firmly rooted in

good ol' mainstream Bollywood. Friendship, separation, loneliness, ambition.... These are themes explored even by her legendary father in those iconic Salim-Javed screenplays. But Zoya has cleverly served them with a contemporary twist that appeals to a new generation. Even her ability to direct ensembles is perhaps a throwback to the golden era of multi-starrers, when one got to enjoy many faces for the price of one ticket....

If she can lay claim to being unconventional, it is in the increasingly crucial area of marketing and publicity. She is known for carefully planning her promotions, and her unusual promotional strategies, such as the entire cast of ZNMD taking a road trip from Bombay to Delhi. For the promotion of *Dil Dhadakne Do*, featuring yet another ensemble star cast comprising of Priyanka Chopra, Ranveer Singh, Anushka Sharma, Anil Kapoor and, of course, her brother, she broke with convention by not having any trailer launch event, and 'instead of hosting a song launch event, the team…hosted a special Sunday brunch where the song was shown. The entire cast and crew and everyone who attended … was dressed in summer brunch outfits and looked their best' (Sur 2015).

I have contended that the collaborative nature of film-making, defined and limited by the redeployment of the familial mode of production, has significantly underpinned any singular directorial vision that one might discern in Akhtar's corpus of work. Her films are informed by the forces of liberalization and globalization, reflexivity and self-referentiality, and attest to a predilection for generic diversification and stylistic conventionality. Her reputation of being an unconventional film-maker is overstated and isn't supported by the close examination of her films. In conclusion, although Akhtar's growing body of work is significant considering the rarity of a commercially successful female film-maker in the Bombay film industry, she is yet to achieve her full potential.

References

Business of Cinema News Network. 2014. 'Farhan Akhtar Multitasking on *Dil Dhadakne Do* Sets.' 4 August. Retrieved 30 June 2015, from http://businessofcinema.com/bollywood_news/farhan-akhtar-multitasking-dil-dhadakne-sets/163354

Chopra, A. 2011. 'In Bollywood, Female Directors Find New Respect.' *New York Times*. 2 September. Retrieved 6 April 2015, from http://www.nytimes.com/2011/09/04/movies/zoya-akhtar-and-farah-khan-bollywood-directors.html?_r=3

Genzlinger, N. 2009. 'A Bollywood Satire.' *New York Times*. 29 January. Retrieved 19 May 2015, from http://www.nytimes.com/2009/01/30/movies/30luck.html?_r=0

Gupta, P. 2015. 'The Mehras Are very Different than the Akhtars: Zoya Akhtar.' *Times of India*. Retrieved 22 May 2015, from http://timesofindia.indiatimes.com/entertainment/hindi/bollywood/news/The-Mehras-are-very-different-than-the-Akhtars-Zoya-Akhtar/articleshow/47386105.cms

Gupta, P.D. 2011. 'Salaam Mumbai.' *The Telegraph*. 22 January. Retrieved 30 June 2015, from http://www.telegraphindia.com/1110122/jsp/entertainment/story_13477408.jsp

Harjani P. 2011. 'Indian Tourists Flock to Spain.' *CNN.com*. 19 September. Retrieved 30 June 2015, from http://travel.cnn.com/mumbai/life/indian-movie-boosts-spanish-tourism-694426

Insider. 2014. 'The Great Indian Traveller.' *Insider.biz*. 20 November. Retrieved 30 June 2015, from http://the-insider.biz/index.php/issues/special-edition-2014/item/331-the-great-indian-traveller/331-the-great-indian-traveller

Kumar, N. and P. Chaturvedi. 2015. 'Urban and Unapologetic—The Cinema of Zoya Akhtar.' *Brave New Bollywood: In Conversation with Contemporary Hindi Filmmakers*, 121–37. New Delhi: SAGE Publications.

Mohamed, K. 2009. 'Review: Luck by Chance.' *Hindustan Times*. 30 January. Retrieved 19 May 2015, from http://www.hindustantimes.com/movie-reviews/review-luck-by-chance/article1-372769.aspx

Mumbai Mirror. 2015. 'Cruise Vacations Have Become a Hit after *Dil Dhadakne Do*'. 19 June. Retrieved 30 June 2015, from http://www.mumbaimirror.com/entertainment/bollywood/Cruise-vacations-have-become-a-hit-after-Dil-Dhadakne-Do/articleshow/47726356.cms

Sahni, D. 2011. 'Review Round-Up: *Zindagi Na Milegi Dobara*.' *The Wall Street Journal*. 15 July. Retrieved 21 May 2015, from http://blogs.wsj.com/indiarealtime/2011/07/15/review-round-up-zindagi-na-milegi-dobara/

Sen, M. 2015. 'Bombay Talkies and the Indian Cinema Centenary.' *South Asian Popular Culture* 13 (1): 1–3.

Shekhar, M. 2011. 'Mayank Shekhar's Review: *Dhobi Ghat*.' *Hindustan Times*. 22 January. Retrieved 30 June 2015, from http://www.

hindustantimes.com/movie-reviews/mayank-shekhar-s-review-dhobi-ghat/article1–653088.aspx

Sur, P. 2015. 'Priyanka Chopra-Ranveer Singh-Anushka Sharma's *Dil Dhadakne Do* Comes Up with Some Unique Promotional Strategy.' 22 May. Retrieved 22 May 2015, from http://www.bollywoodlife.com/news-gossip/priyanka-chopra-ranveer-singh-anushka-sharmas-dil-dhadakne-do-comes-up-with-some-unique-promotional-strategies/

Vaishnav, A. 2015. '5 Reasons Why Zoya Akhtar is Bollywood's Smartest Director.' *Huffington Post.* 1 May. Retrieved 19 May 2015, from http://www.huffingtonpost.in/anand-vaishnav-/why-zoya-akhtar-is-most-s_b_7106716.html

Film References

Akhtar, Z. 2009. *Luck By Chance.* Excel Entertainment and Reliance Big Pictures.

———. 2011. *Zindagi Na Milegi Dobara.* Eros International and Excel Entertainment.

———. 2013. *Sheila Ki Jawaani.* Viacom 18 Motion Pictures.

———. 2015. *Dil Dhadakne Do.* Junglee Pictures and Excel Entertainment.

Kagti, R. 2007. *Honeymoon Travels Pvt. Ltd.* Excel Entertainment.

———. 2012. *Talaash.* Aamir Khan Productions and Excel Entertainment.

Kunder, S. 2010. *Tees Maar Khan.* Hari Om Entertainment Co., Three's Company Production and UTV Motion Pictures.

Nair, M. 1988. *Salaam Bombay!* Cadrage, Channel Four Films and Doordarshan.

———. 1996. *Kama Sutra: A Tale of Love.* Channel Four Films, Meerabai Films and NDF International.

Rao, K. 2011. *Dhobi Ghat.* Aamir Khan Productions.

CHAPTER 12

Urban Dreams: Sudhir Mishra's Representations of Social and Political Change

Pavithra Narayanan and Clare Wilkinson

In a column published in *Outlook* in 2006, Sudhir Mishra proposes that the purpose of cinema 'is to help make sense of the times we live in'. As a writer and director, Mishra has been reflecting upon the struggles of men and women entangled in India's political and social realities since the early 1980s. In 14 films from 1983 to 2013, he has returned repeatedly to two overriding themes: the beauty and poignancy of dreams that shatter in the face of events and relationships in contemporary Indian life, and the pain and inevitability of personal and political betrayal. Although featuring many successful actors from the commercial realm, directorial, rather than star, authority marks Mishra's artistic endeavours.[1] He is linked, by the virtue of professional association, friendship and sensibility, with film-makers such as Vidhu Vinod Chopra and Ketan Mehta. Unlike Chopra, who has made a prominent mark as a producer as well as a director, and unlike Mehta, who is a prolific director in both film and TV, Mishra is a focused film-maker, conceiving, writing and directing his own work. Primarily interested in exploring urban experience in Mumbai and latterly Delhi, his films span social and cultural divides from the travails of working-class life in Mumbai's down-at-heel neighbourhoods to conspiracies and recriminations in the boardroom of the modern Indian corporation. Politics suffuse his films, whether the familial, gendered politics of the household or the sprawling, pervasive structures of institutional and group power. At the same time, however, he is fascinated by intimacy and the deeply emotional transactions of personal life.

In his most ambitious and most critically acclaimed project, *Hazaaron Khwaishein Aisi* (2005, in India; henceforth, *Hazaaron*), his ability to mesh these disparate strands reaches its peak.[2] Expanding beyond the urban settings in which he is most at home into the fractious countryside, Mishra chronicles the turbulent 1970s alongside the ebb and flow of love and friendship among three St. Stephen's College graduates. While this film features prominently in the essay to follow, we also draw out some of the most compelling elements in other selected films in his oeuvre. In our discussion of *Dharavi* (1991) and *Khoya Khoya Chand* (2007), we hope to show how the crafting of his films adds subtlety and power to his way of making sense of the Indian experience.

Sudhir Mishra's Films: An Overview

Mishra is a well-respected writer as well as a director, sharing the writing credit on Kundan Shah's satirical 1983 film *Jaane Bhi Do Yaaro* early on his career. Between 1987 and 1996, he made five films, including three with the National Film Development Corporation of India (NFDC) that won National Awards (*Yeh Woh Manzil To Nahin* 1987, *Dharavi* 1991 and *Main Zinda Hoon* 1988). The last film from this period, *Is Raat Ki Subah Nahin* (1996), was an important influence on the wave of gangster and crime films that followed in the late 1990s and onwards.[3] After a seven-year hiatus, three films appeared in 2003 — *Calcutta Mail*, *Chameli* and *Hazaaron* (2003–05). Since 2003, Mishra has made nine films, including the short films *The Ball* (the latter part of a 2011 anthology titled *Mumbai Cutting*) and *Kirchiyaan* (2013).

Cast members of Mishra's films include mainstays of character acting like Saurabh Shukla and others prominently associated with parallel or art cinema (Rajat Kapoor, Deepti Naval, Shabana Azmi); others have built careers acting in both popular and offbeat films (Om Puri, Irrfan Khan). Mishra often works with certain actors and technicians more than once: Shukla has appeared in six of his films, Chitrangada Singh in three and Deepti Naval, Kay Kay Menon and Shiney Ahuja in two. Music directors who have scored and composed multiple films with Mishra include Shantanu Moitra for *Hazaaron*, *Inkaar* and *Khoya Khoya Chand* and Rajat Dholakia for *Dharavi* (for which he won a National Award) and *Yeh Woh Manzil To Nahin*. In five films, a close collaborator was Mishra's partner, film editor Renu Saluja.

With the important exception of *Hazaaron*, Mishra's films unfold in and are defined by urban space. Police lock-ups, fetid streets and noisy bars comprise the milieu of the city's underlife, while coolly designed offices and apartments constitute the private spaces of middle- and upper-classes work and leisure. Rapid-fire conversations bounce across courtyards and in and out of shadowed rooms and dusty lanes; declarations and accusations are traded over nightclub tables, in stark rooms with cheap plastic chairs and in well-appointed drawing rooms. Vehicles also provide the settings for dialogue and interaction — cars, taxis or even police vans — reminding us that traversing the city is as elemental an experience for its residents as residing or working in it. Mishra, as both story and dialogue writer, stamps each film with its own distinct linguistic rhythms, whether this is the idiosyncratic, colloquial Hindi of *Dharavi* or *Yeh Saali Zindagi* (2011) or the elegant and evocative Urdu of *Khoya Khoya Chand*.

Back Bay, with its expanse and grandeur, provides a recurrent reference point for his Mumbai films, but its scenic possibilities are compounded by its importance as public space for promenading and recreation for all strata of city society. Playing with scale, however, can yield very different results: A pull-back shot on *Dharavi* illustrates its vastness within the even larger Mumbai landscape, while confining the two protagonists of *Chameli* for the first half of the film within a colonnaded stretch of a South Mumbai road shrinks the social and moral forces that shape their lives into a momentary singularity.

Mirroring the interconnective complexity of the city settings are the labyrinthine plots that propel characters past, away and towards each other. *Is Raat Ki Subah Nahin* starts with its characters situated all over the city, engaged in simultaneous acts of subterfuge and double-dealing that will, over the course of one night, force them into unintentional collision. Similarly, in *Yeh Saali Zindagi*, characters moving along parallel paths are made to converge via a tightly choreographed, non-linear sequence of scenes. The opening (in which Irrfan Khan as Arun is shown apparently dying from an accidental gunshot wound) leads to an extended flashback of the events leading up to it, and the film culminates with a postscript that comes temporally after the opening scene. In between, a myriad of new characters are introduced, and their histories and characteristics fleshed out via still more short and funny flashbacks. As actions and their unintended consequences pile up, the eventual outcome becomes ever more difficult to anticipate, imparting a zest and ingenuity to scenarios and characters that in other hands might become hackneyed. Also pointing out Mishra's divergence from the 'generic forms' of Hindi cinema, Ranjani Mazumdar argues that his supple treatment of time and memory in the film *Chameli* (e.g., Chameli's narrating, subverting and recalling the past) produces a 'typically urban experience of a constant play of complex pasts and memories' (Mazumdar 2007: 204).

It is tempting to assign Mishra's films to the realist stream of film-making, most associated with parallel or art cinema. But to do so neglects those elements of commercial cinema that resonate throughout his work, whether the abiding concern with intense personal relationships or the use of music and songs. Songs enjoy a life separate from the films in which they are picturized, worming their way into public consciousness on the radio, through recordings, and now via mobile phones and the Internet. The import of this is that the music of Mishra's films reaches an audience that is far broader than the one that watches them. Within the films, songs add facets and depth to the emotional resonance of the story, like the way they have so often operated in Hindi films generally. With some key exceptions, for example, the picturization of the song 'Bhaage Re Mann' on Kareena Kapoor in *Chameli*, Mishra does not often permit the song to draw the viewer too far from the narrative. Rather, he prefers to provide a diegetic rationale for a performance (a street music festival, a bar singer or a film song sequence encapsulated within the film). The range of music in Mishra's films is quite broad, including jazz, rock, and Indian folk and classical music. Urdu lyrics lend intensity and bite to songs, and thoughtful use of distinctly Indian song forms gives subtle inflections to the scenes they accompany. In Jaideep Varma's 2013 documentary on Mishra, *Baavra Mann: A Film on Sudhir Mishra* (henceforth, *Baavra Mann*), music director Shantanu Moitra and lyricist Swanand Kirkire describe grafting a *qawwali* (an ecstatic musical performance of devotional poetry from the Sufi Muslim tradition) on to a piece of pop dance music to lend dignity and splendour to the first sexual encounter between two of the lead characters in *Hazaaron*.

The hunger to chase one's dreams and the equally powerful temptation to betray both friends and foes provide the propulsive force to Mishra's films. Some ambitions are aspirational and personal (Rajkaran's [Om Puri] desire to become a man of substance in *Dharavi*); others aim at nothing less than the transformation of culture and society (Siddharth's [Kay Kay Menon] commitment to revolutionary action in *Hazaaron*). Almost all are predicated upon either naivety or self-delusion. For this reason, Mishra's protagonists find themselves confronted with choices that involve or instigate compromise and treachery. Particularly wounding are the grudges that develop between mentor and protégé: Rahul (Arjun Rampal), the advertising executive Pygmalion of *Inkaar*, viciously undermines the fast-rising Maya (Chitrangada Singh) when he (falsely) believes that she has discarded him; haughty film star Prem Kumar (Rajat Kapoor) abandons both of his 'discoveries' Nikhat (Soha Ali Khan) and Zafar (Shiney Ahuja) once he learns of their affair (*Khoya Khoya Chand*), notwithstanding that his own relationship with Nikhat was exploitative and selfish. Only love can flourish untainted by ambition. Thus, in *Yeh Saali Zindagi*, the audience is encouraged to be sympathetic towards Arun's (Irrfan Khan) perfidy with respect to his business partner and their criminal associates because he does everything for the slim chance of love with the heroine Priti (Chitrangada Singh). At the other extreme, unexamined loyalty and constrictive moral codes risk initiating utter devastation; for example, Ramanbhai's (Ashish Vidyarthi) implacable determination to seek revenge for every slight in *Is Raat Ki Subah Nahin* leads to the death of both his allies as well as his enemies.

It would be a mistake, however, to assume that the choices that protagonists face are entirely dictated by their actions as individuals. Rather, the structural and historical constraints within which characters must operate comprise the framework within which each film's story unfolds, be these conventional behavioural and ethical strictures, or the suffocating power of the family, the community or the state. The characters in Mishra's films, in keeping with these questions and realizations, are considerably more complex and flawed than their counterparts in commercial Hindi film. Many are unlikeable, while even the most sympathetic are subject to crucial errors in judgment—which is entirely what we would expect in any thoughtful exploration of the contrary forces of desire and capitulation in modern day India.

In order to give a more precise idea of how Mishra tackles the issues and stories that interest him, we now move on to in-depth analyses of the three films that Mishra himself regards as among his best work (*Baavra Mann* 2013). We commence with short accounts of *Dharavi* and *Khoya Khoya Chand*, and then go on to a sustained reflection on Mishra's arguably best film, *Hazaaron*.

Dharavi

In *Dharavi*, Mishra gives us a protagonist whose fall from a position of status and security within the world of the *basti* (colony, settlement) contains echoes of the trials of Job, only slightly tempered by our appreciation that naivety and hubris play at least some role in his fate.[4] Rajkaran Yadav (Om Puri) lives in a top-floor, one-room dwelling with his wife, Kumud (Shabana Azmi), and son. He is paying off a loan that helped him buy a taxi, yet he acts with all the assurance of a full proprietor, keeping his car meticulously clean, and dressing proudly in a starched white uniform to go to work. Mishra uses two devices to acquaint the audience with Rajkaran's confident and empowered point of view. The first is Rajkaran's narration of his arrival in the city and the consolidation of his fortunes. In addition to regaling his passengers with his history, we hear Rajkaran's voice giving a first-person voice-over. With the camera shooting over Rajkaran's shoulder as he drives his taxi, he describes his philosophy of life and success: '[In] the ocean every wave has a name; catch the wave at the right time and it'll work out' (*Dharavi* 1992). The use of first-person narration does not just establish the presumptions upon which Rajkaran operates; it also prompts us to accept Rajkaran's authority to tell his story (Kozloff 1989: 45). Shortly afterwards, Rajkaran is transported into a fantasy scene in which he flirts with the heroine of the Hindi melodrama that he was watching with the rest of the community at the film's start. These interludes continue to punctuate the film as Rajkaran, in the position of the Hindi film hero, happily and casually receives the respect and attention of the seductive screen heroine. Rajkaran is, in effect, a distillation of the hungry, hopeful outsider for whom Bombay has been and still remains the place to realize one's dreams (Ganghar 1996; Mazumdar 2007: 47–48). But Rajkaran is not content to keep his ambitions to himself; brimming with self-confidence, he brashly proclaims his faith in the ability of the individual to rise up by his own efforts in the glowing terms of someone we already anticipate will come to learn the hollowness of such conviction.

Rajkaran has inveigled three of his fellow slum dwellers to join him in the purchase of a small dyeing factory in Dharavi. Almost inevitably, one of them fails to make good on his contribution, causing Rajkaran to embark on ever more damaging and dangerous actions to keep his dream alive. As each pillar of his 'castle in the air' is knocked away, Rajkaran is unable to fully comprehend the vice in which he is trapped. Forever hoping for the best, based on little more than the conviction that he is a hardworking man who merits the rewards of a just world, Rajkaran becomes deeply indebted to one of the dominant criminal families that rules Dharavi. When the police maliciously destroy the factory, Rajkaran loses his taxi that he had used as collateral.

We are reminded that Rajkaran has nowhere to go. He wants nothing more to do with his home village, declaring that there is nothing there for him, even as his mounting losses make the city scarcely more comfortable. In any case, the pleasures of the countryside are never far away. Signs advertise 'country liquor' on the walls of a shop and traditional musicians play in the local bar and during religious festivals (a striking image that bookends the film is of a turbaned man in rural dress playing a *chikara* [traditional stringed instrument]). The village even follows him into Dharavi in other more sinister ways, as he strives unsuccessfully to avoid relying on his fellow caste members from the village to secure his factory loan.

In a denouement of equal parts of tragedy and absurdity, a rival gang eliminates Rajkaran's creditors in a bloody assault and destroys his beloved taxi in the bargain. Rajkaran is fortuitously liberated from the immediate bond (we do not know what happens to the debt he is still paying off for the taxi itself), but the one precious thing he owned at the film's outset is irretrievably gone. Alienated by his egotism and rashness, his wife has already deserted him for her first husband. Simultaneously, we see his mother (Pramod Bala) riding a train back to her village in a recapitulation of the sequence in which she is shown coming to the city. Her disappearance to the 'nothing there' of the village is tantamount to her permanent departure from Rajkaran's life, and the duplication of the shot suggests a return to beginnings, as Rajkaran now is as lacking in resources as he was when he first arrived in the city. In a wry coda, Rajkaran is shown working as a taxi driver, in a rented cab, expounding his latest plan to get back into the factory business.

The intention surely cannot be to celebrate Rajkaran's pluck, for he barely seems to register the profundity of his loss, both material and emotional. Tellingly, his own narrative voice, so certain and declarative at the outset, is absent; Rajkaran's self-assured claim to authorship of his own story is by now both ridiculed and nullified (Kozloff 1989: 45–48). In addition, costume, which is an important materialization of character in film (Street 2001), highlights the lack of fit between Rajkaran's pipe dreams and his reality; the tidy white clothes he wore to drive his own taxi in the start of the film have now been swapped for wrinkled khaki. In giving way to the film's version of his story rather than his own, Rajkaran's powerlessness is confirmed.

The betrayals that litter Rajkaran's path are multifaceted: the betrayal of friendship and expectation among his associates; his own failure to stand by his kin and his compromise of his principles of self-reliance in going to the unscrupulous Tiwari brothers for a loan. But Rajkaran's greatest mistake is to assume that the world he inhabits operates according to justice and merit as opposed to being warped by atavistic loyalty and remorseless cruelty. Rajkaran is quite prescient about the inability of his brother-in-law Chaskar's (Virendra Saxena) followers to stand behind him in his grass roots organizing against the local power brokers; he is though utterly blindsided by the contempt and cynicism with which the Tiwaris treat him. There is, in sum, very little in which to have faith, other than the assurance that the powerful will obliterate the powerless. The only grace note of the conclusion is Rajkaran's wife's decision to return to her disabled first husband, Shankar (Mushtaq Khan). While Rajkaran lives in the dream world of the Hindi melodrama, Shankar, already a broken man, lives in a real world in which the stuff of film illusions is fashioned — a studio filled with incomplete painted film posters. Kumud's decision seems less like a sacrifice than a gesture of compassion that has no parallel in the rest of the film.

Khoya Khoya Chand

Described by Mishra as his most personal and favourite film (*Baavra Mann* 2013), *Khoya Khoya Chand* is an exquisitely crafted and distinctly oblique view of the Hindi film industry of the 1950s and 1960s. Mishra has stated elsewhere his respect for and appreciation of the achievements of film-makers of the era, and takes full opportunity in this film to bring it to life in full recognition of both its brilliance and its blemishes. The atmosphere and mores of the period are lovingly recreated in the costumes, settings and above all, Urdu dialogues and haunting songs.

The plot is like a nested set of boxes; the film we see is—as we learn by the conclusion—a film within a film, and that film includes even more films, shown in the process of production. The film charts the rise of two fictional luminaries of the film industry, who apart from wanting desperately to 'make it' in the film world are also seeking release from the psychological grip of painful childhoods. One is the tragically exploited heroine, Nikhat (Soha Ali Khan), daughter of an unscrupulous and ambitious mother (Alka Pradhan); the other, the determined but complicated Zafar (Shiney Ahuja), son of a Lucknow patrician (Yusuf Hussain) whose many marriages sowed trauma among his wives and by extension Zafar. Lacking the connections that would guarantee a foothold in the industry, each must secure the patronage and thus the loyalty of more powerful figures. Superstar Prem Kumar (Rajat Kapoor) takes both of them under his wing, but the terms of Nikhat's 'contract', being sexual in nature, are emotionally fraught. A sequence of betrayals propels the plot along, commencing with Kumar's pragmatic alliance with an acceptable bride that shatters Nikhat. Soon thereafter, Zafar and Nikhat begin an affair that infuriates Kumar.

Nikhat and Zafar's love story comes to grief when she puts loyalty to her duplicitous relatives over marriage to Zafar. She also refuses to appear in his directorial debut, a film that is based on his family life and his attempt to exorcise its demons. The film's failure presages Zafar's exile from Bombay, compounded by a bitterness and resentment that ruins even his long friendship with loyal Shaymol (Vinay Pathak). Nikhat, a survivor by nature, enjoys fame and success, but begins to fall apart from the strain of her separation from Zafar and the squandering of her gifts on a new variety of commercial film that arrives in the 1960s.

To flesh out the world of the 'golden era' of Hindi film, Mishra made use of film veteran narratives of the day-to-day experience of making films, and the life that went on around film-making (*Baavra Mann* 2013). The importance and availability of such sources does not mean, however, that we should evaluate the recreations of films and film-making on grounds of authenticity. It is critical that the films within the film are pastiches (Dyer 2006), imitations that capture the present moment's retrospective understanding of what films meant at the time (Dyer 2006: 128). The exaggerated melodramatic delivery, the rough and ready effects, and the overstated costumes immerse the viewer in the past of film-making at the same time as they elicit an ironical distance from it, lending credence to Mishra's decentred approach to the real lives and loves of his characters. Lifting the veil from the actual operations of film-making (using period cameras and lights) stresses the artificiality of the moral order of the 1950s and 1960s films, as the film's actors, in character, adopt roles so at variance with their off-screen experience.

For the heroines, the obvious mismatch comes from the emphasis upon sexual restraint on screen compared to the necessity of using sexual favours to get on in the business. Both Nikhat and Ratanbala (Sonya Jehan), her chief rival, suffer for their deviation from normative Indian female sexuality, but it is very apparent that Mishra is entirely sympathetic towards them. In fact, he marks the consummation of Zafar and Nikhat's love, hidden in a tent on location while the crew and cast search for her, through the folk device of shadow puppets on the tent wall, with running figures and rearing horses scaled down to suit the telling of a fairy-tale romance. The utter lack of cynicism in this scene and others tempers the wry nostalgia and moments of parody in the rest of the film.

The recurrence of the same characters again and again in scenes of filming, partying and script negotiation (among other activities) reinforces the smallness of the film world, which at times seems as oppressive as the joint family Zafar has sought to escape. Certainly Nikhat is an echo of the young wife of Zafar's father, who earnestly desires that Zafar will release her from the household, but whom he refuses to help—either because he does not care enough or feels powerless to do so. As the film moves towards its conclusion, however, the various slates are wiped clean. The example is set as Shaymol enlightens Zafar about Nikhat's decline since his departure and all that he has done to help her. In response to Shaymol's embittered declaration that he did not betray Zafar (it being understood that Zafar had made no commitment to Nikhat that could be betrayed), Zafar tells him that 'no-one means to betray anyone; it's just the circumstances' (*Khoya Khoya Chand* 2007). This singular insight offers a clue to a kind of understanding that almost no other character in Mishra's films is able to discover, that is, the way in which society, moral strictures, and the random play of chance and opportunity corrupt the choices of individuals no matter their declared intent. In addition to Mishra giving us 'a hero who is not always a hero, a villain who is not just a villain but has compassion...the heroine is not virginal and has ambition' (*Baavra Mann* 2013), another novel perception of the film could be that through acknowledging the power of circumstances and accepting and forgiving one's vulnerability to them, one can make a new start. And indeed this is exactly what Nikhat and Zafar do, making a film as a labour of love that is, in fact, the story of their own love, the very film we have been watching all along. Unlike most Hindi film romances, *Khoya Khoya Chand* does not end with a wedding. It does though conclude with the 'marriage' of Nikhat's self and her persona that throws into doubt the presumption that all popular Hindi films must necessarily deal with untruth.

Perhaps this scenario 'works' because *Khoya Khoya Chand* portrays a world unto itself. Assuredly, there are glimpses of India beyond the film set and film circles, but these are comparatively few. Instead, we are reminded that film-making can be about the world and yet be strikingly detached from it (a detachment which is compounded by distancing effects, like pausing the film while a narrator describes how this was the moment in which Zafar and Nikhat met). According to Rupleena Bose (2009), the result is to disengage Muslim culture and the Muslims who created and preserved it from the larger political context from which it came and to which it would, nostalgically, refer. Instead, the politics here are contingent on measures of success and loyalties that have no

clear real-world equivalent; it is not Zafar's religion or his community that governs how he will fare, it is whether he can safe-
guard the trust of people to whom he is a stranger. In this sense,
the film world is dramatically different from the settings of other
Mishra films.

Hazaaron Khwaishein Aisi

Before its release in 2005, Mishra's *Hazaaron* (made in 2003) earned
much critical acclaim at several international film festival venues,
including Berlin, Italy, Canada, Turkey, the United States and
the United Kingdom. Fellow film-maker Ashutosh Gowariker
described this movie as 'Indian cinema's first great political epic'
and Shekhar Kapur called it 'The most important film to come
out of India in a long time' (Bhayani 2004). But its low box-office
receipts show that the film did not have a wide viewership in
India. In fact, even in its script stage, *Hazaaron* was not popular
among the Bollywood elite. Well-known actors rejected the script,
says Mishra, describing it as the 'worst script they've ever read
in their lives' (*Baavra Mann* 2013). In 1997, the film received partial funding from French producer Joel Farges, but it took five
years before another producer, Pritish Nandy, agreed to finance
the film. Completed in 2003, the film was not released until 2005.
Not surprisingly, *Hazaaron* has nothing in common with box-
office hits of that year, such as Anees Bazmee's *No Entry*, Shaad
Ali's *Bunty Aur Babli*, David Dhawan's *Maine Pyaar Kyun Kiya*,
Madhur Bhandarkar's *Page 3* and Sanjay Leela Bhansali's *Black*.
These star-packed Bollywood blockbusters revolve around stories about extramarital affairs of doctors and newspaper men,
endearing crooks, celebrity lifestyles and the relationship between
a visually and hearing impaired woman and her teacher who
has Alzheimer's. On the other hand, set against the 1960s and
1970s political backdrop of the Naxalite movement, the Indian
Emergency era and the revolutionary spirit of youth who reacted
to the violence and betrayals by the state, Mishra's *Hazaaron* with
relatively unknown actors, Kay Kay Menon, Chitrangada Singh
and Shiney Ahuja, unravels a story about an India that was, and

continues to be, marked by injustices, strife, opposing ideologies and political repression.

Produced 28 years after the two-year Emergency period, Gautam Chintamani notes that *Hazaaron* is Bollywood's only 'cinema of Emergency'.[5] The Mumbai film industry's reluctance to address the brutal realities of the Emergency era, Chintamani (2012) adds, is because it prefers 'safe' wars like the independence struggle that 'clearly demarcates between the good and the bad when it comes to people but more importantly it is risk-free of antagonizing the Nehru–Gandhi family'. The battles portrayed in *Hazaaron* are neither safe nor popular. Today, while there may be a sense of indignation about issues such as press censorship and arrests of politicians, journalists and citizens during the Emergency period, movements such as the Naxalite peasant struggle for social, economic and political justice have little support from a public that embraces India's attempts to reposition itself within the neoliberal capitalist order. In keeping with his interest in complicated and intense relationships, Mishra situates the sociopolitical context of the film within the framework of a story that focuses on characters and family, personal journeys and love. The film can thus be described as what Deborah Mistron (1984: 47–49) terms a 'revolutionary melodrama', a 'hybrid sub-genre', which draws on conventional codes of melodrama (family and romance) to reconstruct historical cataclysms that led to political and social changes. However, *Hazaaron* departs from traditional revolutionary melodramas, including the Mexican films that Mistron analyses, as well as films such as Ketan Mehta's *The Rising: Ballad of Mangal Pandey* (2005) and Richard Attenborough's *Gandhi* (1982) because the story is not about a historical past with nationalism as a centripetal force to enlist public loyalty to the nation-state. Rather, *Hazaaron* underscores the failures of a post-independent Indian state.

Mishra's directorial style of placing the politics in *Hazaaron* as a backdrop to a love story necessitates the viewer to extract, fill in and deduce evidence of a socially and politically diseased system. He provides signifiers or what Nick Lowe (1986) calls, 'plot coupons', a narrative device which relies on many metaphorical representations (coupons) that can be redeemed later to construct historical meanings and to understand their significance. For example, at first glance, the story appears to be about the tumultuous relationship between the three main characters, Siddharth Tyabji (Kay Kay Menon), Vikram Malhotra (Shiney Ahuja) and Geeta Rao (Chitrangada Singh). Their journey takes them from the cities of Calcutta and Delhi to the village of Bhojpur, where the privileged lives of the urban protagonists, their families and friends stand in sharp contrast to the realities of the non-metropolitan working poor. Each of these pieces are metaphorical coupons that lead the viewer to a larger story about India; when the coupons are redeemed, Bhojpur becomes the country itself, a place where the poor are exploited, where state authorities abuse their power and a place that 'no one gives a damn about' (*Hazaaron*).

The opening of *Hazaaron* contains the most overt acknowledgment of the state of the nation two decades after India gained political freedom in 1947. Using archival footage of Jawaharlal Nehru's 'Tryst with Destiny' speech delivered on the eve of Indian independence, a narrative text plainly states that Nehru's 'dream had soured', and as his daughter, Indira Gandhi, took the helm, 'India was being pulled in a thousand different directions'. Acknowledging that he had also believed in Nehru's dream of a new, more inclusive India, Mishra informs the viewer that the story is about his 'imaginary siblings' lives in those times' (*Hazaaron*). The narrative cuts to a silent, black and white scene of violence; the transition into colour reveals a street full of blood. This opening provides the audience the first cue that *Hazaaron* is a political film, but the director quickly takes his place behind the camera and begins to direct a story about a romantic love triangle between Siddharth, Vikram and Geeta.

Mishra employs the epistolary form of storytelling to introduce his main characters, to locate their geographical and political positions, and to reveal that both Siddharth and Vikram love the same woman, Geeta.[6] The letters, written in English and read out in voice-over mode by the protagonists, make it clear that the film is about, and primarily for, urban-, middle- and upper-class youth with an English education. The epistolary format, with complementing visual images, also serves as a mechanism to organize political events for the viewer. Interestingly, this narrative device which holds the film together was inserted into the film only after its completion (*Baavra Mann* 2013). Starting with a student protest with Siddharth at the centre, the viewer is presented with the first 'Dear Geeta' letter from Siddharth: 'Calcutta was awe-inspiring. I am now back in Delhi, my beliefs totally strengthened. We have to change the world, and change it fundamentally' (*Hazaaron*). Dressed like Che Guevara in camouflage and khakis, Siddharth appears absolute in his convictions. He says that he admires 'the best and brightest of Bengal' who joined the Naxalite movement, 'did not take the comfortable roads their parents laid down for them ... [and] went down the dirt and muddy roads to the village' (*Hazaaron*). Siddharth's words reveal his self-absorption; his vision of the revolution is limited to his own class, privileged youth who are mirror-images of himself. The letter ends in an imperative for the, as yet, unseen woman: 'Geeta, I have now become a card holder member of the party — eventually, you must also.... Love, Siddharth' (*Hazaaron*).

The introduction to Vikram also starts with a protest that he watches from a rooftop not with empathy, but merely as a concern of inconvenience. Vikram is presented as antithetical to Siddharth, but as soon as his voice-over begins, the viewer is made aware that they both have something significant in common. His 'Dear Geeta' letter opens with: 'First and foremost, I still love you' (*Hazaaron*). Vikram complains that he is stuck in Meerut because the 'Muslim–Hindu sibling rivalry' has delayed trains. The town's apathy towards those who died in the riot matches Vikram's moral numbness. Driven by materialist ambitions, he scoffs at the ideals of his Gandhian father and at the 'rich kids playing this "let's change the world game"' (*Hazaaron*).

Mishra presents Geeta's character not through the world of letters but through her interactions with Siddharth and Vikram. The audience catches their first glimpse of Geeta nodding enthusiastically at the radical rhetoric in a student play that includes Siddharth as one of the actors. The scene cuts to her walking down a road; Vikram pulls up beside Geeta in a Jeep and offers to drive her to meet Siddharth. The dialogue that ensues reveals that she is not averse to Vikram's affection and company, but she loves Siddharth. While the director establishes the ideologies of the two men, Geeta appears to have no political convictions of her own. With this final introduction, Mishra begins a tangled and troubled love story of three individuals, their insecurities, conflicts and journeys. Each character is a distinct representation of different principles and practices: Siddharth believes in Leftist ideals, Vikram is a capitalist and Geeta evolves into a grass-roots activist. It is solely from the vantage point of these urban class protagonists that Mishra lays out the events that took place between 1969 and 1977.

Mishra's characters counter representations of heroes in Bollywood's revolutionary melodramas such as Ashutosh Gowariker's *Lagaan: Once Upon a Time in India* (2001), Mani Ratnam's *Yuva* (2004), Rakeysh Mehra's *Rang De Basanti* (2006) and Prakhash Jha's *Raajneeti* (2010). *Hazaaron* does not reify myths about camaraderie, male bravery, courage and sacrifice; protagonists do not cast aside their petty differences and fight together for a just cause; and struggles do not end in victory. In the first half of the film, Siddharth embodies the persona popularized by the 1970s films such as Prakash Mehra's *Zanjeer*, Yash Chopra's *Deewaar* and Ramesh Sippy's *Sholay*—the angry young man whose activism is shaped by an authoritarian government, a corrupt state and an unjust system. However, for all his spirit and glassy-eyed quest to save the world, in the face of real danger, Siddharth almost instantly transforms from a leader to a coward and chooses self-preservation over confrontation. The audience witnesses an idealist devolving into a frightened man who does not hesitate to use the women of the village, comrades, Vikram, Geeta and finally his privileged status to save himself. At the end of the film, although Siddharth apologizes to Geeta for leaving her, his parting words, 'You have to, I suppose, get over your first love in order to be free' (*Hazaaron*), refer to his decision to break away from his attachment to an ideal, not Geeta. Geeta never curtailed his freedom; she was always only an extension of his life as a student, as an activist and as a lover.

Siddharth was in love with his own idea of change. While he recognizes that the people's movement in Bhojpur did result in change, 'that no one can rape a lower caste woman in those parts so easily anymore' and that such change is 'about a leap of about 5,000 years' (*Hazaaron*), he dismisses these significant social transformations. His declaration, 'The world hadn't changed in ways that *I* [authors' emphasis] wanted it to' (*Hazaaron*), underscores his tragedy, the loss that Wendy Brown (1999: 26) refers to, when 'We come to love our Left passions and reasons, our Left analyses and convictions, more than we love the existing world that we presumably seek to alter'. Siddharth's irony to bear is that all that he achieved through his idealism was to motivate Geeta towards carving out a life without him. Mishra's decision to punish Siddharth's character with such severity, rather than reward him for his idealism, however short-sighted and short-lived, appears harsh and, perhaps, demoralizing. But Mishra likely cannot justify glorifying extreme Left-wing intellectuals like Siddharth, intellectuals who, Walter Benjamin (1934: 5–6) described 'have nothing to do with the worker's movement … [and momentarily] mimic the proletariat'. Siddharth's character is Mishra's passing nod to student activists of the 1970s and a word of caution to the youth of today: To bring about revolutionary change, we need to be committed to more than just an idea or ideal.

The director also enacts poetic justice on Vikram who is apathetic to the injustices around him. Vikram has a definite understanding of the exploitative ways the capitalist class empowers and ensures their hegemonic positions and applies this knowledge to acquire capital and power. His life centres on corrupt and destructive business collaborations; he has no qualms about negotiating deals that would leave villages in ruins. Using his middle-class status to justify his material values, he tells Geeta, 'Siddharth was born with a silver spoon in his mouth—he can afford to do the things he does; we can't' (*Hazaaron*). Vikram rightly meets his fate in Bhojpur at the hands of power structures he refused to rise against. Fearful of being punished for losing Siddharth, a high-target prisoner, the Bhojpur police decide to use Vikram as a substitute; a merciless beating on the head leaves Vikram in a vegetative state, a state that symbolizes his moral and ethical numbness. Vikram personifies the Indian population who play an integral role in India's neocolonial problems. The message Mishra appears to deliver is that our existence is no better than Vikram's vegetative state if we do nothing to fight injustice and alter unequal power relations.

The failures of Siddharth and Vikram are offset by Geeta's actions; unlike Siddharth, the violence Geeta encounters and the injustices she witnesses only strengthen her conviction to choose a path that Siddharth once admired. Both Geeta and Siddharth are protected by their class privilege; although Geeta decides to return to the village, she does not want their son to grow up in a 'dangerous' place and she sends him to live with her parents in Delhi. While Siddharth exemplifies the wealthy radical student activists who entered traditional professions, Geeta represents the urban youth who were influenced by social movements and became grass-roots activists. Mishra has earned a reputation for writing strong roles for women.[7] In *Hazaaron* as in *Chameli* and *Inkaar*, the female image and the female body are not just sites of violence; they are also sites of contestation, courage and resistance. Both Siddharth and Vikram are saved by the very bodies that are bound to inequitable and violent patriarchal structures. However, *Hazaaron* distances personal injustices; instead, it focuses on epistemic violence and repression and systems of patriarchy and power; thus, the film does not pointedly address Geeta's rape by her husband and the police. Geeta's experiences in conjunction with other forms of violence including caste oppression, police brutality and forced sterilization serve to underscore the grotesque injustices, inequalities and tyrannies that plague the nation. When the film does call attention to a personal injustice, the scene serves to highlight moments of solidarity and humanity. For instance, when a wealthy landlord's son rapes a woman, the villagers decide to collectively seek vengeance. Moments later, the landlord suffers a heart attack; instantly, the villagers' response is to help their oppressor rather than watch him die. Siddharth, who is narrating this incident to Geeta in a letter, interprets the villagers' compassion as duty, a reaction to long-existing differential power

relations. Siddharth's admission that he is 'still trying to understand' the significance of the villagers' act of kindness (*Hazaaron*)
perhaps reflects his narrow understanding of the role that violence plays in resistance movements. He perceives violence as an
inevitable and necessary course of action, as Frantz Fanon (1965:
27) pointed out, 'to change the order of the world', but he seems to
forget that physical violence by the oppressed classes is not gra-
tuitous violence fuelled by hate and resentment. Thus, although
Siddharth recognizes the inhumanity of the oppressor, he fails to
appreciate the humanity of the oppressed; had the villagers emulated the landlord and remained impervious to his pain, their collective action for justice would have had little meaning.

Addressing the legitimacy of the Naxalites' use of violence
to free and defend themselves, their families and land, in a 2010
guest column titled 'Heart of Darkness', Mishra (2010) writes, 'We
have failed to see it as a valid militancy, because at the heart of it
is desperate poverty.' He chides the government for its negligent
and militaristic attitude towards India's tribal communities; at the
same time, he also calls for 'Naxals ... to give up violence'. Like
René Maublanc who was convinced that 'the proletariat needs
allies who come from the bourgeois camp' (Benjamin 1934: 6),
Mishra believes that the Naxalites' war against injustice, discrimination and poverty can be won only by solidarity across class and
caste lines. 'The answer to the Naxal crisis', according to Mishra
(2010), 'is dependent on urban Indians reaching out. They owe
a great responsibility to the disadvantaged, because if a nation
is to progress, it must take all people along with it'. Mishra's
political positions come across clearly in *Hazaaron*. He seems to
consciously interlink the lives of his urban protagonists with the
villagers of Bhojpur to illustrate that they are interdependent on
each other and collective action is imperative to accomplish what
Siddharth set out to do — 'to change the world, and change it fundamentally' (*Hazaaron*).

Mishra offers a film that teaches without preaching and persuades without invasion; but the overt politics, the anti-heroic
male representations, the unconventionally strong female protagonist, combined with the lack of collective memory about the

Emergency era and apathy towards revolutionary struggles may be some reasons why *Hazaaron* is not a popular film. A decade after its release, the sociopolitical issues Mishra unsparingly exposes in *Hazaaron* continue to remain relevant. Wedded to neoliberal forms of development, India has seen an exponential rise in ruthless forms of capitalist exploitation, socio-economic inequalities, and large-scale destruction of lives, livelihoods and lands. The aberrant methods of state control and violence of the Emergency period have now become normalized and justified under pretexts of national security and growth. Revolutionary forces in various parts of the country are locked in battles for justice with corporate, state, military and paramilitary forces. Rape, corruption, religious and national fundamentalism, and the iniquitous caste system are some of the many dark problems that beset the nation. It seems fitting that *Hazaaron* ends on the outskirts of Bhojpur, where trucks stormed through the trees with state authorities who arrested, persecuted and raped the villagers; as the final shot captures the peaceful quiet of a distant tree line, a contemporary audience may wonder, how long before the trucks come again through the trees.

A Final Word

Hazaaron, as well as other Mishra's films, illustrates that dreams cannot be eradicated and in dreams is birthed hope. But how does hope persevere in the face of the inescapable facts of social existence? From the films with which he began his career to the recent *Inkaar*, Mishra has been unflinching in his examination of what happens when people must choose between compassionate love and ambition in the struggle to make something meaningful of their lives. His work challenges the viewer to ask what it will take to confront the gross injustices and inequalities that stifle and destroy dreams on a daily basis. For his own part, Mishra does not spell out answers, but rather believes that 'if there is a loss of faith he has to narrate that' (*Baavra Mann* 2013). That his 'narrations' are so rich and compelling come from the fact that they are intelligent but never cold. Here is where Mishra's deft commingling of elements drawn from both the art cinema and mainstream Hindi film-making come to the fore. The dialogues, music, the consummate acting and the visual storytelling combine to impress upon the audience a deeply humane perspective on contemporary India. Indeed it is his ability to invest incisive and even painful reflections with deeply felt emotion that makes his films vital and essential viewing.

Notes

1   In Jaideep Varma's documentary on Sudhir Mishra, Mishra himself describes direction as 'an act of imposition' (*Baavra Mann* 2013).
2   The film was produced in 2003 but not released until 2005. We are choosing to use the release date in this essay.
3   Director Anurag Kashyap refers to this influence in Jaideep Varma's documentary about Sudhir Mishra, *Baavra Mann* (2013).
4   The Hindi word *basti* is somewhat misleadingly translated as 'slum', creating the impression of a disorderly space of lumpen inhabitants while failing to emphasize the structural implications for inhabitants of living in an illegal and unofficial settlement. Mumbai's so-called slums house a significant cross section of blue- and white-collar labour, service industry workers and small manufacturing industries. Appearances aside, residential and work spaces are orderly and often scrupulously maintained. Yet, access to water, waste disposal and electricity are significant challenges, and despite the indispensability of slum dwellers to the functioning of the city, their rights are tenuous at best.
5   In her article, '"Come and See the Blood on the Streets": Cinematic Representation of Student Activism in India and Mexico', Sonya Surabhi Gupta compares *Hazaaron* with Jorge Fons' Rojo Amanecer, Mexico's first feature film that deals with the 2 October 1968 Tlatelolco massacre of hundreds of unarmed protestors, mostly students by government armed forces (Gupta 2009: 110).
6   Commenting on the epistolary format, Gupta (2009: 120) notes that the letters from Siddharth and Vikram to Geeta offer Vikram, not Siddharth, an opportunity to offer counter statements.
7   Alka Kurian (2012) provides a detailed gender analysis of films that deal with the Naxalite movement in her book chapter 'Radical Politics and Gender in Govind Nihalani's *Hazaar Chaurasi Ki Maa*, Sudhir Mishra's *Hazaaron Khwaishein Aisi* and Gangavihari Borate's *Lal Salaam*'.

References

Benjamin, W. 1934. 'The Author as Producer.' Translated by John Heckman. Reprint, *New Left Review* I/62 (July–August 1970): 1–9. Retrieved 20 May 2015, from http://newleftreview.org/I/62/walter-benjamin-the-author-as-producer

Bhayani, V. 2004, August 18. 'Sudhir Mishra Film Only Indian Entry at Edinburgh.' 18 August. Retrieved 25 May 2015, from http://www.indiaglitz.com/sudhir-mishra-film-only-indian-entry-at-edinburgh-hindi-news-10261

Bose, R. 2009. 'Writing "Realism" in Bombay Cinema: Tracing the Figure of the "Urdu Writer" through *Khoya Khoya Chand.*' *Economics and Political Weekly* 44 (47): 61–66.

Brown, W. 1999. 'Resisting Left Melancholy.' *Boundary 2* 26 (3): 19–27.

Chintamani, G. 2012, June 30. 'Who's Afraid of the Big Bad Emergency? Bollywood.' Retrieved 20 May 2015, from http://www.firstpost.com/bollywood/whos-afraid-of-the-big-bad-emergency-bollywood-361738.html

Dyer, R. 2006. *Pastiche: Knowing Imitation.* New York: Routledge.

Fanon, F. 1965. *The Wretched of the Earth.* London: MacGibbon & Kee.

Ganghar, A. 1996. 'Films from the City of Dreams.' In *Bombay, Mosaic of Modern Culture,* edited by Sujata Patel and Alice Thorner, 210–24. New York: Oxford University Press.

Gupta, Sonya S. 2009. '"Come and See the Blood on the Streets": Cinematic Representation of Student Activism in India and Mexico.' *Contemporary Perspectives* 3 (1): 106–24.

Kozloff, S. 1989. *Invisible Storytellers: Voice-over Narration in American Fiction Film.* Berkeley, CA: University of California Press.

Kurian, A. 2012. *Narratives of Gendered Dissent in South Asian Cinemas.* London: Routledge.

Lowe, N. 1986. 'The Well-tempered Plot Device.' *Ansible* 46. Retrieved 15 May 2015, from http://news.ansible.uk/plotdev.html

Mazumdar, R. 2007. *Bombay Cinema: An Archive of the City.* Minneapolis: University of Minnesota Press.

Mishra, S. 2006, December 4. 'Thirsting for Pyaasa.' *Outlook.* Retrieved 11 May 2015, from http://www.outlookindia.com/article/thirsting-for-pyaasa/233289

———. 2010, May 30. 'Heart of Darkness.' Retrieved 11 May 2015, from http://shekharkapur.com/blog/2010/05/heart-of-darkness-guest-column-by-sudhir-mishra/

Mistron, Deborah E. 1984. 'A Hybrid Subgenre: The Revolutionary Melodrama in the Mexican Cinema.' *Studies in Latin American Popular Culture* 3: 47–56.

Street, S. 2001. *Costume and Cinema : Dress Codes in Popular Film*. New York: Wallflower Books.

Film References

Ali, S. 2005. *Bunty Aur Babli*. Yash Raj Films.

Attenborough, R. 1982. *Gandhi*. International Film Investors and NFDC.

Barjatya, S. 1989. *Maine Pyaar Kiya*. Rajshri Productions.

Bazmee, A. 2005. *No Entry*. Narsimha Enterprises and Sahara One.

Bhandarkar, M. 2005. *Page 3*. Lighthouse Entertainment.

Bhansali, S. 2005. *Black*. SLB Films Pvt Ltd and Applause Entertainment.

Chopra, Yash. 1975. *Deewaar*. Trimurti Films Pvt Ltd.

Gowariker, A. 2001. *Lagaan: Once Upon a Time in India*. Aamir Khan Productions, Ashutosh Gowariker Productions Pvt. Ltd and Jhamu Sugandh Productions.

Jha, P. 2010. *Raajneeti*. Prakash Jha Productions, UTV Motion Pictures and Walkwater Media.

Mehta, K. 2005. *The Rising: Ballad of Mangal Pandey*. Kaleidoscope Entertainment and Maya Movies.

Mehra, P. 1973. *Zanjeer*. Prakash Mehra Productions.

Mehra, R. Omprakash. 2006. *Rang De Basanti*. ROMP and UTV Motion Pictures.

Mishra, S. 2013. *Inkaar*. Viacom 18 Motion Pictures.

——. 2013. *Kirchiyaan*. Large Short Films.

——. 2011. *Mumbai Cutting*. Sahara One Motion Pictures and White Cloud Productions.

——. 2007. *Khoya Khoya Chand*. Holy Cow Pictures.

——. 2005. *Hazaaron Khwaishein Aisi*. Pritish Nandy Communications.

——. 2003. *Chameli*. Pritish Nandy Communications.

——. 2003. *Calcutta Mail*. Sanghmitra Arts.

——. 1996. *Is Raat Ki Subah Nahin*. Plus Films.

——. 1992. *Dharavi*. 1992. Doordarshan and NFDC.

——. 1988. *Main Zinda Hoon*. Doordarshan.

Ratnam, M. 2004. *Yuva*. Madras Talkies.

Sippy, R. 1975. *Sholay*. Sippy Films.

Varma, J. 2013. *Baavra Mann: A Film on Sudhir Mishra*. Films Division. Retrieved 17 September 2016, from https://www.youtube.com/watch?v=eLuQpo22B30

13

Ashutosh Gowariker: Narrativizing the 'Nation'

Tutun Mukherjee

Two powerful technological mediums that the West made available to India during the colonial period were the printing press and cinema. It is significant that both as mass media became powerful instruments for fostering anti-colonialism and the 'imagining of a nation'. As Benedict Anderson (1983) famously describes, 'a nation is an imaginary construct, a creation of a geo-political and cultural idea where none exists, and forging ideological constructions to link a self-defined cultural group with the State-to-come' (p. 6). While the print medium provided exhortative rhetoric to inspire Swadeshi sentiments (reclaiming 'own land'), cinema worked in more subtle and subliminal ways to kindle communitarian emotions to fight 'evil' and restore the sway of the 'sacred'. With the freedom struggle gaining momentum, the binaries of good and bad and the context of 'a testing time' became very clear in the film narratives of the time. Hence, as has been said of Hollywood cinema, Hindi cinema too can be called the historian of the India's changing destiny and its social-cultural shifts as 'an unwitting recorder of national moods' (Rollins 1983: 1).

Indeed, the earliest films made by Dhundiraj Govind Phalke, who was fondly called 'Dadasaheb', which revived and reconstructed myths of 'heroes' who overpower evil with determination, were each a deliberate and careful activation of the metaphoric depths of the medium with its potent psycho-social impact to stamp enduring images on the mind. The historic *Raja Harishchandra* (1913) retells the story of a king reduced to abject destitution as a test of his dharma. The narrative shows not only the loss of wealth, dominion and power of the king but also, more importantly, of his identity. A king becomes a 'nobody' and dwells in the cremation ground where only death or nothingness prevails. Finally, after undergoing inexplicable travails, Harishchandra regains all that he lost with additional acclamation because of his indomitable spiritual power and unswerving sense of dharma throughout the horrific experiences. Phalke followed with more films like *Mohini Bhasmasur* (1913), *Satyavan Savitri* (1914), *Lanka Dahan* (1917), *Shri Krishna Janma* (1918), *Kaliya Mardan* (1919) — all retellings of well-known episodes from *puranas* and epics that Phalke's audience could easily identify and relate to, thus triggering collective memory and historical consciousness about crises that could be overcome with courage and faith in oneself. These films are categorized as mythologicals. Actually, what is common to all is their use of mythemes to trigger collective memory of earlier fights against evil and deliberately mythicize the historical context as a critical time when people need moral reinforcement to persevere towards the attainment of their goal. Preeti Kumar (2015) writes that Phalke's *Kaliya Mardan* showed Krishna vanquishing the serpent Kaliya, to the background chorus of Vande Mataram, the revolutionary song of the Indian Freedom Movement. Also, in the retelling of episodes from the Mahabharata in *Bhakta Vidur* (Kanjibhai Rathod, 1921), the wise man Vidura appears in dhoti and cap, thus drawing a parallel with Gandhi. The film also included a song on the *charkha* or the spinning wheel invoked by Gandhi as a symbol of self-reliance and of the Indian National Congress. Preeti Kumar writes that 'allied to a significant moment in the life of a nation' stories about heroes are pivotal in the process of reviving memory towards the construction of a discourse of national self-identity (Kumar website). As Patrick Colm Hogan remarks, 'we rely on metaphors to understand the nation. Needless to say, nationalists draw on a variety of models to represent the nation' (2011: 135). However, it is important to remember that the revival of myths during the Indian freedom struggle presented majorly Hindu models for interpreting the historical situation, and to a large extent the National Congress Party is also allied to this construction of the 'nation' and 'national identity'. Even Raja Ravi Varma's oleographs of Hindu deities initially printed at Phalke's studio were also seen as supporting the Hindu-led freedom movement. It isn't surprising, therefore, that Bombay cinema's role as a major producer and disseminator of ideology was used to promote 'Hindutva ideology' and till date has been targeted for this by some critics (see Khan 2011). Nevertheless, the entire endeavour did extend positive support to the nationalist struggle of the time. Famous scriptwriter J. Michael Straczynski (1999) once remarked that 'the point of mythology or myth is to point to the horizon and to point back at ourselves: this is who we are, this is where we came from, and this is where we're going'. He bemoans the fact that societies are ignoring and forgetting their myths which is a cultural loss. This, however, cannot be said of Hindi and regional films in India whose diegesis continue to draw heavily on mythemes.

This chapter will focus on some films directed by Ashutosh Gowariker, which have left a mark on the history of Indian filmmaking. Gowariker as a model and actor in theatre, TV and cinema was comfortable in front of the camera, but always wanted to direct films and, thus, fulfilled in his life what is stated in his blog as what he was 'destined' for (refer to Gowariker's blog[1]). His debut as director was *Pehla Nasha* in 1993, followed by *Baazi* in 1995, both mediocre formula thrillers in the typical Hindi cinema style that had mediocre commercial success. The first films provided hands-on experience with the basics of film-making and whetted his appetite for meaningful cinema as he searched for a definite direction for his kind of cinema. This chapter will discuss his directorial signposts like *Lagaan: Once Upon a Time in India*

(2001; henceforth, *Lagaan*), *Swades* (2004), *Jodhaa Akbar* (2008) and *Khelein Hum Jee Jaan Sey* (2010)[2] which do indicate a certain path he is trying to follow as he develops a directorial style of his own. Evidently his choice was not art, parallel or alternate cinema but commercially viable yet meaningful and inspiring cinema. He had, therefore, to first learn to negotiate the precarious balance between 'cinema with a purpose' and 'cinema as formula entertainment' to ensure that his films don't flip either into complex expressivity or crass commercialism. As every film-maker knows, there is no golden rule that assures artistic and commercial success of any film, no matter how big the production or how good the director may be. Keeping the huge market for Hindi cinema in mind, the target audience remains an enigmatic and amorphous mass and can be neither under- nor over-estimated. Until its release, one can never be sure if a film is pitched right and will click with the audience and thereby the 'box office'. Big budget–big banner–multi-star films can flop at the box office while small-budget niche films can become runaway successes. Inevitably, however, the reason for the success is a well-knit, well-made film with a topical and appealing story. As film-making is a truly democratic endeavour, depending on the input of every component that creates a film, the final success also depends on the balanced output of the entire team. Failure of one link in the chain would impact the end product.

In a brief conversation during 'Bimal Roy Film Society' meeting in Mumbai on 23 February 2006, Ashutosh Gowariker credited Bimal Roy and Mahboob Khan as the two most powerful influences on his film-making. It is noteworthy that Roy's *Do Bigha Zamin* (1953), Khan's *Mother India* (1957) and Gowariker's *Lagaan* (2001) highlight the theme of the integral bonding between people and their land although the cinematic treatment is different in each film. Ancient literature available to us, such as *Krishi-Parashara*, Kautilya's *Arthasastra*, Panini's *Ashtadhyayi*, Tamil Sangam literature, *Manusmriti*, Varahamihira's *Brihat Samhita*, *Amarakosha*, *Kashyapiya-Krishisukti*, Surapala's *Vrikshayurveda*, to mention a few, all describe India as agri-dependent civilization, and its society and culture deriving from such values. All the three films mythologize 'land' as nurturer, haven, heritage and identity. Although each film spins away in different trajectories with their plots, all show that despite agriculture being the source of economic sustenance for the society from ancient times, the modern-day situation and laws are not farmer-friendly. Exploitation thrives and pulverizes the peasants in its grip. Ironically, even in the year 2015, 68 years after Independence, the situation remains unchanged. The misery of the farmers has not alleviated, their issues don't seem to have received adequate attention nor have their problems been politically addressed. Incidents of landless or debt-ridden farmers committing suicide are frequent occurrences. Films such as *Do Bigha Zamin, Mother India* and *Lagaan* could very well represent the current situation. Hence, their contemporaneity remains undiminished. The remarkable feature is that the films are able to link the ancient past and the immediate past with the present through the slow unravelling of the mythical bond of the land and its people.

Made soon after Independence, *Do Bigha Zamin* shows the gradual transformation of the society from agri-dependence to urbanization, when loss of land leading to the loss of traditional livelihood drives villagers to the cities in search of jobs. Rendered rootless, they become the flotsam in the urban jungle and part of the 'unintended city' (see Jai Sen 1976). Shambhu Mahto owes the zamindar 65 rupees. When he somehow manages to collect the money, accounts are manipulated to show a much larger sum. The case goes to court that depends on definite proof and witnesses. Shambhu's protest that God is his witness is received with scornful laughter. Shambhu forfeits his hereditary land and journeys to the city where he pulls the rickshaw and his son becomes a shoeshine to bring few annas home. The grim struggle for survival depletes their lives of hope and joy. Unable to resist the pull of the land, they return to the village to gaze through the iron grills of the gate at the factory being built on their land. Shambhu picks up a lump of earth from his land and is chased away as thief by the watchman. The family walks away towards the ever-receding horizon. The story written by another maestro, Salil Choudhury, is a poignant narrative of alienation, dehumanization, helplessness of poverty and the process of 'othering'. Khan's *Mother India*, made 10 years after Independence, elaborates the adversities to be confronted with moral and spiritual strength. The plot is a resurrection of Khan's earlier film *Aurat* (1940) but with a changed context to combine what M.K. Raghavendra describes as 'optimistic nationalism of the Nehru era...a "national" epic replete with Soviet-style lyrical agrarianism' combined with the Nehruvian slogan of 'modernization' (2008: 36). In a flash-forward, the protagonist Radha, now an old woman, is invited to dedicate the village canal to the people. She is honoured as a 'survivor' in life's battle and the film rewinds to describe her past full of hardships and sorrow, a helpless and illiterate woman face-to-face with avaricious cunning that claims 3/4 portions of her land's produce. Radha doesn't surrender to circumstances but confronts life with intrepidity, even to the extent of shooting her son to save dharma. Her elder son is now a member of the political hierarchy. She is bestowed the virtues of Bharat Mata and symbolizes the creation of a more secular myth of Nation as Mother. Neither film tries to flag any specific ideology, though *Do Bigha Zamin* is regarded as the frontrunner of the neo-realist or new wave cinema in India in which the misery of displacement and loss of livelihood are not glossed over or romanticized. Both films are quite brutal in presenting the indifference of nation's so-called 'builders' to the plight of the poor, especially farmers who are the backbone of the country. Neither film shies away from showing selfish ruthlessness and corrupt human behaviour gaining an upper hand, though *Mother India* moves more towards the melodramatic paradigm which was to become the overwhelming trend of Hindi cinema. Both films narrate realistic issues of ordinary lives, their joy in the possession of land, their simplicity yet stoic acceptance of sorrows to be faced. Herein lie their heroism and nobility.

Gowariker's *Lagaan* (2001) acknowledges the influence of the two great masters through its theme, characterization and music. But the narrative and the outcome are definitely more romantic. The forerunners are invoked from the opening scenes as the dark monsoon clouds in the overcast sky are welcomed by the farming folk with joy as the harbinger of the fecundity of the land. The songs 'Hariyala Sawan Dhol Bajata Aaya' and 'Dharti Kahe Pukar Ke' and 'Dukh Bhare Din Beete Re Bhaiya' of the earlier films resound in the wonderfully choreographed 'Ghanana Ghanan' of *Lagaan*, as do the songs of celebration of Krishna's birthday or Holi. The simple joys of community life are shown to emphasize the shared roots of culture and belief which should translate as collective strength, but often do not. In *Lagaan*, meaning land taxes, the villagers of Champaner grapple with severe drought and the inexorable demand for land taxes by the zamindar and colonial masters. This means that most of the harvest surplus is gone and there is minimal food left for the farmers themselves. When their pleas for waiving—or even deferment—of taxes in view of the drought fail they don't despair but accept what appears to be a hopeless challenge to defeat the British at their own game. It is a desperate gamble. If they can defeat the British in a game of cricket which they have absolutely no idea about, their land taxes will be waived for three years. But if they lose, they must pay triple *lagaan*, which would lead to their total ruin. The spirit of resilience of 'never say die' that pushes them is like that of Shambhu or Radha, not to be overcome by terrific odds. What follows is not a mere game of cricket, but a 'Once upon a time' mythical battle of epic proportions if the high stakes are taken into account. It becomes an extraordinary fight to establish 'justice' and 'humanity' that the underdogs or, in this case, the 'ordinary heroes' ultimately win. Clearly, *Lagaan* is a 'fairy tale'; it doesn't share the cynical realism of *Do Bigha Zamin* and is closer to the 'feel good' and 'all's well that ends well' mood of *Mother India*. It also exudes certain amount of national confidence of the post-globalization era when Hindi cinema, with its new branding as 'Bollywood', emerged as a serious contender in the world's cinema circulation network.

The point to note is that the use of religious mythemes is in place in all the three films. *Do Bigha Zamin*'s protagonist is Shambhu, invoking the autochthonous Shiva who swallows poison to secure others' happiness; here too Shambhu/ Shiva's wife is Parvati; their son is Kanhaiya, as the playful child Krishna was fondly called, to contrast the loss of childhood and innocence of this child yoked to the grim battle for survival. *Mother India*'s Radha invokes Krishna's beloved as the symbol of love; she is also Lakshmi the goddess of the household and the Earth mother. *Lagaan*'s hero is 'Bhuvan' meaning the world, and his lover is Gauri, another name for Shiva's wife. Bhuvan's 'mai'/ mother represents a strong symbol for Earth mother or land. All three films stress the deep bonding of land with its people and I argue that all of them narrativize the nation by making the 'space' tangible as India. This is strengthened through careful cinematography that captures Indian landscape through seasons, pans the land and the sky in seamless shots, shows the skin colour of the characters to match that of the earth, their costumes and rituals; Hindu festivals as well as those celebrating rites of cultivation provide occasions for songs and dances imperative for Hindi melodrama. Worth mentioning here are the painterly shots and carefully edited sequences of *Do Bigha Zamin* which are not matched by the other two films though the camera work of Faredoon Irani in *Mother India* and Anil Mehta in *Lagaan* is praiseworthy. The characters speak a dialect that is a fusion of rustic and standard to be meaningful for a pan-Indian audience. In addition, *Mother India* and *Lagaan* have their share of songs of romance. All three films received critical acclaim at home and abroad and became paradigms of cinematic excellence. Balraj Sahni, a brilliant actor, is understood to have said, 'I shall die happy to know I acted in *Do Bigha Zamin*'; Nargis became the iconic personification of Mother India; *Lagaan* launched Aamir Khan's production company and created his image as a discerning actor. *Lagaan* earned Ashutosh Gowariker his place among filmmakers of repute and indicated the path for the kind of cinema he would pursue. Gowariker's next film *Swades* (Own Country), released in 2004, was inspired by K. Shivaram Karanth's novel *Chigurida Kanasu*, which had been made into a Kannada film earlier. Gowariker explains that the plot of his film also derives from the real-life story of two 'Non-Resident Indians' or NRIs Aravinda Pillalamarri and Ravi Kuchimanchi who returned to India from the United States and developed the pedal power generator to light remote, off-the-grid village schools; Gowariker spent considerable time with them to understand their motivation and their success.

Swades is a journey of discovery of his country and its people for NRI Mohan Bhargava (Shah Rukh Khan) who grew up in the United States and works as a project manager at NASA. After the death of his parents, Bhargava travels to India hoping to renew contact with his nanny. He learns that she lives in her village Charanpur. Mohan Bhargava's physical journey into the rural interiors of the country that is his own but from which he has been alienated is also an inward journey of finding his roots and identity. The director adopts the process of *ostranenie* or what the Russian linguists explain as 'defamiliarization', that is, to present common and familiar things in an unfamiliar or strange ways to nuance perception as gradual awareness. This leads the way to sensitive inner perception of a metropolitan Indian venturing into domains never seen or experienced before. The variety of people he meets acquaints him with equally varied temperaments, interests, attitudes and living conditions—some amusing and some harsh such as the helpless and hopeless poverty, caste[3] discrimination, child marriage,[4] illiteracy, child labour,[5] general disregard of progress, pessimistic apathy to change. Bhargava settles down in the village and the adjustment isn't easy, nor is it easy to understand the rigid attitudes of the people, their complacencies about being 'the best in the world' although this is just an unsubstantiated boast. Bhargava shocks them by saying their country is not the best but has the potential to become so if they take upon themselves the onus to improve their condition and stop shifting blame on others or wait for others to do their work for them. He decides to work as a catalyst of change. For instance, he persuades the villagers not to shift the school away from the village by convincing them about the importance of education of their children and wins the appreciation of the schoolteacher Gita who is a childhood friend. The decisive point in Bhargava's life comes after his visit to the adjacent village to collect rent on Gita's behalf from the tenant Haridas. He returns empty-handed unable to insist on the payment of rent on seeing Haridas's abject poverty, his struggle to even feed his children. The reason for his desperate condition is the village elders not allowing Haridas to change his profession from that of a weaver to a farmer. The mire of prejudice and caste-entrenched mind-set, regressive and self-centred thinking, reluctance to advancement and lack of openness to knowledge hinder rather than enhance life here. Gowariker brings into the diegetic discourse the difficulties in the path of development that, however, are resolvable with a positive attitude and little initiative. But such awareness cannot be imposed; it must emerge from within. It is the success of the script, direction and acting that the motivating rhetoric, hard-hitting and inspiring, does not become pedantic. Bhargava spends time with the children to introduce them to the marvels of science that can be harnessed for humanitarian purposes, and to extend their horizon of knowledge by literally taking them into the fascinating galactic world of stars and planets with the help of a small telescope. Bhargava is determined to do his bit to improve the quality of life for the villagers and drive home the fact that they must themselves solve the problems they face and that the solutions to remove their backwardness lie within their power. He taps the energy and enthusiasm of the villagers who merely lack proper ideas and guidance in the implementation of those ideas. He garners support to build a reservoir to both store water from the perennial spring from the hill and set up a small hydroelectric power plant to provide electricity to the village and, thus, make it self-sufficient and self-reliant. That this is not a pipe-dream has been proved by the real-life enterprise of Aravinda Pillalamarri and Ravi Kuchimanch mentioned above with whom Gowariker spent quality time to understand the entire process of their endeavour. In the film, as his hydel project nears completion, Bhargava's vacation from work is also over. When he prepares for his return to the United States, his nanny is reluctant to leave the village at her age to travel to a strange land and live among alien people; Gita whom he loves chooses to stay behind too to fulfil her promise to her father to keep the village school going. Back in the United States, Bhargava is restless and disturbed as images of his homeland, the poverty and helplessness of the people and their desperation impinge on his consciousness. The people, the sights and sounds, the colour and smell of India beckon him. Shah Rukh Khan does credit to the role and projects a finely tuned portrayal of the protagonist Mohan Bhargava. The film ends by showing Mohan Bhargava back in the village after finishing his project and resigning his lucrative and prestigious job at NASA, and thereby disproves the parody (used in the film) of the acronym NRI as the 'Non-Returning-Indian'!

Swades is a motivating film that justifiably received critical acclaim, although the box-office returns didn't match that of *Lagaan*. The similarity between the two films in terms of cinematographic style and thematic concern for 'inspirational films' that convey message and also entertain seem to indicate the cinematic path Gowariker has embarked upon and is set to follow regardless of monetary gain. What he wants to make are meaningful films. The epigraph for *Swades* is a quotation from Mohandas Karamchand Gandhi exhorting the people to not 'hesitate to act because the whole vision might not be achieved, or because others do not share it, is an attitude that only hinders progress', meaning, 'nothing attempted is nothing gained'. Champaner won a battle for self-respect and rights; Charanpur gains in self-confidence and self-reliance. Very importantly, Swades is an appeal to successful Indians abroad to answer the call of their mother country. Both films carry positive and compelling ideas and stress that myths are replayed in different forms through human life. The mythemes in *Swades* as for his later film *Khelein Hum Jee Jaan Sey* are nationalist in spirit just as the first films of the Silent Era were.

Frank Kermode once remarked that 'myths are agents of stability, fictions the agents of change. Myths call for absolute, fictions for conditional assent. Myths make sense in terms of a lost order of time; fictions, if successful, make sense of here and now' (1967: 39). Thus juxtaposed, the two present the key components of fictionality. Gowariker's cinema attempts to weave such strands of fictionality towards certain empirical stabilities which he believes are foundational for a cohesive and peaceful nation. Hence, the next notable film in Gowariker's cinematic journey is the spectacular and epic recreation of the historical regime of the great Mughal emperor Akbar recounted through the lens of romance.

Jodhaa Akbar, made in 2008, develops as a bildungsroman, narrativizing young Akbar's gradual political maturation and his attempt to forge a spirit of religious tolerance, even promoting a new religion to reduce hostility between the two factions of Hindus and Muslims and the struggle for dominance of one group over the other, and building the 'Ibadat Khana' as a common hall for prayers for all religious groups. Perhaps the most significant act of all was the abolition of the detested 'jizya' tax levied on Hindus embarking on pilgrimages, which, as is shown in the film, wins for him a place in the hearts of the people as 'Shahenshah-e-Hindustan'. This also wins Jodha's approbation and she returns to Akbar and is proclaimed 'Malika-e-Hindustan'. Akbar, though illiterate, had immense curiosity about different faiths, knowledge systems and philosophical issues, and encouraged debates and discussions on these subjects. Through a shrewd blend of diplomacy, intimidation and brute force, Akbar had secured his empire extending from the Hindu Kush to the Deccan. Often kings and emperors married many wives to forge political alliances. This becomes the plot that Gowariker develops through his version of Akbar's reign. The film narrative takes off from the Akbar's decision to marry Jodha Bai the princess of Amer to strengthen ties with the Hindu Rajputs. Although the identity of 'Jodha' as the name of the Hindu princess Akbar marries is contested as some documents refer to her Islamic name Mariam-uz-Zamani, Gowariker claims to have historically authenticated the basis of his narrative. It becomes clear from the beginning that keeping the Indian 'box office' in mind, the story would develop more as a family drama and romance and less as a historical re-telling except for retaining the kernel of wisdom of topical relevance for contemporary India: Akbar's method of sustaining an empire that could be torn asunder by religious antagonism. Thus, Akbar learns the tenets of 'nation-building'.

The film shows that Jodha is forced by family circumstances (clan disputes) to accept the inter-religious marriage with Akbar but refuses to remain a pawn in the political game and compromise her dignity and self-respect. She extracts a promise from the emperor that she won't be forced to change her religion nor be coerced into conjugality. Even her family is shocked at these 'impertinent demands' as Jodha's ploy for the marriage proposal being rejected assuming the emperor's refusal. Akbar, however, surprises all by accepting these demands and, thus, the narrative underlines 'hero' Akbar's sensitivity and respect for women in the prohibitively patriarchal set-up of both Hindu and Muslim societies. Akbar learns to respect and gradually love and admire his wife, her beauty, dignity, intelligence and her religion. He allows her to retain her faith, build a Krishna temple within his fort and hold festivities. History endorses that Akbar participated in these religious ceremonies. The film shows the lead pair as strong-willed yet greatly attracted towards each other whose romance blossoms in an enticing manner — imaged as the thrust-and-parry of fencing allowing Jodha to be the winner when Akbar is momentarily distracted, and through domestic tensions and misunderstandings so typical of the Indian domestic domain that audience sympathy is immediately secured for the daughter-in-law who on entering a 'new and strange' household confronts hostility of certain kinds. The prime plotter is Akbar's wet nurse Maham Anga, who enjoys immense power due to Akbar's indulgence for nursing him through childhood when his father Humayun was in exile and his mother was with her husband. Maham Anga as the mother-in-law by default, rules over the domestic domain including the harem keeping the private–public strictly separate but overlaps the boundaries herself to participate in court proceedings, advise young Akbar on statecraft and influence his decisions. Sensing Akbar's attraction and admiration for the strong-willed Jodha, Maham Anga plans to poison his mind against her. Mindful of his unquestioned trust in her which was the source of her power-play, Maham Anga swallows the insult when Akbar had her son cruelly killed for insubordination. She, in fact, pretends to support his decision and action. Akbar falls prey to her evil machinations and sends Jodha back to her parents', till the queen-mother Hamida Banu Begum takes up her position as the true 'mother-in-law' in control of the inner quarters, reveals the web of deception to Akbar and pushes him towards reconciliation with Jodha Bai. Realizing the grave injustice he had committed, Akbar visits

Amer to apologize and request Jodha's return. Jodha asserts her will again and says she will return when convinced of his sincerity about respecting human values. Akbar learns to gauge grass-roots sentiments of his people regarding law and order and governance, pricing of goods and such other problems of his subjects by walking incognito among them. The uncompromising severity of his nature, usual for such times, is hinted at through the cruel deaths for treachery and insubordination he orders, and the banishment of the conniving clergy and his foster mother. But Gowariker has been accused of disregarding Akbar's merciless massacre of Chittor which is surely a black spot in his otherwise illustrious reign. Gowariker's Akbar is a brave, fearless man and an excellent fighter, more spiritual than fanatically religious, an astute statesman who learns to manage the political and court intrigues of the Ulemas and religious factions. But most of all, Akbar is a charming and sensitive lover who wins the heart of his wife Jodha Bai. Gowariker's film romanticizes Akbar but is able to present him as a complex individual who gradually grows in stature and wisdom to become one of the most successful rulers of the largest empire in India.

Hindi films make no claim to historical authenticity but are constructed as narratives of desire. Neither is Gowariker treading a new path with his fictionalizing of history. Besides myths, history too provided stories for Hindi cinema from 1940s onwards and was presented with the usual romantic angle like Sohrab Modi's *Sikandar* (1941), A.R. Kardar's *Shahjehan* (1946), V. Shantaram's *Dr. Kotnis Ki Amar Kahani* (1946). The biggest blockbuster was K.A. Asif's *Mughal-E-Azam* (1960) which had taken 10 years to complete. Asif's film questions Akbar's justice when confronted with the problem of his only son Salim's (future emperor Jahangir) love for Anarkali, a beautiful dancing girl of the court. The emperor's will which has the honour and respect of the dynasty and the realm in mind, cannot overlook the difference in 'class' — a dancing girl cannot be the future empress of Hindustan — and, therefore, he intervenes to separate the lovers forever. *Mughal-E-Azam* was a landmark film in terms of its magnificent cinematography, acting, and unforgettable songs and dances. It also showed fine crowd-management shots and fighting sequences. The battle scenes despite the absence of any special effects were presented convincingly. This was followed by another romantic film *Taj Mahal* (1963) based on Jahangir's son Shahjehan's love for his queen Arjumand Banu in whose memory he built the splendorous tomb. *Jodhaa Akbar* recalls both the spectacle of *Mughal-E-Azam* and the lyrical charm of *Taj Mahal*. Despite the usual slough of criticisms and the banning of the film in some sectors for alleged misrepresentation of 'Jodha Bai' and the so-called distortion of Rajput history, Gowariker's *Jodhaa Akbar* was declared a massive hit. It must be acknowledged that it was not strictly the history but rather a well-made compact film—with brilliant cinematography, music, crowd sequences and a correct mix of intrigue, violence, passion and populist appeal—which was really the reason for its box-office success. For contemporary India, the marriage of a Hindu princess with a Muslim king was acceptable for the sake of peace, prosperity and the spirit of 'secularism' they would build together, as the film prophesies. Hrithik Roshan delivers one of his best performances, getting into the skin of the character of Gowariker's 'Akbar'. Aishwarya Rai, not known for her acting prowess, looks gorgeous and manages a credible romantic chemistry with Roshan. History helps to augment the 'spectacular' in terms of costumes, jewellery and splashes of brilliant colours, rich sets in castles and forts, battle scenes, and also serves to recall a time when political stability was carved by the tact and understanding of two individuals whose love surmounted all obstacles. Gowariker's subtle message seems to be that empire- or nation-building needs the will to understand people's problems and address them with wisdom, and promoting awareness for collective welfare that should not be derailed by differences of religion and sects. Peter Brooks, in his book *Reading for the Plot* (1984), refers to Freud's analyses of the masterplot in *Beyond the Pleasure Principle* and agrees with both Tzvetan Todorov and Roland Barthes,

> [T]he narrative is the articulation of a set of verbs. These verbs articulate the pressure and drive for desire. Desire is the wish for

the end, for fulfillment, but the fulfillment must be delayed ... [to] understand it in relation to the origin and the desire itself. (111)

Brooks explains that the unfolding story is 'inhabited' by the reader's (in this case, the spectator's) desire, not necessarily individual desire but 'transindividual and intertextually determined desire' taking into account his/her 'expectations for, and of, narrative meanings' (1984: 112). Brooks holds that the plot of a narrative 'mediates meanings within the contradictory human world of the eternal and the mortal', just as Freud's master-plot describes the temporality of desire seeking fulfilment in fictional narratives. Thus, persuasive desire, crafted skilfully in a traditional storytelling style finds ready response from the receptor. As a successful narrative, the film represents the eternal within the temporal to make sense of the 'here and now'. One would say that Gowariker's *Jodhaa Akbar* brings the past alive as an allegory of nation-building.

A forgotten chapter of 'nation-building' constitutes what is referred to as the 'Agniyug' (Fiery Epoch) or the turbulent phase of the freedom struggle during the first quarter of the twentieth century comprising incidents when freedom fighters adopted armed nationalist movement against the British, a 'violent' uprising running parallel to the 'non-violent' movement. It began in Bengal involving charismatic people like the Ghosh brothers Aurobindo and Barin, Pramathanath Mitra, Chittaranjan Das, Bipin Chandra Pal, Sakharam Ganesh Deuskar, Khudiram Bose, Prafulla Chaki, Nalini Gupta, Satyen Bose, and so on supported by two organizations, 'Anusilan Samiti' and 'Jugantar Party' which had underground cells both in Calcutta and Dhaka that soon spread all over Bengal. A section of this group supported violent insurrection. There were 'dacoities' to collect money; looting government treasuries and armouries; acquiring arms, ammunition and bombs. Gowariker's next film, *Khelein Hum Jee Jaan Sey* (2010) dramatizes the Chittagong Armory Raid of 1930 and is based on the book *Do or Die* (2000) by Manini Chatterjee. The film traces the life of the legendary revolutionary Surjo Sen who being a school teacher was fondly referred to as 'Master-da'. The film opens with a group of young revolutionaries—Ganesh Ghosh, Lokenath Baul,[6]

Ambika Chakraborty,[7] Ananta Singh,[8] Kalpana Datta[9] and few others led by Nirmal Sen after his release from jail and accompanied by Pritilata Waddedar[10] — meet Master-da to plan their course of action. Each is assigned the task of collecting information about the British cantonment. They also undergo rigorous training in martial arts, shooting and making bombs. Master-da's plan of looting Chittagong Armory and Auxiliary Force Armory and simultaneously disrupting telephone, telegraph and train connections was put into action on 18 April 1930. The looting is successful in the sense that guns are found but are useless without ammunition and hence burned, and the communication lines are disrupted. Surjo Sen takes a military salute, hoists the National Flag and proclaims a Provisional Revolutionary Government in place. The revolutionaries then split into smaller groups and carry out attacks on British installations. For example, Pritilata Waddedar attacks the European Club and kills the British officers before committing suicide by swallowing cyanide. The revolutionaries are relentlessly pursued by the British police and the army. Many are shot dead and their bodies burned with petrol. Sen is surrounded when he is in hiding in his sister's house. Nirmal Sen is wounded in the ensuing gun-fight. He persuades Master-da to flee while he holds off the attack till he dies. Finally, Sen is captured by the police, tortured in captivity where his teeth and limbs are broken with hammers and then is dragged unconscious to be hanged in Chittagong Central Jail. Later, as homage to Sen's martyrdom, a revolutionary from his group Haripada killed the police super who had led the hunt and final attack and torture on Sen.

The film *Khelein Hum Jee Jaan Sey* ('We Play with Heart and Soul', KHJJS) is an admirable tribute to a forgotten chapter of Indian history and the heroic young people who put their lives at stake for the sake of freedom. Despite the inspirational input, the film did not fare well either with the critics or at the box office, though the effort to re-live history was generously praised. The story-telling lacks grip and becomes too meandering. The Gowariker touch is evident in some well-crafted incidents and scenes with passionate and poignant appeal as, for example, of the young hearts surrendering to the hypnotic patriotic appeal of

'Vande Mataram', combining their innocence and zeal with their idealism, their pledge to secure a free motherland at the cost of their lives. They play the game of life and death fearlessly for the cause they believe in. It is indeed a lesson for contemporary Indians who are complacent about their freedom. The producers of the film went on record to say they didn't recover even 10 per cent of their costs but are proud to give a good film and not a poor one (KHJJS on Wikipedia). It is also reported on the KHJJS Wikipedia page that

> MovieTalkies rated the film 4.5 out of 5 and noted 'Gowariker this time manages to keep a running subtext that underlines the drama with a national emotional resonance right till the heart-wrenching denouement that will bring a lump to the throat of even the most hardened hearts, while the story actually unfolds as a thriller with the planning and execution of five attacks on the British in a single night and its aftermath, a first for Indian cinema. At a time when our cinema needs true calibre to distinguish itself as an art form rather than a medium of lowest common denominator entertainment, *Khelein Hum Jee Jaan Sey* stands as a lighthouse, shining high.

In the words of the influential theorist of nationalism and national identity[11] Ernest Renan:

> A nation is a soul, a spiritual principle. Two things which in truth are but one, constitute this as soul or spiritual principle. One lies in the past, one in the present. One is the possession in common of a rich legacy of memories; the other is present day consent, the desire to live together, the will to perpetuate the value of the heritage that one has received in an undivided form.... A large aggregate of men creates a kind of moral conscience which we call nation (Renan 1996).

In the choice of subjects for his films, Gowariker has indicated his commitment to represent narratives of community and nation-building, encompassing different aspects. In the treatment of the subject, he deploys cues from archives of memory that link the predicaments of the present to the solutions from the past. He seems to subscribe to the view that a nation as an idea emerges from traditions of political thought and social-cultural beliefs which contribute to various nationalist discourses to present the 'idea of nation' as persisting through time.

Gowariker's film *Mohenjo Daro* was released in August 2016. The film attempted to recreate the intriguing Indus Valley Civilization that vanished inexplicably. The film offers an explanation that a series of natural devastations may have forced the people to migrate towards the fertile Ganga-Jamuna belt. However, despite much hype and few commendable visuals, the film was disappointing in almost all aspects and failed to meet audience expectations. The narrative did not captivate as it could not connect the past with the contemporary context, the magic of romance was missing and there were unforgivable and glaring flaws in detailing and acting unexpected from a director of Gowariker's calibre. This only emphasizes the fact that the audience cannot be taken for granted. However, Gowariker is a promising director so one can only wish him wiser from the lesson and await his next venture.

Notes

1   http://www.ashutoshgowariker.com (accessed 24 August 2016).
2   https://en.wikipedia.org/wiki/Khelein_Hum_Jee_Jaan_Sey (accessed 24 August 2016).
3   https://en.wikipedia.org/wiki/Caste_system_in_India   (accessed 24 August 2016).
4   https://en.wikipedia.org/wiki/Child_marriage (accessed 24 August 2016).
5   https://en.wikipedia.org/wiki/Child_labour (accessed 24 August 2016).
6   https://en.wikipedia.org/wiki/Lokenath_Bal (accessed 24 August 2016).
7   https://en.wikipedia.org/wiki/Ambika_Chakrabarty (accessed 24 August 2016).
8   https://en.wikipedia.org/wiki/Ananta_Singh (accessed 24 August 2016).
9   https://en.wikipedia.org/wiki/Kalpana_Datta (accessed 24 August 2016).
10   https://en.wikipedia.org/wiki/Pritilata_Waddedar (accessed 24 August 2016).
11   https://en.wikipedia.org/wiki/National_identity   (accessed   24 August 2016).

References

Anderson, B. 1983. *Imagined Communities: Reflections on the Origins and Spread of Nationalism*. London: Verso.

Brooks, P. 1984. *Reading for the Plot: Desire and Intention in Narrative*. New York: Knopf.

Hogan, P.C. 2011. 'The Narrativization of National Metaphors in Indian Cinema.' In *Analyzing World Fictions: New Horizons in Narrative Theory*, edited by Frederick Lois Aldama, 135. Austin: University of Texas Press.

Kermode, F. 1967. *Sense of an Ending: Studies in the Theory of Fiction*. London: Oxford University Press.

Khan, S. 2011. 'Recovering the Past in *Jodhaa-Akbar*: Masculinities, Femininities and Cultural Politics in Bombay Cinema.' *Feminist Review* 99: 131–46.

Kumar, P. 2015. 'Reconfiguring India: Narrating the Nation through Great Men Biopics.' *The IAFOR Journal of Media, Communication and Film*. I (II). Retrieved 12 April 2015, from http://iafor.org/archives/journals/media/media-journal-vol1-issue2-contents/Narrating-the-Nation.pdf

Raghavendra, M.K. 2008. *Seduced by the Familiar: Narration and Meaning in Indian Popular Cinema*. New Delhi: Oxford University Press.

Renan, E. 1996. 'What is a Nation?' In *Becoming National: A Reader*, edited by Geoff Eley and Ronald Grigor Suny, 41–55. New York and Oxford: Oxford University Press. Retrieved 11 April 2015, from http://www.nationalismproject.org/what/renan.htm

Rollins, P.C. 1983. *Hollywood as Historian: American Film in a Cultural Context*. Lexington: University Press of Kentucky.

Sen, J. 1976, April. 'The Unintended City.' Life and Living, Seminar 200. Retrieved 23 September 2015, from http://www.india-seminar.com/2001/500/500%20jai%20sen.htm

Straczynski, J.M. (1999) Retrieved 12 January 2015, from http://www.brainyquote.com/quotes/quotes/j/jmichaels413161.html

Film References

Asif, K. 1960. *Mughal-E-Azam*. Sterling Investment Corp.

Gowariker, A. 1993. *Pehla Nasha*. Ahlan Productions.

———. 1995. *Baazi*. Aftab Pictures.

———. 2001. *Lagaan: Once Upon a Time in India*. Aamir Khan Productions, Ashutosh Gowariker Productions Pvt. Ltd and Jhamu Sugandh Productions.

Gowariker, A. 2004. *Swades*. Ashutosh Gowariker Productions Pvt. Ltd., Dillywood and UTV Motion Pictures.

———. 2008. *Jodhaa Akbar*. Ashutosh Gowariker Productions Pvt. Ltd. and UTV Motion Pictures.

———. 2010. *Khelein Hum Jee Jaan Sey*. Ashutosh Gowariker Productions Pvt. Ltd. and UTV Motion Pictures.

———. *Mohenjo Daro*. Ashutosh Gowariker Productions and Disney India, forthcoming.

Kardar, A.R. 1946. *Shahjehan*. Kardar Productions.

Khan, M. 1940. *Aurat*. National Studios.

———. 1957. *Mother India*. Mehboob Productions.

Modi, S. 1941. *Sikandar*. Minerva Movietone.

Phalke, D. 1913. *Raja Harishchandra*. Phalke Films.

———. 1913. *Mohini Bhasmasur*. Phalke Films.

———. 1914. *Satyavan Savitri*. Phalke Films.

———. 1917. *Lanka Dahan*. Phalke Films.

———. 1918. *Shri Krishna Janma*. Phalke Films.

Rathod, K. 1921. *Bhakta Vidur*. Kohinoor Films.

Roy, B. 1953. *Do Bigha Zamin*. Bimal Roy Productions.

Sadiq, M. 1963. *Taj Mahal*. Pushpa Pictures.

Shantaram, V. 1946. *Dr. Kotnis Ki Amar Kahani*. Rajkamal Kala Mandir.

14

Madhur Bhandarkar and the New Bollywood Social

Ulka Anjaria

Madhur Bhandarkar is often referenced as distinct from mainstream directors for his disruption of Bollywood generic conventions, evinced in his 'dark and real' stories (I. Chatterjee 2014) on 'serious issues' (Sharma 2014: 52), the lack of conventional song-and-dance sequences in his films (Garwood 2006: 177–180), his representation of queer sexuality (Singh 2014: 95, 105) and his heroine-centred stories (Moin 2014: 652). But despite these qualities and the interest in Hindi film studies in the margins of the mainstream industry and in feminism and sexuality in Bollywood, there is surprisingly little scholarship that investigates the aesthetics and generic qualities of Bhandarkar's films. He seems to fall into a gap that has arisen in the field in the recent years between the realist impulse evident in film-makers like Vishal Bhardwaj, Abhishek Chaubey, Anurag Kashyap and others, who tend to move away from Bollywood conventions, and the lavish over-the-top formula films that define a classically Bollywood aesthetic such as those of Yash Chopra and Karan Johar.

Yet this in-betweenness might be seen as a particular mode of aesthetic, formal and political experiment in what many identify as a changing Bollywood cinema. Indeed, Bhandarkar has often been criticized for failing to achieve flawless films (I. Chatterjee 2014) despite winning the National Film Award three times. His films have never done very well at the box office, with the exception of *Chandni Bar* (2001) and *Page 3* (2005) — and even those were only semi-hits.[1] His particular predicament seems to be that his films are neither gritty and realist enough nor melodramatic and spectacular enough. Indeed, he seems to be profoundly aware of the vacillations of representation that are necessary for a commercial, melodramatic and non-realist mode such as popular cinema to represent social concerns. Upon closer look, his films portray an acute awareness of the possibilities and limitations of popular cinema through extended experiments with realism and political film-making.

A Socially Conscious Film-maker

Nine out of Bhandarkar's 11 films (as of early 2015) have a straightforward social message. Of these, four (*Chandni Bar*, *Satta*, *Fashion* and *Heroine*) explicitly raise issues of gender and sexuality by centring on a female protagonist even as those themes also lie at the background of films such as *Page 3* and *Corporate*. The nine social films can also be divided roughly in half based on the milieux they primarily represent: four (*Page 3* [2005], *Corporate* [2006], *Fashion* [2008] and *Heroine* [2012]) focus on the lives of the rich and glamorous, three (*Chandni Bar* [2001], *Traffic Signal* [2007] and *Jail* [2009]) on the downtrodden and socially marginalized and two (*Aan: Men at Work* [2004; henceforth, *Aan*] and *Satta* [2003]) are somewhere in the middle centring on the corruption of the political elite and the underworld who are certainly rich though not particularly glamorous. Yet characters from other milieux are interspersed throughout both sets of films. Thus, *Traffic Signal* offers glimpses into the sordid lives of Mumbai's socialites through their car windows as they await the light change at the Kelkar Road traffic signal, and conversely, *Page 3* and *Corporate* offer snatches of otherwise absent subaltern perspectives through the witty ruminations of drivers, office peons and security guards; as these figures—never named or otherwise individuated—stand waiting on their employers at their various professional and social engagements, they exchange light banter that exposes the superficiality and hollowness of the lives of the wealthy (a formula which seems to have anticipated the wily chauffeur Balram Halwai in Aravind Adiga's Booker Prize-winning novel *The White Tiger* [2008]). Thus, if we consider Bhandarkar's oeuvre as a whole we see a commitment to representing not only individual social ills but the larger social landscape of contemporary Mumbai, spread as it is across multiple gaps of wealth and social standing. This interest allows him to identify, along with the stark inequalities that characterize the city, common concerns that cross social divides such as the suffering of women, the violence of capitalism, the straining of the social contract, hypocrisy and jealousy as features of human nature and even questions of body image—which, he shows, affect the poor as well as the rich (in *Traffic Signal*, a young dark-skinned boy spends his paltry earnings on fairness cream with dreams of changing his complexion).

The female-centred films stand out for their investment in representing modern gender crises in urban India and for breaking the pattern in Bollywood of representing women as side characters—as pretty accessories at worst and secondary protagonists at best—in male-oriented plots.

Satta is striking not only for its female lead but for the way Anuradha (Raveena Tandon) is characterized as a protagonist who abides by none of the popular cinematic logic that keeps female characters silent sufferers in the face of oppression. At numerous times throughout the film, Anuradha boldly raises her eyes to those who try to silence her—her husband, her in-laws, campaign workers, politicians, even her lover—and directly refutes their insults in extended speeches that bespeak not only her moral high ground but her keen understanding of their hypocrisy. Hypocrisy is, in this film as in so many others of Bhandarkar's, a key theme, which often manifests itself in gender inequality, and Anuradha seems to have an endless fount of speeches she uses to shame her attackers into acknowledging their own. Mumtaz (Tabu), the protagonist of *Chandni Bar*, is much less articulate—she probably speaks a dozen lines of dialogue in the whole film—but her life and those of the other dancers at the beer bar where she works also buckle under the hypocrisies of patriarchy. Even more so than Anuradha, Mumtaz is subject to insult by almost everyone she meets; she is always referred to as 'tu' (rather than the more formal 'tum' or 'aap') and everywhere she goes men treat her with contempt. In the few cases when she dares to speak out she is accused of offending men's honour. Unlike *Satta*, *Chandni Bar* ends on a bleak note; although Mumtaz has come far in making a life for herself and her children after the death of her husband Pottya (Atul Kulkarni), her son becomes involved in street gangs and her daughter becomes a bar dancer, suggesting that the myth of self-making is brutally hollow.

Corporate, *Fashion* and *Heroine* pursue the questions of gender and sexuality in different ways; the three films represent the cost of fame and money on the lives of women. The protagonists of *Fashion* and *Heroine* are ridden with anxiety which veers precari-ously into mental illness—an anxiety that largely reflects the shal-lowness of the new glamour industries. But even where he is so critical of these industries, Bhandarkar is sensitive to the way in which a critique of contemporary India's new forms of desire and aspiration could quickly revert to traditionalist patriarchy, where women's desires are circumscribed because of the immorality they might spawn. Thus, in *Corporate*, we are asked to respect Nishi's (Bipasha Basu) ruthless ambition even as we see the intense cor-ruption and moral turpitude of the corporate world in which she works. In *Fashion* as well, although Meghna (Priyanka Chopra) is driven to alcoholism and other self-destructive behaviour by the selfishness and greed of the fashion industry, her decision to leave Mumbai and give up modelling altogether is not presented as a solution. Rather, *Fashion* suggests that the choice between domes-ticity and capitalism is a false one and ends up hurting women; the ideal is to integrate both so that women can live a rich and sat-isfying life while still holding on to dreams of making it big. Here this conflict is resolved when Meghna's parents finally accept her desire to be a model (they had earlier disowned her), suggesting that the social problem is not in the fashion industry itself but in a patriarchal culture that has little room for women's aspirations.

In *Heroine*, it turns out the film industry is so destructive for Mahi (Kareena Kapoor) that she does have to leave it altogether in order to reclaim herself; here Bollywood is presented as ironically antithetical to female desire. This film is much more fragmented and disjointed than *Corporate* or *Fashion* and we know much less about Mahi than we did about Nishi or Meghna. Some have suggested — and box office returns seem to confirm this — that this is because *Heroine* is a failed film (R. Chatterjee 2012), but there is something suggestive about reading it not as a repetition of the same topic of the perils women face in capitalist India but as a sort of return or revisiting of this theme through the vexed trope of cinephilia (discussed further below). Whereas *Fashion* touches on some questions of stardom, *Heroine* more explicitly asks its audience to consider what it means to act at all: both the kind of acting that is required of film stars at work and the kinds of performances that are necessary to manage desire in the new India more broadly. This is captured in the novel's plot when in order to recover her failing career Mahi leaks a sex video of herself; the sex tape, once understood as a violent invasion on private desire, here is recast as a performance of that invasion and the question of the 'privacy' of desire is no longer the operative one. New India — the movie suggests — epitomized by the film industry, requires that participants constantly 'act' and 'perform' various versions of themselves and suggests that this requirement might leave no room for a real self to emerge. Mahi's bipolar diagnosis is thus mentioned but not made a central element of the film (unlike in *Woh Lamhe* [2006], for instance), serving more as a metaphor for all of the different selves that she must increasingly be than as a literal diagnosis.

Sexuality is also an important theme in Bhandarkar's films, most evident in his representation of queer characters. Some scholars have criticized his stereotypical depiction of queer characters (R. Chatterjee 2012) and certainly there are several gay male characters in particular who seem to be represented only for comic relief — especially in *Dil Toh Baccha Hai Ji* (2011). However, these should not overshadow the variety of representations of queerness in Bhandarkar's oeuvre as a whole. The gay prostitute in *Traffic Signal*, for instance, is depicted with sympathy as he develops a camaraderie with Noorie (Konkona Sen Sharma), a female prostitute working at the same bus stand—one that is belied by their initial competition over clients. Similarly, the one-night liaison between the protagonist Mahi and Promita in *Heroine* goes a significant way in destigmatizing lesbian love, even though it does little to redeem that love or rope it in to Bollywood domesticity. *Fashion* too, although peppered with gay stereotypes in its minor characters, represents Rahul Arora (Samir Soni) as a gay fashion designer struggling with parental and social pressures to start a family. He ends up suggesting a marriage of convenience with his best friend, the female fashion model Janet Sequeira (Mugdha Godse), to which she agrees not only because of their friendship but as an acknowledgement of her own precarious relationship, as a fashion model, with middle-class domesticity. By connecting these two characters in this queer plot the film makes the radical move of presenting modelling as a sort of queer subjectivity as well. Indeed throughout his films, Bhandarkar extends queerness beyond gay or lesbian characters: in the intense female friendships in *Chandni Bar*; in Anuradha's taking of a lover while still legally married in *Satta* and then her decision, at the very end of the film, to live alone; and in Dominic (Ranvir Shorey)'s unrequited love of Noorie in *Traffic Signal*. All these suggest forms of intimacy outside of the heteronormative family and the traditional structure of Bollywood domesticity.

Bhandarkar's films also seem to evince interest in questions of masculinity, although this theme lies much deeper under the surface of his films. It does help to explain, however, what seem to be his two outlier films: *Aan*, whose 'social' message strangely supports police encounter killings and *Dil Toh Baccha Hai Ji*, which does not seem to have a social message at all. *Aan* is curiously subtitled 'Men at Work', suggesting some investment in questions of masculinity—but in the film masculinity is for the most part inseparable from 'aan [honour]', which suggests, through what Anustup Basu (2010) calls 'the encounter genre' (177), that heroism resides in doing what one thinks is right even if it is illegal. (The theme of encounter killings, with similar treatment, briefly appears in *Page 3* as well [Sarma 2014: 88].) The 'men' of the subtitle thus deserve that appellation primarily because they display an unrestrained amount of masculine valour in the form of long, extended physical fights with seasoned criminals and because they participate in the murder—some at point blank range—of around two dozen underworld criminals: they are honourable because they take the law into their own hands. *Dil Toh Baccha Hai Ji*, although a very different kind of film, was, like *Aan*, a flop; and although it might easily be dismissed for its weak plot and infantile humour, can alternatively be seen as an attempt to subject modern masculinity to the same scrutiny to which *Fashion* and *Heroine* subject modern femininity. The three-hero structure replicates a pattern initiated by *Dil Chahta Hai* (2001) and that has since been taken up by a myriad of films—a structure that suggests that there is no longer a viable unitary figure that might epitomize masculine heroism, but that films have to represent different models for masculinity side by side (in this case: the nice guy, the playboy and the dork) in order to capture the diversity of men's experiences in the twenty-first century. It also suggests that the nature of manhood must be rethought in a middle-class and post-patriarchal context (in this film at least, there are no authoritarian parents or other modes of societal repression) when sex, for the most part, is readily available to both men and women. What makes these films outliers is how disconnected these potentially interesting commentaries on masculinity are from Bhandarkar's other social critiques: thus, in *Aan* we have a film that exonerates the kind of extra-legal police actions strongly condemned in *Chandni Bar*, in which Pottya is unjustly killed in a police encounter; and in *Dil Toh Baccha Hai Ji* middle-class entitlement runs freely (as when Naren [Ajay Devgan] bribes a police officer to release a rich drunk driver from jail), where elsewhere in Bhandarkar's oeuvre that same entitlement is subject to intense satire and social critique.

Historians of Hindi cinema might be reluctant to call these films 'social' in the way the term has been used in the past, although they do seem to conform to Ravi Vasudevan's (1995) definition of the social as 'the genre used to address the problems of modern life' (307). But politically speaking, Bhandarkar's films neither resemble the working man's films of the 1970s nor do they — with the exception of *Corporate* — excoriate the evils of capitalism. In fact, many of them might even be seen to celebrate capitalism.[2] And when they do represent socially marginalized protagonists they do so without the possibility for insurgency or revolt: *Chandni Bar* renders Mumtaz as a perpetual victim; *Traffic Signal* and *Page 3* end by suggesting that the characters' exploitative lives will continue forever; and where there is justice, as in the ending of *Jail*, it is solitary rather than collective. Yet at the same time, Bhandarkar's films are clearly more political than the fanciful romances of the 1990s or the 'neoliberal' plots of India's new middle-class films. It is precisely this transgression of these deep-seated categories that marks his work as distinct from some of his contemporaries.

Realism and Naturalism

Critics often claim that Bollywood films do not abide by the conventions of cinematic realism (Chakravarty 1993: 80–81), even as there is some sense among critics that post-2000 Hindi popular cinema has undergone a realist turn (Gopal 2011: 54; Naresh and Prakash 2015: 1; Srivastava 2009: 706–707). Contemporary Bollywood realism is often characterized by more believable plots, fewer song and dream sequences, more relatable, nuanced characters, and increasingly, stories located in realistic settings such as contemporary Indian cities rather than on fantastic sets in rural landed estates. But the problem with this definition is that it conflates realism with the 'realistic' and thus overlooks longstanding debates among realist writers and film-makers about how best realism might serve the cause of political representation. For instance, Leftist writers and film-makers have traditionally coupled their representations of the harsh lives of the poor with a representation of a better future, even if that future has not yet been realized. Thus, realism attains a utopic dimension that is often not, in fact, realistic.

Bhandarkar's realism, by contrast, veers towards what has been identified in literary studies as 'naturalism', which is the representation of the poor not as an immanent proletariat but as suffering under oppressive conditions to the point of reducing their humanity to the realm of what Giorgio Agamben (1998) calls, in the context of the Nazi concentration camps, bare life. In naturalism, plot and character succumb to external environmental or circumstantial forces. We see elements of this in the plotlessness of several of Bhandarkar's films. For instance, *Traffic Signal* has an entirely episodic plot with almost no narrative movement. The film centres around a community of characters who cluster around a busy traffic signal in Mumbai; the overt political impulse is in bringing their lives to the screen, as conveyed in the film's dedication:

> This film is dedicated to the multitudes of people working at the traffic signals in the country…. We do not intend to demean, mock, ridicule or make value judgments on the professions or lifestyles of these people…. As a matter of fact we are genuinely moved and overawed by the grit and determination shown by these people in their day to day struggle for survival at the traffic signals.

'Grit', 'determination', 'day-to-day struggle' and 'survival' accurately convey the politics of this film, which is that of persistence in the fate of hardship. The mode of the film bends to that politics so that it too is structured around repeated patterns: showing the characters plying their wares to the cars every day as they stop at the traffic signal, showing the repeated patterns—a male car passenger who calls women vendors close to stroke their hands in sexual pleasure, a beggar who acts mentally ill, and so on—that constitute the unvarying days for those who make their living at the traffic signal. Even when the signal is demolished due to development the local gangster Silsila (Kunal Khemu) simply finds another intersection where he will set up his enterprise again. The trope of this film, therefore, is the repeated and continual nature both of the lives of those who make their living at the traffic signal and, more broadly, of development in the city at large (i.e., you can demolish one slum but another will quickly appear).

An episodic structure is found in *Jail* as well, which is also a film that seeks to humanize the characters it represents. *Jail* offers a much more realistic representation of prison life than anything seen in Bollywood before; but the film's realism goes beyond that. *Jail* has almost no plot to speak of — or, more accurately, the story lies precisely in the lack of plot: Parag (Neil Nitin Mukesh) is wrongly jailed and despite repeated appearances before the court his application for release on bail is continually refused. Thus, he embarks upon a seemingly endless cycle of jail life (waking, eating, talking, working and sleeping) — itself monotonous and repetitive — punctured by sporadic appearances in court where his bail plea is denied and after which he has no choice but to return, a little more dejected each time, to jail. This cycle constitutes the film's 'plot' in its characterization of the difficult and debased lives of India's prisoners. Like *Traffic Signal*, *Jail* ends on a plea for respecting the human rights of India's 3.7 lakh prisoners, the majority of whom, the titles announce, 'have not been found guilty'.

Bhandarkar incorporates this naturalist impulse into other films in more minor but still significant ways — evinced in *Page 3*'s repetitive, cyclical and episodic representation of one socialite soirée after another, many of which have no bearing on the film's plot, and in *Chandni Bar*'s representation of the repetitive life of the bar dancer, which one character describes as: 'Wahi sala beer bar, wahi dhuan, wahi customers…, wahi jhuti hansi. Roz ka wahi chakkar hai [The same damned beer bar, the same smoke, the same customers…, the same fake smiles. Every day is the same cycle]'. In all these examples the sheer monotony of life becomes a significant element of the films' political critiques. In *Chandni Bar* Mumtaz's life acquires a harried inevitability, so that, as mentioned above, despite her attempts to improve the futures of her children they end up pushed back into their family histories. The last shot of Mumtaz in that film, doubled over in tears and pain after having witnessed her adolescent son shoot and kill two people, stands for the sheer helplessness that is central to the naturalist imagination.

Cinephilia

The self-referential plots and aesthetics of recent Bollywood films have generated many forms of cinephilia: from films about films such as Farah Khan's *Om Shanti Om* (2007), to films that satirize Bollywood such as Punit Malhotra's *I Hate Luv Storys* (2010) and even to individual postmodern scenes such as when Chulbul Pandey (Salman Khan) interrupts a fight scene to dance to the villain's catchy ringtone in Abhinav Kashyap's *Dabangg* (2010). These are akin to the form of cinephilia we see in *Heroine*, which is set in the Bollywood film industry, and, in which, despite watching the self-destructive spiral of the protagonist, there is a pleasure in having access to Bollywood 'behind the scenes'. The film plays off that voyeurism, implicating its own viewers in the media frenzy that makes life at times unlivable for its heroine. We also see Bhandarkar's cinephilia in his own repeated cameos in some of his films. In *Fashion*, Bhandarkar appears very briefly in the background of a film shoot and one actress says to another, 'He must be doing a film on fashion—he makes *realistic* movies.' In *Heroine*, Bhandarkar never actually appears on screen but as a journalist comes out of a trailer she says, looking back, 'Bye, Madhur', and the protagonist Mahi asks her: 'You were interviewing my director?' In an early scene in *Jail*, we see a billboard for Bhandarkar's film *Corporate* as the protagonist drives down a Mumbai street; and in *Traffic Signal* we see the lights of 'Chandni Bar' in the background of the Kelkar Road intersection.

However, cinephilia in Bhandarkar's films also takes another form, which is the repeated use of actors and actresses across a range of films. This is akin to the form of cinephilia by which Shah Rukh Khan plays a character named Rahul in *Dil To Pagal Hai* (1997), *Kuch Kuch Hota Hai* (1998) and *Kabhi Khushi Kabhie Gham* (2001); the cinephilic pleasure lies in recognizing that the repetition of the character establishes a moral continuity that exceeds any individual film. This is a widespread practice in Hindi popular cinema but it occurs mostly with leading actors and actresses; what distinguishes Bhandarkar's use of a repeated cast is how often he does it with minor characters and lesser stars. In fact, his heroes and heroines always change from film to film but they are propped up by a repeated set of supporting actors that includes, among others, Atul Kulkarni, Manoj Joshi, Suchitra Pillai, Mugdha Godse, Shrivallabh Vyas, Rajpal Yadav, Ranvir Shorey and Naseer Abdulla. Konkona Sen Sharma and Raveena Tandon also appear in more than one film, although they both also have a lead role. But of all of these recurring actors and actresses Kulkarni and Joshi are most interesting for the nature of their roles and what they say about the politics of cinephilia in twenty-first century Bollywood.

Manoj Joshi appears in seven Bhandarkar films: *Satta, Chandni Bar, Aan, Page 3, Corporate, Traffic Signal* and *Dil Toh Baccha Hai Ji*. He plays very small, neutral roles in three of these: in *Chandni Bar* he helps Mumtaz get her son released from jail; in *Corporate* he plays a flamboyant film director; and in *Dil Toh Baccha Hai Ji* he plays a waiter. *Aan* is his only negative role. But in the remaining three films Joshi's roles consistently constitute a moral centre, even though in none of these is he a protagonist. His role of moral minor character suggests a logic that transcends individual films. In *Satta*, he plays an incorruptible police chief, so righteous that when another policeman urges him to pander to the politicians he reads him the Sanskrit slogan on the front of his police cap—'Sadrakṣaṇāya Khalanigrahaṇāya' or 'To protect the good and destroy the evil.' In *Traffic Signal* Joshi plays a government engineer who refuses to be bribed to support the extension of a flyover being pushed through by a developer eager to clear the land in front of his development. While in *Satta* he works with Anuradha to successfully bring about justice, in *Traffic Signal* he is shot by a gunman hired by the local land mafia and paid off by the MLA; after his death, the flyover is constructed without hindrance. In *Page 3* Joshi plays Bosco, chauffeur to one of the wealthy characters and he acts as a sort of wise subaltern who initiates a running commentary among the other drivers on the lives of the rich, revealing—in a few pithy lines of dialogue—the absurdity of the latter's existence.

Atul Kulkarni's roles are even more developed than Joshi's; he is the minor character par excellence in Bhandarkar's filmography. He appears in four films—three of which are heroine-centred and, thus, Kulkarni's status as minor character is inseparable from the question of what it means to have a female protagonist in Bollywood more generally. In *Chandni Bar* he plays a hot-headed, passionate, but at heart kind gangster; his impulsiveness ends up costing him his life, but before that he proves to be an adequate lover for our protagonist Mumtaz. After hearing that she had been raped by her uncle he goes and stabs the uncle; and he marries her, which although does not remove her from the life of a bar dancer forever, gives her a few years of domestic respite from a world in which she is never quite comfortable. In *Satta* and *Page 3*, Kulkarni's characters play more explicitly supportive roles for the female protagonists. In *Satta*, he plays a politician more righteous than most; certainly, for a majority of the film he does not seem to hold all the outdated notions of patriarchy and a woman's place that characterize Anu's husband, Vivek, and his parents. It is he with whom Anuradha has an extramarital affair. But he is not merely a repository for morality either. As a politician, he is presented as intelligent but also ruthless, upright but also ambitious and when he gets the opportunity to rise to the top of the party's ranks and become chief minister he is willing to forego all of his earlier principles in order to do so. At that point, Anuradha turns against him; thus, his downfall enables her success. In *Page 3*, Kulkarni plays more of an outsider; as a crime reporter he provides a foil to Madhavi's (Konkona Sen Sharma) social reporting; he is, in this way, the conscience of the film and it is only when Madhavi moves closer to his perspective — that is, when socialite reporting and crime reporting come together in the Madh Island human trafficking and pedophilia stand-off with which the film ends — that she gains some redemption from her otherwise futile work.

In the uses of both these actors we see an investment in a moral order that is generally absent in Bhandarkar's otherwise bleak and naturalistic plots. But it is notable that this morality emerges not only 'within' individual films but 'across' films (Anjaria and Anjaria 2008), suggesting that even as Bhandarkar tells realistic stories about contemporary social issues, he is attentive to the excesses of meaning that distinguish popular cinema from its realist or documentary counterparts. He thus presents cinephilia as an unlikely vehicle for political film-making.

Notes

1   *Corporate* (2006), *Traffic Signal* (2007) and *Fashion* (2008) were all aver-age at the box office, *Heroine* (2012) was below average, *Satta* (2003), *Jail* (2009) and *Dil Toh Baccha Hai Ji* (2011) were all flops and *Aan: Men at Work* (2004) was a 'disaster'. All box office rankings are from http://www.boxofficeindia.com/ (accessed 16 April 2015).

2   Sarma (2014) argues that even *Corporate*, which follows the 1970s theme of 'present[ing] the industrialists ... as villains', is still very different from that generation of films in that

> the film does not have even a single character who identifies with and fights for the exploited and marginalised masses. Even those characters who evoke the audience's sympathy cannot be termed virtuous in the real sense. The sensitive characters either unquestionably become a part of the corrupt corporate world or mutely accept their subordination to that world.... Unlike the films of the 1970s and 1980s, which portray the 'angry man,' *Corporate* silences even the faint voice of opposition, and hence, ends on a completely pessimistic note. (89–90)

References

Adiga, Aravind. 2008. *The White Tiger*. New York: Free Press.

Agamben, Giorgio. 1998. *Homo Sacer: Sovereign Power and Bare Life*. Translated by Daniel Heller-Roazen. Stanford: Stanford University Press.

Anjaria, Ulka and Jonathan Shapiro Anjaria. 2008. 'Text, Genre, Society: Hindi Youth Films and Postcolonial Desire.' *South Asian Popular Culture* 6 (2): 125–40.

Basu, Anustup. 2010. 'Encounters in the City: Cops, Criminals, and Human Rights in Hindi Film.' *Journal of Human Rights* 9 (2010): 175–90.

Chakravarty, Sumita S. 1993. *National Identity in Indian Popular Cinema: 1947–1987*. Austin, TX: University of Texas Press.

Chatterjee, Ishani. 2014. 'Madhur Bhandarkar: A Different Kind of Bollywood Director.' *News House*, 13 October. Retrieved 16 April 2015, from   http://www.thenewshouse.com/blog/madhur-bhandarkar-different-kind-bollywood-director

Chatterjee, Rituparna. 2012. '"Heroine": Madhur Bhandarkar's 15 Terrible Caricatures of Bollywood.' *IBN Live*, 21 September. Retrieved 4 May 2015, from http://ibnlive.in.com/news/heroine-madhur-bhandarkars-15-terrible-caricatures-of-bollywood/293828-8-66.html

Garwood, Ian. 2006. 'The Songless Bollywood Film.' *South Asian Popular Culture* 4 (2): 169–83.

Gopal, Sangita. 2011. *Conjugations: Marriage and Form in New Bollywood Cinema*. Chicago, IL: University of Chicago Press.

Moin, Arif. 2014, May. 'Portrayal of Women in Hindi Films with Special Reference to Muslim Characters.' *Excellence International Journal of Education and Research* 2 (5): 644–53.

Naresh, Suparna and Jagadeesh Prakash. 2015. 'Marketing Films Through Social Realities: Shyam Benegal's "Welcome to Sajjanpur": A Case Study.' *International Journal of Scientific and Research Publications* 5 (2): 1–8.

Sarma, Mriganka Sekhar. 2014. 'Death of the Villain: Neoliberalism and Contemporary Hindi Cinema.' *The Clarion* 3 (1): 84–91.

Sharma, Preeti. 2014. 'Changing Trends in Hindi Cinema: 1990–2013.' *Research Insight* 1 (1): 49–57.

Singh, Anita. 2014. 'Fear of the Politics of Noah's Ark: Technologies of Heterosexual Coercion and LGBTQIA Packaging in Bollywood Films.' In *Gay Subcultures and Literatures: The Indian Projections*, edited by Sukhbir Singh, 89–110. Shimla: Indian Institute of Advanced Study.

Srivastava, Neelam. 2009. 'Bollywood as National(ist) Cinema: Violence, Patriotism and the National-Popular in *Rang De Basanti*.' *Third Text* 23 (6): 703–16.

Vasudevan, Ravi S. 1995. 'Addressing the Spectator of a "Third World" National Cinema: The Bombay "Social" Film of the 1940s and 1950s.' *Screen* 36 (4): 305–24.

Film References

Bhandarkar, M. 2001. *Chandni Bar*. Shlok Films.

———. 2003. *Satta*. Metalight Productions.

———. 2004. *Aan: Men at Work*. Firoz Nadiadwala.

———. 2005. *Page 3*. Lighthouse Entertainment.

———. 2006. *Corporate*. Sahara One Motion Pictures.

———. 2007. *Traffic Signal*. Madhur Bhandarkar Motion Pictures and Percept Picture Co.

————. 2008. *Fashion*. Bhandarkar Entertainment and UTV Motion Pictures.

————. 2009. *Jail*. Bhandarkar Entertainment, Maxwell Entertainment and Mirah Entertainment.

Bhandarkar, M. 2011. *Dil Toh Baccha Hai Ji*. Baba Arts, Bhandarkar Entertainment, Panorama Studios.

————. 2012. *Heroine*. Bhandarkar Entertainment and UTV Motion Pictures.

Part III

Gendered Cinema: Bollywood's Women, Gender Politics and Representation

15

Finding Femininity: Homi Adajania and Representations of Urban Womanhood

Sharanya

This chapter explores the work of Hindi cinema director Homi Adajania. Adajania, who made his first feature film *Being Cyrus* in 2005, followed it up with *Cocktail* in 2012 and more recently in 2014 with *Finding Fanny*. Adajania's background includes everything from scuba-diving to advertising (Menon 2006) and the spaces between his films in the arc of his film-making are indicative of this. According to Homi Adajania, 'Real life has an underbelly that is stark and sombre. Ugliness and beauty, darkness and light, morbidity and fun are two sides of the same coin. Cinema has the capacity of flipping that coin' (Menon 2006). Adajania's films, to varying degrees, attempt to demonstrate aspects of this 'reality', but in doing so distort the very definition of what 'real life' has come to mean, technically and textually, in contemporary Hindi cinema. This chapter will first elaborate on the details of Adajania's filmic oeuvre and then examine his stylistic and thematic concerns across the three films, focusing especially on his representation of unruly and domestic

291

spaces and the relationship between these spaces and women in his films, protagonists who often seem to mirror, and affect, them. Adajania's thematic and stylistic preoccupations are read primarily through the vocabulary of mise en scène and cinematography. The chapter also seeks to locate Adajania's work within the larger framework of popular Hindi cinema, and Bollywood, and suggest intersections and interstices in those debates that Adajania's work appears to exist in.

The Unruly and the Domestic: Women and Spaces in Adajania's Films

Ackbar Abbas, whilst examining the unstable relationship between the city, cinema and the cinematic, notes that the city emerges from the image but 'it is exactly the instability of the cinematic image that allows it to evoke the city in all its errancy in ways that stable images cannot' (Abbas 2003: 145). Acknowledging this city as an 'exorbitant' one that 'is neither securely graspable nor fully representable', described by Calvino, Benjamin and Borges as 'invisible', 'phantasmagoric', and 'labyrinthine', Abbas notes that 'It is as much a physical presence as it is idea and dream' (Abbas 2003).

This city, or the spaces falling errantly out of such a city, could be read as the backdrop to Adajania's films. All his films deal with the urban in so far as acknowledging it as a forceful presence determining the trajectories of the incomplete or unfulfilled lives of his various protagonists, but the urban itself only briefly relies on the stock shots of megapolises like Mumbai in *Being Cyrus* or London in *Cocktail*. The filmscapes secure themselves within the unravellings of the domestic within the interior even as the external world, the dry, hot, inhabited roads of Goa, the dangerous and treacherous pavements of suburban London or the indifferent streets of Mumbai, offers no respite. The women in Adajania's films find themselves placed in a similarly precarious manner in these spaces: their identities fluctuating between tropes of the demure and the deviant. Sangeeta Datta suggests, 'The new cinema movement of the 1970s and 1980s made attempts to explore women's subjectivity, her familial and civic role. Today we may well ask, where is the woman at work?' (Datta 2000: 79). This question holds true for Adajania's films, although frequently filmed in the realm of the 'outside', depicting women maintaining or working in the domestic (the lives of their husbands, the household or both) and rebelling against them or attempting to, none of the women barring Meera and Veronika, the protagonists in *Cocktail*, are shown to be at work. In *Cocktail* too, the only occasion Veronika is shown to be working becomes the premise for a conversation between the two women about Gautam's, the male protagonist's, place in the household and the friendship.

Cocktail (2012) was written by Bollywood director Imtiaz Ali of *Rockstar* (2011) and, more recently, *Highway* (2014) fame and his brother, director and writer Sajid Ali. It is evident that the script and dialogue are not a product of Adajania's worldview; *Cocktail*, the most commercially successful of Adajania's films, does not aspire to or carry any visible strains of the peculiar dark humour that characterizes both *Being Cyrus* and the later *Finding Fanny*. Set in contemporary London, the film tells the story of three friends, Meera, Gautam and Veronika. Meera (Diana Penty) arrives in London as a bewildered girl who finds herself briefly in a sham marriage with Kunal (Randeep Hooda). She is rescued from streets by the relentlessly reckless and 'free-spirited' Veronika (Deepika Padukone). Gautam (Saif Ali Khan), who first encounters a hostile Meera stranded at the airport in his endless attempts to flirt with all women, has a one-night stand with Veronika and eventually moves in with her. They become best friends but this friendship is quickly destabilized when Gautam's mother (Dimple Kapadia) arrives to see her son's fictitious fiancée; Meera is pushed forward quickly by Gautam as his fiancée before they all take off on holiday. During this time, Meera and Gautam fall in love while pretending to be a couple but Veronika, curiously enough, warms up to Gautam's mother; the latter's project of finding Veronika a husband makes Veronika feel cared for. The rest of the film follows a confession from Meera and Gautam about their love that

Veronika is forced to accept in the light of her easy-going ways, causing her to re-embody 'the bad girl ways' marked by a return to heavy drinking, drugs and an accident. All is settled eventually; Gautam and Meera get married with Veronika's blessing.

In *Cocktail*, Veronika is introduced to us as a glam icon; quick, grainy cuts of her applying make-up, drinking wine in dim light, in flashy, claustrophobic space, her body depicted in fragments, eventually settling on her speeding through the streets of London in the evening and her hair streaming out in the wind. The camera follows her in the next shot, moving up from her ankles to finally reveal who she is, dressed up, out on the streets of London and standing out in a crowd. Meera appears on-screen for the first time in the interiors of an aircraft, in her salwar kameez, heavy jewellery and sweater. When they meet in front of a mirror in a washroom their starkly different reflections, a crying Meera, a drunken Veronika, are presented to us as images that may be disturbed but well retained as essences in the film.

In London, Meera quickly adapts to Veronika's lifestyle; she finds a job as a designer, swiftly swaps her traditional salwar kameezes for casual T-shirts, tops and jeans and goes out partying with Veronika, even as Veronika is established as the more carefree and 'liberated' of the two, unlike Meera, she drinks frequently, has one-night stands and does not care about expired milk in her fridge. Veronika's flat through the first half is frequently shown as a littered but imaginative space scattered with fairy lights, inspiring phrases like 'DREAM', bright clothes, film projectors and photographs. Meera, even as she makes herself at home sets up a Hindu prayer space, picks up stray clothes and cleans up after Veronika.

Following the trip with Gautam's mother, Veronika abandons her wild ways and begins dressing, in her words, like 'marriage material, the sweet Indian bride', cooking dishes she cannot remember names of and is reduced to calling them by their ingredients ('that yoghurt thing') and trying to emulate what she calls 'the *ada*, the Indian thing'; an innate essence of 'Indianness' she perceives in Meera. They stand, once again, in front of a mirror, this time, not so dissimilar in appearance or demeanour but Veronika still perceiving a lack, an essential quality of being 'Indian' in herself. She asks Gautam, 'If I wear Indian clothes, grow my hair out, get groomed in the Indian way, in short if I become like Meera, do you think your mother will accept me?' The spaces taking precedence here are more reflective of the domestic: Gautam confronts Meera and reveals the truth about their relationship to Veronika in her kitchen, Meera and Veronika end their friendship in the kitchen and then argue in the hallway. If the close-ups were of the bright details of Veronika's room earlier in the film, now those very details are dull and in shallow focus.

Meera's loneliest and most estranged moments in London look similar: she is outside the realm of the domestic, either in a crowded airport, a busy street in central London, in a cramped discotheque or framed against the window in Kunal's room. Ranjani Mazumdar, addressing the work of the 'panoramic interior' aesthetic in Bollywood, specifically in the work of Karan Johar and Farhan Akhtar, concludes that

> *The panoramic interior expresses a crisis of belonging, fear of the street, and the desire for the good life – all at once* [...] The shadows of the uncanny, the fear of the street corner, the overwhelming crowd, the chaos of the marketplace, the violence in the street, and the city of strangers remain just outside, threatening to invade [...]. (Mazumdar 2007: 148)

The invasion here is especially an invasion of belonging; if Veronika has been sullied, as per the film's characters by being the woman on the street, Meera is the traditional woman who needs to be protected from the violence of the external world. Veronika, however, slips between these two dichotomous modes set up by the film, 'like Meera' and 'desi' or her opposite, in lack, till the last frame.

Mazumdar takes up this dichotomy astutely as a theme recurring across 'Bombay' cinema more broadly, citing Chatterjee who notes that the Eurocentric 'materiality'/'spirituality' dichotomy of the West/East translated into everyday life, where 'social space gets divided into *ghar* and *bahir*, the home and the world. The 'world' is the external domain of the material while the 'home'

remains the spiritual self with woman as its representation (238)'
(Mazumdar 2007: 82). While this dichotomy holds true in terms of
the spatial division in Adajania's films, the representations of the
women inhabiting those spaces indicates a more complex reworking of this even as the matrix itself appears to be the same. Shilpa
Phadke, Sameera Khan and Shilpa Ranade, in their noteworthy
sociological endeavour to wrestle with the role of women loiter-
ing in public space in contemporary Mumbai, expand on this
dichotomy specifically in terms of sex work but also more broadly
on women being in public acknowledging that 'the public woman
is not so much a direct threat to "good" women as much as an
illustration of what might happen to good women should they
break the rules' (Phadke, Khan and Ranade 2011: 28). While the
public and private spaces depicted in *Cocktail* are indicated to be
London, it is noticeable that the spatial politics contextualizing
the 'public' woman in urban India that Phadke, Khan and Ranade
have identified are transposed upon the urban Indian woman in
London through Adajania's film-making. The particular spati-
alities of contemporary London, in other words, have no bearing upon either Meera or Veronika because the notions of how
the 'public' and 'private' women must behave have been carried
through, unchanged.

Finding Fanny (2014) is a black comedy that problematizes this
binary in interesting ways, much as *Being Cyrus* does. It follows a
road trip that five people and a cat undertake from the tiny, iso-
lated village of Pocolim in Goa. Rosalina (Dimple Kapadia) is the
self-professed matriarch or 'puppet-master' of the village whose
son Gabo (Ranveer Singh in a cameo) married the village belle
Angie (Deepika Padukone) and, at the altar, choked on his wedding cake and died. Gabo's best friend, the mechanic Savio (Arjun
Kapoor), rattled at not having been chosen by Angie instead
leaves for Mumbai and returns to Pocolim after some years.
Angie's closest friend is the postman and church choir's eldest
member, Ferdinand, or Ferdie (Naseeruddin Shah), who receives
his own undelivered letter containing a marriage proposal to his
sweetheart Stephanie Fernandes, or Fanny, from 27 years ago.
Angie offers to help him find Fanny and together, in the car of the

eccentric painter Don Pedro (Pankaj Kapur), the crew set off on a trip that turns accidentally into an adventure. The film ends, however, with Ferdie and Rosalina getting married as well as Angie and Savio, eventually.

Pocolim is shown in its entirety to include not just the quirky interiors, whether they are living rooms and office spaces, of various characters but also backyards, gardens and village paths. Indeed, the film opens with Angie's voiceover introducing the various characters, but before we see Ferdie we have heard the howl of dogs and his choral practise and seen neatly-composed shots, a recurring and important cinematographic element in *Being Cyrus* too, albeit with a different purpose, including the candles he uses for prayers the faded, framed black and white photographs of his choir, the lonely dimly-lit space of his post office, his quaint clock made of seashells and the organized, overpowering clutter of his living room; the slide show of intricately composed photographs indicating a long, solitary idiosyncratic life above all else. Pocolim too, is similarly introduced: we see quick snapshots of characters in various public spaces such as a woman sewing on a machine amidst clothes lines on a street, a dog resting on the steps of a house framed through the bars of the gate, an abandoned gateway overgrown with weeds. In all the shots described here, movement appears almost an afterthought and incidental because the shots are primarily indicators of stillness and solitude. Life does not move on because there is nowhere it can move to. The stale quality of the disordered interiors captured in the mise en scène also heightens the loneliness of the urban life fostered by a small village like Pocolim and the particular seclusion of the women who live there.

Fanny, Angie and Rosie are all framed as women who are most comfortable in the realm of the domestic. Both Angie and Rosalina are introduced, like Veronika in *Cocktail*, through sexualized shots of their back, their arms and legs lacking perhaps only the quick rhythms of 'Angrezi Beat' and the powerful glamour factor. They are occupied outdoors—Rosie, elaborately dressed, on her way somewhere, and Angie going about her chores and pottering about in the garden. However, these outdoors are framed as part of 'home', that is, Pocolim and the entire community contained within it. Their loneliness is framed and voiced aloud by Angie only in the stifling interiors of their home, when they sit, perfectly framed in yet another still, across each other at the dining table, Angie falling asleep in the drowsy afternoon heat and Rosie concerned by little other than her tea and her cat. All characters engage with their loneliness in the dark recesses of their home spaces; if Angie and Rosie have the comfort of their home, Savio has his car, Ferdie his room and Don Pedro his canvas.

The 'outdoors' leads them to deviate from their roles as matri-archs and nurturers of other people's, frequently men's dreams even as life goes on as usual for the men. In a field that could be anywhere, Angie and Savio spend an unsatisfying night together, bringing to the fore her need for intimacy and her confused ambivalence about it. In the same field, while Don Pedro paints his muse Rosie at last, his happiest moment being when he walks into the sunset with his painting held high above him, Rosie allows herself to be vulnerable to Don Pedro's painting escapades and feels irrevocably used and alone afterwards; she is framed as a lone, tired figure against the endless field. Fanny, finally, is 'found' in another village during her funeral procession when we learn that she has been married five times and that Ferdie per-haps never stood a chance at happiness with her. Fanny's secrets, her dalliances with men, her desperation to keep her life full and occupied, come to the fore only at her grave; once again, outside life and its domesticity itself.

It is worth noting, then, that one of the sites that is positioned as the exterior, the unknown place where things fall apart and the centre fails to hold, is the interior of the car. Rather than the vari-ous unfamiliar geographical locations the car takes them to, the interior of the car becomes the site that causes estrangement and unfamiliarity. Fights break out in the car, tempers run high, the cat is thrown out the window because of Ferdie's allergies and, in what is possibly the darkest moment of the film, Don Pedro gets shot in a tussle over a gun discovered in the glove compartment of his car but the characters remain oblivious to this death right till the end of the film.

In *Being Cyrus,* a noirish thriller written by Adajania and writer Kersi Khambatta, a pair that collaborated again later on *Finding Fanny* which is said to be 'the first major Indian film to be made in English, which for many Parsis today is their mother-tongue' (Jain 2011), this established interior/exterior binary is possibly complicated the most; an interesting fact given that it was Adajania's first feature film. It is the story of the narrator, a young man named Cyrus Mistry (Saif Ali Khan) from Jamshedpur who arrives at the doorstep of the once-eminent pottery artist Dinshaw Sethna (Naseeruddin Shah) and his wife Katy Sethna (Dimple Kapadia) in the small town of Panchgani. Over the course of the year that he spends with them, Cyrus and Katy grow close even as Dinshaw begins to lose his mind slowly. We are shown that Cyrus begins to run small errands for Katy in Mumbai including visiting her father-in-law Fardoonjee, who lives with Dinshaw's brother Farrokh (Boman Irani) and his wife Tina (Simone Singh). Fardoonjee, starving, ill and uncared for is grateful for the treats and monetary assistance from Katy but even more grateful, perhaps, for Cyrus's company. Through the film, Cyrus's exact occupation in the Sethna household, other than helping with chores, remains unclear; occasional flashbacks of him being abused as a young orphan and shots of him fiddling with a microscope in a small room in the sprawling Sethna mansion are juxtaposed mysteriously with other more regular shots of him around the Sethnas that do not seem to lie outside the retrospective narrative unlike the former shots.

Everyone is unhappy, it seems — Tina in her loveless marriage, Farrokh and Katy in their clandestinely conducted affair and even Dinshaw and Fardoonjee when their deteriorating memory isn't failing them; everyone, that is, except for Cyrus. Mysteries begin to unravel when Katy sends Cyrus to kill Fardoonjee and Tina to clear the way for her and Farrokh. Cyrus feeds Fardonjee a resplendent meal, stabs him, shoots Farrokh — who, in turn, plans to kill Cyrus — plants Katy and Dinshaw's fingerprints (explaining, thus, the long hours spent with instruments, photographs and the microscope) all over the flat and leaves having left no proof of his existence. Tina alibis out and Katy and Dinshaw go to prison for life. It is then revealed that Tina and Cyrus (or Xerxes, which we learn later is his real name) are siblings and this has all been Tina's doing to inherit Farrokh and Fardonjee's money. Tina attempts to plan a similar undertaking with yet another family but Xerxes escapes.

The two women are protagonists in this film, a feature that is repeated in his subsequent films. Katy and Tina are both shown to be housewives who are unhappy in their marriages, although for completely different reasons; Tina and Xerxes's plan is discovered only at the end of the film. Both women spend their time indoors for the most part. The outside world is not the town of Panchgani but the streets and cafes, and police stations, of Mumbai. Interestingly enough, their moments of transgression, such as Katy's phone conversations with Farrokh during their affair or Tina's indulgence in magazines and smoking when Farrokh isn't around, take place within the domestic threshold of the house too, but these spaces are carved out as time 'away' from the oppressive routines of housewivery rather than as 'spaces' to retreat to. Katy and Tina both move within their houses to reorient themselves with their transgressions; we see Katy stray from the corridor to the gardens while Tina after ensuring that Farrokh has indeed left for work changes into her dressing gown and moves from the kitchen, a space of labour, to the sofa in the living room, a space of leisure. Indeed, these sequences are juxtaposed in the film, along with shots of Farrokh reclining on his office chair, intensifying the irony of the hierarchies of pleasure. The music in this juxtaposed sequence, a playfully romantic instrumental track, helps to heighten this irony not unlike in other Adajania films. Adajania's compositional shots make powerfully evident the darkness that lurks within domestic quarters. Stills are central to the film's cinematography; stills of objects on which Dinshaw and Katy's fingerprints are planted, of lifeless bodies being modelled on the floor with chalk lines drawn around it and of Fardoonjee being ill-treated. These stills highly resemble those to be found later in *Finding Fanny*, as elaborated upon previously. They reveal possibilities and dreams as much as facts about the eerie psyche of the domestic realm.

References

Abbas, Ackbar. 2003. 'Cinema, The City, and the Cinematic.' In *Global Cities: Cinema, Architecture and Urbanism in a Digital Age*, edited by L. Krause and P. Petro, 142–57. New Brunswick, NJ: Rutgers University Press.

Casetti, F. 2013. 'What is a Screen Nowadays?' In *Public Space, Media Space*, edited by C. Perry, J. Harbord and R.O. Moore, 16–40. Palgrave Macmillan. Retrieved 30 April 2015, from www.palgraveconnect.com. lib.exeter.ac.uk/pc/doifinder/10.1057/9781137027764.0006

Datta, S. 2000. 'Globalisation and Representations of Women in Indian Cinema.' *Social Scientist* 28 (3/4): 71–82. Retrieved 30 April 2015, from http://www.jstor.org/stable/3518191

Dwyer, R. 2011. 'Zara Hatke ("Somewhat Different"): The New Middle Classes and the Changing Forms of Hindi Cinema.' In *Being Middle-class in India: A Way of Life*, edited by H. Donner, 184–209. New York and Oxon: Routledge.

Jain, P. 2011. 'Such a Long Journey: Portrayal of the Parsi Community in Films.' *Visual Anthropology* 24 (4): 384-90. DOI: 10.1080/08949468. 2011.583573

Massey, Doreen. 1994. *Space, Place and Gender*. Minneapolis, MN: University of Minnesota Press.

Mazumdar, R. 2007. *Bombay Cinema: An Archive of the City*. London and Minneapolis, MN: University of Minnesota Press.

Menon, J. 2006. 'Being Homi.' *Verve* 14 (4). Retrieved 30 April 2015, from http://www.verveonline.com/41/people/homifull.shtml

Niyogi De, E. 2012. 'Empire, Media, and the Autonomous Woman: A Feminist Critique of Postcolonial Thought.' Oxford Scholarship Online. Retrieved 30 April 2015, from http://0-www.oxfordscholarship.com. lib.exeter.ac.uk/view/10.1093/acprof:oso/9780198072553.001.0001/ acprof-9780198072553

Ostepeev, L. 2008. 'My Name Is Johnny: Bollywood Noir.' *Metro Magazine: Media & Education Magazine*, 158: 68–71. Retrieved 30 April 2015, from http://search.informit.com.au/documentSummary;dn=52024491152 3233;res=IELLCC

Phadke, S., S. Khan and S. Ranade. 2011. *Why Loiter: Women & Risk on Mumbai's Streets*. London: Penguin.

Film References

Adajania, H. 2014. *Finding Fanny*. Illuminati Films and Maddock Films.
———. 2012. *Cocktail*. Eros International and Illuminati Films.

Adajania, H. 2005. *Being Cyrus*. Miracle Cinefilms, Serendipity Films and Times Infotainment Media.

Anand, V. 1970. *Johny Mera Naam*. Trimurti Films Pvt. Ltd.

Raghavan, S. 2007. *Johnny Gaddaar*. Adlabs Films.

16

Gender Politics and Small-town India: The Cinema of Abhishek Chaubey

Krupa Shandilya

A bhishek Chaubey (born in 1977) is part of a group of young directors who are invested in recreating the local in Bollywood cinema as is evident in all of his cinemas. With the economic liberalization of the Indian economy in 1991, Bollywood cinema has been increasingly concerned with depicting the lives of the South Asian elite, both in the diaspora and in India. Sangita Gopal terms this cinema the New Bollywood, as its preoccupation with the global constitutes a decisive break from the themes and conventions of pre-liberalization Indian cinema.[1] This global turn is visible both in the content of these films, which took on subjects such as premarital sex, divorce and homosexuality, and in the language deployed, namely Hinglish, an admixture of Hindi and English.

Abhishek Chaubey's cinema represents a radical departure from that of the New Bollywood for it focuses on depicting unconventional romantic liaisons and feminist female characters who live in small towns in India. In this focus on the local, his cinema constitutes an essential part of what I term the second wave of post-liberalization cinema. This includes Anurag Kashyap's *Gangs of Wasseypur* (2012), Vishal Bhardwaj's *Omkara* and *Haider* (2014), Maneesh Sharma's *Shuddh Desi Romance* (Pure Indian Romance; 2013) and *Band Baaja Baaraat* (Bands, Horns and Revelry; 2010) and Anand Rai's *Tanu Weds Manu* (2011).

Chaubey's first cinematic venture, *Omkara*, reflects this preoccupation with the local. *Omkara* retells the story of Shakespeare's *Othello* in the context of caste-ridden Uttar Pradesh, in the dialect of the region, *Khariboli*. Chaubey, who co-wrote the script with Vishal Bhardwaj, explains that he wants to create 'characters that are rooted in reality. When Clint Eastwood wears a cowboy hat, he makes it cool but he's really just playing a character that is uniquely American. We also must make our uniquely Indian characters cool. Like Langda Tyagi [the Iago character of the film]' (Singh 2009). Thus, Langda Tyagi's character in the film is an upper-caste man, whose insecurities stem from physical disability, rather than from his race. Like Iago, Langda's dragging limp prevents him from displaying the masculine prowess expected of a man who is the commander of a group of political gangsters.

Just as Chaubey nuances Iago's character to fit within his milieu, in *Kaminey*, his next venture as scriptwriter, the protagonist Charlie is similarly a man of his milieu. Set in the Mumbai underworld, *Kaminey* narrates the story of twins who get embroiled with an international drug lord and a petty local politician. Just as Langda Tyagi's Hindi is peppered with Khariboli, Charlie similarly deploys a Hindi slang, commonly known as *Bambaiya* Hindi, in order to convey the milieu of this world.

Chaubey's vision is more fully reflected in his next two films *Ishqiya* (2010) and *Dedh Ishqiya* (2014), both of which he has scripted and directed. Hence, we see in these films not only a preoccupation with the local, but also strong feminist female protagonists whose sexual desires drive the plot. Both films are set in small towns in Uttar Pradesh and, like his other films, are steeped in the specificities of their milieu—caste-Hindu society of Gorakhpur in *Ishqiya* and the refined Urdu-speaking Muslim elite of Mahmudabad in *Dedh Ishqiya*.

Ishqiya tells the story of Khalujaan and Babban, two small-time thieves on the run from their boss Mushtaq, who seek shelter, and subsequently fall in love, with a beautiful widow named Krishna. Krishna manipulates the men's affection and cons them into an elaborate kidnapping plot to seek revenge on her husband, Vidyadhar, whom she believes is still alive. Over the course of the film we realize that Vidyadhar thought it necessary to fake his death so that he could better control a caste-conflict and gain political power. The film ends with the death of Vidyadhar and the two men walking away into the sunset with Krishna.

As I have argued elsewhere, the film's unconventional plot represents a new genre of Hindi cinema, the 'desi feminist noir', which focuses on the dark machinations of a femme fatale from a small town, who is rewarded rather than punished for her transgressions of the patriarchal order.[2] Likewise, the character of Krishna represents a new type in Hindi cinema, the desi feminist femme fatale who is rewarded rather than punished for her manipulation of men:

> While the traditional femme fatale is a proto-feminist figure who rejects the heteronormative conventions of patriarchal society only to be punished for her transgressions,[3] the desi feminist fatale who drives this genre is rewarded rather than punished for her infractions of the patriarchal order. This femme fatale is feminist because she rejects the institution of marriage in favor of sex and erotic playfulness, and in doing so inaugurates a feminist narrative trajectory of romance characterized by unconventional romantic liaisons. (Shandilya 2014: 99)

While I have considered the femme fatale's role in terms of the film's genre, I turn now to thinking about her unconventional sexual relations and their implications for how we read the tradition/modernity dichotomy as it has been articulated in Bollywood cinema.

To begin with, Krishna is depicted as a sexual, sensuous, widowed protagonist who seeks both romance and sex, and in this, defies Hindi cinema's conventions of Hindu widowhood, established and perpetuated by Ramesh Sippy's landmark film *Sholay*

(Embers; 1975). In *Sholay*, Jai, a small-time crook, falls in love with an upper-caste widow, Radha, who follows the sartorial conventions of widowhood in her white sari and lack of ornamentation. In addition, her character is framed in terms of the moral order of upper-caste widowhood, which, from at least the nineteenth century, designated asexual purity for the widow.[4] In keeping with this, Radha is de-sexualized and presented as chaste. Thus, Radha's romance with Jai is understated and devoid of sexual content, and Jai's death at the end of the film ensures that it will remain unfulfilled. The film's conclusion decisively removes the possibility of widow remarriage, and thus conforms to the mores of Hindu caste society.

Ishqiya's parallel with *Sholay* is self-conscious. In an interview, Chaubey declares that 'Krishna is a typical small-town woman yet also a femme fatale in a polyester sari who could very well fit into a Western movie', and further recounts that 'Arshad Warsi [Babban in *Ishqiya*] had told him she's like *Sholay*'s Thakur [landowner]' (Bhattacharya 2014). In an interesting inversion, Krishna is likened not to the widow of *Sholay*, but to the landowner who deploys Jai and Veeru to avenge his son's death, for in *Ishqiya*, Krishna convinces Khalujaan and Babban to avenge her husband's disappearance through seduction.

In *Sholay*, romance and sex are separated in the two female protagonists — Radha is allowed romance but not sex and Basanti is allowed romance laced with sexual undertones. In contrast, in *Ishqiya* the two are conjoined in the same character, Krishna, who uses sex to seduce Babban and romance to seduce Khalujaan. This becomes evident as the film nears its conclusion. Once the men have discovered Krishna's treachery, they decide to kill her and run away with the money. When Babban is unable to pull the trigger, he asks Khalujaan to do the needful. Khalujaan responds:

> KJ: *Mujhe is haramzadee se ishq ho gaya hai.*
> Babban: *Yeh sahi hai Khalu. Tumhara ishq ishq aur hamara ishq sex.*
> (KJ: I've fallen in love with this bitch.
> Babban: That's right, Khalu. Your love is romance and mine is sex!)

Babban's declaration makes Krishna's tactics of seduction clear. Krishna's combination of sex and romance defies Bollywood cinema's conventions of chaste widowhood. In addition, it also nuances her portrayal as a femme fatale, for right after this exchange between the men, the camera pulls to a close up of Krishna and we see her shed a single tear. Krishna's remorse at her manipulation of the men suggests that unlike the traditional femme fatale, she harbours feelings of real affection for the men.

This interpretation is reinforced by the end of the film when she chooses Khalujaan and Babban over her husband. Although her manipulation of the men has been a ploy to secure Vidyadhar, when she finally confronts Vidyadhar over his faked death, he declares that he had to choose the cause over her. Krishna's original plan for revenge on Vidyadhar involves killing him and then committing suicide through self-immolation. The film, however, resists this traditional depiction of chaste widowhood through self-immolation, for at the last moment, Krishna is rescued by Khalujaan and Babban.

As Krishna leaves the house, an old widow arrives with a burning torch which she hands to Krishna. This moment is significant for multiple reasons. First, the old widow had previously introduced Khalujaan and Babban to Krishna and had, thus, set forth the film's plot. In this, the old widow plays a crucial—albeit subtle—role in the film's narrative trajectory, for her appearance at the climactic moment brings the story full circle; having assisted Krishna with avenging her husband, she now assists her in getting rid of him, so that she might take two lovers who satisfy her romantic and sexual desires. Second, her presence at this moment suggests a radical reworking of the imaginary of the Hindu widow who is meant to be an upholder of tradition, for here she encourages Krishna to take a decisively un-traditional step. Finally, Krishna's decision to light the fire overturns the notion of sati (self-immolation) as the widow's primary duty, for here the widow kills her husband and walks away with two lovers.

In her book on romance in Hindi cinema, Sangita Gopal argues that new possibilities for romance emerge in the films of the New Bollywood. She writes: 'If romantic love and the arranged marriage had been the two opposing norms of conjugality in Indian cinema, serial monogamy emerges here as a third option' (Gopal 2011: 78). In *Ishqiya*, we see a fourth option: the ménage à trois. This conclusion disrupts the romantic conventions of Bollywood cinema by depicting a sexual widow and rewarding her for transgressive desires. The conclusion of the film further defies patriarchal conventions of romance by rejecting monogamy in favour of polyamory.

Chaubey's next film, *Dedh Ishqiya*, is not so much a sequel to *Ishqiya* (although promoted as such) as it is an extension of its themes, namely the feminist femme fatale in small-town India. Like *Ishqiya* and *Omkara*, the film is set in Uttar Pradesh, this time in the fictional town of Mahmudabad.[5] Once again, we meet Khalujaan and Babban on the run from Mushtaq, to whom they owe a considerable sum of money. In an effort to repay him, Khalujaan and Babban hatch a plan to trap a wealthy widowed heiress, Begum Para. While Khalujaan, posing as a prince, woos Begum Para, Babban poses as his servant and woos Begum Para's maid-in-waiting, Muniya.

Although the men plan to ensnare the women, it is the women who manipulate and outsmart the men. Over the course of the film, we realize that the women are lovers and that the proposed marriage to a man is a ploy to extract money from him. The women plan to elope with the money and set up a dance school for girls, a utopian feminist space that stands outside of heteronormative coupledom. Once again, Chaubey's cinema explores unconventional romantic liaisons, in this case a lesbian romance which is gestured to but never fully articulated as such by the film.

In the context of Chaubey's cinematic oeuvre, *Dedh Ishqiya* is certainly the most daring departure from the conventions of Bollywood cinema, which, like most mainstream cinema, shies away from depicting homosexual relations onscreen. While the films of the New Bollywood, such as *Dostana* (Friendship; 2008) and *Girlfriend* (2004), do tackle homosexual relationships, their portrayals are coloured by misogyny and homophobia. The homosexual desires of the characters are either portrayed as a joke, a ruse that assists heterosexual couple formation as in the case of *Dostana* or as a twisted evil that disrupts heterosexual relationships, as seen in *Girlfriend*.

In contrast, *Dedh Ishqiya* resists these patriarchal conventions by delighting in the depiction of a lesbian relationship that is allowed to triumph over the heterosexual relationships in the film. Babban tells Khalujaan:

> *Sabke chehre pe naqab hai. Yeh tumhari jaan-e-hayaat jo hai, uske chehre pey bhi hai. Yeh jalsa, muqabla, shohar ki talash, nikkah, sab drama hai* (Chaubey, *Dedh Ishqiya*).

> (Everyone wears a mask. Your darling [Begum Para] included. The gathering, the competition, the search for a husband, the wedding, all of that is drama.)

This statement reveals that heterosexual coupledom in the film is a mere fraud meant only to facilitate lesbian coupling, and that the lesbian bond is the only relationship in the film that is not tainted by self-serving interests. The depiction of lesbian desire in the film is similarly positive as it is conveyed through sensual caresses, soft lighting and extended close-ups of languorous looks exchanged between the women.

The subtlety of its portrayal is often lost to cinemagoers, many of whom are oblivious of the film's lesbian subplot. Hence after the release of the film, film critics took it upon themselves to educate viewers.[6] In an interview, Chaubey explains that the romance between two women was necessary for narrative resolution, but its depiction could not be too overt to account for the sensibilities of a conservative audience. He says,

> [A]fter discussions with a few learned friends, we got the perfect pitch. Eventually, the hint was so subtle that if you got it, you left the theatre with a sly smile, and if you wanted, you could ignore it and still have plenty left with to enjoy. (Bhattachrya 2014)

I have argued elsewhere that the film's obfuscation of desire is not merely a ploy to avoid censorship and backlash from political conservatives, but has significant feminist implications:

[The film's articulation of] female sexual desire through a politics of (in)visibility…are illegible to those who recognize women's desire only when they are structured by the 'dominant configurations [of] pleasure, identity, and visibility' (Gopinath 2005: 152). In doing so, [it]…destabilizes the correlation between westernization and sexual expression that the films of the New Bollywood insist on (Shandilya 2014: 109).

Thus, as we see, the scopic (in)visibility of homosexuality in the film defies multiple patriarchal conventions of Bollywood cinema — First, the notion that homosexual desire is deviant, aberrant and can only be dealt with through humour or violence. Second, that female sexual desire, when it is expressed, is largely the product of the female protagonist's 'Westernization'.

In its insistence on portraying unconventional sexual relationships in the small-town milieu, the film reconfigures Bollywood's imaginary of the small town, which has largely been seen as a provincial backwater untouched by the modernizing influences of the city. In films of the pre-liberalization era, the Indian village featured prominently as an idyllic pastoral space. This village had no specific geographic location or history, but rather was created as a generic village that was meant to simultaneously represent every village and no village. It was often represented as the heart of the 'true' India — pure, innocent and childlike, features which became characteristic of the village belle who inevitably falls in love with the city-bred hero and convinces him of the evils of city life, specifically of its modernization and Westernization. This is usually accomplished through a narrative doubling — the hero protagonist must decide between the Westernized city girl and the innocent village belle.

This trope remained popular in films of the post-liberalization era but assumed a slightly different form. For instance, the 2001 film *Lagaan: Once Upon a Time in India* (henceforth, *Lagaan*) portrayed its protagonist Bhuvan as having to choose between the village belle Gauri and Elizabeth, who is literally an English woman. The film's setting in the British Raj necessitates that Bhuvan chooses the chaste, Indian woman over the morally correct but nevertheless white (and hence unacceptable) British woman. But one could also read Bhuvan's choice as allaying anxiety about Westernization in the post-liberalization era. As film scholar Gita Rajan argues, in films of the post-liberalization era such as *Lagaan*, a composite modern Indian masculinity needs to be reasserted through both physical prowess (the game of cricket) and heterosexuality.[7]

In this context, *Ishqiya* and *Dedh Ishqiya*'s depiction of the small town nuances the generic village by situating the film in a specific sociocultural milieu. Further, its portrayal of sexual, sensuous women who initiate unconventional romantic relationships even as they live in small-town India subverts the dichotomy of the innocent village and the evil city.[8] In an interview with *Mumbai Mirror*, Abhishek Chaubey recounts his own upbringing in an Orthodox Brahmin family in Faizabad. He declares that while men headed the family in the outside world, the true decision-makers were the women, 'In the outside world they play supporting roles, but all major decisions are taken when the husband and wife have their heads on the pillow and she's telling him what has to be done' (Bhattacharya 2014).

This, as we have seen, is indeed reflected in Chaubey's cinema, where small-town women drive the plot of the film. It remains to be seen whether *Udta Punjab* (Flying Punjab; 2016), Chaubey's forthcoming film set in Punjab depicting the time of Partition, reiterates the thematic concerns of his other films. In an interview, Chaubey declares that '[*Udta Punjab*] is not *Ishqiya* 3 but a film set in Punjab with an ensemble cast and one kickass woman character' (Bhattacharya 2014). This suggests that the film might explore the feminist themes of *Ishqiya* and *Dedh Ishqiya*. Thus, Chaubey's fascination with sex and the small-town seems, at least at the moment, to be a defining feature of his cinema.

Notes

1 'One of my central suggestions in this book is that the postnuptial couple produced by new Bollywood serves as a ground for elaborating on the citizen-subject of the emerging post-liberalization state' (Gopal 18).

2   The 'desi feminist noir' is characterized by all the elements of film noir, such as the murky distinction between good and evil, the law-lessness of the streets and the femme fatale. However, in these films the figure of the femme fatale is used to forward explicitly feminist trajectories of love, romance and sex (Shandilya 2014: 97–98).

3   As Elizabeth Bronfen argues,

> [The femme fatale of film noir is] a particularly resilient con-temporary example of tragic sensibility…. [S]he functions both as the screen for fantasies of omnipotence and as the agent who, by ultimately facing the consequences of her *noir* actions, comes to reveal the fragility not only of any sense of omnipo-tence that transgression of the law affords, but, indeed, of what it means to be human. (Bronfen 2004: 105)

4   Feminist historian Tanika Sarkar reconstructs the material history of the nineteenth century widow who refused sati and argues that nationalist discourse required her to withdraw from all sexual desire and embrace a life of 'ascetic widowhood', so that she could represent the spiritual Indian nation untouched by colonialism: '[S]trict ritual observances root [the widow's] body in ancient India, thus miracu-lously enabling her to escape foreign domination…. Ergo, the nation needs ascetic widowhood' (Sarkar 2001: 42).

5   'I make UP-centric regional films, if I can make them intelligible to people in Tamil Nadu without losing out on realism, why not?' (Bhattachrya 2014).

6   As stated in Moifightclub (2014),

> This is a strange scenario. I read review after review after review, every damn possible review of *Dedh Ishqiya*. Just to figure out one thing—to see if anyone has written about the homage scene in the film, and the inspiration behind the film's spoiler, or scratched it beyond the surface. And I was extremely disappointed to see that not a single reviewer has mentioned it.

7   'Gowariker connects sportsmen to the nation by constructing a com-plex complementarity between a good citizen and normative hetero-sexuality. Such a complementarity, however, can be enacted only at this moment of globality' (Rajan 2006: 1111).

8   As Mahesh (2010) states,

> I wanted to make an entertaining rural film, which was real-istic yet fun, a commercial film that breaks the basic norms of

such a genre—family-oriented, urban movies with happy end-
ings. I basically wanted to change the audience's perception of
a commercial film and *Ishqiya* was just that.

Film References

Bhardwaj, V. *Omkara*. Big Screen Entertainment, Panoramas Studios and
 Shemaroo Video Pvt. Ltd.
———. 2014. *Haider*. UTV Motion Pictures and Vishal Bhardwaj Pictures.
Chaubey, A. 2014. *Dedh Ishqiya*. Shemaroo Entertainment and Vishal
 Bhardwaj Pictures.
———. 2010. *Ishqiya*. Shemaroo Entertainment and Vishal Bhardwaj
 Pictures.
Gowariker, A. 2001. *Lagaan: Once Upon a Time in India*. Aamir Khan
 Productions.
Kashyap, A. 2012. *Gangs of Wasseypur*. Jar Pictures, AKFPL and Bohra
 Bros Productions.
Mansukhani, T. 2008. *Dostana*. Black Dog Jib Productions and Dharma
 Productions.
Razdan, K. 2004. *Girlfriend*. SP Creations.
Rai, A. 2011. *Tanu Weds Manu*. Bohra Bros Productions, Paramhans
 Creations and Movies n' More.
Sippy, R. 1975. *Sholay*. United Producers and Sippy Films.
Maneesh S. 2013. *Shuddh Desi Romance*. Yash Raj Films.
———. 2010. *Band Baaja Baaraat*. Yash Raj Films.

17

Women in the Dark World: Sriram Raghavan and Hindi Film Noir

Swetha Sridhar

As a genre (or a style), film noir has received scant attention from the commercial Hindi film-making industry, that is, Bollywood. In spite of movies such as *C.I.D.* (Raj Khosla 1956), *Manorama Six Feet Under* (Navdeep Singh 2007), and *No Smoking* (Anurag Kashyap 2007), the genre by and large remains largely under-represented. It is in this context that one needs to understand the success of Sriram Raghavan, as both writer and director, who is often credited with bringing noir to the consciousness of the average film-goer.

There is rarely any consensus on what specifically allows for a film to be categorized as a noir. To summarise,[1] some scholars argue that particular characteristics of the cinematic narrative, such as the lighting, characters or editing styles, make up the genre. On the other hand, it is posited that noir as a genre refers to a set of recurring patterns that allow for labels to be used in production, marketing and distribution, but more importantly, creates a set of expectations for the audience. The genre has less to do with a group of artefacts than a constantly evolving discourse that structures aesthetics and ideology. Most commonly associated with the cinematic tropes of the masculine and loner detective, the femme fatale, the decay of urban life and the criminal underbelly of life, the genre of film noir is effectively mobilized by Raghavan to tell stories that are at once locally rooted but appeal to an international narrative aesthetic. Fay and Nieland believe that noir is not a genre that is embedded in the American post-War depression situation, but open to a narrator with a critical voice. Film noir, truly considered, is no longer representative of a uniquely American malaise, but an international phenomenon that traverses complex international geo-political terrain and is, thus, a distinctively hybrid form (Fay and Nieland 2009). It is this aspect that allows for a common thread to be drawn between Sriram Raghavan's range of movies—from the honour-among-thieves plot that is *Johnny Gaddaar* (2007) to the James Bond-esque plot of *Agent Vinod* (2012) to the revenge plot of *Badlapur* (2015). Bhatia writes about Raghavan's approach to noir and reasons that,

> [It] isn't straight-up noir: The screen isn't shrouded in shadow, there's no fatalistic voice-over, and novelist and screenwriter Raymond Chandler's rule about someone who 'is not himself mean' going down mean streets is soon discarded. Instead, what we get is a sprinkling of noir themes and tropes: the pervasive fog of bad luck; the idea that once fate plays a hand, there's not much you can do about it.... (Bhatia 2015)

Raghavan's work can be classified more specifically as neo-noir, which is distinguished from classic noir by a more expansive understanding of the city-scape and is often characterized by a journey into the underbelly of one's own mind to interrogate questions of identity, belonging and memory. Where classic noir was seen as a response to the effects of the Great Depression and the Second World War, neo-noir is a reaction to changes that are resulting in a social upheaval since such as liberalization and the emergence of a global village (Conrad 2007). Dimendberg (2004) suggests that noir can be understood as an articulation emerging from the tension between the dissolution of the 1920's American urbanism by the Second World War, and the breakdown of 1950's America by the spectacle of post-modernism. An expansive reading of this formulation allows us to understand the genre as a reflection of the 'hollow spaces of capitalism', paying close attention to spaces, places and characters in transition, and less as an American stylistic cycle. This seems to suggest that despite definitions of genre and style, perhaps the most useful way of interpreting noir is to understand it as a commentary on the sociocultural transitions of the twentieth century. To this end, the label 'desi noir' (Chopra 1996) comes closest to describing the corpus of Sriram Raghavan's work. Sandilya (2014), in her work, suggests 'desi noir' as a place-holder for cinema of post-liberalization India, which articulates the tensions of modernity and heteronormativity in a language distinct from that of 'Bombay Noir' or the 'Indian Social'.

Continuing with the established tropes of the neo-noir films, Raghavan's films do contain many of the same themes of 'alienation, pessimism, moral ambivalence and disorientation'. This is evident when one considers *Johnny Gaddaar*, the story of a drug deal gone wrong when the money involved goes missing. The attempt to unveil the identity of the thief drives the narrative of the movie, with each of the five members of the gang suspecting the other. Critically though, although the members of the gang are in the dark, the audience know who the *gaddar* (traitor) is from the outset, and the motivations behind the theft. As the movie reaches its climax, the characters and the audience become painfully aware of the conflicting interests and ambitions that drive human behaviour and the consequences (often unintended) of following certain paths.

Given the nature of the issues that neo-noir addresses, it is oft characterized by a lack of closure in the narrative, leaving audience only with a heightened sense of identification and lack of moral boundaries.

Agent Vinod, an espionage thriller plotted around a RAW agent Vinod's (Saif Ali Khan) voyage through the maze of conspiracies to uncover a plot to create global unrest exemplifies such ambiguity. RAW is left clueless after Rajan (Ravi Kishan), one of its agents and Vinod's friend, sends an incomplete message before dying, and this sets the eponymous Agent Vinod off on a globetrotting mission which takes him from Russia to Morocco and from Latvia to Pakistan. Indeed, Raghavan's careful crafting of his characters ensures that audiences are left unclear about the protagonist of the story and ambiguous about the moral rightness of the characters' actions. Raghavan, in his capacity as director, comments on this in an interview with the *Times of India* in 2015,[2] as he says, 'The viewer is trained to root for the hero. We do that. Gradually, the viewer's perception is destroyed. They may ask that how can a hero do this or that?' The concept of the hero is turned further on its head in the exchange between Liak (Nawazuddin Siddiqui), the antagonist, and Raghu (Varun Dhawan), the protagonist, of Badlapur, where Liak points out that at least his crimes were committed in the heat of the moment, unlike Raghu's, which were the result of cold-blooded calculations.

Raghavan's work is notable for the manner in which it explores the consequences of being 'pulled into' the noir world, rather than the make-up of characters that exist entirely in the noir world a priori — be it Raghu from *Badlapur* or Sarika (Urmila Matondkar) from *Ek Hasina Thi*. Raghu's entry into the noir world is predicated on the death of his wife and child right at the beginning of the movie, and his determination to avenge their deaths makes up the rest of the plot of the movie. Although the plot seems fairly simple and unremarkable, Raghavan shows skill in how Raghu charts the hitherto unknown territory — an exploration that the audience make with Raghu. Similarly, Sarika, whose whirlwind romance turns sour when she is framed for her boyfriend's underworld crimes, embarks tenuously into the noir world when she's released from prison, ready for revenge. Perhaps Raghavan's approach to plotting is summed up in this quote about plotting *Badlapur* from an interview with *Bollywood Hungama* in 2015[3] — 'Yes, in a sense it's a tale of lost innocence, almost like a short story where the basic characters play out their karma in a tightly wound plot.' This feeds into the self-reflexive quality that neo-noir cinema often exhibits (Conrad 2007) as directors like Raghavan work quite consciously within the framework of noir and are aware of the fact that they are adding to the canon.

As one examines his work, one considers the work of Borde and Chaumeton who theorize that film noir is but a '"series" — one united not by visual style or narration but rather by a consistency of an emotional sort: namely the state of tension created in the spectators by the disappearance of their psychological bearing' (Borde and Chaumeton 2002). Further, I look to Frank's (1996) conception of noir as an impression of real life and lived experience, and Schrader (1972) who writes that film noir is defined neither by conventions of setting nor by conflict, but by qualities of mood and tone. It is this that leads me to explore the possibility that Sriram Raghavan's success as a director of noir cinema in Bollywood stems from his particular way of 'doing' cinema.

Central to Raghavan's way of doing cinema is the manner in which he uses the female characters in his plots as a means of building the genre, and its implications in the larger Indian sociocultural milieu. At the outset, a disclaimer is mandated. There is a great amount of feminist academic debate about whether women in noir occupy an empowered space or are a representation of the misogynistic social norms that allow for the creation of such cinema. This chapter does not seek to enter into this debate; rather, by exploring the manner in which Raghavan scripts the women in his movies over the nature of his doing so, the chapter speaks how femininity, morality and noir are co-constructed in Raghavan's cinematic world.

With a few exceptions, most of the women in noir films can be categorized into three types (Blaser and Blaser 2008). The 'femme fatale' — an independent and ambitious woman who attempts to breaks free of convention, often with violent results — are seen as women who seek to advance themselves by manipulating their sexual allure and by controlling its value. The 'nurturing woman' is the second trope, often dull, featureless and serving only to be an indicator of the futility and stultifying nature of marriage as an institution. The last of the three tropes is the 'marrying woman' who is seen as constantly pushing the hero to accept his conventional role as husband and father, often serving as the counterpoint to the femme fatale. One of the major contributions of neo-noir as a genre is the blurring of the three tropes, and Raghavan's cinema makes extensive use of these characters. What draws all of these women together is the sense that they are all 'trapped' in the noir world and, in their own way, are striving to make the best of their situation — be it Iram from *Agent Vinod* or Mini from *Johnny Gaddaar*.

The femme fatale is a trope that constantly recurs in the three movies as Mini from *Johnny Gaddaar*, Iram from *Agent Vinod* and Jhimli from *Badlapur*. These women act as foils against which the masculinity of the lead characters is established, something that is highlighted in the interactions between Liak and Jhimli — the beaten-down criminal and the prostitute from *Badlapur*, respectively.

Iram represents a particular kind of femme fatale common to the later film noir — a 'nurturing redeemer' who does not threaten the hero because she does not intend to marry or domesticate him. Although Iram aspires to a life of normalcy represented by a family in the traditional sense, at no point is there any indication that she expects this from Vinod. This new type of femme fatale gives the hero something that his male friends cannot: a safe romantic alternative to the threatening marrying type (because she is not a potential wife) or even an idealized vision of the past (a function previously served by the 'good woman'). She becomes a human connection that the broken and world-weary agent makes, and thus the 'nurturing' femme fatale becomes a source of comfort, understanding and redemption.

What is evident from a reading of these characters is the strength of their allure that then becomes a demonstration of their strength as characters themselves. Through an expression of sexuality, subtle or otherwise, the women's other deficiencies (as it were) are forgiven, and the strength derived from her allure transcends the image of her demise. In other words, the image that the audience is left with at the end of a sequence is less a lesson about the costs of transgression, and more an exposition of the various ways in which hyper-sexualized femininity is exerted as a tool. In the song 'Jee Karda' from the movie *Badlapur*, Raghavan makes a pointed comment about the same where he juxtaposes a brooding, well-muscled and bare-chested Raghu, seen exerting in a space made to look like a warehouse or an abandoned gym with an image of Jhimli applying lipstick while looking on coquet-tishly, even as men dance and express physical anguish over Misha's (Raghu's wife) death. The idea of Jhimli's sanction to be there derives from the strength that she wields even as she holds on to her sexuality, or perhaps the strength she wields because of it. In other words, the sexuality of Raghavan's characters is not linked entirely to the body but to the objects that construct these characters as desirable.

Another site of tension that Raghavan repeatedly showcases, albeit very subtly, is the family and the marital relationship. Two of his characters — Radhika Apte's Koko in *Badlapur* and Rimi Sen's Mini in *Johnny Gaddaar* — serve to highlight the highly fraught nature of the institution. Mini especially can be read as a charac-ter typical to most noir cinema — the housewife yearning for inde-pendence from her husband. Such characters are traditionally seen as using their sexuality to manipulate men rather than submitting to the requirements and demands of a husband and the traditional family unit, thus creating alternatives for themselves (Blaser and Blaser 2008). The audience is initially led to believe that she is Vikram's girlfriend based on a risqué conversation that the two of them have about the colour of her clothes. However, in few scenes we come to realise that she is actually married to Shardul, Vikram's business partner and friend. At no point it is made explicit what prompts Mini to leave Shardul, other than her love for Vikram. Women who are seen as transgressing the boundaries of conven-tional behaviour within the institution of family meet with and deserve apt punishment, as do the men who succumb to their sexual charms. It may be argued that Mini and Vikram exemplify this tendency — Vikram's desire for Mini and his dreams of a better life in Canada with her set in motion a series of consequences that cannot be stopped. However, throughout the movie, the audience empathize with Mini, as they do with Jhimli, as, to use Harvey's (1998) idea, 'despite the ritual punishment of acts of transgression, the vitality with which these acts are endowed produces an excess of meaning which cannot finally be contained.'

At the same time, Raghavan sets up a contrast with Varsha (Ashwini Kalsekar), Prakash's wife and Seshadri's (another

member of the gang) romance for his late wife. The latter is especially interesting, given how Janey Place (1998) makes an argument for the good woman as a mirage—the audience knows close
to nothing about Seshadri's dead wife other than his recollection
of her; she functions as a constant foil to his protégé's relationship with his girlfriend, and not as a realistic alternative or pre-
scription for behaviour. Furthermore, Varsha is initially seen as
removed from the noir world inhabited by her husband and his
cronies, and her being drawn into the noir world coincides with
the breaking apart of her family unit, further reifying the ideas of
fragility and destruction that Place uses to describe the family in
noir. On the whole, Raghavan's characters serve to reinforce the
notion common to a lot of film noir that relationships are 'broken,
perverted, peripheral or impossible, rather than life-affirming
and spiritually enriching' as argued by Harvey[4] (1998).

These characters not only represent a move away from the social
norm and convention, but their 'in-between-ness' is also characterized by their grappling with larger issues as it were. Part of the
tension that we see emanating from Iram pertains not just to the
tension that she shares with the RAW agent Vinod, but more fundamentally from the question of who she really is and what her
affiliations are. Throughout the movie, tension arises from the fact
that her identity is in flux—a fact that matters more than Vinod's
constant metamorphosis from one undercover identity and costume to another. In the end, as the audience is convinced of the reality of her 'Pakistani-ness', she achieves 'redemption' in the manner
familiar to most femme fatales—death, sacrificing her life for the
larger cause, the thwarting of the terrorist plot in this instance.

In part, Raghavan's exploration of issues such as these stems
from the larger trend that can be seen in post-liberalization cinema
in India. In this context, Rachel Dwyer takes into consideration the
transformation of the Indian cinematic imaginary in this period,
allowing for aspirations of upward mobility, the emergence of the
middle class, contestation in public life and so on (Dwyer 2014).
This coincides with what Vasudevan posits about the role of these
new genres and narrative styles in addressing newly formed and
acknowledged subjectivities (Vasudevan 2010). It is against this

background that Indian cinema and its themes must be viewed. Transforming from a cinema culture with nationalist conscience to a cinema that interrogated many of the contemporary happenings in Indian society; and given noir's function as a response to upheaval of modernization and globalization, Bollywood's expansion allowed for directors like Sriram Raghavan to emerge. Vasudevan (2010) further makes an argument for Indian cinema of the post-liberalization period investing greater importance to 'Hollywood economies of narration' often eschewing Indian narrative formulae of song, dance and comic asides, in favour of pure narrative entertainment. It's no surprise that Raghavan's narrative aesthetic found a niche in this changing landscape. A quick glance at any of his cinema evidences a careful absence of any formulaic elements of Bollywood cinema; songs are used at key points as background score or a narrative device, but never as an intrusive element in the plot. With *Agent Vinod*, this idea was reiterated with Rajeev Masand calling attention to the skilful use of the song 'Raabta',

> [E]ven as bullets fly in the lobby of a seedy Eastern European motel with Saif Ali Khan dodging them with choreographed skill, darting from corner to corner to save Iram, love blooms between the two as the ballad plays in the background muting the sound of gunfire. (Masand 2012)

Further, Raghavan's characters, especially the romantic couples in his film, can be read as exemplifying the trends that Kona (2011) sees in post-liberalization romance in Indian cinema. In his cinema, '...coming togetherness is bound to the individualism rooted in a capitalist ethic where you have the means to acquire what you desire; the "freedom" is about being able to afford the love as much as it is a politics of desire,' as demonstrated by the romance between Mini and Vikram, whose romance is about each other as much as it is about their plan to get rich quick and elope. The question of gender is crucial to a discussion of post-liberalization cinema. It becomes evident that women's role within the narratives speaks to a sensibility where free market liberalism comes into conflict with social mores, for control over the bodies of women, and the value of the labour they provide: literally, in the case of prostitutes like Jhimli, but also more obliquely, where Iram contributes not by fighting or strategizing but by being an undercover 'companion' or dancing in a mujra sequence. In this manner, Raghavan's work also fits into the circuits of desire and consumption that mark the emergence of a post-1991 'New Bollywood' (Gopal and Moorti 2008).

Tejaswini Ganti (2012) asserts that the commercial outcome of cinema is often seen as an indicator of social norms and sensibilities, as well as an indicator of how closely the audience identifies with the narrative on screen; perhaps Raghavan's track record stands testimony to the ambiguity with which audiences respond to his work. He has a self-confessed tenuous relation to the box-office as articulated in an interview with *Bollywood Hungama* in 2015: 'I've never been bothered much about what the box-office would think of me. Even *Ek Hasina Thi* and *Johnny Gaddaar* didn't set the box-office on fire. But people still remember those films fondly.'

Nonetheless, it must be said that Raghavan's craft stands testimony to his love for cinema in general — his narratives are peppered with references to earlier movies such as the clips from *Parwana* (Jyoti Sarup 1971) in *Johnny Gaddaar*, *Sholay* (Ramesh Sippy 1975) in *Badlapur* and *Thalapathi* (Mani Ratnam 1991) in *Agent Vinod*, and he draws stylistic inspiration from a wide variety of sources. At its heart, Raghavan's craft treads the fine line between being a refined viewer of cinema himself, and a film-maker with his distinct style, establishing in Bollywood, the beginnings of the noir.

Editor's note: Ketan Mehta's underrated *Aar Ya Paar* (1997) was an addition to the corpus of noir in Hindi films in the 1990s. *Samay* (Robby Grewal 2003), a dark cop drama, starring Sushmita Sen fared better with critics but failed commercially. However, it was with *Jism* (Amit Saxena 2003), a rehash of *Double Indemnity* (Billy Wilder 1944), that noir found a larger audience.

Notes

1 Refer to Fay and Nieland (2009) for a detailed exposition of this debate.

2   Raghavan, Sriram, interview by Rajesh Naidu. 'I Followed the Hitchcockian Approach of Providing as Much Information as Possible to the Viewer' (10 March 2015).
3   Raghavan, Sriram, interview by Subhash K Jha. *I Was Very Pissed Off with the Poor Performance of Agent Vinod* (18 February 2015).
4   Perhaps nowhere is this more evident than the anguish that Sarika goes through as a result of her romantic involvement with Karan, in Raghavan's debut film *Ek Hasina Thi*.

References

Bhatia, Uday. 2015. 'Shadowy Past.' *Livemint*, 3 March. Retrieved June 2015, from http://www.livemint.com/Leisure/aKSH2CAjNVd4io-VhFghNKM/Shadowy-past.html

Blaser, John J. and Stephanie L. M. Blaser. 2008. 'No Place for a Woman: The Family in Film Noir.' *Film Noir Studies*. Retrieved June 2015, from http://www.filmnoirstudies.com/essays/no_place.asp

Borde, Raymon and Etienne Chaumeton. 2002. 'Towards a Definition of Film Noir.' In *A Panorama of American Film Noir*, by Raymon Borde and Chaumeton Etienne, 5–14. San Francisco, CA: City Lights Publishers.

Chopra, Anupama. 1996. 'Bye-bye Bharat.' *India Today*, March.

Conrad, Mark T. 2007. 'Introduction.' In *The Philosophy of Neo-Noir*, edited by Mark T Conrad, 1–4. Lexington, KY: University of Kentucky Press.

Dimendberg, Edward. 2004. *Film Noir and the Spaces of Modernity.* Cambridge, MA: Harvard University Press.

Dwyer, Rachel. 2014. *Picture Abhi Baaki Hai: Bollywood as a Guide to Modern India.* Gurgaon: Hachette India.

Fay, Jennifer and Justus Nieland. 2009. *Film Noir (Routledge Film Guidebooks): Hard-Boiled Modernity and the Cultures of Globalization (English).* New York: Routledge.

Frank, Nino. 1996. 'The Crime Adventure Story: A New Kind of Detective Film.' In *Perspectives on Film Noir*, edited by R. Barton Palmer. New York: G.K. Hall.

Ganti, Tejaswini. 2012. *Producing Bollywood: Inside the Contemporary Hindi Film Industry.* Durham and London: Duke University Press.

Gopal, Sangita and Sujata Moorti. 2008. *Global Bollywood: Travels of Hindi Song and Dance.* Minneapolis, MN: University of Minnesota Press.

Harvey, Sylvia. 1998. 'Women's Place: The Absent Family of Film Noir.' In *Women in Film Noir*, edited by E. Ann. Kaplan, 22–33. London: British Film Institute.

Kona, Prakash. 2011. 'Notions of Gender in Hindi Cinema: The Passive Indian Woman in the Global Discourse of Consumption.' *Bright Lights*

Film Journal. Retrieved 20 August 2016, from http://brightlightsfilm.com/notions-of-gender-in-hindi-cinema-the-passive-indian-woman-in-the-global-discourse-of-consumption/#.V-QRLPB97IU

Masand, R. 2012. Online movie review. Retrieved 20 August 2016, from http://www.rajeevmasand.com/reviews/our-films/guns-n-poses/.

Place, Janey. 1998. 'Women in Film Noir.' In *Women in Film Noir*, edited by E. Ann. Kaplan, 47–68. London: British Film Institute.

Sandilya, Krupa. 2014. 'The Long Smouldering Night: Sex, Songs and Desi Feminist Noir.' *New Cinemas: Journal of Contemporary Film* 12 (1 and 2): 97–111.

Schrader, Paul. 1972. 'Notes on Film Noir'. *Film Comment* 8–13.

Vasudevan, Ravi. 2010. *The Melodramatic Public: Film Form and Spectatorship in India*. New Delhi: Permanent Black.

Film References

Agent Vinod. 2012. Directed by Sriram Raghavan. Produced by Saif Ali Khan and Dinesh Vijan. Performed by Saif Ali Khan, Kareena Kapoor Khan, Ram Kapoor, Adil Hussain and Prem Chopra. Illuminati Films, Eros Entertainment.

Badlapur. 2015. Directed by Sriram Raghavan. Produced by Dinesh Vijan and Sunil Lulla. Performed by Varun Dhawan, Huma Qureshi, Nawazuddin Siddiqui, Radhika Apte and Yami Gautam. Eros International.

Ek Hasina Thi. 2004. Directed by Sriram Raghavan. Produced by Ram Gopal Varma and R. R. Venkat. Performed by Saif Ali Khan, Urmila Matondkar and Seema Biswas. R. R. Movie Makers.

Johnny Gaddaar. 2007. Directed by Sriram Raghavan. Produced by Adlabs Films Ltd. Performed by Neil Nitin Mukesh, Dharmendra, Rimi Sen, Vinay Pathak and Zakir Hussain. Adlabs Films Ltd.

Kashyap, A. 2007. *No Smoking*. Eros International.

Khosla, R. 1956. *C.I.D.* Guru Dutt Films Pvt. Ltd.

Ratnam, M. 1991. *Thalapathi*. G.V. Films Ltd.

Raghavan, S. 2004. *Ek Hasina Thi*. R. R. Movie Makers.

———. 2007. *Johnny Gaddaar*. Adlabs Films Ltd.

———. 2012. *Agent Vinod*. Illuminati Films, Eros Entertainment.

———. 2015. *Badlapur*. Eros International.

Sarup, J. 1971. *Parwana*. Ambika Chitra.

Singh, N. 2007. *Manorama Six Feet Under*. Shemaroo Entertainment.

Sippy, R. 1975. *Sholay*. Sippy Films.

CHAPTER 18

'There Is No Greater Joy than Telling a Story One Believes In' — Our Brother Onir

Nandini Bhattacharya

The title of this chapter borrows a sentence from independent film-maker Onir's interview given to the *Times of India* (2012, March 10). Onir said in another part of that interview,

> I think, this [National] Award is a victory for independent film makers. We made this film on a budget of 1.5 crores and we got the award for the best Hindi film in an industry which has seen films with a budget of 100–150 crores in 2011. The National Award validates the art of storytelling.

Without questioning the optimistic point of view expressed by the film-maker himself, in what follows, I wish to excavate the true daring of India's first film-maker to take on LGBT rights as a cinematic story without financial backing, without the assurance of a guaranteed audience and against great personal and societal odds. While I may seem to be mythologizing a film-maker who does come after other doyens of cinematic daring (Satyajit Ray, Ritwik Ghatak and Shyam Benegal are some of Onir's own-acknowledged models), I hope this essay will establish the magnitude and challenge of what Onir has accomplished.

I would like to claim, particularly, that one of the frameworks within which Onir's films—beginning with the groundbreaking *My Brother...Nikhil* and concluding (for the purposes of this essay) with *I AM*—operate is that of telling the story of 'fraternity' in its various senses within the Indian sociocultural matrix as well as the private familial one. The contention is curiously enough supplemented by the fact that several of Onir's films deal titularly and thematically with relations between brothers and sisters (*My Brother ... Nikhil, Sorry Bhai!*, the Megha episode in *I AM* and so on), or that privately and publicly Onir acknowledges his strong sense of familial connections, especially with his sister, the National Award-winning editor Irene Dhar Malik who not only edits his films but also seriously introduced him to good cinema in the first place.[1]

'Fraternity' is defined by the *Oxford English Dictionary* as follows: 'A group of people sharing a common profession or interests; A male students' society in a university or college; A religious or Masonic society or guild; The state or feeling of friendship and mutual support within a group' and so forth. Leaving aside the second very North American culture-specific denotation of fraternity, the other three broader definitions extend the meaning of 'brother' well beyond the consanguinary or familial into the professional, the vocational, the ethical and ideological, and the communal. I propose that Onir's auteurial intervention in Hindi cinema has been, at least thematically, in rerouting the conventional affective plot of a film—social or romantic—into a deeper, focused exploration of the idea of fraternity in the senses described above by the *Oxford English Dictionary*. And in re-centring this at best hidden strain (pun intended) within the feudal family romance of Hindi cinema (as Madhava Prasad said in 1998), and showcasing and highlighting the potential of the 'fraternal' romance in Hindi cinema or in cinema in general, Onir transcended Hindi cinema's tendency to bury this crucial affective connection and its potential in the playful graveyard of the 'sister/brother' subplot in his inaugural career moves. He revealed, instead, something both psychically and culturally essential about filial, fraternal and sibling relationships, and roles that speaks not only to homosexual experiences and identities of Indians, but also to the lateral tensions and bonds within the hetero-normative family that rival and challenge the hetero-patriarchal romances that usually overshadow them.

A few words about Onir's technique and style are in order, though, before we can take the concepts above any further. In an interview conducted with Onir on 30th November 2014, I asked him what inspired or determined him to make movies. With many gestures at the huge difficulties of financing, patronage, networking and insider status that shape commercial film-making in India, the answer Onir gave pointed at a sort of instinctually divergent view of life and society themselves, far transcending the conditions, practices and traditions of film-making per se. Referencing Shyam Benegal's classic film *Junoon* (1978) as his first significant cinematic experience, Onir described his encounter with 'real' cinema as follows:

> I think subconsciously, when I was in class eight, I saw this film by Shyam Benegal called *Junoon*. I did not really understand it then but it kind of stayed with me and made me fascinated with the medium; I was drawn to it and wanted to be part of it but it was not very conscious.

Comparing the pervasive presence of Bollywood films that most Indian spectators grow up with to an ongoing fair or festival, or to the experience of routine Sunday market-going among Bengalis especially (this is the ethno-linguistic community Onir comes from, of course), Onir described his initiation into cinema as both magical and liminal, as well as an intensely visual experience. He referred to the searing texture of cinematic image and movement as what Metz and others have famously described as a grand syntagmatic psychodrama (Metz 1982; Mishra 2001).[2]

With characteristic humility, Onir also described his film-making enterprise as a collective collaboration and expressed reservations about a director calling a film 'their' film, since so many people contribute to the making of any single full-length film.

However, when pushed on the question of his very own signature film-making style, he acknowledges that those who know him well, such as his favourite actor and collaborator Sanjay Suri, can vouch for his brushstrokes on the visual canvas of his films, and have led him to recognize certain patterns and habits—perhaps predilections and intentions—even in his cinematic corpus. He listed them as his unique tracking and panning techniques, as avoidance of the shot reverse shot method of classical narrative cinema and as the tendency towards the disquisitional or dialectical film (as French film-maker Eric Rohmer, for instance): 'I have started to realize that I like my characters to stand next to each other and not look at each other but to look out at nature, or the night or something and **talk**....'[3] Without putting too fine a point on it, I would flag this comment by the director about the textural laterality of his images and mise en scène for when I return to the observations made about Onir's resistant, decentring response vis-à-vis the hierarchical hetero-patriarchal (or feudal family) romance of much commercial cinema.

Acutely aware of the materiality and texture of the moving image, Onir also places a premium on the interweaving of sound, image and light in scenes in *My Brother ... Nikhil*, saying,

> They [the actors] sounded beautiful. It had a different texture; the night is night. You don't need to always see; cinema is also about sound, about voices, about you know just texture, and it's there right from *My Brother Nikhil*; very often I don't feel the necessity of always seeing a person, or of close-ups that some people are obsessed with.

Eschewing, therefore, many conventions of cinematic realism, Onir's own reportage suggests his investment in cinema as a medium for narrative and affective 'flows' rather than episodic linearity.

Of course, my point is not necessarily that a certain spatial and compositional indirection argues for a singular, identifiable political and aesthetic trajectory in film-making—film language is, after all, enunciatory and not individually owned—but a film-maker's technique and cinematic voice can be compared, respectively, to tactics and strategies. Hence, Onir's stylistic choices such as his use of colour — 'I like also a lot to play with color codes…characters I feel also have favorite colors [sic]' — might indicate sensorial choices that might, in turn, point to ideological as well as discursive enunciations. The same applies to names for his characters; Onir likes to play with names. Below I quote at some length from our interview:

> I try and find names which have a certain…. I'll give you an example; in *Shab*, two of my lead protagonists have double names — dual personalities and double names — and their names question the meaning of social values. So for me names are also very important, and I realized that…it also mattered to people because when I was doing *I AM*, and the first story was 'I AM AFIA,' I had wanted a very well-known director to write a song. He came to the office and he said, *Is ka kahaani kya hai?* [What is the story?] So I told him it is the story of a single mother, and he said *Afia ka matlab kya aapko maloom hain?* [Do you know what Afia means?]) So I said yeah it means noble, a girl born on a Friday, and he said *Aap aise aurat ko kaise yeh naam de sakte hain?* [How can you give this name to a woman like this?]. So I said *ki kyun, mujhe toh,* [Why, as for me] I really like her, I love her, and I think that she is noble. And, he turned around and he saw the poster of Omar, which is the gay guy in the film. And he said *yeh toh different kism ka film lag raha hai,* [This looks like a different kind of film] and I said different how? He said, *Omar ka matlab aapko maloom hain?* [Do you know what Omar means?]. I really didn't know the meaning of the names, I just like some of them. And he said '*Yeh toh Muhammad ka* [this is Muhammad's] third nephew or something like that'.

Onir was quite good-humoured as he said all this to me, but the prior exchange pointedly sounds the note of anxiety surrounding the cultural and communal ownership of names. And in this regard, Onir further continued to explicate his interest in names in the following language:

> Names also very often signify a political identity; you know, Abhimanyu [in *I AM*] had a reason for being Abhimanyu, you know. Similarly, consciously I chose names in that film…. I feel very often in Hindi film you don't have [sic] representation of the minority communities, unless they are stereotypes, and here they

were Muslims without being not very…they were not wearing topis, they were not wearing burkhas, they were not doing namaz, just like Abhimanyu and Megha were not going to a temple, so I feel that it is very important for characters to be normalized, to be shown without their…like even when I did a film like *Sorry Bhai* the girl was Aliya, ok? And nowhere in the film is there any reference that she is a Muslim. For me she is just another **girl**, you know, like one of my **friends**, and I don't want that whole thing of how you constantly try to bracket people because of what religion they come from or whatever. And that is something I have again done very consciously in *Shab*, to use names in a way where it is always slightly political.

None of this should seem especially surprising coming from an avid follower of the French New Wave, Andrei Tarkovsky, Luis Bunuel and Pedro Almodovar. Indeed, the joyous sensorium of Onir's films is marked very much by a riot of colours, textures, moods and premonitions such as those characteristic of the European film-makers he has admired and learned from. However, many of Onir's conscious film-making decisions are marked not only by a riotous sensorial cornucopia—a queer aesthetic some might call it even, especially if they know that Onir is Bollywood's first and one of its only openly gay film-makers—but also by what is perhaps usually its inverse, namely a universe of resource scarcity. This explains his respect for Iranian film-makers, in particular, who excel in the singular magic of film-making with very limited resources and under massive disciplinary statist surveillance. Hence, another one of Onir's idols is Jafar Panahi, whose films he especially admires for conveying so much so economically. Onir admires especially the delicate indirection and minimalism that Iranian cinema deploys, in part necessitously, but 'beautifully', in his words. He does acknowledge his interest in some Hollywood films but insists on the paintbrush and palette of cinema being much wider and much more transnational. In his words, it is not that he does not love some Hollywood film-makers but they do not captivate him. And for Onir, to be captivated is a complex brew of political, sensorial, aesthetic and ethical achievements, in part imbibed from his film-making training in Berlin, at the feet of European cinema, where he learned the kind of self-discipline and economization of time, material and alliances that have enabled him to survive as a largely independent film-maker.

And when it is a question of production and film financing, certainly Onir has been a tremendous innovator in the history of Hindi cinema. After all, Onir's films are frequently crowd-funded, and *I AM* was entirely so. In this sense, he is also a populist and not 'avant garde' film-maker by his own free confession.[4] Still, while he would freely admit also to the tremendous commerciali-zation of art as a default dimension of the contemporary national culture industry, Onir yet stands firm by his recognition that an entire capitulation to that behemoth is the slippery road to medi-ocrity and cultural inanition. Entirely aware of the compromises that he has to make as a working film-maker in Bollywood, he nevertheless says,

> when I meet young students who think Bollywood and Hollywood are all there are—you know Spielberg and Yash Chopra—that makes me sad because there is so much more; I think what very often causes people to forget that cinema is not it's like there are bestsellers and real literature, that the line is thin, but there is a difference, you know there is. Especially in India people forget there is cinema, which is a form of art, which you need to learn, which you need to develop, and nurture in a certain way, where the only way to evaluate is not how much money it will generate. You know that is what is really sad and alarming about a society where everything is only valued in terms of how much money it can generate.

A final question to consider about Onir's craft is that of the distinc-tion routinely made between 'commercial' and 'non-commercial' film-making. Onir categorically opines that the distinction between commercial and non-commercial cinema is a distinction without a difference, and that the more meaningful distinction for him is that between 'mainstream' and 'non-mainstream' film-making. He clarifies that rather than budget, viewership, audi-ence segmentation, formula and revenue generation—that are all criteria that might well apply as meaningful distinctions in other ways across the commercial/non-commercial, mainstream/

non-mainstream spectrum—the true difference between his kind of films and others is that between mainstream versus the non-mainstream film. He insists, therefore, that while he is a non-mainstream film-maker, he is most certainly also a commercial film-maker. What meaningfully differentiates a non-mainstream film from a mainstream one is, in his view, not commerce, but content, and content alone.

He says, for instance:

> We constantly talk of cinema not being time-bound. So why should the definition in terms of the viewership decide what is mainstream and what is not?... I mean it does not destroy me if my films are not accepted, but it does make me sad, and I keep trying and hoping to bridge the gap.... When a film follows a certain formula and has a certain star cast it is perceived as a commercial film which is supposed to do certain commerce; even it fails it will still be a 'commercial' film. Whereas a film which has a certain kind of content, no big stars, not backed by a studio, has no item number there, no actress sitting around and doing nothing, is not considered 'commercial'. So there are certain symbols that are considered 'commercial' by the industry. I constantly tell them that this is a three crore film doing a sixteen crore business, how is it not a commercial film? Whereas a hundred crore film doing a hundred crore business, where was the commerce? It is also all about shares in studios now, so if you sign in certain actors your shares go up so it doesn't matter that the film does not make money as long as your shares go up.

This would be borne out also by his astute rejection of the dichotomy of 'commercial' versus 'non-commerical', or 'art' or 'avant garde'. Thus, for Onir it is time to pry the distinction between commercial and non-commercial films away from criteria of viewership, audience segmentation (captive and aspirational), revenue generation, budget, etc. He believes that the category of commercial is generated largely by the financial flows of how a film is made, distributed and exhibited, and not by content, intent, style or subject matter. While it is true that content does matter in so far as adherence to formula matters—the minute the content shifts to anything that's challenging, things get volatile— the real matter is whether the non-default content touches upon social issues uncommon in the mainstream, whether for the audience or for the industry.

In one of the few extant academic readings of Onir's films, Shukla and Rai speak of Onir's 'resistance to the essentialized notions of "SEX" as merely being a biological phenomenon of reproduction, resistance to the psychological terrors of the past, resisting...normative sexual orientation and resisting...child abuse...' (Shukla and Rai 2013: 1). But one should go a bit further than a hagiography of Onir as the film-maker who defies norms and expectations in all the hallowed ways of the so-called 'avant garde' director. Instead, it is refreshing to hear from him that the way he distinguishes his film-making from that of others is along the lines of someone who works within the constraints and norms imposed by a homogenizing and hetero-normative industry without bowing out of the game, for that would truly lead to becoming irrelevant. He says,

> [W]hen I look at my own work I think I am actually so much more in that commercial space, be it in term of actors I've worked with, be it in terms of the way music is used, or be it in terms of the entire film. Except for the content of the film, I don't think mine are really films that challenge the structure of filmmaking, are not revolutionary in terms of film language or something like that, and that way I think I am much more commercial. I am 'indie' largely because of the **way** my films are financed.

Another sense in which Onir asserts his independence is in his freedom from patronage, either as a film-maker or as an initiate, because he is in some ways entirely free of the nexus even of the Film and Television Institute of India cognoscenti and their *doxa* by having trained abroad, having avoided the big studios and still been able to make a film about gay rights, and having been able to do without big 'stars'. His is an interesting populist space, one that is probably most closely recognizable through the example of 'parallel' film-makers of the 1970s but without their state funding. Thus, while he is acutely aware of the networks and camaraderie of other aspiring Young Turk directors, he also recognizes both the benefits and the snares of their profession that lead to limitations, especially when it comes to non-heteronormative themes.

Having travelled, therefore, the arc of Onir's stylistic, ideological and industry-related tactics and strategies as a contemporary Bollywood film-maker, I return now to the representational critique that is at the heart of his film-making. I called his mode, his intervention, the 'fraternal' model. How far is that sustained by the analysis above of Onir's inspirations, practices and goals? The 'fraternal' model is not a question of sympathy towards gyno-centric film-making alone, though that certainly is true for someone who would say,

> In most Hindi films, if it is a woman-centered film that's different, but otherwise women always are the counterpart of the male. You know, women very, very rarely have an identity of their own. So for example in my films very often it is the other way around. It's 'my brother' Nikhil it's not 'my sister' Anu. It is very often the women who are stronger characters and are the ones who are the driving forces, you know not like most Hindi films where women are mainly passive. Women are changing the courses [*sic*].

In addition to that, and the entire scuttling of industry best practices through methods such as crowd-sourcing and return to earlier innovations in film-making such as natural, unmediated location filming and crowd-casting such as Ray's, though, the fraternal model is a question of the critique of an ethos of communalized gender normativity and subjectivity that for many have made Onir merely the poster child 'gay' film-maker of the Hindi industry.

What does it really mean, though, to be 'indie', commercial and non-mainstream, besides being independent of financiers, of the lineaments of the hardboiled hetero-patriarchal feudal family romance, and indeed even of the plot and genre-driven aesthetics of heteronormativity itself? Ironically, it is from the platform of commerce rather than from aesthetic elements — style, formula and so forth — that one best returns to my characterization of Onir as offering what I have called the 'fraternal' orientation in Indian cinema. If we now recall the *Oxford English Dictionary*'s definition of 'fraternity', we will remember that it consists largely of communities, be they professional, vocational, ethical or ideological. It is these social and ethical values of community spaces and practices that the art and craft of Onir's film-making situate at the heart of a pioneering 'fraternal' and, perhaps, 'lateral' model of film-making.

Keeping his gaze squarely on the distinction between 'mainstream' and 'non-mainstream' rather than on 'commercial/non-commercial' has allowed Onir to maintain a strategic footing in at least two worlds, perhaps four: living cinema versus an attenuated bloodless version of it ignored by popular audiences, and straight versus queer worlds. Indeed, it is his strategic adherence to the concept of the mainstream that allows Onir's films to raise questions of gender justice and sexual ethics. Let us now return to the sobriquet of 'fraternity' in interpreting Onir's work. As we know, what is most often said about Onir is that he is a 'gay' film-maker. Sometimes expressions like 'concerned with social justice issues' alternate with the flat moniker of 'gay' in referring to Onir, but the reality is that Onir has had to pay a price for being, or being perceived as, India's quintessential 'gay' film-maker.

He relates an anecdote about this himself:

> I met an actress the other day, and she told me that a very well-known film-maker came to her and said Oh I want you to act in this film that I am doing ... issues-based, you know the Onir kind of film. So I said you should have told him that you are anyways doing an Onir film so why do you need to do an Onir kind of film.... People tend to label you so quickly, that anyone who has any kind of gay content in their film, is now immediately making an Onir kind of film.... But I know I make things difficult for myself. If I would just shift a little, make my identity invisible, or a joke, things would be much easier for me, but somehow, I just can't.... Where people get hung up is actually the content. Very often Onir film means **gay** ... **so**, I try to camouflage. Which I didn't do in my first film, and which I now know it was a mistake not to do in *I AM*, and now I have learned that I have to use the same trick ... and that's also what I have learned from Iranian cinema, you don't just go tom-toming about what you want to say, you just don't talk about it and it's [after a pause] **there**.

In January 2011, Onir was charged with molesting an aspiring male actor and the case attracted national attention; the actor apologized in print after Onir filed a defamation case against him. In the ensuing melee, though, one of the casualties was a nuanced critical understanding of what it means to be a gay man and an artist. Onir is not a 'gay' film-maker though he is gay and he makes films about gay people and LGBT issues in contemporary India. Rather, he is a film-maker for whom issues of gender and sexuality rights and justice top the priority list of film content. From *My Brother … Nikhil* to *I AM*, Onir's films provoke and suggest different ways of imagining affect, filial dynamics, familial power relations, gender roles and relations, and identity struggles. Thus, *My Brother…Nikhil* offers such a re-reading of family, fraternity, filiation, hetero-patriarchy and hetero-normativity. A persecuted HIV-positive gay man finds his staunchest ally in his sister, who stands between him and the society that rejects and hates him in a posture meant to be read as the film's own activist staging of the non-normative outcomes of normative affective belonging. In locating advocacy for the 'public secret' of the pariah gay man — a subject theoretically without familial existence or public meaning in a traditional Indian society — in a sister and not the parents, the film argues the breakage of hetero-patriarchal kinship flows in favour of lateral solidarities as transferring private traumatic affect to the realm of public activism and advocacy as well as re-reading a certain kind of 'public' problem as the proper object of a womanhood endowed with values of compassion, 'sisterliness', and empathy for a brother.

While crowd-sourcing and other innovative financing practices are what mark this non-mainstream commercial film-maker's methods, his singular social vision synchronizes with his commercial ingenuity and singularity. His films are not merely woman-centric, nor are they even about a rights-based individualism. They are about community: imagining it, building it, broadening it and representing it. A film-maker who has originally and single-handedly introduced and instituted these techniques, aesthetics and economies of independent film-making — and who also keeps justice and ethics at the forefront of content of his art of cinema — is truly one of the most notable of contemporary Bollywood directors.

Notes

1   Onir stated in his personal interview (on 30 November 2014) with me
that

> when I was in class ten my sister took to me this film festi-
> val in the ice skating rink in Calcutta where I saw *Charulata*
> and *The French Lieutenant's Woman*, and at that point I was like
> okay this is what I want to do.... I think it was not so much the
> ambience of the film festival because I don't remember any-
> thing, but both the films made an impact. I think that maybe I
> was seeing so much of this Bollywood, and then suddenly I see
> this thing which at that point of time I honestly didn't under-
> stand so much, but it kind of captivated me. Partly also I was
> influenced by Didi [older sister Irene] because I admire her so
> much, so okay she wants to get into films so I also want to do
> something like that.

2   Following Metz's Sausseurian analysis of the cinema as a grand
syntagm linking both the spectatorial unconscious and cultural
consciousness, Mishra argues in his book for understanding Indian
cinema as a re-telling of foundational cultural and national arche-
types based on a syntax of enduring collective mythologies.

3   Onir enthusiastically reflected as follows:

> I realized that in *My Brother Nikhil* they were looking out at the
> sea, in *Sorry Bhai* they were looking out at the sea, and in *Shab*
> they are constantly looking out at the night; into the night or
> the mountains.... I [also] realized that the texture and color of
> my films are not really what is very prevalent in the Hindi film
> industry. Either they distinctly have a different texture and
> color, or it is all much more muted and people speak.... I think
> I try to make it as less filmy as possible.

Asked for an example of a particular shot of such panoramic film-
making, and of such textures and colours, he cited *My brother ...
Nikhil* where in wanting to capture the sea as an existential panoramic backdrop for the human drama unfolding next to it, but lacking the necessary budget to light up an entire beach, he opted for a
blue-filtered light and a darker image, where shadows and indistinct
voices and murmurs conveyed the intended meaning far better than
more naturalist, well-lit filming (connoisseurs of film will of course

find here echoes of Satyajit Ray's well-known preference for natural lighting and crowd-cast actors). Laughing, Onir then said,

In India, a lot of viewers were like, you know, *O kucchh garbar hai* [Something is not right]. You know the shoot is dark, whereas I was looking more towards audience which is much more involved towards, you know, **cinema**, let me put it that way.

4   Leaving aside the fact that most Indian film-makers would consciously avoid the terms 'art' and 'avant garde' like the plague, because those terms come trailing associations of what Onir humorously calls 'Don't touch me!'

References

Metz, Christian. 1982. *The Imaginary Signifier: Psychoanalysis and the Cinema*. Bloomington, IN: Indiana University Press.

Mishra, Vijay. 2001. *Bollywood Cinema: Temples of Desire*. New York: Routledge.

Sahu, Deepika. 2012. 'This is a Victory for Independent Filmmakers: Onir.' *Times of India*. 10 March. Retrieved 12 June 2015, from http://timesofindia.indiatimes.com/entertainment/hindi/bollywood/news/This-is-a-victory-for-independent-filmmakers-Onir/articleshow/12198112.cms

Shukla, Manjair and Maessh Rai. 2013. 'Reclamation of Identities Through Screen: A Study of Onir's I AM', *Research Scholar: An International Refereed e-Journal of Literary Explorations* 1 (3): 1–7. Retrieved 11 June 2015, from http://www.researchscholar.co.in/downloads/44-manjari-shukla.pdf

Film References

Benegal, Shyam. 1979. *Junoon*. Filmwala's.

Onir. 2005. *My Brother…Nikhil*. Four Front Films.

———. 2008. *Sorry Bhai!*. Puja Films, Anticlock Films and Mumbai Mantra.

———. 2010. *I Am*. Anticlock Films.

CHAPTER 19

Location and Agency in Crafting Habib Faisal's Authorship

*Monika Mehta**

Introduction

Auteur theory has undergone a number of shifts. Initially, in the famed *Cahiers du Cinéma*, it emerged as a term used to identify and to praise European 'art' directors for the stylistic and/or thematic features visible in their oeuvres. At this juncture, the discussion on auteurs found its match in the discerning cinephile.

Later, auteur theory expanded its terrain to accommodate choice directors working in commercial cinema, more specifically, Hollywood directors as well as their aficionados. As industrial analyses became more prominent in film studies, an auteur began to be viewed as one element in the processes of film production,

---

* I thank Lisa Patti for carefully reading multiple drafts of this chapter and offering generative suggestions.

marketing, distribution and reception (Hayward 2012). In the context of Indian cinema, this history of auteur theory has primarily recognized the work of Satayjit Ray, who is identified with 'art' films. The vast majority of art and commercial film directors in India (with whose work audiences are more familiar) have received little scholarly attention. A new and generative analytical turn has shifted discussions from appraisals of auteurship to considerations of authorship. This critical turn enables us to reflect upon how varied film industry personnel or production houses leave their imprints on film, and to examine relations amongst these diverse, unequal signatures (Caldwell 2008; Gray and Johnson 2013).

In this chapter, I explore in what ways authorship is a productive critical lens for analysing post-economic liberalization Bombay cinema which has witnessed a number of changes with the entry of corporations, including the intensification of kinship and social networks (Ganti 2012). My analysis expands studies of auteurship in two ways: First, auteur studies generally build their arguments by identifying and analysing stylistic and/or thematic consistencies in a director's films; these investigations are tethered to the filmic texts. I extend this mode of analysis by considering how the representations of Habib Faisal's biography and industrial relationships add to his authorship. I argue that both informal and formal networks, structured by sex, gender and class, are critical to building Faisal's successful career. Second, auteur studies primarily focus on film directors. Like recent journalistic and scholarly works (see Kipen 2006; Price 2010), my chapter draws attention to screenwriting as a vital site for studying creative authority. This is particularly important in Faisal's case given that his screenplays and dialogues have garnered acclaim. There is a consistent narrative about his work as a screenwriter and director. In both cases, his authorship is signalled by the presence of strong female characters and an attention to nuances of locations, characters, language and class.

I track the role of location and class in Faisal's films and in the discussions of his life that emerge in tandem with them, examining how they enable and define his authorship. I then analyse the construction of female agency in his films which is a sign of his stamp on these works. This textual analysis is accompanied by a consideration of Bombay cinema's industrial transformations, specifically Yash Raj Films' strategy to diversify their offerings in the 2000s. Finally, I investigate the extent of Faisal's authorship as he works for/with Yash Raj, Planman Motion Pictures and Walt Disney.

Building a Middle-class, Male Signature

Biographies and auteur studies of Bombay film directors generally recount tales of impassioned men, devoted, and at times, consumed by film-making. Their signatures are inscribed in pre- and post-production decisions (e.g., casting, production crew, setting/ locations) as well as in their creative choices (e.g., shots, lighting, camera-work, script, dialogue, music). In comparison to these monumental, riveting tales, biographical information on Habib Faisal appears prosaic. Interviews conjure an urban, middle-class figure who, following Indian social norms, wanted to become a doctor, for whom 'IIT [Indian Institute of Technology] and IIM [Indian Institute of Management] were glamorous' ('Film-making happened accidentally, says Habib Faisal' 2012). Failing at competitive medical school exams, he joined Kirori Mal College at Delhi University and developed an interest in theatre, writing and directing. Later, he studied mass communication at Jamia Millia Islamia and worked as an assistant director on *Electric Moon* (1992) directed by Pradeep Kishen and written by Arundhati Roy. Subsequently, he went to Southern Illinois University in the United States and earned a Masters of Fine Arts Degree in cinema and photography. These biographical details affirm a middle-class ethos in which education is a key component, signalling respectability.

This information also links Faisal to his successful male peers and prominent male stars. Homosociality, registered via collegiality, common alma maters and shared experiences of Delhi in Faisal's biographical text shape and propel his career. In an interview, Faisal refers to the third floor of Yash Raj Films as a 'mini-Delhi…. Shaad (Ali), Kabir (Khan) and I studied at KM college, while Maneesh (Sharma) is a Hansraj product' (Guha 2012).

A number of Faisal's colleagues in the film industry, including Tigmanshu Dhulia, Maneesh Sharma, Dibakar Banerjee, Kabir Khan, Shaad Ali, Jaideep Sahni, Anurag Kashyap and Imtiaz Ali arrived in Bombay in the mid-1990s–2000s via Delhi and/or Delhi University. Kirori Mal College, Faisal's alma mater, is known for its famed alumnus, Amitabh Bachchan, who features on their website. Shah Rukh Khan's biographies dutifully note that he studied at Hansraj College at Delhi University and Jamia Millia Islamia, actively participating in theatre during this period. Like Faisal, Khan worked with Pradeep Kishen and Arundhati Roy; he had a cameo as a gay character in the telefilm *In Which Annie Gives It to Those Ones* (1989) directed and written by them. Culled from a repository of personal and professional experiences, this biographical information enables Faisal to belong to an industry where informal associations — real and imagined — are critical to one's career. For audiences, this information bears an imprint of middle-class respectability. More importantly, Faisal's emergence from and experience of this milieu are key components of his authorship, providing a sheen of authenticity to the middle-class characters that often feature in his screenplays and directorial ventures.

After completing his studies in the United States and returning to India, Faisal initially shot features for the television channel NDTV. Later, he was offered a position as a cameraman and worked for NDTV for five years. In 2004–05, Faisal directed two television shows, *Lavanya* and *Kareena Kareena*. While the former interrogated the institution of marriage, the latter followed the life and times of its female protagonist. Both television shows contribute to defining two key elements in Faisal's authorship, namely female agency and the re-working of the family drama.

Faisal's entry into Yash Raj Films was enabled by his association with Tigamanshu Dhulia who had acted in *Electric Moon* (1992) and was familiar with Faisal and his work from his college days. Dhulia introduced Faisal to Shaad Ali (Like Faisal, a Kirori Mal alumnus) who was directing films under Yash Raj. Initially, Fasial was given a non-contractual position as a screenplay and dialogue writer at

Yash Raj ('What I Did in *Band Baaja Baaraat'* 2012). His writing credits under Yash Raj include *Salaam Namaste* (co-author of screenplay, 2005), *Jhoom Barabar Jhoom* (screenplay and dialogues, 2007), *Ta Ra Rum Pum* (screenplay and dialogues, 2007), *Band Baaja Baaraat* (screenplay and dialogues, 2010), *Ladies vs. Ricky Bahl* (dialogues, 2011), *Ishaqzaade* (screenplay, dialogues and co-author of story, 2012), *Daawat-e-Ishq* (writer, 2014) and *Bewakoofiyaan* (writer, 2014). Faisal won both Filmfare and Screen awards for 'Best Dialogue' for *Band Baaja Baaraat*. His directorial debut, *Do Dooni Chaar* (2010) took place under Planman Motion Pictures; he penned the story as well as the dialogues and co-wrote the screenplay. *Do Dooni Chaar* won the National Film Award for 'Best Feature Film in Hindi'; Faisal took home the Filmfare award for 'Best Dialogues'. His second and third directorial ventures, *Ishqzaade* (2012) and *Daawat-e-Ishq* (2014) were produced by Yash Raj.

Faisal's oeuvre emerges at a period of key shifts in the Bombay film industry. The impact of these changes is visible in the production and distribution strategies of Yash Raj Films, the company under which Faisal has generated nearly all his filmic work. The changes which have occurred in the last decade or so include: hiring new directors, writers, marketing executives, production crew; introducing new stars; creating a new brand Y-Films which would market films directed at youth; producing television shows; and setting up an office in Los Angeles to produce Hollywood films. Following a strategy employed by the US majors, Yash Raj Films diversified its offerings, targeting varied audiences. In addition to its staple big-budget Hindi films (reigning stars, spectacular song sequences, foreign locations), it introduced small films (new stars and directors, largely domestic locations, innovative, 'real' stories) and Y-Films (new stars, stories focusing on the lives of middle- and upper-class urban youth; Yash Raj Films, n.d.). Through this assortment of films, Yash Raj sought to woo the burgeoning multiplex and diasporic audiences, and to retain its 'All-India' audience.

The changes in Yash Raj's production strategy can be attributed to two powerful new competitors: domestic and international corporations who had entered the Bombay film industry, and had access to more resources for film production, and in the case of Hollywood majors, a much wider exhibition network. The entry of domestic and foreign corporations has been paved by policies of economic liberalization which I discuss elsewhere (see Mehta 2005). Initially, Sony, Fox and Walt Disney entered the Indian film market as distributors or producers of Indian films. These avenues allowed them to forge ties with exhibitors. This industrial strategy allowed them to show not only Indian films that they had produced or distributed, but also Hollywood films. The shifts at Yash Raj can be read as judicious financial moves aimed at a rapidly changing media environment, but such a reading would overlook the way in which these choices and broader industrial changes impacted the narrative structure of Hindi films. Faisal's entry into Yash Raj Films is a part of these shifts.

Faisal's work as a screenwriter and director is enabled and modified by Yash Raj Films, Planman Motion Pictures and Walt Disney. In an interview, Fasial notes that he and Siddharth Anand, the film's director, disagreed about a scene in *Salaam Namaste*. Anand was appalled that the film's hero would cook breakfast for the heroine; Faisal convinced him to retain the scene (Guha 2012). This anecdote underscores Faisal's agency and his progressive view on gender relations. More importantly, it reveals production as a site of negotiation that does not always favour the screenwriter. Studies of Bombay film productions as well as my own work on censorship indicate that scripts are routinely revised and subject to demands for changes by the producers, director, actors as well as vagaries of production and post-production (e.g., Central Board of Film Certification and protesters). The screenplay also follows a form (e.g., segmentation by scene) and abides by genre parameters (Price 2010). In the context of Bombay cinema, story, screenplay and dialogues are often considered distinct forms of labour and can involve two or more people, multiplying authorial imprints. Given that songs are central to Hindi films, the lyricist is an additional writer whose work contributes to the script. Decisions about the content of the songs, and their placement and visualization can involve the production house, director, choreographer, composer and/or lyricist.

Yash Raj Films generally supplies and/or approves a film's stars, lyricist(s), choreographer, playback singers and production crew for directors who work under the banner. For example, both Faisal's *Ishaqzaade* and *Daawat-e-Ishq* starred Parineeti Chopra who had a three-film contract with the production house. *Do Dooni Chaar*'s producer Arnidam Chaudhri admits that he was happy with the eventual casting of Rishi Kapoor and Neetu Singh which Faisal desired; however, Chaudhri confesses that he first tried to convince the younger Juhi Chawla to take the role ('*Do Dooni Chaar* About the State of Teachers' 2010). A production account of *Do Dooni Chaar* describes Walt Disney's entry as follows: 'Walt Disney came on board, showed immense faith and made this their first live-action Hindi film' (Pandey 2011). Given that Disney is listed as the film's distributor and not its producer, one wonders in what sense did they 'make' this film. This statement unwittingly points to the critical role of distributors in 'making' films and building reputations of directors. Disney's powerful and wide exhibition network paved the way for *Do Dooni Chaar*'s release which brought recognition and accolades for Fasial. Auteur studies generally suggest that in spite of the imposition and control exerted by production houses, directors stamp films with their vision. Certainly, Yash Raj, Planman and Walt Disney regulate Faisal's work, but they also provide the industrial structure which allows him to make films and circulate them. Auteur studies point to a singular vision of a director, and David Kipen's 'Screibher Theory' seeks to install the screenwriter as the film's 'real' author. Diverging from these arguments, my analyses of Faisal's oeuvre show multiple and, at times, competing signatures of the screenwriter(s), director, production house and stars.

Re-framing Family and Romance

Family drama and romance have been key genres in the Yash Raj collection and are readily identified with the production house. After the stupendous success of *Dilwale Dulhania Le Jayenge* (1995), the 'family-love' story virtually defined the production house.

Faisal's work as screenwriter and director seeks to rework both family and romance. In doing so, it seeks to engage audiences at home and abroad who consume a steady diet of Hollywood romance comedies.

Faisal's initial screenplays and dialogues written for Yash Raj Films were set in diasporic contexts. They narrated romantic and marital troubles, and featured strong female protagonists. In *Salaam Namaste*, Amber Malhotra (Preity Zinta), defying Indian cultural values as represented in the 1990s and early 2000s Hindi family films, lives with her boyfriend and, despite his objections, has their child. The film invokes the family in conversations via a phone call that Amber makes after her break-up. This phone call affirms the importance of the family; however, the film is not driven by parental desires, authority or surveillance. Preity Zinta's star image as an independent, outspoken woman matched the character Faisal and Siddarth Anand had created. *Salaam Namaste*'s free-spirited characters, lively dialogues, casting, Western sartorial choices, glossy Melbourne locations, affluent interiors and fresh song–dance sequences indicate a seamless blend and execution of the writers', director's and production house's visions.

In *Ta Ra Rum Pum*, Faisal re-inserts the idiom of class which had been erased from Yash Raj family romances in favour of Indian cultural values. Rajveer Singh (Saif Ali Khan), Radikha Banerjee (Rani Mukerjee) and their two children lose their gargantuan house and expensive belongings when Rajveer is unable to compete as a race car driver. They move to a more economical and sparse one-bedroom apartment in Jackson Heights. Both Rajveer and Radikha need to work as taxi driver and piano teacher, respectively, to make ends meet. Radhika's father (Victor Banerjee) features as an urbane, wealthy figure against whose wishes she marries Rajveer, but his role and authority are minimal. The film reveals a dissonance amongst the production house, director and screenplay writer. The vistas of Manhattan, designer clothing, and a remodelled and embellished Jackson Heights as well as exuberant and at times lavish song sequences, typical Yash Raj features, are incongruent with Faisal's screenplay and dialogues. Moreover, the narrative of demoted diasporic characters who needed to labour and save money did not follow the rules of diasporic representation in Yash Raj Films and, more generally, of the 1990s and early 2000s family films.

The visual and aural articulations of class complement each other in Faisal's directorial debut *Do Dooni Chaar*. Unlike Yash Raj Films, an established institution in the Bombay film industry, *Do Dooni Chaar*'s producer, Planman Motion Pictures headed by Arindam Chaudhuri, only emerged in 2004. Prior to *Do Dooni Chaar*, Planman had produced six small-budget films in Hindi and Bengali and earned critical acclaim. *Do Dooni Chaar*'s focus on middle-class life and realist aesthetic matched both the production house's previous line-up as well as its budget. *Do Dooni Chaar*'s production account approvingly notes Disney's support of the film, '[I]t was heartening to see a Hollywood studio that understands there are Indian films that are not "Bollywood-ized"' (Pandey 2011). In the context of contemporary Bombay cinema, *Do Dooni Chaar* was unconventional in opting for yesteryear stars and following a realistic aesthetic. However, I would argue that Walt Disney distributed the film because its 'heartwarming' family story narrated in a linear, realist mode was the norm in Hollywood, and the global arena. Moreover, the film's thematic content matched its brand image as a family corporation.

Pandey's production account relates the long hours and hardwork put into the script: Faisal's insistence that while the films' stars were from Bombay, the rest of the cast had to be chosen from Delhi so that they would be able to speak Hindi with a Delhi accent, and Faisal's determination to use 'real' locations instead of sets despite poor weather conditions and his injury (Pandey 2011). This narrative foregrounds two key features of Fasial's authorship, namely attention to language and location. The film's reviews add well-developed characters and strong female protagonists to this list. In interviews, Faisal shares that he drew upon his own experiences of growing up in Delhi in a middle-class family in which his father's modest income as a teacher restricted their access to consumer goods; like *Do Dooni Chaar*'s Duggals, they could not afford a car and had to make do with a scooter ('*Do Dooni Chaar* About the State of Teachers' 2012).

Do Dooni Chaar is steered by the divergent demands of middle-class morality, patriarchal obligations and consumer desires. Delhi is not framed by shots of India Gate or Rasthrpathi Bhavan which confirm its political status as India's capital. Rather, references to Lajpat Nagar and Kirori Mal College define and structure the Duggals' middle-class life. The family lives in a small Delhi Development Authority (DDA) flat in Lajpat Nagar. Santosh Duggal (Rishi Kapoor) teaches mathematics at an ordinary school and supplements his income by tutoring at the Chatwal Coaching Center. By meticulous accounting, his wife Kusum Duggal (Neetu Singh) manages the home and its finances; she carefully tucks money in a tin box and dreams of buying a new fridge. Their daughter Payal (Aditi Vasudev) is embarrassed to go to Kirori Mal College on her father's dilapidated scooter, and wants to have a car, ipod and brand name t-shirts. Meanwhile, their son Sandeep (Archit Krishna) goes to an English-medium school and makes unlawful money by betting on cricket matches, an immoral activity for which he is 'punished'.

The female protagonists both figuratively and literally steer the film. Payal drives them to a family wedding rather than her meek father. At the venue, Santosh's sister asks him to give a present which matches her in-laws' status. While Santosh frets, Kusum sells her gold bangles for a suitable monetary gift. Later, when Santosh decides to buy a car, Payal carefully inspects the various models and asks appropriate questions. Payal accompanies her father to McDonald's so that he can accept a bribe for passing a student and, thereby, pay for the car. The story ends on a happy note preserving both middle-class morality and aspirations. The student's relatives pay Santosh to tutor him and with the money, the Duggals bring home their car.

Do Dooni Chaar's realist aesthetic and plot gestures to the 1970s middle cinema which explored middle-class concerns and ethos such as getting a good education, finding a decent job and flat, maintaining one's morals, to name a few. These films' locations, sets, costumes, cinematography and song sequences were modest and muted in comparison to the larger-than-life Amitabh Bachchan actions films that dominated the period. Unlike 'art' films of this period, the stories were not politically charged. These films featured both character actors and stars (who were given the opportunity to show their acting skills), and they were financed by relatively small production houses. In citing this cinema, and its most notable director, Hrishikesh Mukherjee, Fasial inserts himself into Bombay cinema's genealogy; this citation assists in establishing Faisal's reputation as a worthy director.

Faisal's later scripts and directorial ventures continued to be set in India and employed a modified realistic aesthetic suited to Yash Raj Films' penchant for the 'good-life' which is often showcased in the song sequences; Faisal is most associated with these films. *Band Baaja Baaraat* reunited Faisal with Maneesh Sharma; they had initially met when Faisal was working for NDTV. Sharma, the film's director, emphatically asserts that he had wanted Faisal to develop his story idea into a screenplay and to write the film's dialogues, and requested producer Aditya Chopra to hire Faisal (Pereira 2011). An unexpected hit of 2010, the film charts the story of an ambitious, middle-class Delhi girl, Shruti Kakkar (Anushka Sharma) who wants to become a top wedding planner. She articulates her career trajectory in spatial terms, an upward climb from middle-class Janakpuri to the elite Sainak Farm. To accomplish her goals she forms a business alliance with Bittoo Sharma (Ranveer Singh) which turns into a romantic entanglement. Faisal's screenplay and dialogues gesture to big budget 1990s family romances by invoking family, love, wedding and, of course, Shah Rukh Khan, but re-route their narrative energies. If the big budget films were driven by male characters and male stars, *Band Baaja Baaraat* places the film's heroine at the helm. Shruti is not the 'good Indian girl' of the 1990s family romances who values her virginity, willingly sacrifices her love and desires for family or who waits for her lover to resolve their story. Rather, Shruti's desires and ambitions propel the story as she convinces her parents to support her dream to become a wedding planner and, in the process, delay her own wedding. Moreover, she first educates Bitto in business and later, in romance, making him a 'man'.

Drawing upon their shared knowledge and experiences of Delhi, Faisal and Sharma worked together to produce a textured film which mapped middle- and upper-class worlds of Delhi. Class is referenced and invoked by recognizable neighbourhoods (Janakpuri, Paschim Vihar, North Delhi campus, Sainik Farm), houses (modest constructions with shared walls versus spacious homes with manicured lawns), streets (narrow and bustling versus wide and relatively empty), characters' mannerisms and speech (a colloquial mixture of Hindi, Punjabi and English versus polished Hindi and English), and clothing (ordinary versus designer). The close nature of their collaboration is expressed in an interview:

> While most may believe that the director is the captain of the ship, Sharma is clear that a good writer is as important. 'A good screenplay and dialogues can be handled by an average director but a bad story cannot be resurrected even by a good director,' reasons Sharma. Faisal is humbled by the thought, but gives credit to Sharma where it is due. 'It's unheard of in Bollywood for a writer to go on recce before the shoot. But Maneesh took me along to Delhi for *Band Baaja Baaraat* and Goa for *Ricky Bahl* so that there were no discrepancies between writing and execution,' says Faisal. (Pereira 2011)

During the film's marketing and even later, its new male star, Ranveer Singh, credited both Faisal and Sharma with training him to act and imbibe the persona of a rough-edged, loud Delhi college student.[1] Faisal played a significant role in the film's marketing, giving television and print interviews. In these interviews, he played and often was cast in the role of Singh's mentor. Both Faisal's inclusion in the location surveys and the film's marketing can be read as an expansion of his authority and authorship. This inclusion and agency needs to be situated in the transformations taking place at Yash Raj which included drawing attention to new writers and directors, and capitalizing on their names. This visibility also is part and parcel of the 'Bollywoodization' of the Hindi film industry where certain Hollywood norms (legal contracts, bound scripts, 'clean' money) and discourses on professionalism, creative authority and value of a good script are signs of a 'global' film industry.

Yash Raj's *Ishaqzaade* offered Faisal the opportunity to occupy the director's chair. The film expanded Yash Raj's offerings and Fasial's repertoire. Yash Raj supplied the films' new stars, Parineeti Chopra and Arjun Kapoor; Chopra had played a small, but significant role in Yash Raj's film *Ladies vs Ricky Bahl*. Moving away from India's metros, this love story is set in the fictional North Indian town of Almore. In interviews, Faisal asserted that *Ishaqzaade*, unlike contemporary love stories, drew attention to the violent opposition to romantic love that crosses community lines. Its charged storyline, which hooked romance to action, stood in sharp contrast to frothy, designer romances associated with Yash Raj and Dharma Productions. Rather, it recalled pre-1990s romance dramas where romantic love is enmeshed in weighty obstacles and/or dangers.

In *Ishaqzaade*, the Chauhans and the Querishis are not only political rivals, but belong to different religious communities, Hindu and Muslim, respectively. Faisal constructs Zoya (Parineeti Chopra) as a feisty girl who wishes to participate in politics while her family is determined to get her married. Zoya's desire to occupy masculine spaces is best articulated in the scene in which she 'trades' her expensive earrings for a gun (Rangan 2012). Following conventions of the romance genre, Zoya and Parma (Arjun Kapoor) are at loggerheads in their initial encounters. Post-altercations, the two seemingly fall in love. Baradwaj Rangan rightly observes, '[L]ove transforms Zoya into a "girl"'; she's distracted and fantasizes about Parma and she puts a bindi on her forehead which in this context signifies Hindu femininity (Rangan 2012). Zoya and Parma decide to get married secretly, participating in both Hindu and Muslim wedding ceremonies.

After they make love, the film delivers an unexpected blow to Zoya and its audiences. Parma cruelly declares that he was simply pretending to love Zoya in order to obtain revenge. The lovemaking scene — a potential sign of Zoya's sexual agency — becomes an act of rape. Later, Parma circulates a video of him and Zoya to bring about the Querishis' downfall. Given the prolific MMS sex scandals, viewers are first positioned to imagine that the video shows Parma and Zoya making love. Later, we discover there is an equally potent and transgressive video: Zoya participating in Hindu wedding rituals with a fuzzy Parma. The scene reminds us that heterosexual marriage reproduces patriarchal tradition, and women are marked as carriers of tradition; as such, by choosing a marital partner from a different religious community, which is to say becoming an agent rather than an object of exchange, Zoya doubly violates tradition. The circulation of this video produces Querishi's loss at the elections as well as Zoya's expulsion from both family and community. The film forcefully foregrounds Zoya's plight: As an agent of a transgressive act, Zoya has 'no place' in the home (natal or marital) or the community.

Distraught and enraged, Zoya picks up a gun and sneaks into Parma's home. Unlike most filmic brides, who enter their marital homes with pomp and ceremony as well as blessings to multiply both wealth and bodies, Zoya comes to kill Parma. She is discovered by Parma's widowed mother who angrily admonishes her son. After his mother's harsh rebuke and her death (she intercepts a bullet fired by her father-in-law which is meant for Zoya), Parma reforms and turns into Zoya's saviour as he helps her escape his family home. Ironically, with Chand Bibi's (Gauhar Khan) help, Parma and Zoya find refuge in a brothel where they learn to love one another and renew their wedding vows. When they leave the brothel to escape to another town, they are cornered by both families. In the family romances of the 1990s, the patriarchal family is strict, albeit ultimately benevolent and agrees with the wishes of their children. In *Ishqzaade*, the male members emerge as callous, terrifying killers. Zoya makes the decision that Parma and she should kill one another rather than die at the hands of their hunters. Faisal earned praise for the film's gritty locations and authentic characters. However, Zoya's decision to renew her romantic and marital relationship with Parma was characterized as regressive and Faisal was often forced to defend this charge, which dented his status as a 'progressive' film-maker. I wish to locate this narrative strand within the context of the romance drama in Indian commercial cinema, where women generally stay with the men they marry. The 'compulsion' and 'demand' of this genre reveal its patriarchal underpinnings, which are reproduced in *Ishqzaade*.

Daawat-e-Ishq reunited Faisal with Parineeti Chopra and brought a new star into the Yash Raj fold, Aditya Roy Kapur. This casting served to consolidate both a key sign of Faisal's authorship and an important component of Chopra's star image: the spunky, strong female. The film follows Gulrez Qadir (Parineeti Chopra), a Muslim shoe salesgirl, who is infuriated by the dowry demands of her second-rate prospective grooms. Her exasperation peaks when her 'modern' boyfriend Amjad's (Karan Wahi) parents also stipulate monetary 'help' as a condition for their marriage and he does not protest. An incensed Gulrez convinces her timid father Abdul Qadir (Anupam Kher), who works as a senior clerk at the high court, to participate in her plan to trap a groom and use the IPC 498a (anti-dowry act) to extract money from him. The film's issue-based plot recalls the 1950s social which engaged with problems such as caste, poverty and women's subjugation. This gesture situates Faisal in the history and lineage of Bombay cinema, adding to his repute and drawing attention to the overlaps between discourses of authorship and kinship.

To execute Gulrez's plan, the film moves between to two cities, Hyderabad and Lucknow. While Hyderabad has been underexplored in Hindi cinema, Lucknow has been primarily linked with the courtesan genre and the Muslim social; these cities are associated with India's largest religious minority, Muslims. This film's investment in the 'minor' is articulated in an early dialogue. When Amjad tells Gulrez that he is going to the United States to study, she affirmatively says, 'New York', and he responds, 'Kalamazoo'. The film's central characters' are Muslims, that is, minorities, and they speak Deccani in Hyderabad and Urdu in Lucknow; in post-Independence India, both languages occupy a less privileged status in relation to Hindi. The bonus features in the DVD as well as interviews inform us that a diction and language instructor was hired to teach Deccani to the cast; the film's credits include the name of the instructor. The film's Muslim characters are a shoe salesgirl, a senior clerk, an aspiring MBA, and middle- and upper-middle class neighbours and parents. These commonplace figures are distant from the dominant past and present representations of Muslims in Bombay films as *tawaifs*, nawabs, avuncular chachas wearing namaaz hats, terrorists or citizens who need to prove their patriotism. Instead, the film's characters are ordinary and organic as opposed to exotic and/or foreign.

The average, lower-middle class lives of the film's characters are depicted visually. Hyderabad is constructed by shots of Charminar which is visible from Gulrez's lacklustre lower-middle class home; the congested streets, through which Gulrez navigates the scooter in order to drop her father at court and to get to her job at the gleaming mall; and the wide and leafy streets on which she walks with Amjad. When the film moves to Lucknow, the site of the con, the film's visual style shifts to match the upper-class guise of its characters. Gulrez and her father stay at a sumptuous five-star hotel and wear expensive clothes. Her prospective groom Taru Haider (Aditya Roy Kapoor) lives with his family in a large, beautiful home. He owns and runs a spacious yet ordinary-looking restaurant which attracts many customers including foreigners. He is often clad in colourful shirts and pants, sports a handle-bar moustache and wears kajal. While wooing Gulrez, he takes her on a tour of Lucknow's tourist sites. The film's eye-catching and, at times, retro turn appears to be Yash Raj Films' handiwork. It highlights the performative aspect of Gulrez's plan. Moreover, it quietly gestures to Lucknow's performative role in Bombay cinema's courtesan genre which features Muslims as tawaifs and nawabs.

In Lucknow, Gulrez and her father successfully convince Taru's family of their pedigree and wealth. Once they agree to get married, Taru secretly gives Gulrez the money that his parents demand. At this show of decency and sincerity, Gulrez wavers, but eventually decides to follow through with the fraudulent marriage, charging Taru and his family with IPC 498a (they recorded the dowry demand), and absconding with their money. The film quickly moves to its resolution at a train-station where a guilt-ridden Gulrez returns the money and confesses that she likes Taru — and he quickly forgives her. It ends with a didactic scene in which Amjad, Gulrez's former boyfriend, realizes his earlier mistake and stands up to his dowry-demanding parents. The film's closing note recalls Film Divisions' short documentaries that sought to educate Indian citizens about social problems. Its hurried storyline reveals the pressures of multiplex screenings and the new normative runt-imes. Hindi films' running time have increasingly shortened to both increase revenues at the box office and to emulate a Hollywood norm. This impacts Hindi films' narrative structure, which find it difficult to accommodate drama, romance, action, humour and 5–6 song sequences — key elements of Bombay cinema's signature.

Signature and Materiality

For the most part, auteur studies focus on film texts and identify signs of a director's creative authority, eschewing discussions of social and economic conditions that produce auteurs. More recent studies, by examining industrial relations, make visible the relations of power and privilege which shape film authorship (see Caldwell 2013). In concert with this new work, my analyses of Faisal's oeuvre, representations of his life and industrial relations show that film is not the vision of a single person. Rather, it bears multiple imprints; these imprints testify to film production as an act of collaboration, unequal negotiation and divergent agendas. My formal analyses of Faisal's work accompanied by a critical industrial and biographical account compel us to track the signs of his authorship on screen (e.g., strong female characters, colloquial dialogues, 'realistic' locations, middle-class characters) and to think about the important role of homosociality (e.g., friendship, shared alma maters, collegiality, citation) in producing male auteurs. The screen has been a focal point for vigorous debates on gender and sex; my analysis invites us to debate representation at the level of the industry with the same rigour and to investigate female authorship in the Bombay film industry.

Note

1   Interview with Ranveer Singh. (n.d.). Retrieved 9 April 2015, from http://www.glamsham.com/movies/interviews/09-ranveer-singh-interview-121014.asp

References

Caldwell, J.T. 2008. *Production Culture: Industrial Reflexivity and Critical Practice in Film and Television*. Durham: Duke University Press.

———. 2013. 'Authorship Below-the-line.' In *A Companion to Media Authorship*, edited by J. Gray and D. Johnson, 349–69. Malden, MA: Wiley-Blackwell.

'*Do Dooni Chaar* About the State of Teachers in India: Faisal.' 2010. *The Indian Express*. 6 October. Retrieved 9 April 2015, from http://archive. indianexpress.com/news/do-dooni-chaar-about-state-of-teachers-in-india-faisal/692894/

'Filmmaking Happened Accidentally, Says Habib Faisal.' 2012. *Times of India*. 10 May. Retrieved 5 April 2015, from http://timesofindia.india-times.com/entertainment/hindi/bollywood/news/Filmmaking-happened-accidentally-says-Habib-Faisal/articleshow/13078457.cms

Ganti, T. 2012. *Producing Bollywood: Inside the Contemporary Hindi Film Industry*. Durham: Duke University Press.

Gray, J. and D. Johnson (eds). 2013. *A Companion to Media Authorship*. Malden, MA: Wiley-Blackwell.

Guha, A. 2012. 'No Such Thing as too Much Spunk, Says Habib Faisal'. *Daily News and Analysis*. 22 April. Retrieved 5 April 2015, from http://www.dnaindia.com/entertainment/report-no-such-thing-as-too-much-spunk-says-habib-faisal-1678987

Hayward, S. 2012. *Key Concepts in Cinema Studies*, 4th edn. London: Routledge.

Kipen, D. 2006. *The Schreiber Theory: A Radical Rewrite of American Film History*. Hoboken, NJ: Melville House.

Mehta, M. 2005. 'Globalizing Bombay Cinema: Reproducing the Indian State and Family'. *Cultural Dynamics* 17 (2): 135–54.

Pandey, A.R. 2011. 'Producing *Do Dooni Chaar*.' 3 February. Retrieved 9 April 2015, from http://aratiraval.blogspot.com/

Pereira, P. 2011. 'Two too Much.' *The Indian Express*. 18 November. Retrieved 9 April 2015, from http://archive.indianexpress.com/news/two-too-much/877315/

Price, S. 2010. *The Screenplay: Authorship, Theory and Criticism*. Basingstoke and Hampshire: Palgrave Macmillan.

Rangan, B. 2012. '"Ishaqzaade"... Shooting Stars.' 6 May. Retrieved 9 April 2015, from https://baradwajrangan.wordpress.com/2012/05/16/ishaqzaade-387553659/

'What I Did in *Band Baaja Baaraat* — Habib Faisal.' 2012, May 11. Retrieved 8 April 2015, from https://www.youtube.com/watch?v=q2mbho6DplA

Yash Raj Films. (n.d.). Retrieved 7 April 2015, from http://yashrajfilms.com/

Film References

Anand, S. 2007. *Ta Ra Rum Pum*. Yash Raj Films

Asthana, N. 2014. *Bewakoofiyaan*. Yash Raj Films.

Faisal, H. 2010. *Do Dooni Chaar*. Walt Disney Studios Home Entertainment.

———. 2012. *Ishaqzaade*. Yash Raj Films.

———. 2014. *Daawat-e-Ishq*. Yash Raj Films.

Sharma, M. 2012. *Ladies vs. Ricky Bahl*. Yash Raj Films.

Glossary

Angrez	The British people
Annas/anas	Indian currency unit, equal to 1/16th of a rupee
Ayah	A maidservant
Babuji	A respectful address for a male and/or father
Badal/megha	Cloud
Bal Bharati, Champak	(Here) Hindi language children's magazines
Balaatkaar	Rape
Bambaiya	Related to the city of Bombay (or Mumbai)
Bhai	(Lit.) Brother, in Mumbai slang, it refers to a gangster
Bindi	A decoration that Indian (especially Hindu) women put on their foreheads; traditionally, also, a dot considered sacred by married Hindu women
Burkhas	An outer garment worn by women in some Islamic traditions to cover their bodies when in public
Chaand	The moon
Chachas	Uncle (lit.); father's younger brother
Chakra	Wheel
Chamatkaar	Miracle
Chawls	Tenements
Chhoti chhoti	Minor

Desi	Usually refers to people (and their way of lives/language) from the subcontinent that includes India, Pakistan and Bangladesh
Desi-ghee	(Here) homegrown and wholesome; (lit.) a kind of clarified butter
Dhamki	Threat
Dhanda	Business
Dharma	Duty
Dhoti	Traditional men's garment in South Asia, particularly India and Nepal
Dukh bhare din beete re bhaiyya	Song from *Mother India*; (lit.) unhappy days are over, brother
Emotional atyachar	Emotional brutality
Gaddar	A traitor
Ghin	Disgust/repulsion
Hatke	(Lit.) different; also common Bollywood parlance to suggest that rather than being a formulaic, this is a different kind of a film
Hazaar	Thousand
Ishq	Love
Janampatri	Birth horoscope
Ji	Hindi term of respect for male
Kaante	Thorns
Kaarobaar	Business
Kala ghoda	(Lit.) A black horse; a neighborhood in Mumbai
Khalujaan	Respectful address for maternal uncle (aunt's husband)
Khariboli	A dialect of Hindi language
Lagan	Tax
Maar	Injury

Mama	Uncle; (lit.) mother's brother
Manohar Kahaniyan, Satya Katha	Hindi magazines
Masala	Spice/spicy; (here) an adjectival term for popular Hindi cinema with its mix of elements such as emotions, action, melodrama and song-and-dance
Miyan	Urdu term of respect for a male
Mughals	(Lit.) Muslim dynasty of India from 16 to 19th century; here, magnates, rich and powerful people
Naadaan	Innocent
Nallah	Gutter
Navrasas	Nine emotions, fundamental to the aesthetics of Indian performing arts
Nawabs	A Muslim nobleman or person of high rank
Paan	A kind of betel leaf to chew, usually served at the end of an Indian meal
Paanch	Five
Parinda	A bird
Paunchy	Slang for someone with a paunch
Prayogshala	Laboratory
Shehnai	An Indian musical instrument
Sikandar	Hindi/Urdu variant for Alexander; (here) a winner
Supari	(Lit.) Betel nut; (here) Mumbai slang for the money paid to gangsters and hitmen
Swadeshi	Related to India
Tamasha	Theatre
Tapori	A street *thug* from Mumbai, known for their peculiar brand of language and dressing
Tawaif	Courtesan

Tuna	A play on *munna*
Ulemas	Muslim scholars who possess specialist knowledge of Islamic sacred law
Yaar	(Informal) a friend
Zameen	Land
Zamindar	A landowner
Zindagi	Life

Filmography

1. Farah Khan Filmography (only as a director)

   - *Happy New Year*. 2014. Yash Raj Films.
   - *Main Hoon Na*. 2004. Eros International.
   - *Om Shanti Om*. 2007. Eros International.
   - *Tees Maar Khan*. 2010. UTV Motion Pictures.

2. Mansoor Khan Filmography (only as a director)

   - *Qayamat Se Qayamat Tak*. 1988. Nasir Husain Films and United Producers.
   - *Jo Jeeta Wohi Sikandar*. 1992. Nasir Husain Films and United Producers.
   - *Akele Hum Akele Tum*. 1995. United Seven Combines and Venus Records & Tapes.
   - *Josh*. 2000. United Seven Combines and Venus Records & Tapes.

3. Farhan Akhtar Filmography (only as a director)

   - *Dil Chahta Hai*. 2001. Excel Entertainment.
   - *Lakshya*. 2004. Excel Entertainment.
   - *Don*. 2006. Excel Entertainment.
   - *Don 2*. 2011. Excel Entertainment and Red Chilies Entertainment.

4. Aditya Chopra Filmography (only as a director)

- *Dilwale Dulhania Le Jayenge*. 1995. Yash Raj Films.
- *Mohabbatein*. 2000. Yash Raj Films.
- *Rab Ne Bana Di Jodi*. 2008. Yash Raj Films.

5. Vidhu Vinod Chopra Filmography (only as a director)

- *Murder at Monkey Hill*. 1976. FTII.
- *An Encounter with Faces*. 1978. Films Division.
- *Sazaye Maut*. 1981. Vinod Chopra Presentation.
- *Khamosh*. 1985. Vinod Chopra Productions.
- *Parinda*. 1989. Natraj Productions and Vinod Chopra Productions.
- *1942: A Love Story*. 1994. Vinod Chopra Productions.
- *Kareeb*. 1998. Vinod Chopra Productions.
- *Mission Kashmir*. 2000. Destination Films and Vinod Chopra Productions.
- *Eklavya: The Royal Guard*. 2007. Vinod Chopra Productions.
- *Broken Horses*. 2015. Reliance Entertainment and Vinod Chopra Productions.

6. Rajkumar Hirani Filmography (only as a director)

- *Munna Bhai M.B.B.S*. 2003. Vinod Chopra Productions.
- *Lage Raho Munna Bhai*. 2006. Vinod Chopra Productions.
- *3 Idiots*. 2009. Vinod Chopra Productions.
- *PK*. 2014. Vinod Chopra Productions.

7. Sanjay Leela Bhansali Filmography (only as a director)

- *Khamoshi: The Musical*. 1996. Polygram Films Entertainment.
- *Hum Dil De Chuke Sanam*. 1999. Bhansali Films and Jhamu Sugandh Productions.
- *Devdas*. 2002. Mega Bollywood Pvt. Ltd.
- *Black*. 2005. SLB Films and Applause Entertainment Ltd.
- *Saawariya*. 2007. SPE Films, SLB Films
- *Guzaarish*. 2010. SLB Films.

- *Goliyon Ki Rasleela Ram-Leela*. 2013. Eros International and SLB Films.

8. Vishal Bhardwaj Filmography (only as a director)

- *Makdee*. 2002. Vishal Bhardwaj Pictures.
- *Maqbool*. 2003. Kaleidoscope Entertainment & Vishal Bhardwaj Pictures.
- *The Blue Umbrella*. 2005. UTV Motion Pictures.
- *Omkara*. 2006. Big Screen Entertainment, Panorama Studios & Shemaroo Videos Pvt. Ltd.
- *Kaminey*. 2009. UTV Motion Pictures and Vishal Bhardwaj Pictures.
- *7 Khoon Maaf*. 2011. UTV Spotboy and VB Pictures.
- *Matru ki Bijlee ka Mandola*. 2013. Vishal Bhardwaj Pictures.
- *Haider*. 2014. UTV Motion Pictures and Vishal Bhardwaj Pictures.

9. Deepa Mehta Filmography (only as a director)

- *Fire*. 1996. Trial by Fire Films Inc. and Kaleidoscope Entertainment.
- *Earth*. 1998. Cracking the Earth Films Inc. and Jhamu Sugandh Productions.
- *Water*. 2005. Deepa Mehta Films, Flagship International and David Hamilton Productions.
- *Heaven on Earth*. 2008. Astral Media, Canadian Broadcasting Corporation (CBC) and Hamilton Mehta Productions.

10. Anurag Kashyap Filmography (only as a director)

- *Paanch*. 2003. Padmini Tele Media and Star Talaash Promotions.
- *Black Friday*. 2004. Mid Day Multimedia Ltd., Big Bang Pictures and Jhamu Sugandh.
- *No Smoking*. 2007. Big Screen Entertainment, Eros Entertainment and Panorama Studios.

- *Return of Hanuman*. 2007. Percept Picture Company and Toonz Animation India.
- *Dev.D*. 2009. Anurag Kashyap Films, UTV Motion Pictures and UTV Spotboy.
- *Gulaal*. 2009. Zee Limelight.
- *That Girl in Yellow Boots*. 2010. Anurag Kashyap Films, NFDC and Sikhya Entertainment.
- *Gangs of Wasseypur 1 & 2*. 2012. Jar Pictures, AKFPL and Bohra Bros Productions.
- *Bombay Talkies (Murabba)*. 2013. Viacom 18 Motion Pictures.
- *Ugly*. 2013. DAR Motion Pictures and Phantom Films.
- *That Day After Every Day*. 2013. Anurag Kashyap Films and Large Short Films.
- *Bombay Velvet*. 2015. Film Team Sri Lanka, Fox Star Studios and Phantom Films.

11. Zoya Akhtar Filmography (only as a director)

- *Luck By Chance*. 2009. Excel Entertainment and Reliance Big Pictures.
- *Zindagi Na Milegi Dobara*. 2011. Eros International and Excel Entertainment.
- *Sheila*. 2013. Viacom 18 Motion Pictures.
- *Dil Dhadakne Do*. 2015. Junglee Pictures and Excel Entertainment.

12. Sudhir Mishra Filmography (only as a director)

- *Main Zinda Hoon*. 1988. Doordarshan.
- *Dharavi*. 1992. Sudhir Mishra. Doordarshan and NFDC.
- *Is Raat Ki Subah Nahin*. 1996. Plus Films.
- *Calcutta Mail*. 2003. Sanghmitra Arts.
- *Chameli*. 2003. Pritish Nandy Communications.
- *Hazaaron Khwaishein Aisi*. 2005, in India. Pritish Nandy Communications.
- *Khoya Khoya Chand*. 2007. Sudhir Mishra. Holy Cow Pictures.

- *Mumbai Cutting.* 2011. Sahara One Motion Pictures and White Cloud Productions.
- *Kirchiyaan.* 2013. Large Short Films.
- *Inkaar.* 2013. Viacom 18 Motion Pictures.

13. Ashutosh Gowariker Filmography (only as a director)

- *Pehla Nasha.* 1993. Ahlan Productions.
- *Baazi.* 1995. Aftab Pictures.
- *Lagaan: Once Upon a Time in India.* 2001. Aamir Khan Productions, Ashutosh Gowariker Productions Pvt. Ltd and Jhamu Sugandh Productions.
- *Swades.* 2004. Ashutosh Gowariker Productions Pvt. Ltd., Dillywood and UTV Motion Pictures.
- *Jodhaa Akbar.* 2008. Ashutosh Gowariker Productions Pvt Ltd and UTV Motion Pictures.
- *Khelein Hum Jee Jaan Sey.* 2010. Ashutosh Gowariker Productions Pvt Ltd and UTV Motion Pictures.
- *Mohenjo Daro.* Ashutosh Gowariker Productions and Disney India, forthcoming.

14. Madhur Bhandarkar Filmography (only as a director)

- *Chandni Bar.* 2001. Shlok Films.
- *Satta.* 2003. Metalight Productions.
- *Aan: Men at Work.* 2004. Firoz Nadiadwala.
- *Page 3.* 2005. Lighthouse Entertainment.
- *Corporate.* 2006. Sahara One Motion Pictures.
- *Traffic Signal.* 2007. Madhur Bhandrkar Motion Pictures and Percept Picture Co.
- *Fashion.* 2008. Bhandarkar Entertainment and UTV Motion Pictures.
- *Jail.* 2009. Bhandarkar Enterainment, Maxwell Entertainment and Mirah Entertainment.
- *Dil Toh Baccha Hai Ji.* 2011. Baba Arts, Bhandarkar Entertainment, Panorama Studios.

- *Heroine.* 2012. Bhandarkar Entertainment and UTV Motion Pictures.

15. Homi Adajnia Filmography (only as a director)

    - *Being Cyrus.* 2005. Miracle Cinefilms, Serendipity Films and Times Infotainment Media.
    - *Cocktail.* 2012. Eros International and Illuminati Films.
    - *Finding Fanny.* 2014. Illuminati Films and Maddock Films.

16. Abhishek Chaubey Filmography (only as a director)

    - *Ishqiya.* 2010. Shemaroo Entertainment and Vishal Bhardwaj Pictures.
    - *Dedh Ishqiya.* 2014. Shemaroo Entertainment and Vishal Bhardwaj Pictures.

17. Sriram Raghavan Filmography (only as a director)

    - *Ek Hasina Thi.* 2004. R.R. Movie-Makers.
    - *Johnny Gaddaar.* 2007. Adlabs Films Ltd.
    - *Agent Vinod.* 2012. Illuminati Films, Eros Entertainment.
    - *Badlapur.* 2015. Eros International.

18. Onir Filmography (only as a director)

    - *My Brother... Nikhil.* 2005. Four Front Films.
    - *Bas Ek Pal.* 2006. Four Front Films, Paramhans Creations & Movies n More.
    - *Sorry Bhai!.* 2008. Puja Films, Anticlock Films and Mumbai Mantra.
    - *I Am.* 2010. Anticlock Films.

19. Habib Faisal Filmography (only as a director)

    - *Do Dooni Chaar.* 2011. Walt Disney Home Entertainment.
    - *Ishaqzaade.* 2012. Yash Raj Films.
    - *Daawat-e-Ishq.* 2014. Yash Raj Films.

Bibliography

A. Appadurai, *Modernity at Large: Cultural Dimensions of Globalization* (Minneapolis, MN: University of Minnesota Press, 1996).

———, ed., *Globalization* (Durham, NC: Duke University Press, 2001).

A. Astruc, 'The Birth of a New Avant-Garde: *La Camera-Stylo*,' in *The New Wave*, ed. P. Graham (London: Seeker & Warburg, 1948), 17–23.

A. Athique, *Indian Media: Global Approaches* (Cambridge: Polity Press, 2012).

A. Bachchan, 'Official Blog of Amitabh Bachchan: Day 265,' 2009. Retrieved 14 July 2010, from http://bigb.bigadda.com/7psl44S

A. Banker, *Bollywood* (Harpenden: Pocket Essentials, 2001).

A. Bazin, *What is Cinema*, Vol. II, ed. and trans. Hugh Gray (Berkeley, CA: University of California Press, 2005[1971]).

A.A. Berger, *Popular Culture Texts: Theories and Texts* (London/New Delhi/Newbury Park, CA: SAGE Publications, 1992).

———, *Narrative in Popular Culture, Media, and Everyday Life* (London/New Delhi/Newbury Park, CA: SAGE Publications, 1997).

A. Chopra, *Shah Rukh Khan and the Seductive World of Indian Cinema* (New York/Boston, CA: Warner Books, 2007).

A. Dirlik, 'The Postcolonial Aura: Third World Criticism in the Age of Global Capitalism,' in *Contemporary Postcolonial Theory: A Reader*, ed. P. Mongia (London/New York: Arnold, 1997).

A. Friedberg, *Window Shopping: Cinema and the Postmodern* (Berkeley, CA: University of California Press, 1993).

A. Kavoori and A. Punanthambekar, eds., *Global Bollywood* (New Delhi: Oxford University Press, 2008).

A. Kuhn, *The Power of Image: Essays on Representation and Sexuality* (London/New York: Routledge, 1992).

A. Nandy, 'The Hindi Film: Ideology and First Principles,' *Indian International Centre Quarterly* 8, no. 1 (1981): 89–96.

A. Owen, ed., *Story and Character: Interviews with British Screenwriters* (London: Bloomsbury, 2003).

A. Rajadhyaksha and P. Willemen, eds., *Encyclopaedia of Indian Cinema* (London: British Film Institute/Oxford University Press, 1999).

A. Sarris, 'Notes on the *Auteur* Theory,' in *Film Theory and Criticism: Introductory Readings*, 6th ed. (Oxford: Oxford University Press, 2004[1962].

A. Willis, 'Locating Bollywood: Notes on the Hindi Blockbuster 1975 to the Present,' in *Movie Blockbusters*, ed. J. Stringer (London/New York: Routledge, 2003).

A.R. Kavi, 'The Changing Image of the Hero in Hindi Films,' *Journal of Homosexuality* 39, nos. 3 and 4 (2000): 307–12.

A.S. Rai, *Untimely Bollywood: Globalization and India's New Media Assemblage* (Durham, NC/London: Duke University Press, 2009).

B. Anderson, *Imagined Communities: Reflections on the Origins and Spread of Nationalism* (London: Verso, 1983).

———, *The Spectre of Comparison: Nationalism, Southeast Asia and the World* (London: Verso, 1998).

B. Nicholas, *Movies and Methods Volume 1* (Berkeley, CA/Los Angeles, CA/London: University of California Press, 1976).

———, *Ideology and the Image: Social Representation in the Cinema and Other Media* (Bloomington, IN: Indiana University Press, 1981).

———, ed., *Movies and Methods Volume 2* (Berkeley, CA/Los Angeles, CA/London: University of California Press, 1985).

———, *Representing Reality* (Bloomington, IN/Indianapolis, IN: University of Indiana Press, 1991).

———, *Blurred Boundaries: Questions of Meaning in Contemporary Culture* (Bloomington, IN/Indianapolis, IN: University of Indiana Press, 1994).

B. Singer, *Melodrama and Modernity* (New York: Columbia University Press, 2001).

C. Acland, *Screen Traffic: Movies, Multiplexes, and Global Culture* (Durham, NC: Duke University Press, 2003).

C. Breckenridge, *Consuming Modernity Public Culture in a South Asian World* (Minnesota, MN: University of Minnesota Press, 1995).

C. Etherington-Wright and R. Doughty, *Understanding Film Theory* (New York: Palgrave Macmillan, 2011).

C. Gledhill, ed., *Home Is Where the Heart Is: Studies in Melodrama and the Woman's Film* (London: British Film Institute, 1987).

C. Gledhill and L. Williams, eds., *Reinventing Film Studies* (London/New York: Arnold, 2000).

C. McCabe, 'Realism and the Cinema: Notes on Some Brechtian Theses,' *Screen* 15, no. 2 (1974): 7–27.

C. Metz, *Language and Cinema* (The Hague: Mouton de Gruyter, 1974).

———, *Psychoanalysis and Cinema: The Imaginary Signifier*, trans. Celia Britton, Annwyl Williams, Ben Brewster and Alfred Guzzetti (London: Macmillan, 1982).

———, *The Imaginary Signifier: Psychoanalysis and the Cinema* (Bloomington, IN/Indianapolis, IN: Indiana University Press, 1986).

D. Arijon, *Grammar of the Film Language* (Los Angeles, CA: Silman-James Press, 1976).

D. Bordwell, *Narration in the Fiction Film* (Madison: University of Wisconsin Press, 1985).

———, *How Hollywood Tells It: Story and Style in Modern Movies* (Berkeley, CA: University of California Press, 2006).

D. Bordwell and K. Thompson, *Film Art: An Introduction* (Reading, MA/ Menlo Park, CA/London/Amsterdam/Don Mills, ON/Sydney: Addison-Wesley, 1979).

D. Bordwell and N. Carroll, *Post-theory: Reconstructing Film Studies* (Madison/London: University of Wisconsin Press, 1996).

D. Bordwell, J. Staiger and K. Thompson, *The Classical Hollywood Cinema: Film Style and Mode of Production to 1960* (London: Routledge, 1988[1985]).

D. Chute, et al., 'Bollywood 101,' *Film Comment* 38, no. 3 (2002, May–June): 28–31.

D. Cook, *A History of Narrative Film*, 3rd ed (New York: Norton, 1996).

D. Elley, *The Epic Film: Myth and History* (London: Routledge and Kegan Paul, 1984).

D. Epstein, *20th Century Pop Culture* (London: Carlton, 1999).

D. Mann, *Hollywood Independents: The Postwar Talent Takeover* (Minneapolis, MN: University of Minnesota Press, 2008).

D. Spoto, *Dark Side of Genius: The Life of Alfred Hitchcock* (London: Collins, 1983).

D. Thomson, *The New Biographical Dictionary of Film*, 4th ed. (London: Little, Brown, 2003).

D. Thomson and I. Christie, *Scorsese on Scorsese*, rev. ed. (London: Faber & Faber, 2003).

E. Branigan, *Narrative Comprehension and Film* (London/New York: Routledge, 1992).

E. Dyja, ed., *BFI Film and Television Handbook 2004* (London: British Film Institute, 2003).

E. Ezra and T. Rowden, eds., *Transnational Cinema: The Film Reader* (London: Routledge, 2006).

E. Rohmer and C. Chabrol, *Hitchcock: The First Forty-four Films* (Oxford: Roundhouse, 1979).

E. Said, *Orientalism* (London: Penguin Books, 1991[1979]).

E. Shohat and S. Robert, 'The Cinema after Babel: Language, Difference, Power,' *Screen* 26, nos. 3 and 4 (1985): 35–58.

———, 'Film Theory and Spectatorship in the Age of the "Posts,"' in *Reinventing Film Studies*, eds. Christine Gledhill and Linda Williams (New York: Hodder Arnold, 2000): 381–401.

———, eds., *Multiculturalism, Postcoloniality and Transnational Media* (New Brunswick, NJ: Rutgers University Press, 2003).

Edward Dimendberg, *Film Noir and the Spaces of Modernity* (Cambridge, M A: Harvard University Press, 2004).

F. Fanon, *The Wretched of the Earth* (Harmondsworth: Penguin Books, 1967[1961]).

——, *Black Skin, White Masks* (London: Pluto Press, 1986[1952]).

F. Jameson, *Postmodernism or the Cultural Logic of Late Capitalism* (London/ New York: Verso, 1991).

——, *The Cultural Turn: Selected Writings on Postmodernism 1983-1998* (London/New York: Verso, 1998).

——, 'Reification and Utopia in Mass Culture,' *Social Text* 1 (Winter, 1979): 130–48.

F. Truffaut, *Hitchcock: The Definitive Study of Alfred Hitchcock* (New York: Simon & Schuster, 1986[1967]).

——, *The Films in My Life*, trans. Leonard Mayhew (New York: Da Capo, 1994[1978]).

G. Andrew, *Film Directors A-Z: A Concise Guide to the Art of 250 Great Film-Makers* (London: Carlton Books, 2005[1999]).

G. Chatterjee, *Mother India* (London: British Film Institute, 2002).

——, *Awara* (New Delhi: Penguin Books, 2003).

G. Gopinath, 'Queering Bollywood: Alternative Sexualities in Popular Indian Cinema,' in *Queer Asian Cinema: Shadows in the Shade*, ed. Andrew Grossman (Binghamton: The Haworth Press, 2000), 283–98.

G. Mast and M. Cohen, eds., *Film Theory and Criticisms: Introductory Readings*, 2nd ed. (New York/Oxford: Oxford University Press, 1979).

G.C. Spivak 'Can the Subaltern Speak?' in *The Postcolonial Studies Reader* (London/New York: Routledge, 1988[1995]), 24–28.

Gilles Deleuze, *L'Image-Mouvement* (*Image Movement*) (Paris: Minuit, de Valck, Marijke, 1983).

H. Bhaba, *The Location of Culture* (London and New York: Routledge, 1994).

I. Bhaskar and R. Allen, *Islamicate Cultures of Bombay Cinema* (New Delhi: Tulika Books, 2009).

J. Baudrillard, *The Gulf War Did Not Take Place*, trans. Paul Patton (Bloomington, IN: Indiana University Press, 1995).

J. Berger, *Ways of Seeing* (London: Penguin Books, 1990).

J. Boorman and W. Donohue, eds., *Projections 3: Film-makers on Film-making* (London/Boston, MA: Faber and Faber, 1994).

J. Butler, *Gender Trouble* (London/New York: Routledge, 1999).

J. Caughie, ed., *Theories of Authorship* (London/New York: Routledge, 1981).

J. Collins, H. Radners and A.P. Collins, *Film Theory Goes to the Movies* (New York/London: Routledge, 1993).

J. Gardner, 'Avatar: Blueface, White Noise,' *Huffington Post*, 2010. Retrieved 19 July 2010, from http://www.huffingtonpost.com/iared-gardner/emavatarem-blueface-white_b_409522.html

J. Gibbs, *Mise-en-scene: Film Style and Interpretation* (London/New York: Wallflower Press, 2002).

J. Hill, *Sex, Class and Realism: British Cinema 1956–1963* (London: British Film Institute, 1986).

J. Hill and P.C. Gibson, *The Oxford Guide to Film Studies* (Oxford/New York: Oxford University Press, 1998).

J. Hollows and M. Jancovich, eds., *Approaches to Popular Film* (Manchester/New York: Manchester University Press, 1995).

J. Hollows, P. Hutchings and M. Jancovich, eds., *The Film Studies Reader* (London/New York: Arnold, 2000).

J. Lyotard, *The Postmodern Condition: A Report on Knowledge* (Manchester: Manchester University Press, 1979).

J. Natoli and L. Hutcheon, *A Postmodern Reader* (New York: State University New York Press, 1993).

J. Stringer, *Movies Blockbusters* (London/New York: Routledge, 2003).

J. Virdi, *The Cinematic Imagination: Indian Popular Films as Social History* (New Brunswick, NJ/London: Rutgers University Press, 2003).

J.G. Shaheen, *Reel Bad Arabs: How Hollywood Vilifies a People* (New York: Olive Branch Press, 2001).

———, *Guilty: Hollywood's Verdict on Arabs after 9/11* (Northampton, MA: Olive Branch Press, 2008).

Jane Feuer, *The Hollywood Musical*, 2nd ed. (London: Macmillan, 1993).

———, 'The Self-reflexive Musical and the Myth of Entertainment,' *Quarterly Review of Film Studies* 2, no. 3 (1977, August): 313–26.

Jim Pine and Paul Wilemen, eds., *Questions of Third Cinema* (London: British Film Institute, 1989).

K. Bhasin and R. Menon, *Borders and Boundaries: Women in India's Partition* (New Delhi: Kali for Women, 1998).

K. Chun, What Is a Ghost?: An Interview with Guillermo del Toro, *Cineaste* 27, no. 2 (2002, Spring): 28–31.

K. Thomson and D. Bordwell, *Film History: An Introduction* (New York: McGraw-Hill, 1994).

K.N. Kotwal, 'Steven Spielberg's *Indiana Jones and the Temple of Doom* as Virtual Reality: The Orientalist and Colonial Legacies of *Gunga Din*,' *Film Journal*, no. 12 (n.d.). Retrieved 30 August 2012, from http://www.thefilmiournal.com/issue12/templeofdoom.html

Kwame A. Appiah, *Cosmopolitanism: Ethics in a World of Strangers* (New York: W.W. Norton, 2006).

L. Althusser, *Lenin, Philosophy and Other Essays*, trans. Ben Brewster (New York: Monthly Review Press, 2001).

L. Badley, R. Barton Palmer and Steven J. Schneider, eds., *Traditions in World Cinema* (Edinburgh: Edinburgh University Press, 2006).

L. Braudy and M. Dickstein, eds., *Great Film Directors: A Critical Anthology* (New York: Oxford University Press, 1978).

L. Gopalan, 'Avenging Women in Indian Cinema,' *Screen* 38, no. 1 (1997, Spring): 42–59.

———, *A Cinema of Interruptions* (London: British Film Institute, 2002).

L. Mulvey, 'Visual Pleasure and Narrative Cinema,' *Screen* 16, no. 3 (1975, Autumn): 6–18.

M. Allen, 'The Impact of Digital Technologies on Film Aesthetics,' in *The New Media Book*, ed. D. Harries (London: British Film Institute, 2002).

M. Driscoll, 'Reverse Postcoloniality,' *Social Text* 22, no. 78 (2004): 59–84.

M. Pendakur, *Indian Popular Cinema: Industry, Ideology and Consciousness* (New Jersey: Hampton Press, 2003).

M. Salisbury, ed., *Burton on Burton*, rev. ed. (London: Faber and Faber Ltd, 2006).

M. Sen and A. Basu, *Figurations in Indian Film* (New York: Palgrave Macmillan, 2013).

M. Strokes and R. Maltby, *Identifying Hollywood's Audiences: Cultural Identity and the Movies* (London: British Film Institute, 1999).

M.M. Prasad, 'Cinema and the Desire for Modernity,' *Journal of Arts and Ideas* 25, no. 6 (1993): 71–86.

———, *Ideology of the Hindi Film: A Historical Construction* (Delhi: Oxford University Press, 1998).

N. Kazmi, *The Dream Merchants of Bollywood* (New Delhi: UBS Publishers, 1998).

N. Lacey, *Images and Representation: Key Concepts in Media Studies* (Basingstoke: Palgrave, 1998).

N. Puwar 'Kabhi Ritz, Kabhi Palladium: South Asian Cinema in Coventry 1940–1980,' *Wasafiri* 43 (2004, Winter): 41–43.

P. Bogdanovich, *This is Orson Welles* (New York: Harper Collins, 1992).

———, *Who the Devil Made It: Conversations with Legendary Film Directors* (New York: Ballantine Books, 1998).

P. Bourdieu, *Distinction: A Social Critique of the Judgement of Taste* (London/ New York: Routledge, 1984).

P. Brooks, *The Melodramatic Imagination* (New York: Columbia University Press, 1976).

P. Chatterjee, 'Beyond the Nation? Or Within?' *Social Text* 16, no. 56 (1998): 57–69.

P. Cook, ed. *The Cinema Book* (London: British Film Institute, 1985).

P. Cook and M. Bernink, eds. *The Cinema Book* (London: British Film Institute, 1999).

P. Duncan, *Film Noir: Films of Trust and Betrayal* (Harpenden: Pocket Essentials, 2000).

P. Fuery, *New Development in Film Theory* (Basingstoke: Macmillan, 2000).

P. Jaikumar, *Cinema at the End of Empire: A Politics of Transition in Britain and India* (Durham, NC: Duke University Press, 2006).

P. Joshi and R. Dudrah, eds., *The 1970s and its Legacies in India's Cinemas* (England: Routledge, 2014).

P. Kaarsholm, ed., *Cityflicks: Indian Cinema and the Urban Experience* (Kolkata: Seagull Books, 2004).

P. Singer, *One World: The Ethics of Globalization* (New Haven, CT: Yale University Press, 2004).

P. Uberoi, 'The Diaspora Comes Home: Disciplining Desire in *DDLJ*,' *Contributions to Indian Sociology* 32, no. 2 (1998, July–December): 305–36.

P. Willemen, *Looks and Frictions: Essays in Cultural Studies and Film Theory* (London: British Film Institute, 1994).

P. Wollen, *Reading and Writings: Semiotic Counter-strategies* (London/New York: Routledge, 1982).

———, *Signs and Meanings in the Cinema* (London: British Film Institute, 1998).

R. Altman, *Film/Genre* (London: British Film Institute, 1999).

R. Applebaum and R. William, eds., *Critical Globalization Studies* (New York: Routledge, 2005).

R. Barthes, ed., 'Death of the Author,' in *Image, Music, Text* (London: Fontana, 1977[1968]).

R. Beellour, *The Analysis of Film* (Bloomington, IN/Indianapolis, IN: Indiana University Press, 2002).

R. Doraiswamy, 'Commercial Hindi Cinema: Changing Narrative Strategies,' *Cinemaya* 23 (1994): 4–12.

R. Dudrah and D. Jigna, *Bollywood: Sociology Goes to the Movies* (London: SAGE Publications, 2006).

———, ed., *The Bollywood Reader* (Berkshire/New York: Open University Press, 2008).

———, *Bollywood Travels: Culture, Diaspora and Border Crossings in Popular Hindi Cinema.* Contemporary South Asia Series (London: Routledge, 2012).

R. Dudrah, M. Elk and B. Fuchs, eds., *Shah Rukh Khan and Global Bollywood* (New Delhi: Oxford University Press, 2015).

R. Dwyer, *Picture Abhi Baaki Hai: Bollywood as a Guide to Modern India* (Gurgaon: Hachette, 2014).

R. Dwyer and J. Pinto, *Yash Chopra* (London: British Film Institute, 2002).

———, eds., *Beyond the Boundaries of Bollywood: The Many Forms of Hindi Cinema* (New Delhi: Oxford University Press, 2011).

R. Dwyer and P. Christopher, eds., *Pleasure and the Nation: The History Politics and Consumption of Public Culture in India* (Delhi: Oxford University Press, 2001).

R. Dyer, *Stars* (London: British Film Institute, 1979).

———, *Heavenly Bodies: Film Stars and Society* (Basingstoke/London: Macmillan Press, 1986).

R. Dyer. 'Entertainment and Utopia,' *Movie* 24, Spring (1977). Reprinted in Bill Nichols, ed., *Movies and Methods*, Vol II (Berkeley, CA: University of California Press, 1987), 220–32.

———, *Only Entertainment* (London/New York: Routledge, 1992).

———, *A Matter of Images: Essays on Representation* (London/New York: Routledge, 1993).

R. Kaur, *Performative Politics and the Cultures of Hinduism: Public Uses of Religion in Western India* (Delhi: Permanent Black, 2003).

———, 'Cruising on the Vilayati Bandwagon: Diasporic Representations and Reception of Popular Indian Movies,' in *Bollyworld: Popular Indian Cinema Through a Transnational Lens*, eds. Raminder Kaur and Ajay J. Sinha (New Delhi: SAGE Publications, 2005): 309–29.

R. Kaur and Ajay J. Sinha, eds., *Bolllyworld: Popular Indian Cinema Through a Transnational Lens* (New Delhi: SAGE Publications, 2005).

R. Mazumdar, 'Ruin and the Uncanny City: Memory, Despair and Death in *Parinda*,' *Sarai Reader 02: The Cities of Everyday Life* (Delhi: CSDS, 2002), 68–78.

———, *Bombay Cinema: An Archive of the City* (Minneapolis, MN/Ranikhet: University of Minnesota Press/Permanent Black, 2007).

R. Stafford, *Understanding Audiences and the Film Industry* (London: British Film Institute, 2007).

R. Stam, *Film Theory: An Introduction* (Malden, MA/Oxford: Blackwell, 2000).

R. Thomas, 'Indian Cinema: Pleasures and Popularity,' *Screen* 26, nos. 3 and 4 (1985): 116–31.

R. Vasudevan, ed, *Making Meaning in Indian Cinema* (New Delhi: Oxford University Press, 2000).

———, *The Melodramatic Public: Film Form and Spectatorship in Indian Cinema* (New Delhi: Permanent Black, 2010).

———, 'The Melodramatic Mode and the Commercial Hindi Cinema,' *Screen* 30, no. 3 (1989): 29–50.

R.J. Emery, *The Directors: Take One and Take Two* (New York: Allworth Press, 2002).

———, *The Directors: Take Three and Take Four* (New York: Allworth Press, 2003).

S. Barbas, *Movie Crazy: Fans, Stars and the Cult of Celebrity* (New York/Basingstoke: Palgrave Macmillan, 2001).

S. Chakravarthy, *National Identity in Popular Indian Cinema, 1947–1987* (Austin, TX: University of Texas Press, 1993).

S. Derne, *Movies, Masculinity and Modernity: An Ethnography of Men's Film-going in India* (Westport, CT/London: Greenwood Press, 2000).

S. Golani, *Decoding Bollywood: Stories of 15 Film Directors* (New Delhi/Bangalore/Chennai: Westland, 2014).

S. Heyward, *Cinema Studies: The Key Concepts* (London/New York: Routledge, 2000).

S. Kakar, *Intimate Relations: Exploring Indian Sexuality* (New Delhi: Penguin Books, 1989).

S. Malpas, ed., *Postmodern Debates* (Basingstoke: Palgrave Macmillan, 2001).

———, *The Postmodern* (London/New York: Routledge, 2005).

S. Neale, 'Melodrama and Tears,' *Screen* 27, no. 6 (1986, November–December): 6–23.

———, *Genre and Hollywood* (London/New York: Routledge, 2000).

S. Patel and T. Alic, eds., *Bombay: Metaphor for Modern India* (Bombay/Delhi: Oxford University Press, 1995).

———, *Bombay: Mosaic of Modern Culture* (Bombay/Delhi: Oxford University Press, 1996).

S. Rohdle, *Promised Lands: Cinema, Geography, Modernism* (London: British Film Institute, 2001).

S. Zizek, *Enjoy Your Symptoms! Jacques Lacan in Hollywood and Out*, 2nd ed. (New York/London: Routledge, 2001).

Sidney Lumet, *Making Movies* (New York: Vintage, 1996).

S.J. Schneider, *501 Movie Directors*, 1st ed. (New York: Barron's Educational Series, 2007).

S.M. Maira, *Desis in the House: Indian American Youth Culture in New York City* (Philadelphia, PA: Temple University Press, 2002).

T. Ganti, *Bollywood: A Guidebook o Popular Hindi Cinema* (London: Routledge, 2004).

T. Letitch, *Crime Films* (Cambridge: Cambridge University Press, 2002).

T. Todorov, *The Fantastic: A Structural Approach to a Literary Genre* (Ithaca, NY: Cornell Press, 1973).

T. Woods, *Beginning Postmodernism* (Manchester: Manchester University Press, 1999).

T.W. Adorno, *Critical Models: Interventions and Catchwords*, trans. Henry W. Pickford (New York: Columbia University Press, 1998).

V. Lal, *Deewar: The Footpath, the City and the Angry Young Man* (New Delhi: Harper Collins, 2011).

V. Lal and Ashis Nandy, eds., *Fingerprinting Popular Culture: The Mythic and the Iconic in Indian Cinema* (New Delhi: Oxford University Press, 2006).

V. Mishra, 'Towards Theoretical Critique of Bombay Cinema,' *Screen* 26, nos. 3 and 4 (1985, May–August): 133–51.

———, *Bollywood: Temples of Desire* (New York/London: Routledge, 2002).

V. Perkins, *Film as Film: Understanding and Judging Movies* (Cambridge, MA: Da Capo Press, 1993).

V. Propp, *Morphology of the Folk Tale* (Austin, TX: University of Texas, 1968).

W. Benjamin, *Understanding Brecht*, trans. A. Bostock (London: Verso, 1998).

W. Higbee and S.H. Lim, 'Concepts of Transnational Cinema: Towards a Critical Transnationalism in Film,' *Transnational Cinemas* 1, no. 1 (2010): 7–21.

Walden Bello, *Deglobalization: Ideas for a New Economy* (London: Zed, 2002).

Walter Benjamin, 'The Work of Art in the Age of Its Technological Reproducibility,' in *Walter Benjamin, Selected Writings, Volume 3, 1935–38*, ed. Howard Eiland and Michael W. Jennings, trans. Edmund Jephcott and Harry Zohn (Cambridge: Harvard University Press, 2000[1936]), 101–33.

William van der Heide, *Malaysian Cinema, Asian Film* (Amsterdam: Amsterdam University Press, 2005).

Wimal Dissanayake, ed., *Cinema and Cultural Identity: Reflections on Films from Japan, India, and China* (Lanham, MD: University Press of America, 1988).

———, ed., *Melodrama and Asian Cinema* (Cambridge: Cambridge University Press, 1993).

W.W. Dixon, *Film Noir and the Cinema of Paranoia* (Edinburgh: Edinburgh University Press, 2009).

Y. Tasker, *Spectacular Bodies: Gender, Genre and the Action Cinema* (London/ New York: Routledge, 1993).

About the Editors and Contributors

Editors

Aysha Iqbal Viswamohan is Professor in the Department of Humanities and Social Sciences, Indian Institute of Technology (IIT), Madras. Her interests include film studies, drama and popular culture. She has a PhD in American Drama, was the recipient of the Canadian Faculty Enrichment Programme fellowship in 2009 and was attached to Simon Fraser University, Vancouver, Canada. She has published over 30 articles in academic journals of repute, including Cambridge, Oxford, Routledge and SAGE. She edited *Postliberalization Indian Novels in English: Politics of Global Reception and Awards* (2013). She is the organizer of *Imaging Cinema*, a popular film workshop (2010–2012 and 2014) at IIT Madras.

Vimal Mohan John has a PhD in film studies from the Department of Humanities and Social Sciences, IIT Madras. He was on an extended fellowship that was awarded to him by the department upon completion of his PhD. His work concerns study of the auteurial practices of film directors and how they mediate gender, cultures and representations. Apart from presenting papers at various national and international conferences, he also publishes academic papers. He teaches as Assistant Professor, Department of English, St. Berchmans College, Kottayam (Kerala).

Contributors

Ulka Anjaria is Associate Professor of English at Brandeis University. She is the author of *Realism in the Twentieth-Century Indian Novel: Colonial Difference and Literary Form* (2012) and editor of *A History of the Indian Novel in English* (2015). She is a recipient of the ACLS/Charles A. Ryskamp Fellowship in 2014 for her current book project on representations of the contemporary in Indian literature, film and popular culture.

Nandini Bhattacharya is Professor of English at Texas A&M University and an affiliate of the Women's Studies, Africana Studies and Film Studies programs here. Her fields of expertise are feminist theory, South Asia studies including cinema, gender and colonialism, and transnational feminisms. Her most recent book is *Hindi Cinema: Repeating the Subject* (2012) and she has taught and published widely on feminism and visual culture, colonial and post-colonial analyses of literature and gender in South Asia.

Nandana Bose is Associate Professor of Film Studies at the University of North Carolina, Wilmington. She has published on Indian cinema in journals such as *Cinema Journal, Celebrity Studies, Velvet Light Trap, Studies in South Asian Film and Media, Feminist Media Studies* and *Journal of the Moving Image*, and anthologies such as *Figurations in Indian Film* (2013) and *Silencing Cinema: Censorship Around the World* (2013). She is currently working on a monograph commissioned by the British Film Institute (BFI).

Ajay Gehlawat is Associate Professor of Theatre and Film at Sonoma State University, California, where he also directs the Film Studies programme. He is author of *Reframing Bollywood: Theories of Popular Hindi Cinema* (2010), editor of *The Slumdog Phenomenon: A Critical Anthology* (2013) and author of *Twenty-First Century Bollywood* (2015).

Jyotsna Kapur is Professor of Cinema Studies and Sociology at Southern Illinois University, Carbondale. She is the author, most recently, of *The Politics of Time and Youth in Brand India: Bargaining with Capital* (2013) and co-edits the journal *Studies in South Asian Film and Media*.

Alka Kurian is Lecturer at the University of Washington, Bothell, where she teaches post-colonial film and literature, human rights and women's studies. Her single-authored book *Narratives of Gendered Dissent in South Asian Cinemas* was published in 2012 and reprinted in 2014. From 2006 to 2014, she co-edited the peer-reviewed journal *Studies in South Asian Film and Media*. She is a Co-director of the Seattle South Asian Film Festival since 2007.

Sudhir Mahadevan is Assistant Professor of Film Studies in the Comparative Literature Department, University of Washington. He received his MA and PhD in cinema studies from New York University and his BA in English from St. Xavier's College in Mumbai. His manuscript titled 'A Very Old Machine: The Many Origins of the Cinema in South Asia' is forthcoming.

Monika Mehta is Associate Professor of English at Binghamton University (The State University of New York [SUNY]). Her research and teaching interests include new media and film studies, cinema in South Asia, theories of nation-state, post-colonial critique and globalization and cultural production. She is the author of *Censorship and Sexuality in Bombay Cinema* (December 2011 and January 2012). She is co-editing *From Bollywood to Hallyuwood: Mapping Power and Pleasure Across Pop Empires* (under advance contract with University of Hawaii Press).

Madhuja Mukherjee teaches film studies at Jadavpur University, Kolkata. Her research involved critical study of the Indian film industry. She works with archival material and is involved with online database projects. Recently, she has researched and published on the soundtrack of Indian films. She is the author of *New Theatres Ltd: The Emblem of Art, The Picture of Success* (2009), and the editor of *Aural Films, Oral Cultures: Essays on Cinema from the Early Sound Era* (2012) and *Voices and Verses of the Talking Stars*

(Readings in Gender Studies Vol. 4) (forthcoming). Mukherjee's first feature-film *Carnival* (2012) had its 'World Premiere' at the 41st International Film Festival Rotterdam, and *Qissa* (2013) written by her (with Anup Singh, director), received the Inalco Jury Award for 'the beautiful script, ...' at the 20th Vesoul International Film Festival of Asian Cinema, France, in 2014. *Kangal Malsat* (2013) described as the 'first graphic-novel in Bengali' was illustrated and narrated by her. Presently, she is working on urban cultures and exhibition spaces.

Tutun Mukherjee is Professor and Head of Comparative Literature at the Centre for Comparative Literature, University of Hyderabad. She has specialized in literary criticism and theory and has research interest in translation, women's writing, theatre and film studies. Her publications cover her diverse interests.

Pavithra Narayanan is Associate Professor of English at Washington State University, Vancouver, where she teaches courses on global and post-colonial literature and theory and documentary film theory and production. Narayanan is the author of *What are You Reading? The World Market and Indian Literary Production* (2012). Her scholarship focuses on social and environmental justice, the intersections between literature and market forces, the politics of nation formation, consequences of neoliberalism and contemporary indigenous and civilian resistance movements. She also produces documentary films.

Soumik Pal is a PhD student in Southern Illinois University, Carbondale. He is majoring in cinema studies and his interests are Indian cinema (especially Hindi cinema), post-colonial theory, neoliberalism and its effects and expressions, and South Asian popular culture.

Varsha Panjwani held a lectureship at the Department of Theatre, Film and Television at the University of York from 2009 to 2013 after obtaining a PhD from the University of York. She currently lectures on Shakespeare, drama and adaptation studies at

Boston University, London, and is an honorary research associate at the University of York. As well as publishing widely on Indian Shakespeare, co-authored drama and disability studies in leading international journals such as *Shakespeare Survey* and in forthcoming collections such as *Shakespeare and Indian Cinema* and *The Diverse Bard*, she has won research grants from the Society of Theatre Research and Folger Shakespeare Library.

Manjunath Pendakur specializes in the political economy of media and has authored a number of books and articles on Canada, India and the United States. He has taught for 18 years at Northwestern University and has held numerous administrative positions at prestigious universities in the United States and Canada. His honours and awards include an endowed professorship at Northwestern University and research grants from The Rockefeller Foundation and John D. and Catherine T. MacArthur Foundation. Pendakur grew up in Karnataka, was educated in Madras and then immigrated to Canada where he obtained his BA and MA degrees from the University of Washington and then PhD in Communication from Simon Fraser University.

Baradwaj Rangan is a film critic and Senior Deputy Editor at *The Hindu*. He won the National Award (Swarna Kamal) for Best Film Critic of 2005. His writings on cinema, music, art, books, travel and humour have been published in various national magazines such as *Open*, *Tehelka*, *Biblio*, *Outlook* and *Caravan*. He has co-written the screenplay for the Tamil rom-com *Kadhal 2 Kalyanam*. He teaches a course on cinema at the Asian College of Journalism, Chennai. His first book, *Conversations with Mani Ratnam*, was published in 2012 and his second, *Dispatches from the Wall Corner*, in 2014.

Krupa Shandilya is Assistant Professor of Sexuality, Women's and Gender Studies at Amherst College. Her book *Intimate Relations: Social Reform and the Late Nineteenth Century South Asian Novel* engages in a comparative analysis in two South Asian literary traditions, namely Bengali and Urdu. Her research and teaching interests include post-colonial literature and theory, feminist theory, South Asian literature and cinema. Her work has appeared in *New Cinemas, Postcolonial Text, Gender and History* and *South Asian Popular Culture*.

Swetha Sridhar is currently pursuing her MPhil in Gender Studies at the Center for Gender Studies, University of Cambridge. She holds an integrated master's degree in Development Studies from IIT, Madras. Her areas of interest include anthropology of culture, media cultures and practice, and questions of identity.

Clare Wilkinson is Associate Professor of Anthropology at Washington State University, Vancouver. Her research and teaching interests include art and media production in India, material culture and theory in anthropology. She is the author of *Embroidering Lives: Women's Work and Skill in the Lucknow Embroidery Industry* (1999) and *Fashioning Bollywood: The Making and Meaning of Costume in Hindi Cinema* (2013).

Sharanya is a PhD drama candidate at the University of Exeter on a split-site UKIERI programme with the National Institute of Advanced Studies in Bangalore. Her research interests lie in inter-sections of urban ethnography, cultural memory, intersections of performance, ethics and violence, and post-colonial poetry. Her thesis is an ongoing attempt to interrogate ethnographic encoun-ters between forms of walking, architecture and memory in con-temporary Delhi. Her non-fiction has appeared in *The Caravan, The Sunday Guardian* and other publications.

Index